Dubai & Abu Dhabi

"All you've got to do is decide to go and the hardest part is over.

So go!"

TONY WHEELER, COFOUNDER – LONELY PLANET

THIS EDITION WRITTEN AND RESEARCHED BY

Josephine Quintero

Contents

Plan Your Trip 4

Explore Dubai & Abu Dhabi 46

Understand Dubai & Abu Dhabi 147

Survival Guide 171

Dubai Maps 203

JOHN BORTHWICK / LONELY PLANET IMAGES ©

RICHARD I'ANSON / LONELY PLANET IMAGES ©

(left) **Burj al-Arab interior (p94)**

(above) **Dubai Aquarium at Dubai Mall (p79)**

(right) **Camel and keeper**

CHRISTIAN ASLUND / LONELY PLANET IMAGES ©

New Dubai p104

Jumeirah p91

Sheikh Zayed Road & Around p77

Bur Dubai p63

Deira p50

Welcome to Dubai & Abu Dhabi

Passengers arriving by air are transfixed by the view: futuristic skyscrapers flanked by a glittering coastline and surrounded by endless desert.

Embracing the Extraordinary

It's little wonder so many entrepreneurial designers and architects love Dubai. Together with a tax-free escape from throttling budgets, stringent building regulations and cookie-cutter specs, this place likes to show off. Tallest building in the world? Tick. Artificial island shaped like a palm? Tick. So-called seven-star hotel? Tick. Largest global shopping mall? Tick... And indoor snow slopes to boot? Tick.

While it's true that recent economic woes have led to some major projects hitting the dust or being scaled down, such as Dubailand, others are being gradually resumed. More superlative-worthy projects to come? Tick. Dubai, a shrinking violet? Never!

Let's Shop!

Before the 1970s, the only time you could shift your credit card into overdrive in Dubai was at the Gold Souq. Serious fashion choice required jetting off to London or New York. Today the city vies with both metropolises as a shopping destination, as well as providing much more than a mere retail experience. While temperatures spiral outside, the malls morph into places to shop, play, eat, drink (coffee) and socialise. If you want a glimpse of a more traditional culture, there are still souqs, particularly in Deira and Bur Dubai.

Feeding Body & Soul

Dubai has a glut of excellent restaurants. Be prepared to be spoiled rotten with cuisine that ranges from East to West, from celebrity-chef-driven to Asian street-style. This is a foodie's fantasy destination, where atmosphere, surroundings and service are an accepted part of the culinary combo. Continue the self-pampering at one of Dubai's spas, with treatments and massages designed to soothe away stress and revitalise the senses. Or flop on a white sandy beach, take a dhow dinner cruise or watch the sunset over rippling red-gold sand in the desert, sharing a vision that was once deeply rooted in Dubai's Bedouin society.

Beyond the City

Travel beyond Dubai to experience another world altogether as a skyscraper skyline is replaced by a more traditional desertscape.

Abu Dhabi is a fascinating and easily accessible destination to the south. This is the emirate that continues to surprise, quietly vying with Dubai with its considerable investment in culture, innovation and architecture. It is also home to the Sheikh Zayed bin Sultan al-Nahyan Mosque, a magnificent must-see sight.

Why I Love Dubai

By Josephine Quintero, Author

I lived in Kuwait for seven years and thought I was pretty savvy about the Arab way of life. How wrong I was. Dubai is a real one-off and full of surprises. There is nothing mundane or matter-of-fact about this place; it is all about drama and extremes – from the architecture to the weather to the food... Ah, the food! I also love the fact that there is a burgeoning, innovative art scene here and in Abu Dhabi. Discovering some fabulous galleries in the dusty Al-Quoz district was a real high point for me – along with travelling to the top of the Burj Khalifa, that is!

For more about our author, see p224.

Above: Dubai skyline from Jumeirah coast

Dubai & Abu Dhabi's Top 10

Dubai Museum *(p65)*

1 Appropriately housed in one of the city's oldest buildings, this museum provides a well-laid-out and comprehensive history of Dubai. Learn exactly how and why, in just a third of a century, this extraordinary destination has risen from being a simple desert settlement to one of the most progressive and modern cities in the Middle East. Many exhibits take the form of lifelike dioramas, while a separate archaeological exhibition covers the ancient history of the region, with a display of exhibits discovered in several excavated tombs.

Bur Dubai

Dubai Souqs *(p52)*

2 Noisy, chaotic and colourful, Dubai's souqs are an enticing reminder that you are, indeed, in a foreign country – something you might forget when you're poolside at your five-star hotel. The small Spice Souq is a heady introduction to Middle Eastern exotic herbs and spices, while Bur Dubai's Textile Souq (p66) is another assault on the senses with its vividly patterned fabrics. Don't miss nearby Hindi Lane (p65), a tiny alleyway flanked by stalls selling brilliantly coloured religious decorations, or the Deira Gold Souq, which has a dazzling display of jewellery at remarkably low prices. DEIRA GOLD SOUQ

Deira, Bur Dubai

1

MICHAEL COYNE / LONELY PLANET IMAGES ©

2

3

RICHARD NEBESKY / LONELY PLANET IMAGES ©

5

JOHN ELK III / LONELY PLANET IMAGES © ARCHITECT: TOM WRIGHT

RICHARD I'ANSON / LONELY PLANET IMAGES ©

Bastakia Quarter *(p65)*

3 Wandering around the maze of narrow lanes in the Bastakia Quarter provides a tangible sense of historic Arabian architecture and culture. The streets are flanked by low-lying traditional buildings, complete with wind towers, arabesque windows and decorative gypsum screens. Punctuated by the occasional splash of dazzling bougainvillea, this evocative area is home to a couple of the city's most characterful guesthouses, as well as cafes, galleries and museums. If you want to learn more about local history, join one of the informative organised walking tours.

Bur Dubai

Dubai Creek *(p68)*

4 Dubai's otherworldly megaprojects got you craving a dose of reality? Walk alongside the Creek and it's easy to imagine life in Dubai half a century ago. The wooden dhows, bustling souqs, stately wind towers and graceful mosques have barely changed over the decades. Wander the streets surrounding the Creek in Bur Dubai and Deira to experience a vibrant multicultural region that has become home to hundreds of thousands of people from across the globe. The most evocative route to cross the Creek is by hopping on one of the traditional *abras* (water taxis).

Deira, Bur Dubai

Burj al-Arab *(p94)*

5 This landmark hotel, with its dramatic design that mimics the sail of a ship, floats on its own man-made island and has become the iconic symbol of Dubai's boom years. If you're not in the ultra-moneyed league that can afford to stay here, you can still indulge in a little make-believe by opting for one of the cocktail or afternoon-tea packages, or by splashing out on a romantic dinner in the underwater restaurant. The interior is all about impact, drama and unadulterated bling, with dancing fountains, gold fittings, giant aquariums and private whirlpool baths your butler can fill with champagne (or caviar) – if you so wish.

Jumeirah

Art Galleries *(p80)*

6 Dubai and Abu Dhabi are rapidly evolving as exciting centres for art in the Middle East. In Dubai, the annual Art Dubai art fair has been instrumental in reviving the city's art culture. Ranging from the dusty industrial surroundings of Al-Quoz to the chic sophistication of the city's financial centre and the boho-chic Bastakia Quarter, the contemporary art scene here is buzzing. It's a similar picture in Abu Dhabi with its dedicated cultural 'island', Saadiyat, which includes branches of leading international art museums the Louvre and the Guggenheim. SHISHAS BY ARTIST MOUNIR FATMI AT ART DUBAI 2012 (P20)

Sheikh Zayed Road & Around

Nightlife *(p31)*

7 Dubai is home to some of the most glamorous, see-and-be-seen nightclubs in the world. Some of the best are in beachside Jumeirah, where you can dance by the sea under the stars, while several of the city's most sophisticated bars top soaring buildings, offering dizzy skyscape views to go with those head-spinning cocktails. If you prefer your ale on tap accompanied by big-screen sports or karaoke, there are plenty of Brit-geared pubs, while live-music lovers may get lucky if their trip coincides with a star billing on the concert circuit in either Dubai or Abu Dhabi. BUDDHA BAR (P111)

Drinking & Nightlife

6

GIOVANNI SIMEONE/SIME/4CORNERS ©

JOHN ELK III / LONELY PLANET IMAGES ©

Shopping Malls *(p37)*

8 The first rule is to realise that, as far as shopping malls are concerned, there are no rules in Dubai. Just arrive without preconceived ideas and be prepared for sights and experiences that go way beyond mere retail therapy. In Dubai, shopping malls represent an integral part of the culture and lifestyle; they are places not just for conspicuous consumption but for extravagant entertainment and world-class dining, Disney-style theme parks and extraordinary architecture. In summer, malls are where everyone retreats to escape the heat, socialise, clinch deals and puff on *sheesha* pipes. SKI DUBAI AT MALL OF THE EMIRATES (P113)

Shopping

Desert Escapes *(p126)*

9 Staying in Dubai, it can be easy to forget that the region's most famous topographical feature has nothing to do with architectural wizardry. Even if you didn't plan on getting sand between your toes, a trip to the desert is highly recommended and there is a wide range of excursions on offer that provide a rare opportunity to experience everything from sandboarding to sleeping under the stars. Alternatively, consider staying at one of the desert resorts or renting a 4WD, which allows you to appreciate the magnificent scenery firsthand.

Day Trips from Dubai

9

CHRISTINE OSBORNE / LONELY PLANET IMAGES ©

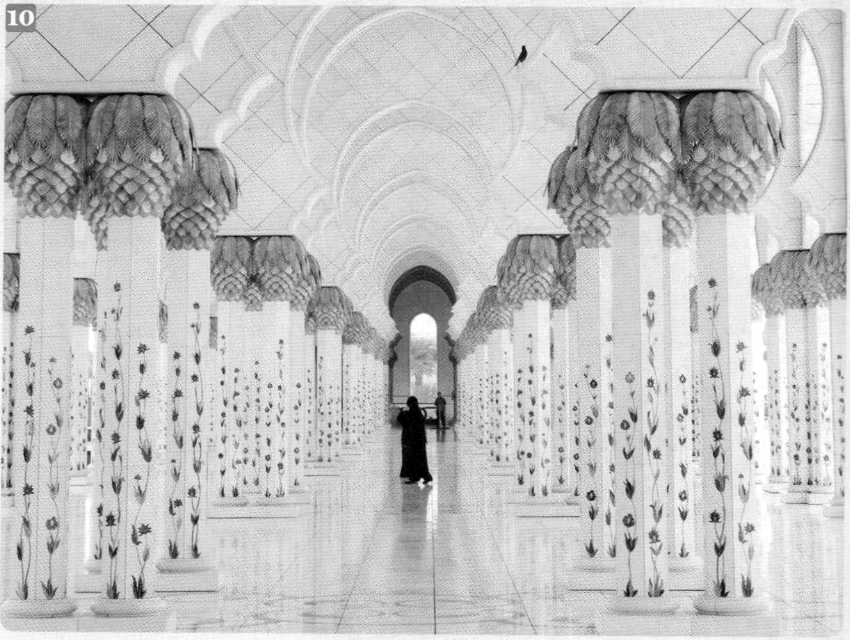

10

PHILIP GAME / LONELY PLANET IMAGES ©

Grand Mosque *(p119)*

10 Don't miss Abu Dhabi's stunning Sheikh Zayed bin Sultan al-Nahyan Mosque, the third-largest mosque in the world. And, yes, it *is* massive, with more than 80 snowy-white marble domes held aloft by 1000 pillars with space for a soul-stirring 40,000 worshippers in its magnificent courtyard and main prayer hall (which also holds the largest handwoven carpet in the world). Intricate inlaid designs of flowers and leaves in marble and semiprecious stones delicately adorn the pillars; massive chandeliers twinkle with thousands of dazzling crystals; and 24-carat gold adornments shimmer throughout.

Abu Dhabi

What's New

Celebrity Dining

It's pretty hard to find anywhere on a par with Dubai when it comes to the number of celebrity chefs bubbling away in the gourmet culinary cauldron. And although one or two have departed (most notably Gordon Ramsay), new names include everyone's kitchen-sink darling Jamie Oliver, while fellow UK-chef Gary Rhodes and Mexican Richard Sandoval both have second restaurants (and concepts). James Martin, another Brit-based culinary star, is also apparently considering neighbouring Abu Dhabi as his United Arab Emirates (UAE) launch pad.

Jumeirah Golf Estates

This impressive new golf course is home of the Dubai World Championship, with courses named after different environmental themes. By 2011 the Earth and Fire courses were completed with Water and Wind still at the planning stage. (p44)

Sleep Pods at Airport

In October 2011 Dubai International Airport became the first airport in the Middle East to offer snooze cubes (modular sleep pods) for weary travellers. (p172)

International Art Museums

Although there have been delays, Abu Dhabi's highly impressive cultural project, Saadiyat Island, is definitely going ahead. When completed, this man-made island will be home to a branch of both the Louvre and the Guggenheim art museums. Check www.saadiyat.ae for an update. (p119)

Al Majaz Waterfront Project

Sharjah's ambitious Al Majaz waterfront project includes sculpture gardens; walking, jogging and cycling paths; restaurants and cafes; and laser and water shows, including a 100m-high dancing fountain. (p126)

Armani Hotel

The iconic Burj Khalifa is a fitting home for the world's first hotel that has been exclusively designed and developed by Giorgio Armani. It's as cutting edge and contemporary as you would expect from this Italian style guru. (p140)

Dubai Sports Complex

The Dh1.1 billion Dubai Sports Complex opened in late 2010 as a multipurpose sports venue with a capacity of 15,000 spectators. Facilities include an indoor aquatic centre, which hosted the FINA World Swimming Championships in December 2010.

One&Only The Palm

Arrive by ferry at this 2011 One&Only hotel newbie with its signature Moorish-cum-Andalucían architecture and exquisite landscaping and hotel facilities. (www.oneandonlyresorts.com; p143)

The Ivy

Arguably London's most revered dining institution, the Ivy opened in the suitably iconic Jumeirah Emirates Towers in late 2011. (p84)

For more recommendations and reviews, see **lonelyplanet.com/dubai**

Need to Know

Currency
United Arab Emirates (UAE) dirhams (Dh)

Languages
Arabic, English

Visas
Citizens of 34 developed countries get free 30-day visas on arrival in the UAE.

Money
ATMs are widely available. Credit cards are accepted in most hotels, restaurants and shops.

Mobile Phones
You can buy a pay-as-you-go mobile with credit for as little as Dh125. Alternatively, local SIM cards are widely available.

Time
Dubai is four hours ahead of GMT. The time does not change during the summer.

Tourist Information
The **Department of Tourism & Commerce Marketing** (DTCM; www.dubaitourism.ae) operates 24-hour information kiosks in the Terminal 1 and 3 arrivals areas of Dubai International Airport.

Your Daily Budget

Budget less than Dh600
- Budget hotel room: Dh300–400
- Excellent supermarkets for self-caterers
- Cheap museum entrance fees, free public beaches

Midrange Dh600–1200
- Midrange double room: Dh500
- Two-course meal in good midrange restaurant: Dh125–200, plus wine
- Top attractions and sights: average Dh100

Top End over Dh1200
- Four-star hotel room: from Dh1000
- Fine dining for lunch and dinner: from Dh800
- Bar tab for wine and beer: from Dh300

Advance Planning

Three months before Double-check visa regulations as these can alter without prior warning. Check date of Ramadan, which changes annually.

One month before Reserve a table at a top restaurant. Check concert-venue websites for what's on during your stay.

One week before Check average daytime temperature.

Useful Websites

- **Lonely Planet** (www.lonelyplanet.com/dubai) Destination information, hotel bookings, traveller forum and more.
- **Dubai Tourism** (www.dubaitourism.ae) Official tourism site of Dubai Government, which provides updated advice on visitor visas.
- **Dubai Community** (www.dubailime.com) Classifieds, culture, events and features.
- **Daily English Language News** (www.gulfnews.com) Regional, local and international news, plus sports and classifieds.
- **Dubai Explorer** (www.liveworkexplore.com/dubai) Geared towards residents with lots of practical info.

WHEN TO GO

The best times are March to April and October to November when temperatures are in the low 30°Cs. Avoid July to August when temperatures average around 43°C with 95% humidity.

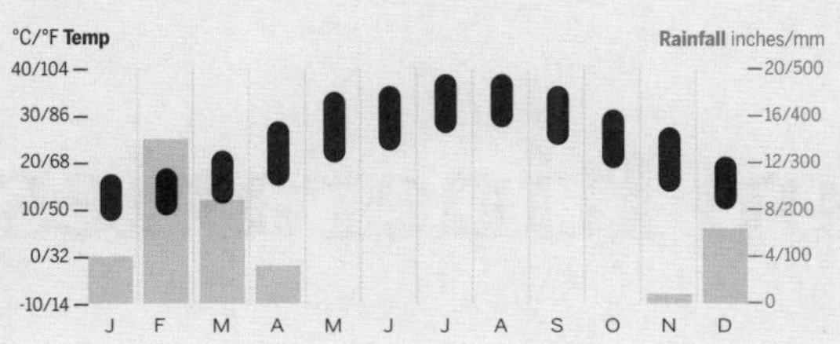

Arriving in Dubai

Dubai International Airport
The metro, buses and taxis to central Dubai are all convenient modes of transport to/from the airport. If you are staying at a four- or five-star hotel, check whether an airport transfer is available.

Metro The Red Line stops at Terminals 1 and 3 and is the most efficient way to get across town by public transport.

Bus Several public buses serve the airport, including the 401 (to Al-Sabkha bus station) and bus 402 (to Al-Ghubaiba bus station).

Taxi A taxi costs between Dh45 and Dh90 depending on your destination.

For much more on **arrival** see p172.

Getting Around

Before you hop aboard a local bus or the metro, you must purchase a rechargeable Nol card from ticket offices in any metro and some bus stations, plus ticket vending machines.

- **Metro** There are two metro lines. The Red Line runs from near Dubai International Airport to Jebel Ali. The Green Line links the Dubai Airport Free Zone with Dubai Healthcare City.
- **Bus** There is a network of 79 bus routes. Buses can be overcrowded and slow.
- **Boat** *Abras* (traditional wooden boats) cross the Creek. There are water buses, which are also good for sightseeing.

For much more on **getting around**, see p173.

Sleeping

Dubai is a luxury travel destination with essentially two types of hotel: the city hotel and the beach resort. Prices are at their lowest in the sweltering summer months of July and August. At other times of the year it is essential to reserve ahead of time. Most hotels offer considerable deductions if you book online. Hotel apartments offer more economical accommodation, while there's a growing number of B&Bs.

Useful Websites

- **Dubai Hotels** (www.dubaihotelsltd.com) Wide range of options, mainly in top-end category.
- **Direct Rooms** (www.directrooms.com) Competitive site for hotel booking with some good deals.
- **Late Rooms** (www.laterooms.com) Especially good for last-minute offers.

For much more on **sleeping**, see p134.

RAMADAN

Muslims are required to fast during Ramadan and everyone, regardless of religion, is expected to observe the fast when in public. That means no eating, drinking or smoking during daylight hours. Government offices cut hours, bars and pubs are closed until 7pm each night, live music is prohibited and dance clubs are closed throughout the month.

Unless you are particularly interested in Islam, you may want to avoid visiting during this holiday, which shifts by a few days each year.

Top Itineraries

Day One

Jumeirah (p91)

Cruise into your day with an early morning stroll on the sand at the **Jumeirah Open Beach**. Next, aim for a perfect balance of spirituality and architecture at the **Jumeirah Mosque** before feeding the body with some healthy soul food at the **Lime Tree Cafe**. Continue in culture mode by enjoying fine artwork at the **Pro Art Gallery**, then indulge with a shopping spree at **S*uce** boutique.

Lunch Taxi to Ravi (p96) for a pack-in-the-flavours Pakistani curry.

Sheikh Zayed Road & Around (p77)

It's the hottest part of the day so time to retreat indoors. Hop in a cab to the **Dubai Mall** and visit the watery wonderland of the **Aquarium** before perusing the shops. Wind up the afternoon by grabbing a restaurant pew at **Souq al-Bahar** overlooking the magical dancing fountains with their soaring Burj Khalifa backdrop.

Dinner Tuck into top Brit-inspired nosh at the Rivington Grill (p83).

Sheikh Zayed Road & Around (p77)

Check out the killer views and cocktails at **Neos**, the high-octane bar at the hotel **Address Downtown Dubai**. Or show off big-time as you belt out your top Susan Boyle number at **Harry Ghatto's** at Jumeirah Emirates Towers.

Day Two

Bur Dubai (p63)

Enjoy breakfast in the tranquil walled garden of the **Basta Art Cafe**. Nip next door to check out the latest exhibition at the **Majlis Gallery** and wander around the historic **Bastakia Quarter**, dipping in and out of the various museums. Enjoy the short stroll to the breezy **Bur Dubai Souq**, via the atmospheric **Hindi Lane**. Check out the textiles, pick up a pashmina (or two) and cool down with a fresh mango juice before heading for a Creekside location for a late lunch.

Lunch Enjoy Middle Eastern fare at Bait Al Wakeel (p69).

Bur Dubai (p63)

Backtrack to the **Dubai Museum** where you can spend a good hour boning up on the history and culture. Then wind your way through the souq to the **Shindagha Heritage Area**, which has been restored with a paved walkway and a couple of excellent museums housed in sumptuous historical buildings. Stay until sunset, when you can revive yourself with a coffee overlooking the passing parade of boats.

Dinner Splash out with a dinner cruise on the Bateaux Dubai (p69).

Bur Dubai (p63)

You'll be so relaxed after wining and dining on the cruise, but if you have the energy, enjoy a grand finale to your evening by stopping by the super-chic **Red Lounge** bar at the Raffles Dubai hotel, to clink glasses overlooking stunning skyline views. Follow that with a quick spin on the dance floor next door at the oh-so-cool **People by Crystal** nightclub.

Day Three

Deira (p50)

Hop on one of the traditional wooden *abras* (water taxis) to cross the Creek and stock up on saffron at the **Spice Souq**. Crisscross your way back to the **Gold Souq**, stopping off en route for a fresh mango-and-orange juice at the **Ashwaq Cafeteria**. After gawping at all that glitz, wander around the **Perfume Souq**, sampling the musky traditional *attars* (perfumes).

Lunch Enjoy a meaty feast at the Afghan Khorasan Kebab House (p56).

Deira (p50)

After all that banter and bustle, take a break and spend the hottest hours of the day having a luxurious massage at **Amara spa** in the Park Hyatt hotel. Cross the road and stroll down to the colourful quayside where wooden boats unload their wares. Head towards central Baniyas Sq, popping in en route at Deira's two historic museums, the **Heritage House** and **Al-Ahmadiya School**. Then follow your rumbling stomach and cab it to the Mövenpick Hotel in Bur Dubai.

Dinner Enjoy fine Indian dining and entertainment at Chutneys (p70).

Deira (p50)

After a leisurely dinner, head to **Chi** nightclub where you can sip stylish cocktails under the stars at one of Dubai's signature nightspots, then get hip-swaying to the stylish repertoire from a chilled line-up of international DJs.

Day Four

Abu Dhabi (p117)

Make an early start and travel to **Abu Dhabi**, a two-hour drive away. Head straight for the magnificent Sheikh Zayed bin Sultan al-Nahyan Mosque as it closes at noon (and all day Friday). You'll need at least an hour of ogling time here. Wind up the morning at the Central Market.

Lunch Enjoy a Lebanese-inspired main at Shakespeare & Co (p122).

Abu Dhabi (p117)

At the hottest time of the day, take some time perusing the shops here, before heading to the **Emirates Palace** for a gawp at all that gold and a frothy cappuccino (sprinkled with gold leaf, of course). If time permits, take a stroll along the waterfront **Corniche** flanked by pristine white sandy beaches, before returning to Dubai.

Dinner Go Italiano with dinner at Hilton's BiCE (p108) in New Dubai.

New Dubai (p104)

Enjoy post-dinner drinks at the fabled **Buddha Bar** in the Grosvenor House hotel and then glide up the elevator to the hotel's 44th floor and the swanky retro-check **Bar 44**, with its sweeping panorama, plus live blues and jazz. Consider some serious hip-swinging action at **Nasimi Beach**, the Atlantis hotel's fabled nightspot a couple of fronds away on the Palm Jumeirah.

If You Like...

Nightlife

Barasti Dance with sand between your toes or chill out in the bar at this spirited hotspot, a favourite haunt for expat revellers. (p111)

Nasimi Beach A winning combo of beachside glamour, big-name DJs, live performers and monthly full-moon parties. (p112)

N'Dulge Circus acts, acrobatics, the hottest tracks and a party crowd. (p112).

Buddha Bar Dress to impress at this see-and-be-seen fashionable haunt with its giant Buddha, sexy lighting and chilled-out sounds. (p111)

Etoiles Abu Dhabi's most luxurious hotel is home to the emirate's most sophisticated nightspot, which attracts a super-chic and stylish clientele. (p123)

A Touch of Luxury

Boating in Style Check out the Creek with glass in hand from the deck of a luxury dinner cruise. (p69)

Special Spa Time Crown your stay with a 'Queen for a Day' luxurious treatment session at the Sensasia Urban Spa (p103) or head for Abu Dhabi's glamorous Emirates Palace spa (p119).

High Tea Reserve a top table for tea accompanied by sumptuous cakes, a glass of bubbly and heady views, 200m above sea level. (p94)

Go for Gold At the Deira Gold Souq prices are fair, the quality superb and the purchase a glittering investment. What are you waiting for? (p52)

Spice souq, Bur Dubai

Top Table Dine at one of the celebrity-chef restaurants in Dubai or Abu Dhabi and let your tastebuds convince you that every soupçon of fame is justified.

Shopping Extremes

Dubai Mall The largest mall in the world packs a serious retail punch, and provides plenty of family-geared entertainment. (p88)

Deira Souqs The antithesis of the modern mall, selling everything from dried lemons and saffron to Kashmiri bed throws and camel-skin slippers. (p52)

Ibn Battuta Mall Another one-off, this themed shopping mall is stunningly decorated in country and regional styles, such as Andalucían, Indian and classic Persian. (p113)

Wafi Mall This mall has some retail gems in a wonderful setting with some fabulous stained glass and extraordinary design features. (p72)

Central Market A delightful small mall on the site of the original souq in Abu Dhabi, with lots of warm wood and a great selection of shops. (p123)

Souq Madinat Jumeirah OK, it is a bit 'Disneyland does the Arabian souq', but the look is sumptuous and the shops enticing with plenty of unusual souvenir scope, plus refuelling spots. (p102)

Mall of the Emirates Another mall with a dizzying number of shops, as well as those famous Alpine-inspired ski slopes and some brilliant dining. (p112)

Culture

Gate Village Smock-and-beret types will love nosing around the exciting contemporary galleries at this Financial District art hub. (p82)

Saadiyat Island Four museums and a performing arts centre are set to open in Abu Dhabi in 2013, when the Louvre Abu Dhabi will set the painterly pace with a collection originating from the Louvre in Paris. (p119)

Al-Quoz A cutting-edge area for predominantly Middle Eastern contemporary art, sculpture and installations. (p80)

Annual Festivals Check out the annual cycle of film, theatre and music festivals in Dubai and its neighbours, as well as big-name concerts, orchestras and dance performances.

Museum Sharjah's Museum of Islamic Civilisation is dedicated to all aspects of Islam and is extraordinarily detailed and well-laid-out. (p125)

Beaches

Kite Beach This is a glorious unspoiled stretch of sand, north of the Burj al-Arab; there are no facilities, so pack a picnic. (p94)

Jumeirah Beach Park Although it costs a few dirhams, this beach has superb family-geared facilities, including playgrounds, a proper park (fronting the sand) and ice creams for sale. (p94)

Jumeirah Beach Residence Open Beach A great place just off The Walk at JBR, with a long stretch of sand and plenty of restaurants nearby. (p94)

Umm Suqeim Beach Overlooking the iconic Burj al-Arab, this is the beach where you shouldn't forget your camera. There are good facilities, including showers, and an enticing white sandy beach. (p94)

Jumeirah Open Beach Good facilities and plenty of towel space on the sand at this long strip lined with a promenade, next to the Dubai Marine Beach Resort & Spa. (p94)

Corniche, Abu Dhabi The beach flanking the Corniche here is glorious with plenty of family-friendly facilities, pristine white sand and convenient cafes and restaurants nearby. (p117)

Bargains

Shopping Festival January is the time for real bargains with many big stores slashing their prices by up to 75%. (p20)

Deira & Bur Dubai Explore the souqs and surrounding streets in Bur Dubai and Deira for some real one-off bargains. (p58 and p72)

Sharjah Everything in Sharjah is cheaper than in its glitzy neighbour. Check out the Central Souq here, particularly its jewellery stores. (p127)

Bastakia Quarter For scintillating gifts, jewellery, crafts and souvenirs check out the gift shops at the Majlis Gallery, the XVA Hotel and the Basta Art Cafe. (p65)

For more top Dubai and Abu Dhabi spots, see

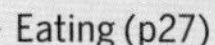

- Eating (p27)
- Drinking & Nightlife (p31)
- Entertainment (p35)
- Shopping (p37)
- Sports & Activities (p42)

Month by Month

TOP EVENTS

Dubai Shopping Festival, January–February

Dubai International Jazz Festival, February

Art Dubai, March

WOMAD, April

Dubai International Film Festival, December

January

A blissful month here when much of the world is suffering post-holiday doldrums and icy conditions. Expect daytime temperatures averaging a pleasant 25°C, though nights can be cool.

Dubai Shopping Festival

Held from mid-January to mid-February, this shopping festival draws hordes of bargain-hunting tourists from around the world. There are huge discounts in the souqs and malls, and the city is abuzz with activities, ranging from live concerts to fireworks. (www.mydsf.com)

Dubai Marathon

With mild January weather and one of the flattest and fastest courses in the world, this full marathon attracts pounding participation from all over the world. (www.dubaimarathon.org)

February

Another warm and winning month, with sun-kissed weather and plenty going on, including many outdoor events. Pack a light jacket or pashmina for those al fresco evenings.

Dubai International Jazz Festival

This increasingly popular event has had locals foot-tapping since 2003. Performances take place over nine days in the outdoor amphitheatre at Dubai Media City and past acts include such musical heavyweights as Kool & the Gang and Alison Moyet. (www.dubaijazzfest.com)

Dubai Tennis Championships

Attracting the big serves of the world's top pros, the men's and women's events are a firm fixture on the international tennis tours. (www.dubaitennischampionships.com)

Emirates Airline International Festival of Literature

A literary event that showcases authors and poets from the Middle East, as well as international best-selling writers such as Wilbur Smith and Margaret Atwood. (www.eaifl.com)

March

The weather might be heating up a fraction, but it is still near perfect in this action-packed month, with warm seas for swimming and plenty of space on the sand.

Art Dubai

Art is becoming big business in the Gulf and the growing number of galleries confirms the trend. Madinat Jumeirah provides a glamorous setting for artists, dealers and gallery owners to canvas their art. (www.artdubai.ae)

Al-Ain Classics Festival

International top talent – from cellist Yo-Yo Ma to Prague's Bennewitz Quartet – perform classical music concerts in the evocative setting of the restored

Al-Jahili Fort in Al-Ain, a 90-minute drive south of Dubai. (www.aacf.ae)

Dubai International Boat Show

Don your deck shoes and head for the International Marine Club to see some fabulous boats go under the hammer; buyers come from all over the yachting world. (www.boatshowdubai.com)

Dubai World Cup

Dubai's racing season culminates in the world's richest horse race but, with no betting allowed, attention turns to the loony fashion-free-for-all of the attendees. (www.dubaiworldcup.com)

April

It's still warm rather than blistering but you'll see more tourists as it is school-holiday time during the Easter break. This is a rollicking good month for music-festival and fashion fans.

Dubai Fashion Week

For the latest local trends, pay attention to the runway during this glam showcase for regional designers. The Spring/Summer collection is presented at a second event in October. (www.dfw.ae)

Chill Out Festival

A weekend event early in the month, this robust line-up of chilled-out performers and DJs takes place at Nasimi Beach at the Palm Jumeirah. Recent line-ups at this beachfront location include Erykah Badu and De La Soul. (www.chillout festivaldubai.com)

WOMAD

Always a global winner, this three-day festival, held in Al-Ain's Al-Jahili Fort and the Corniche in Abu Dhabi, has attracted global giants such as Jamaica's Jimmy Cliff in 2011. (www.womadabudhabi.ae)

May

Temperatures are inching up the barometer and can nudge 35°C-plus, so air-conditioned malls provide welcome relief. There are one or two crowd-pulling events this month.

Al Gaffal Traditional Dhow Race

This traditional dhow race, between the small uninhabited island of Sir Bu Na'air and Dubai Marina, has a winner's purse of Dh500,000. Held on the last Saturday of the month, it's a photographer's favourite. (www.dimc.ae)

July

It is going to be hot, hot, hot – so be sure to don the floppy hat and sunscreen. Ironically, this is low season so you can get some seriously good flight and hotel deals.

Dubai Summer Surprises

Despite the sizzling time of year, a combination of free kids' entertainment and major sales in shopping malls draws plenty of tourists for this, the more family-focused little sibling of the Dubai Shopping Festival. (www.mydsf.com)

October

Temperatures have started to cool considerably, although you can still expect some toasty warm days early in the month. Nights are perfect for dining al fresco in shirtsleeves or for overnight desert trips.

GITEX

Snap up some gadget bargains at this international consumer electronics fair held over five days at the Dubai International Convention and Exhibition Centre. (www.gitex.com)

Swim the Burj

Benefiting the not-for-profit organisation Médecins Sans Frontières (Doctors Without Borders), this charity event draws hundreds of swimmers to complete the 1km circle around the iconic Burj al-Arab hotel. (www.swimburjalarab.com)

Middle East International Film Festival

Stars, directors, critics and cinephiles descend upon Abu Dhabi to meet, mingle and present the latest flicks from around the region in a warm-up to the Dubai International Film Festival. (www.meiff.com)

Diwali

Lights, candles and firecrackers illuminate this magical festival of light, which brings together the ever-growing community of Indian expats in Dubai. Look for traditional sweets in supermarkets, particularly in Deira and Bur Dubai.

November

Sharjah World Book Fair

This major regional book fair presents the latest tomes in Arabic, English and other languages. Readings, workshops and symposia supplement the exhibits. (www.swbf.gov.ae)

Abu Dhabi Grand Prix

The Formula One racing elite tests its mettle on this wicked new track. (www.yasmarinacircuit.com)

December

UAE National Day

The birth of a nation in 1971 is celebrated across the country on 2 December with a range of events, from boat parades to fireworks, concerts to horse shows and traditional dances to military parades.

Dubai International Film Festival

This excellent non-competitive film festival is a great place to catch international indie flicks as well as new releases from around the Arab world and the Indian subcontinent. (www.dubaifilmfest.com)

Mubadala World Tennis Championship

This three-day championship, held in Abu Dhabi's Zayed Sports City, has big cash prizes and attracts grand-slammers from the international circuit. (www.mubadalawtc.com)

(Top) Abu Dhabi Grand Prix
(Bottom) Opening night party of the Dubai International Film Festival

With Kids

Arab culture reveres children and Dubai and Abu Dhabi offer plenty of entertainment for youngsters, much of it extravagant in novelty value (but not in cost). Waterparks and other adrenalin-fuelled activities are an obvious choice, while hotel pools and beaches are tamer options.

PHILIP & KAREN SMITH / LONELY PLANET IMAGES ©

Junior Foodies

When spirits and feet start to drag, there's plenty of ice cream and kid-friendly meals to pick them back up – look for the symbol throughout this book. If you're not sure where to eat, malls are a sure bet; most listed in this book have surprisingly good food courts. All hotels have at least one restaurant suitable for families, usually the 24-hour cafe or the buffet restaurant. Discerning young diners may like to ease themselves into Middle Eastern cuisine with a *shwarma*, essentially a hot chicken wrap and suitably tasty (and messy) to be a big hit with most youngsters.

Themed Attractions

One of Dubai's latest children's attractions is the extraordinary KidZania (p80), an interactive miniature city with offices, a school, a racetrack, a fire station, a hospital and bank, and other real-world places. Older kids can head for nearby Sega Republic (p90), an indoor game park with themed areas and motion-simulator rides, while space cadets can get starry-eyed at the space-themed amusement park Stargate, at Za'abeel Park (p67). If you want to crank up the pace a notch or two, take the kids to Ferrari World Abu Dhabi (p119) and have a spin around the Junior Grand Prix.

Budding Artists

At **Café Ceramique** (www.cafe-ceramique.com; Festival City) children get to select a ceramic object of their choice – a mug is generally a good bet, and sketch, then paint a design of their choice. The masterpiece may then be collected a week later after it has been glazed. It's a great concept for wannabe artists.

Nature Lovers

Kids fascinated by the underwater world shouldn't miss the mesmerising Aquarium & Underwater Zoo (p79) at Dubai Mall, or the labyrinth of underwater tanks and fish-filled tunnels at the Lost Chambers (p106). Children can also get up close and

NEED TO KNOW

- **Formula & disposable nappies (diapers)** Sold at pharmacies and most supermarkets.
- **Babysitting** Peekaboo (www.peekaboo.ae) has créches and play centres for children aged zero to seven years at several shopping malls.
- **Kids clubs** Many hotels have kids clubs and activities. Ask at reception.
- **Strollers & car seats** Bring your own.
- **Transport** Children under five years of age travel free on public transport.

personal with dolphins at Dolphin Bay (p115) or the Dubai Dolphinarium (p67) at Creekside Park. Back on dry land, the Ris al-Khor Wildlife Sanctuary (p80) offers junior twitchers the chance to see flamingos and other exotic birds through binoculars while, further afield, Al-Ain Wildlife Park (p129) has a petting zoo, giraffe rides and spacious enclosures for animals. Abu Dhabi also has the educational (and fascinating) Falcon Hospital (p120).

Chilled-Out Kids

Pint-sized winter-sport enthusiasts can cool down with a trip to the Dubai Ice Rink (p90) at Dubai Mall, or do the Alpine bit and tackle the snow slopes at Ski Dubai (p113) at Mall of the Emirates. Both are also conveniently located for parents who want to indulge in a little kid-free retail therapy.

Playgrounds & Parks

Provided it is not the serious sunburn season of July and August, Dubai has several parks with picnic areas and playgrounds where children can let off steam. One of the biggest, best and greenest is Creekside Park (p67), with attractions such as a cable-car ride, botanical garden, tandem bikes, a science museum and even a dolphinarium. Skateboard fiends may prefer to swoop by Za'abeel Park (p67), which also has a jogging track and space-age theme park, while tots can feed the ducks and enjoy the grassy lawns at Al-Safa Park (p93) in Jumeirah. Alternatively, head for the beach road here and at Jumeirah Beach Park, which flanks the sand and has playgrounds, barbecue pits, volleyball nets and picnic sites for those tired of sand in their sarnies.

Keeping the Teens Happy

OK, so they've done the ski slopes, disco-danced at the ice rink, splashed around at the waterparks and enjoyed a fashionable strut around the malls. Is there more to prevent teens succumbing to total Facebook-deprivation meltdown? Fortunately, yes! For the ultimate holiday pic to impress their pals back home, consider sandboarding, camel riding, an overnight desert safari or even a trekking trip to the Hajar Mountains. All are offered by several tour companies based in Dubai (p126). Budding musicians may want to join a drum circle held at a desert camp (p131), while Olympic-runner wannabes can complete a lap or two with the Dubai Road Runners (p103). Scuba diving is another option; young divers over 12 years of age are eligible for open-water dives with Al Boom Diving (p102). There's also tennis (with courts at many midrange to top-end hotels), volleyball and swimming. Children up to 17 years of age can even go rock climbing at the youth gym SkillZ (p103). And, yes, it is a rock-climbing wall – Dubai has not suddenly sprouted a mountain!

Cool Down at the Waterparks

Probably the most appealing entertainment for hot and bothered kids visiting Dubai in summer is a trip to the waterpark. For some of the best spine-chilling slides, a visit to dramatically positioned Aquaventure (p115) is a suitable launch pad, while the original family favourite, Wild Wadi Waterpark (p102), has gentler options in addition to thrill-seeking hold-onto-your-shorts options.

For Free

There is no denying that Dubai and Abu Dhabi can easily tempt you to part with loads of dirhams (the Gold Souq comes glitteringly to mind...). Fortunately there are still plenty of freebie attractions, as well as some cheapie options such as museums, art galleries and beaches.

JOHN ELK III / LONELY PLANET IMAGES ©

Men's traditional dance, Shindagha Heritage Area (p66)

Souq Time

Wandering around the souqs in Bur Dubai (p66) and Deira (p52) has to be one of the most enjoyable and insightful experiences here and, unless you succumb to the persuasive vendors, it will cost you nothing more than shoe leather. Note that if you are interested in making a purchase, start off your barter by offering half the quoted price. Choose from the textile, perfume, spice, general or gold souq for your exploration, and on no account miss the colourful bustle of Hindi Lane (p65). If you opt to visit souqs on both sides of the Creek, the traditional *abra* (water taxi) crossing costs just Dh1. Look for traditional coffeehouses tucked away between the stalls for your midmorning pick-me-up. It will cost you a fraction of the cost of that half-pint of latte-froth back home and is sure to deliver twice the caffeine kick.

Traditions & Customs

Unabashedly geared towards tourists, Bur Dubai's Heritage and Diving Villages (p66) on the Shindagha waterfront nonetheless provide real insight into the region's Bedouin traditions and maritime past. These working villages/museums are particularly entertaining for families, with the only possible cost being the inevitable tasting of freshly made traditional sweets and pastries, or the purchase of handcrafted souvenirs. Come here in the evening for the most atmosphere and don't forget your camera.

Museum Cheapies

Dubai and Abu Dhabi may not have the sheer number of museums of other major tourist destinations, but at least those that are here are free or very cheap. In Bur Dubai, the free Traditional Architecture Museum (p66) provides a fascinating glimpse of traditional Arabic building techniques, while the nearby Sheikh Saeed al-Maktoum House (p66) is an architectural gem and provides history buffs with a jaunt back in time for just Dh2. Over the Creek in Deira, the Heritage House (p52) provides a peek at an early wealthy

NEED TO KNOW

➡ **Happy Hour** Take advantage of happy hour and drinks' promotions offered by many bars.

➡ **Hotels** Prices plummet to up to 50% in July and August.

➡ **Self-Catering** Hotel apartments are an inexpensive option and mean serious savings compared to eating out.

➡ **Transport** Travel by the reasonably priced metro whenever possible.

pearl merchant's residence with the only cost being the non-obligatory coffee and snacks (Dh1). Next door is the original Al-Ahmadiya School (p53), dating from 1912, which features dioramas of classrooms and Quran lessons.

Peruse the Art

Don your sunhat and sunblock, shift into exploring mode and head for the industrial-zone confusion that is Al-Quoz (p80), home to many of Dubai's most exciting art galleries. Many of the galleries feature contemporary young artists primarily from the Arab world; others have Tate Modern–style installations. It also costs nothing to check out canvases at Gate Village in the city's Financial District (p82), where you'll find some of the most exclusive galleries this side of New York. The Bastakia area of Bur Dubai is home to still more galleries and art museums, such as the British-run Majlis Gallery (p65), which also runs inexpensive art classes; and the Al Serkal Cultural Foundation (p65), which holds monthly exhibitions of mainly Middle Eastern artists.

The Great Outdoors

Although many of Dubai's beaches have been sadly swallowed up by luxury hotels, there are still some free sandy strips where you can take a dip without doling out the dirhams. These include Jumeirah Open Beach (p94), Kite Beach (p94), Umm Suqeim Beach (p94) and Jumeirah Beach Residence Open Beach (p94), where your most expensive outlay will be industrial quantities of sunblock.

Dubai's green spaces may be sparse but they offer a welcome respite from the city's congested centre. Creekside Park (p67) has pleasant views, a cable car and botanical gardens, while Za'abeel Park (p67) covers 51 hectares with landscaped gardens, picnic areas and a large lake. Jumeirah's Al-Safa Park (p93) has grassy lawns for strolling, while Mushrif Park, on the airport road (behind Mirdif), is Dubai's oldest and largest park, covering some 500 hectares. Bird lovers can head for the Ras al-Khor Wildlife Sanctuary (p80), home to flamingos and other exotic birds.

Budget Grub

Good food at cheap prices is relatively easy to find in Dubai, given the large numbers of expat workers here. The ubiquitous *shwarma* fast food is the most obvious choice but if you prefer a tablecloth, check out the inexpensive Indian restaurants in Bur Dubai (p67) and Deira (p54) as well as Middle Eastern restaurants, particularly Lebanese, which offer mezze of generally excellent value for quality and quantity.

Sights for Free

One of the most spectacular free sights is the choreographed dancing fountains at Dubai Mall (p79) with the lit-up drama of the Burj Khalifa (p79) as a soaring backdrop. Similarly iconic, the Burj al-Arab is best viewed from one of the outdoor cafes at another scenic winner: the traditional Arabian-style Souq Madinat Jumeirah (p102). Dubai's extraordinary shopping malls cost nothing to wander around. Don't miss the dramatic waterfall and exterior aquarium at Dubai Mall (p79), the stained-glass pyramids at Wafi Mall (p72) and the view of the ski slopes at the Mall of the Emirates (p106).

Eating

The culinary landscape in Dubai and Abu Dhabi mirrors the population rather than local Emirati culture. In fact, there is little indigenous cuisine (camel-milk chocolates don't count!). It's hard to go wrong with Middle Eastern restaurants, while Indian cuisine is also a good bet, particularly if you're on a tight budget. Asian food is also well represented, with good Thai and lots of Japanese on offer.

Wining & Dining

Enjoying a glass of wine with dinner is not standard practice in Dubai and Abu Dhabi. There are essentially two types of restaurant here: the hotel restaurant and the independent. Only hotels are licensed to serve alcohol, which is why they house the city's top dining rooms and why they are so popular. Alas, because they fall under the umbrellas of giant corporate hotel chains with strict S&P (standards and procedures) manuals that effectively flatten individuality, many of these top-end spots lack the uniqueness and eccentricity you might find in a first-class Western restaurant. Head to the independent restaurants when you want ethnic authenticity; head to the hotels when you want splash and panache – and a big glass of vino to wash it down.

Vegetarian Dining

Dubai and Abu Dhabi are good for vegetarians, with lots of Asian and subcontinental cuisine on offer. The idea of organic food is still quite new, so plan to eat conventional produce or shop for yourself at the Organic Foods & Cafe (p88). Many of the Indian restaurants, particularly in Deira and Bur Dubai, are vegetarian so typically have several pages of menu choice. Even those that are not dedicated vegetarian restaurants still do fantastic things with vegetables, paneer (cheese) and rice. You can also fill up fast at Lebanese restaurants with all-veg mezze, while Thai places have plenty of coconut-and-chilli spiced veg curries and soups. Vegans may be more challenged, but certainly won't be limited to a few lettuce leaves and a carrot stick. Fine-dining places may have less choice; check websites in advance.

Farsi Food

Iranian migrants moved to Dubai in droves around the 1920s; their influence on the culture, architecture and cooking remains. Dubai is the perfect place to sample the deeply underrated traditional Persian cuisine.

Your appetite will be initially tantalised by soft, warm-from-the-oven bread rolled around cheese and herbs. Soup is also a staple of a traditional Persian meal, and the preparation of rice is superb, ranging from the fluffy and light *chelo* rice to the herb-saturated *pollo* rice and the sticky *kateh* rice.

The closest thing Iran has to a national dish is the *chelo kebab,* a dish of grilled lamb or chicken which has been marinated in onions and lime. Look for hearty lamb stews on the Persian menu which typically incorporate subtle spices and combinations of okra, aubergine (eggplant) and spinach. Finally, wash everything down with *dogh,* a yogurt drink like the Indian lassi, and finish your meal with *falooda,* an icy dessert of frozen vermicelli noodles, rose water and cherry syrup.

The following choices are a good bet for enjoying an authentic Persian dining experience.

Iranian Club (see the boxed text, p110) So authentic, women have to cover their heads.

Pars Iranian Kitchen (p96) Delightful al fresco setting and authentic tasty dishes.

Shabestan (p54) Sophisticated, pricy and superb Persian cuisine.

Special Ostadi (p69) A spit-'n'-sawdust authentic Iranian restaurant.

NEED TO KNOW

Price Ranges

In our listings we use the following price codes to represent the cost of a main course.

$	under Dh50
$$	Dh50–100
$$$	over Dh100

Opening Hours

➡ Restaurants are generally open from noon to 3pm and from 7.30pm to midnight; inexpensive cafe-restaurants are generally open from 9am to midnight.

➡ Most restaurants open seven days a week, with the exception of Friday lunch, when some smaller local eateries close.

Reservations

➡ Make reservations for hotel restaurants. Be prepared to give your mobile number, and expect a call if you're late.

➡ Make weekend bookings – Thursday and Friday nights, and Friday brunch – for top tables at least a week ahead.

Tipping

Many restaurants, particularly in hotels, tack on a 10% service charge, but depending on the hotel, the employees may never see this money. Leave an additional 10% to 15% in cash, under the ticket, particularly at low-end restaurants. If service is perfunctory, it's OK to leave a mere 5%.

How Much?

Street food, such as *shwarma*, costs around Dh4; an inexpensive curry at a cheap Indian restaurant costs about Dh10. At midrange restaurants, mains run from Dh50 to Dh100, at top-end spots more than Dh100. Alcohol will send your bill sky-high – from Dh20 to Dh40 for a bottle of beer, or Dh25 to Dh100+ for a glass of wine.

Listings

Please note that the restaurant listings in this book are ordered by author preference.

Finest Fast Food

Prepared authentically, the best fast food ever invented just has to be the *shwarma*, the staple food of the Middle East. Although it has different names in other countries – gyros in Greece and döner kebap in Turkey – it's only known as *shwarma* in Dubai and Abu Dhabi (or *shawarma*, *shawerma*, *chawerma*, but let's not get too pedantic). While the Greeks might disagree, this hand-held meal originated in Turkey, where döner literally means 'one that turns', referring to the vertical rotisserie the *shwarma* meat is cooked on. Strips of marinated meat (usually chicken or lamb) and fat are placed on a huge skewer that rotates in front of the grill. Dubai is blessed with an enormous number of *shwarma* joints but the rule is to eat at those that are busy; they always offer the freshest choice.

Fine Dining

If you have reserved a table at one of the top restaurants in Dubai or Abu Dhabi, do dress up. Casual wear, particularly jeans and trainers, is not recommended. At worst you may be turned away at the door, and at best, you'll feel uncomfortably underdressed. If you don't have a reservation, call to ask if there are any seats for walk-ins or last-minute cancellations.

Meals with a View

Not only can you enjoy a plentiful choice of fine-dining restaurants here, but you can also relish a stunning view (along with your meal). These range from the steely modernity of dramatic high-rises to the evocative, old-fashioned feel of traditional dhows.

Aquara (p108) Sleek yachts bobbing against a backdrop of skyscrapers in Dubai Marina.

Rivington Grill (p83) Grab a table on the terrace and watch the fabulous dancing fountains while you dine.

Shabestan (p54) Gaze at the ballet of dhows on the Creek.

Thiptara (p83) Dine on a lakeview deck beneath the world's tallest tower.

Vu's (p85) Top-of-the-world vistas from Jumeirah Emirates Towers.

Eating by Neighbourhood

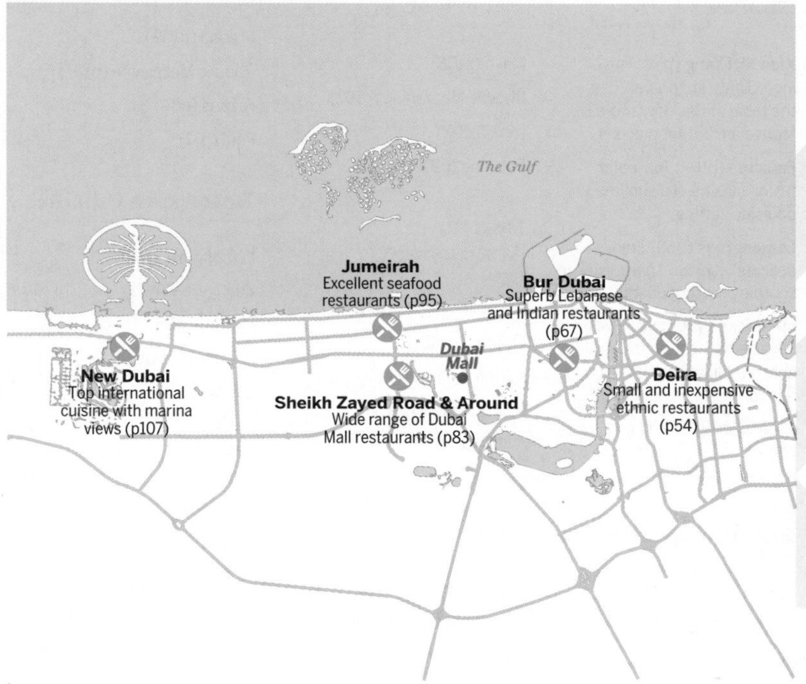

Self-Catering

The small grocery stores around Dubai are good for a box of washing powder, but they're not much fun to browse if you're a foodie trying to suss out Dubai's culinary landscape. The closest thing you'll find to a farmers market is the Fruit and Vegetable Market (Map p206) next to the Fish Market in Deira. There are several major supermarket chains with branches throughout town. Carrefour has probably the biggest selection but the quality tends to be better (and prices higher) at Spinneys. Both stock many products from the UK, North America and Australia and are predictably popular with Western expats; they even have separate 'pork rooms' that are off limits to Muslims. Choithram is cheaper and caters more to the Indian and Pakistani communities. Many markets are open until midnight; some never close.

Lonely Planet's Top Choices

Xiao Wei Yang (p54) Fresh ingredients are prepared at the table at this down-to-earth Mongolian hotpot place.

Eauzone (p107) Top-notch fusion cuisine in a sublime poolside setting.

Lemongrass (p69) Enjoy delicately spiced Thai cuisine in soothing surroundings.

Lime Tree Cafe (p95) Sunshiny flavours meet organic ingredients equalling healthy, happy diners.

Asha's (p69) This succulent, spicy Indian cuisine is pure papadum perfection.

Best Cheap Eats

Noodle House (p85)

Lime Tree Cafe (p95)

Ravi (p96)

Lemongrass (p69)

Xiao Wei Yang (p54)

Best Indian Cuisine

Chutneys (p70)

Khazana (p70)

Asha's (p69)

Indego (p107)

Tiffinbites (p108)

Best Gourmet Experiences

Maya (p108)

Rhodes Mezzanine (p107)

Nina (p108)

Eauzone (p107)

Best for Atmosphere

Bastakiah Nights (p71)

Thiptara (p83)

Karma Kafe (p84)

Bait Al Wakeel (p69)

Awtar (p69)

Best for Foodie Treats

Bateel (p74)

Organic Foods & Cafe (p88)

Souq al-Bahar (p79)

Candylicious (p88)

Best for Brunch

Thai Kitchen (p56)

Aquara (p108)

Sezzam (p109)

Spectrum on One (p85)

Spice Island (p55)

Best for Dessert

Mazina (p109)

Rhodes Mezzanine (p107)

Fazaris (p84)

Paul (p71)

Best Asian Cuisine

Lemongrass (p69)

Zheng He's (p95)

Pai Thai (p96)

Noodle Bowl (p97)

Sho Cho (p121)

Best for Steaks

Fire & Ice (p70)

Tribes (p109)

The Meat Company (p96)

Rhodes Mezzanine (p107)

Marco Pierre White Steakhouse & Grill (p122)

Best for Gourmet Dining

Traiteur (p54)

Shabestan (p54)

Peppercrab (p67)

Al-Mahara (p95)

Sayad (p122)

Drinking & Nightlife

Dubai is a destination famed for its see-and-be-seen nightlife. The best nights are Thursday and Friday – Dubai's weekend nights – when expats burn off steam from their 12-hour-a-day working week. Plan to head to hotels that are licensed to serve alcohol and which, unsurprisingly, are home to most of the best bars and clubs. Note that Abu Dhabi's best bars are also found in its licensed hotels, while Sharjah is totally 'dry'.

Which Bar?

Finding the right bar can be tricky. Dubai is the playground of the parvenu as much as it's a city of expat workers. Choosing an appropriate bar depends on the type of folk you want to meet. Want to get a sense of the social lives of resident workers? Follow the expats. Want to show off that new Marc Jacobs outfit you just bought? Follow the glam crowd. And then there are the niche bars, places frequented by, say, Russian oligarchs and British footballers. Occasionally, you'll spot a random *dishdasha*-clad local breaking ranks with his countrymen (and the law) by drinking alcohol alongside Westerners, but this is an anomaly.

Ordering Drinks

Alcohol is expensive, but that doesn't stop rowdy Westerners from downing pint after shot after pint. Nurse your drinks or you'll shell out a lot of dirhams. Long waits at the bar are common at crowded venues. Conversely, waiters are trained to upsell guests. If you hear 'Would you like another round?', make clear exactly who at the table wants one or you may wind up with a full table of glasses – and a hefty bill. The same applies if you order a bottle of wine; waiters often empty a bottle into one person's glass rather than divvy the last of it up between everyone's, then look at those whose glasses are empty and ask, 'Another bottle?' Also, be wary when you order a bottle of wine from a restaurant wine list as cheaper wines will usually be slipped between far more expensive bottles, which could easily add a couple of zeros to your bill if your index finger wavers during ordering!

Pick 'n' Mix Bars & Pubs

From gritty to glam, multicultural Dubai has plenty of bars and pubs to match your mood. Plan to visit a beach bar in Jumeirah or Dubai Marina to see the sun set over the Gulf, a quintessential Dubai experience; head to a fancy spot, whether it be a dance club or a lounge, to ogle at arrivistes in impossibly high heels; or choose an expat bar to catch a buzz with overworked Westerners laughing too loudly. If you like to make your own discoveries, put down your guidebook and wander the ethnic backstreets of Deira, find a bar in a no-star hotel, maybe an Iranian or Filipino club, and soak up the colour. Alas, this method cannot be recommended for women, single or in groups. There's much prostitution going on in these places and unless you're dressed with nun-like modesty, boozed-up patrons may mistake you for an easy girl.

Sheesha Cafes

If you're not up for drinking, hit the mellow *sheesha* cafes and play a game of backgammon. This is where you'll spot the locals. Emiratis don't like to be around alcohol, but they sure love coffee. Dubai's *sheesha* cafes also provide great insights into local culture. Even if you don't smoke, it's worth reclining languorously and sampling a puff to better understand this traditional male-dominated Middle Eastern pastime. *Sheesha* cafes are open until after midnight, later during winter months. The going rate is Dh20 to Dh60 for all you can inhale.

Ramadan Restrictions

If you are planning on partying during your visit then ensure you avoid Ramadan.

NEED TO KNOW

Costs

It's enough to give anyone the hiccups. You could pay anything from Dh20 to Dh40 for a pint of beer here or Dh25 to Dh100+ for a glass of wine, depending on quality and vintage. Hotels add a 10% service charge.

Opening Hours

- Many bars and clubs are open seven days a week, although some close one day a week.
- Alcohol service is illegal between 4pm and 6pm on Friday and Saturday.
- Hotel bars are generally open from around 11am to 3pm and from 6pm to midnight.
- Smaller venues may close at 1am.
- Clubs open later, from around 8pm to 3am, but don't really get going until 11pm.

Cover Charges

Cover charges range from Dh50 to Dh300 depending on whether there's a big-name DJ. Ladies should look out for specified 'Ladies' Nights' offered at many bars around town; these generally offer up to two free drinks, including cocktails.

Listings

Please note that the drinking and nightlife listings in this book are ordered by author preference.

Although most bars remain open in the evening (it is still legal to serve alcohol after sundown), live-music venues and nightclubs with dancing generally close for the entire period – even background music must be kept to a minimum.

Big-name DJs

DJs spin nearly every night of the week (except during Ramadan), with regular one-off dance events. The repertoire is global – funk, soul, house (lots of house), trip-hop, hip hop, R&B, African, Arabic and Latino. Clubbers come out in force when big-name DJs like Pierre Ravan, Roger Sanchez and Joey Negro jet in for the weekend, but even on a regular old Tuesday, you can find ardent club kids grooving beneath disco balls to house music, the preferred sound in Dubai. Thursday and Friday are the big nights out, when marauding expats join gyrating tourists on the dance floor. For up-to-date details on what's happening in the club world, check out the following websites.

- **www.dubailook.com**
- **www.platinumlist.ae**
- **www.timeoutdubai.com**
- **www.ohmrecords.com**
- **www.infusion.ae**

Club Policies

The door policies obviously vary according to the venue but it is not unusual for top clubs to restrict entrance to advance reservations only, particularly if a top international DJ is spinning the discs. Always check websites first. Some clubs are also guilty of unabashed racist policies, particularly against southern Asians, while others turn away groups of single men, especially on busy nights.

Overall, the Dubai nightclubbing scene is an opportunity for the local fashionistas to strut their stuff, so be prepared to seriously dress up or risk feeling seriously frumpy, or, worse still, being turned away at the door. Beachside venues are generally more informal although there will still be plenty of designer tags and attitude on display.

Transport Tips

- It's best not to criss-cross the city on a weekend; traffic is abominable on Thursday and Friday nights and taxis can be hard to come by.
- Stick to a particular area or two for your nightlife entertainment, such as Dubai Marina, Jumeirah, Downtown Dubai, Deira or Bur Dubai.
- Under no circumstances should you *ever* get behind the wheel of a car if you've had even one sip of alcohol because...
- Dubai has a zero-tolerance policy on drink-driving and you could be imprisoned for up to a month if you are caught under the influence behind the wheel.

Buying Alcohol

One of the most common questions among first-time visitors here is: 'Can I buy alcohol?' The answer is yes – in some places.

Drinking & Nightlife by Neighbourhood

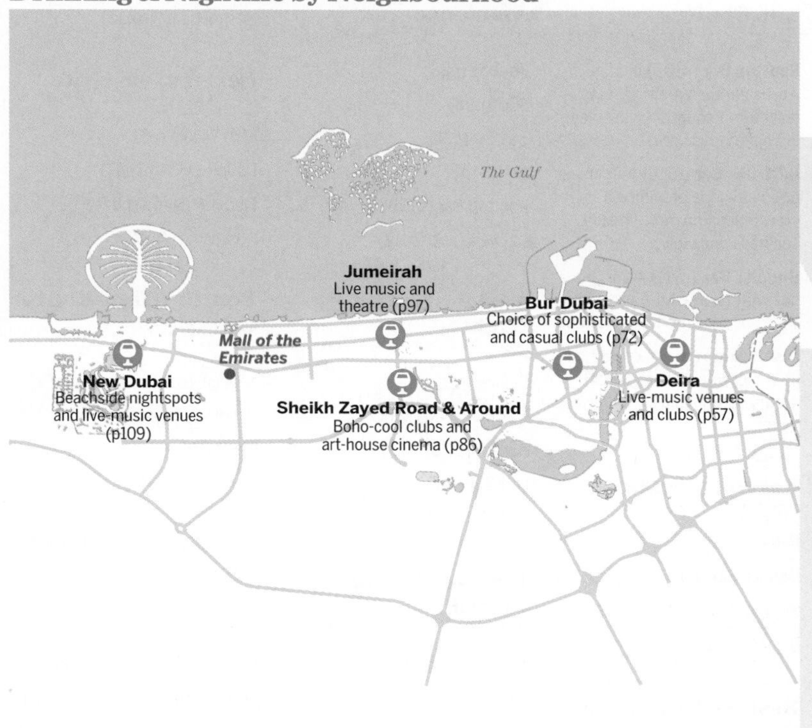

When arriving by air, you can, as a non-Muslim visitor over 18, buy certain quantities of booze in the airport duty-free shop upon arrival (the limit is 4L of spirits, wine or beer). With the exception of 'dry' Sharjah, where alcohol and even *sheesha* (water pipe) smoking is banned, you can also purchase alcohol in bars and clubs that are generally attached to four- and five-star hotels for on-site consumption. Expat residents can acquire an alcohol licence, which entitles them to a fixed monthly limit of alcohol available from alcohol stores. The only store where you can officially buy alcohol without a licence is at the Barracuda Beach Resort in the northern emirate of Umm al-Quwain, north of Sharjah, about an hour's drive north of Dubai. Note that you are not officially allowed to transport alcohol through 'dry' Sharjah, although most people just seem to take the risk anyway.

The Sin Tax

How exactly do the authorities decide on those sky-high booze prices? Yes, it's all down to a hefty *haram* (literally 'forbidden') tax. Consider the following (or go teetotal) during your trip.

- ➡ A bottle of Californian plonk that costs US$10 wholesale automatically incurs a 50% import tax, upping the importer's price to $15.
- ➡ Add a 33% profit for the importer, and now it costs $20.
- ➡ The Dubai-based purchaser (ie the hotel that sells it to the consumer) pays a 30% tax. Now it costs US$26 – at wholesale.
- ➡ The hotel then marks up the price 200% to make its profit and pay its employees. Now it costs about $75.
- ➡ At the moment of sale, the public pays an additional 20%, jacking up the final retail price to a whopping $90.

Lonely Planet's Top Choices

Rooftop Bar (p109) Indulge in a little gentle hip-swinging to chilled-out sounds while enjoying panoramic views.

BiCE Sky Bar (p110) Immensely popular venue providing a crowd-pleasing mix of heady cocktails and views.

Buddha Bar (p111) A gorgeous bar with candlelight and sumptuous decor for true romantics.

Irish Village (p57) A congenial Irish pub with blarney decor, a leafy setting and regular live music.

Best for Cocktails

Red Lounge (p72)

Uptown Bar (p97)

Skyview Bar (p97)

Bar 44 (p111)

Best for Panoramic Views

Maya (p111)

Rooftop Bar (p109)

Bar 44 (p111)

Skyview Bar (p97)

Red Lounge (p72)

Neos (p86)

Best for Smoochy Ambience

Koubba (p98)

360°(p98)

Bar Zar (p98)

Ku-Bu (p57)

Rooftop Bar (p109)

Catwalk Club (p112)

Best for Ladies' Nights

Blends (p111)

Nasimi Beach (p112)

Barasti (p111)

Left Bank (p97)

1897 (p111)

Best for the Glam Crowd

Buddha Bar (p111)

Red Lounge (p72)

Cin Cin (p86)

Cristal (p122)

Etoiles (p123)

Best for Special Promotions

Bar Zar (p98)

Terrace (p57)

Hive (p87)

Nasimi Beach (p112)

Best for Pub Grub

Irish Village (p57)

Double Decker (p87)

Fibber Magee's (p87)

Nezesaussi (p87)

Best for High-Rollin' DJs

N'Dulge (p112)

People by Crystal (p72)

Chi (p72)

Zinc (p87)

Best for Waterfront Views

Terrace (p57)

Ikandy (p86)

Sho Cho (p98)

Nasimi Beach (p112)

Best for (Relatively) Economical Drinks

Irish Village (p57)

Old Vic (p72)

Cooz (p72)

Belgian Café (p122)

Entertainment

Generally you don't come to Dubai if you're after full-on highbrow entertainment. Live performances tend to be light fare – musicals, cabaret or touring shows. That said, you can find some serious stars on the concert circuit both here and in neighbouring Abu Dhabi: Tom Jones, Paul McCartney and Britney Spears all played to sell-out audiences in 2011.

Movie Time

If you want to catch a movie, you've got plenty of high-tech multiplexes to take in the blockbusters; almost all are in shopping centres. Alternative and art-house cinemas are practically nonexistent (there's one screen at Reel Cinemas in Dubai Mall that screens non-mainstream fare). Galleries and alternative venues, such as the XVA Cafe (p71), occasionally run one-off film nights. Also check out the **Alliance Française** (Map p214; ☎04-335 8712; www.afdubai.org), which shows weekly films in French and occasionally hosts festivals. Indie screenings are usually free and promoted in *Time Out*. Another good site to unearth upcoming screenings is www.artinthecity.com.

The Dubai International Film Festival (p22), usually held in December, is arguably the cinematic highlight of the year. There's also the Middle East International Film Festival (p21), held in Abu Dhabi in October, which is seen as a warm-up for the Dubai event. The other weeks of the calendar can be disheartening. The only independent cinemas are dedicated to Tamil, Hindi and Malayalam films, while English-language films are restricted to the unadventurous multiplexes.

Live Music

Dubai's live-music scene is finally generating a buzz. Although cover bands still predominate, there's an increasing pool of local talent hitting the stages of such venues as Chi (p72), Barasti (p111), Fridge (p98), Jambase (p98 and the Irish Village (p57). Homegrown bands to keep an ear out for include metal band Nervecell; the hip-hop collective The Recipe; Arabic folk trio Dahab; hard-rock band Nikotin; and reggae rock by Sho. Dubai-based quintet Juliana Down gained serious cred when they warmed up the crowd at a 2011 concert of Guns N' Roses in Abu Dhabi. Meanwhile, long-term favourite Sandwash released the album *Master Blaster Hole* in 2010, a crisp pop-punk selection of edgy and experimental compositions.

Concert Venues

International top talent also comes to town, although many bypass Dubai to give concerts at the swanky Yas Arena in Abu Dhabi, where big names like Paul McCartney appeared in 2011. Still, it was Sting, Carlos Santana and Elton John who gave the inaugural concerts at Dubai's Meydan Racecourse in early 2010. Other venues that have hosted big stars (such as Robbie Williams, Tom Jones and Jamie Cullum) include the Dubai Media City Amphitheatre, Dubai Festival City Arena and the Sevens Stadium.

Unfortunately, several fledgling music festivals, such as Dubai Desert Rock Festival and Desert Rhythm, have been postponed 'until further notice'. Thankfully the Dubai International Jazz Festival is an exception and celebrated its 10th anniversary in 2012, with James Morrison, Jason Mraz and Jools Holland included on the star-studded line-up.

Meanwhile, you might also want to keep an eye out for Middle Eastern and subcontinental stars. When you see big posters and hear multiple radio ads for acts you're unfamiliar with, do a quick Google search to find out where they're from. There's a reason they're so popular. Lebanese, Indian,

NEED TO KNOW

Costs

Costs vary wildly, depending on whether you're hearing a jazz trio in a snazzy bar where a glass of wine can easily cost Dh50, or attending a big-name concert with tickets typically starting at Dh200.

Music Bans

Dancing and loud music in public places is strictly forbidden. This includes beaches, parks and residential areas; dancing is restricted to licensed venues only. If you are doing some gyrating at a bar without a music licence, you may be unceremoniously asked to stop.

Door Policies

These obviously vary according to the venue but it is not unusual for top clubs to restrict entrance to advance reservations only, particularly when a top international DJ is spinning the discs. Always check websites first.

Entertainment Hours

- ➡ Clubs open late, from around 8pm to 3am, but don't really get going until 11pm.
- ➡ Concerts kick off late, generally not before 10pm.

Drinking

It is worth repeating in this section that Dubai has zero tolerance of drinking and driving, so if you intend to have a drink at the concert venue bars, leave the car at home.

Pakistani and Iranian acts draw big crowds of expat locals... This is the stuff you can't hear back home. Check *Time Out* and *7 Days* magazines for the latest line-up.

The Arts

Dubai's performing arts scene is still in its infancy, but there are some new venues that give hope for an increasingly bright future. The Dubai Community Theatre and Arts Centre (DUCTAC; p112) is one of the few spaces that also trains the spotlight on local talent.

Hitting the Town

For entertainment listings, your safest bet is the weekly *Time Out* magazine, although the freebie *7 Days* is also worth a glance. Look for free guides and leaflets promoting clubs, dance parties and gigs; find them at bars, cafes, Virgin Megastore (p61) and Ohm Records (p74). The same places should also have copies of *Infusion*, an excellent free biweekly pocket-sized mag covering clubs, bars, movies, music, fashion and other lifestyle topics.

As usual, the most current information is on the web. *Infusion*'s website (www.infusion.ae) has an up-to-the-minute party schedule. The same goes for the online club guide on www.platinumlist.ae, which also lets you book tickets to the major events.

Otherwise, for tickets to concerts and other shows, phone the *Time Out* ticketline on ☎800 4669 (☎+971 4 210 8567 from overseas). Or buy online at either www.timeouttickets.com or www.boxofficeme.com.

Stained-glass dome of Wafi Mall (p72)

Shopping

Dubai loves to shop. The city has just about perfected the art of the mall, which is the de facto 'town plaza': the place to go with the family, hang out with friends and be entertained. Dubai malls have ski slopes, ice rinks and aquariums. They look like ancient Persia, futuristic movie sets or a little bit of Disneyland, surrounded by desert.

NEED TO KNOW

Opening Hours

Malls in Dubai open from 10am to 10pm Sunday to Wednesday, from 10am to midnight Thursday to Saturday (weekends), and later during the Dubai Shopping Festival and Ramadan (often until 1am). Traditionally, souqs and non-mall stores close a few hours during the afternoon for prayer, lunch and rest, and don't open on Fridays until late afternoon, but that's changing. These days many remain open all day. Malls get packed on Friday nights.

Returns

Try before you buy and ask about return policies, especially for gifts. Many stores offer returns for store credit only. When in doubt, consider a gift certificate, which generally has an extensive expiration period and with international chains can often be used online.

Websites

➡ **www.quickdubai.com** Great for gifts, including last-minute essentials such as cakes and flowers.

➡ **www.sukar.com** A private online shopping site offering top discounts on known brands. You will need an invite – persevere, you won't be sorry.

➡ **www.souq.com** A local version of eBay with some top bargains and plenty of variety.

➡ **www.nahel.com** A great range of products, including electronics, perfumes and watches.

➡ **www.berrybehaved.com** Includes home-decor items and stylish accessories.

➡ **www.emiratesavenue.com** Great for the latest electronics, including TVs and iPhones.

Listings

➡ The listings in this title are in order of author preference.

How to Find a Bargain

The range of stores – high-street to designer, electronics to carpets – is amazing, but true bargains are as rare as tulips in Tonga, except during the Dubai Shopping Festival (p73). The souqs in Deira and Bur Dubai can equal good prices, providing you are willing to haggle. In general, cut the first suggested price by half and start from there. The Deira Gold Souq is one of the cheapest places in the world to buy gold and, because the regulations regarding authenticity are very strict here, you can be sure that if you are considering a 24-carat bauble, then it is undoubtedly genuine. Small Indian- or Asian-run department stores are also good places to pick up bargain basics, as long as you're not looking for anything of fashion catwalk calibre. And don't miss the Dubai Flea Market (www.dubai-fleamarket.com), held on the first Saturday of the month at Al-Safa Park in Jumeirah, where you can find just about everything – including the kitchen sink.

Main Malls

Dubai Mall (p88) The shopper's Shangri-La, Dubai Mall is the largest shopping mall in the world.

Mall of the Emirates (p112) Another whopper, probably most famous for its indoor ski slope.

BurJuman Centre (p72) Especially good for high-end fashion.

Mirdif City Centre (p58) Opened in 2010 with a superb range of shops, plus a massive play station for kids.

Ibn Battuta Mall (p113) Covers six country-themed courts on one easy-to-navigate level.

Deira City Centre (p58) One of the first malls to open here.

Dubai Festival Centre (p61) A pretty canalside setting, plus great restaurants and shops.

Marina Mall (p113) More than 400 shops on the breakwater, plus a huge activity centre for kids.

Abu Dhabi Mall (p123) A tempting choice of boutiques, designer stores and international chains.

Best Buys

BEDOUIN JEWELLERY

Bedouin jewellery is brilliant in Dubai and with the steady popularity of boho ethnic chic, makes a great gift. Look for elaborate silver necklaces and pendants, chunky earrings and rings, and wedding belts, many of which incorporate coral, turquoise and semiprecious stones. Very little of the older Bedouin jewellery comes from the

Shopping by Neighbourhood

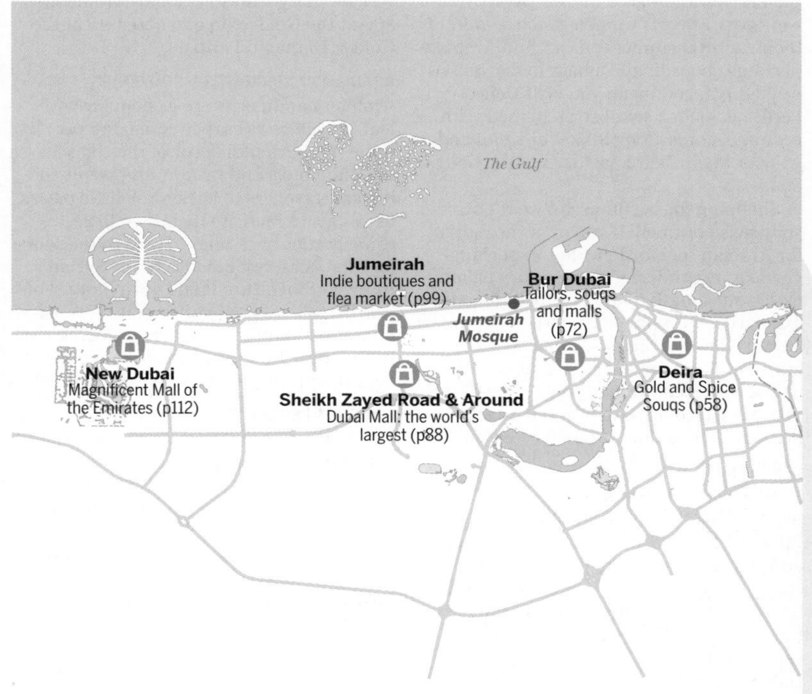

Emirates; most of it originates in Oman, Yemen and Afghanistan.

EXOTIC DELICACIES

Fragrant Iranian and Spanish saffron costs far less here than it does back home. Buy it in Deira's Spice Souq or in supermarkets. Honey from Saudi Arabia and Oman is scrumptious. Look for it in speciality shops in Satwa, in the Spice Souq and in supermarkets. Its colour ranges from light gold to almost black.

CARPETS

Dubai is a carpet-lover's paradise. Fine Persian carpets, colourful Turkish and Kurdish kilims, and rough-knotted Bedouin rugs are all widely available. Dubai has a reputation in the region for having the highest-quality carpets at the best prices. Bargaining is the norm. If you can't secure the price you want, head to another store. When you buy a carpet, ask for a certificate of authentication guaranteed by the Dubai Chamber of Commerce & Industry, so you can be sure that the carpet actually comes from where the vendor says it does.

KITSCH SOUVENIRS

The ultimate kitsch souvenir used to be a colourful mosque clock with an irritating call-to-prayer alarm. Now the souqs and souvenir shops overflow with wacky, kitsch gifts – glass Burj al-Arab paperweights, wooden Russian dolls painted as Emiratis, Barbie and Ken dolls in Emirati dress, key rings strung with miniature towers, camel-crossing-sign fridge magnets, and coffee mugs and baseball caps with Sheikh Zayed or Sheikh Mohammed waving to the crowd.

PERFUME & INCENSE

Attars (Arabian perfumes) are spicy and strong. Historically, this was a necessity: with precious little water, washing was a sometimes-thing, so women smothered themselves in *attars* and incense. As you walk past Emirati women, catch a whiff of their exotic perfume. You can find Arabian-perfume shops in all Dubai's malls, but we highly recommend you visit Deira's Perfume Souq, a small stretch lined with perfume stores along Sikkat al-Khail and Al-Soor Sts in Deira, just east of the Gold Souq.

Shopping for perfume can wear out your sense of smell. If you're in the market for Arabian scents, do what top perfumers do to neutralise their olfactory palate: close your mouth and make three forceful exhalations through your nose. Blast the air hard, in short bursts, using your diaphragm. Blowing your nose first is probably a wise idea.... Some people incorrectly say to smell coffee grounds, but all this practice does is numb your sense of smell.

TEXTILES

Vendors at Bur Dubai Souq and along nearby Al-Fahidi St carry vibrant, colourful textiles from the Indian subcontinent and southeast Asia. They're remarkably cheap, but quality varies. Silk, cotton and linen represent the best value. Dubai's tailors work quickly, and their rates are very reasonable. Prices start at around Dh35 for a shirt or skirt. Draperies may cost as little as Dh10 apiece.

ELECTRONICS

If it plugs into a wall you can buy it in Dubai. Because of minimal duties, Dubai is the cheapest place in the region to buy electronics and digital technology. The selection is huge. Research products of interest before hitting the stores though; sales staff don't always know enough. For the lowest prices and no-name brands, head to Al-Fahidi St in Bur Dubai and the area around Al-Sabkha and Al-Maktoum Hospital Rds, near Baniyas Sq, known as the Electronics Souq. If you want an international warranty, shell out the extra money and head to a mall, Carrefour or Jumbo Electronics.

GOLD & GEMS

The City of Gold's glistening reputation grows from low prices and the sheer breadth of stock. There are a whopping 700 jewellery stores in Dubai, with nearly 300 at the Gold Souq and about 90 at the Gold & Diamond Park.

ARABIAN HANDICRAFTS & SOUVENIRS

Arabian handicrafts are as popular with Dubai visitors as carpets, gold and perfume. The Oriental decor of the city's top-end hotels and restaurants seems to inspire travellers to pack away little pieces of exotica to recreate their own little genie bottles back home. Head to the souqs for Moroccan coloured lanterns, Syrian rosewood furniture inlaid with mother-of-pearl, Arabian brass coffee pots, Turkish miniature paintings, and embroidered Indian wall hangings and cushion covers dotted with tiny mirrors.

GOURMET PRODUCTS

The de rigeur gift for any proper gourmet, Bateel dates (www.bateel.ae) are the ultimate luxury food of Arabia. Bateel dates will spoil you for the more standard variety, for ever. The dates come from Saudi Arabia, which has the ideal growing conditions: sandy, alkaline soil and extreme heat. Quality control is tight: Bateel has its own farms and production equipment. The dates sold here are big and fat, with gooey-moist centres. Because they have a 70% sugar content, dates technically have unlimited shelf life, but you'll find they taste best around the autumn harvest.

At first glance, Bateel boutiques look like a jewellery store, with polished-glass display cases and halogen pin spots illuminating the goods. A closer look reveals perfectly aligned pyramids of dates – thousands of them. Bateel plays to its audience with gorgeous packaging that might leave the recipient of your gift expecting gold or silver within.

The stuffed dates make a great gift – try the candied orange peel and caramelised almonds. If you miss your chance in town (there are several branches), you can stock up at the airport as you leave Dubai. A cardboard box will set you back Dh120 per kilogram, a fancy box Dh200, and a little beribboned sampler of five or seven perfect dates around Dh30.

Lonely Planet's Top Choices

Ajmal (p74) Exotic Arabian essential oils and perfumes sold in exquisitely beautiful bottles.

S*uce (p99) Sassy avant-garde fashions from a wide range of young international designers.

Candylicious (p88) Realise your ultimate sweet dream at this colourful giant-size candy store.

United Designers (p58) Showcasing exciting young local designers with totally original fashion.

Ginger & Lace (p113) Sexy fashions in silky fabrics with lots of floral and lace.

Best Cut-Price Shopping Streets

Khalid bin al-Waleed Rd, Bur Dubai (Map p210)

Al-Fahidi St, Bur Dubai (Map p210)

Al-Hisn St & 73 St, Bur Dubai (Map p210)

Al-Rigga Rd, Deira (Map p206)

Al-Satwa Rd, Satwa (Map 218)

Best for Gifts

O' de Rose (p99)

Camel Company (p102)

Bateel (p74)

Lata's (p102)

Best for Accessories

Marami (p88)

Blue Cactus (p100)

Topshop (p101)

Forever 21 (p114)

Ginger & Lace (p113)

Best for Electronics

Al-Ain Centre (p74)

Jumbo Electronics (p114)

Bang & Olufsen (p75)

Fono (p114)

Best for Women's Fashion

If (p99)

S*uce (p99)

Luxecouture (p100)

Ginger & Lace (p113)

Bauhaus (p114)

United Designers (p58)

Best Shopping Festivals

Dubai Shopping Festival (p73)

Dubai Summer Surprises (p73)

Global Village (p73)

Art Dubai (p20)

Best Shopping Malls

Dubai Mall (p88)

Mall of the Emirates (p112)

BurJuman Centre (p72)

Mirdif City Centre (p58)

Best for Body Beautiful

Faces (p74)

Lush (p60)

Ajmal (p74

Best Mall Entertainment

Ski Dubai (p113)

Dubai Ice Rink (p90)

Dubai Fountain (p79)

Dubai Aquarium & Underwater Zoo (p79)

Best 'Faux' Souqs

Souq Khan Murjan (p72)

Souq al-Bahar (p88)

Souq Madinat Jumeirah (p102)

Sports & Activities

Before the boom, Emiratis spent their free time watching camel races, riding horses and boating. Today, sports and activities in Dubai and Abu Dhabi have broadened to reflect the new population. You could spend an afternoon skittering across the surf on a kiteboard or enjoying a luxury spa treatment. And if you can't stand the sweltering heat – there's always Ski Dubai.

Health & Fitness

The health-and-fitness set is composed primarily of Western expats. With so many people working so hard to continue wearing their skinny jeans, they gravitate to health clubs, yoga studios and fitness centres, and Dubai is full of sore muscles. Consequently, massage and beauty-treatment schedules at day spas fill up fast: book ahead. If you prefer swimming in salt water instead of chlorine, check out one of the public or paid beaches.

Day Spas & Massage

Though you can get a good rub-down at most sports clubs, for the proper treatment book a dedicated spa. Dubai's spas like to incorporate food into their treatments – berries, chocolate, even gingerbread at Christmas. If you're dubious, more-conventional treatments are also available. Make reservations as far in advance as possible for top spas such as Amara (p61) and the Oriental Hammam (p115). Ask if a spa treatment includes use of the pool and grounds. If it does, make a day of it – arrive early and wait poolside. Note: facials look best the next day, so if you have a fancy dinner engagement and want to look great, get the treatment the day before. Most spas offer manicures and pedicures, but if you want a dedicated nail salon, try **Nail Spa** (www.thenailspa.com); there are several branches around town, including one in the Mercato Mall in Jumeirah (Map p218).

Dancing

Strictly Come Dancing fans can take classes in everything from the foxtrot to the nightclub two-step at the renowned US-founded **Arthur Murray Dance School** (www.arthurmurraydubai.com) with branches in New Dubai (p115) and Souq al-Bahar (p79). Private classes are also available.

Skiing

The largest indoor ski slope in the world, **Ski Dubai** (p113; www.skidxb.com), located at the Mall of the Emirates, is an essential for winter-sport enthusiasts. You can also take lessons and learn how to snowboard.

Running

The winter months are cool enough for running nearly anytime during the day; in summer you've got to get up with the sun to jog with no fear of heatstroke. There are excellent jogging tracks in Al-Safa Park (p93) and Za'abeel Park (p67), and along Jumeirah Beach (p94). Prefer running with company? Check out the Dubai Road Runners (p103) or the **Dubai Creek Striders** (www.dubaicreek-striders.com; Sheikh Zayed Rd). If you're into the more social aspects of running (read: drinking afterwards), look into Dubai's 'hashing' clubs at www.deserthash.org. The Dubai Marathon (p20) takes over city streets in January.

Water Sports

DIVING

Diving around Dubai means mostly nosing around shipwrecks on the sandy seabed of the Gulf at a depth of between 10m and 35m. The better sites are generally a long way offshore and mostly for experienced divers. Creatures you might encounter include clownfish, sea snakes, Arabian angelfish and possibly even rays and barracuda.

For novices, the sites off the United Arab Emirates (UAE) East Coast (Khor Fakkan and Dibba; see p132) are most suitable. Also popular are dive spots still further north, off the rugged Musandam Peninsula, which is actually part of Oman. However, fast-flowing currents here require a higher level of experience. In recent times, the eastern shores have been beleaguered by the red tide (see the boxed text, p164), so be sure to ask dive operators about conditions. A day's diving includes two dives and costs around Dh300 to Dh450, including the boat ride and equipment.

For details on the top dive and snorkelling sites in the UAE and the Musandam, consult the 180-page *UAE Underwater Explorer* (www.explorerpublishing.com).

KITESURFING

Kitesurfers congregate at northwest-facing Kite Beach (p94), aka Wollongong Beach, where there's a designated launch and recovery area. It's about 3km north of the Burj al-Arab, past Umm Suqeim Hospital in the district of Umm Suqeim 1. Novices should take a few lessons (about Dh300 per hour). Qualified instructors can be found at **Duco Maritime** (☎050 870 3427; www.ducomaritime.com).

SURFING

Jumeirah's Open Beach is home to Dubai's longest-standing surf school, with lessons available daily from 9am to 5pm, depending on surf conditions. Board rental is Dh50 an hour or Dh200 a day. For details, see **Surf Dubai** (☎050 622 3020; www.surfingdubai.com).

WATERSKIING

Waterskiing in the polluted Dubai Creek is not recommended. Instead, head to Dubai Marina or Abu Dhabi. Waterskiing at a Gulf-front five-star hotel with its own beach club costs around Dh150 for 20 minutes – which, if you're a novice, is a long time. Nonguests must also pay a daily admission fee for access to the hotel grounds and beach club (usually about Dh75 to Dh250). Try Le Meridien Mina Seyahi (p94), where beach access costs Dh150 (Dh250 on Friday and Saturday) and waterskiing Dh150.

BOAT CHARTER

To get a perspective on just how far the city now stretches, see it from the water. **Dubai Creek Golf & Yacht Club** (Map p208; ☎04-205 4646; www.dubaigolf.com; near Deira side of Al-Garhoud Bridge) offers boat charters aboard skippered 33ft vessels. A one-hour Creek cruise costs Dh800, while three-hour trips taking in the Palm Deira are Dh2200. The six-hour trip (Dh3800) goes down the coast to the Palm Jumeirah via the Burj al-Arab.

WATERPARKS

Dubai has two waterparks: Wild Wadi Waterpark (p102) and Aquaventure (p115).

Gyms

Nearly every hotel in Dubai has a gym, but the equipment is often chosen by people who don't work out. The worst have only a few stationary bikes and a cumbersome all-in-one machine with too many cables and pulleys that constantly need adjusting. The best have a full complement

NEED TO KNOW

Planning Ahead

Dubai and Abu Dhabi host some top sports events over the year and it's imperative that you reserve your place and book tickets in advance, especially for such grand-slam events as Abu Dhabi's Grand Prix.

Time of Year

If you are planning to attend or participate in an event, bear in mind the time of year, as this can dramatically impact the cost of your stay with hotels and flights costing considerably more outside the midsummer months.

Buying Tickets

Check websites for relevant reservations procedures. The following sites are good sources of ticket info and booking:

- www.boxofficeme.com
- www.itp.net/tickets
- www.dubaisportscity.ae

Costs

Costs obviously vary wildly depending on the event, but you can reckon on spending around Dh2000 on a three-day Grand Prix pass, Dh230 on a top rugby match and Dh230 on a ticket for a golf tournament such as the Omega Dubai Desert Classic.

of top-end circuit- and weight-training equipment. Admission to gyms generally costs about Dh100 for a one-day pass; it's twice that at a top-end hotel, but you'll gain access to the resort's grounds, tennis courts and swimming pool. If you're going to a hotel gym, get your money's worth by making a day of it.

Golf

Dubai has become a big golfing destination and boasts several championship courses designed by big names – such as Greg Norman, designer of **Jumeirah Golf Estates** (www.jumeirahgolfestates.com), the first phase of which opened in November 2009 in time to stage the European Tour's first Dubai World Championship. Overall, clubs don't require memberships but green fees can soar to Dh850 for 18 holes during the peak winter season (roughly mid-November to late March), although they drop the rest of the year, especially in summer. Proper attire is essential. If you're serious about golf, reserve your tee times as soon as you book your hotel and flight.

Desert Rallying & Sandboarding

Off-road driving in the desert (also disturbingly known as 'dune bashing') is hugely popular. At weekends, the city's traffic-tired workers zip down the Dubai–Hatta road and unleash their pent-up energy on the sand dunes, such as the ruby-red heap of sand halfway to Hatta nicknamed 'Big Red'.

All the major car-hire companies can provide 4WD vehicles. Expect to pay around Dh500 for 24 hours for a Toyota Fortuner or a Hummer H3, plus CDW (Collision Damage Waiver) of Dh60 and an extra Dh12 for personal insurance.

We strongly recommend a few hours of training before you drive off-road for the first time. **Desert Rangers** (Map p220; www.desertrangers.com; 4hr driving course per car Dh1800, sandboarding adult/child Dh250/160) provides basic and advanced courses. It also organises half-day sandboarding safaris with a camel ride included in the price.

Desert Camping

If you've hired a 4WD, the possibilities for camping are fantastic. You can head to the windswept sand dunes of Liwa, the wadis near Hatta, the mountains of Ras al-Khaimah or the East Coast beaches around Dibba. If you don't have a 4WD, you can still find some beautiful spots within walking distance of well-paved roads.

Make sure you are adequately equipped and are carrying a fully charged mobile phone (preferably a GPS), sunscreen, insect repellent and plenty of water.

Don't even consider camping between May and September when the days are scorching and the nights hot and humid.

Spectator Sports

HORSE RACING

The single biggest sport among elite Emiratis is horse racing, with races held at the superb **Meydan Racecourse** (p89; www.meydan.ae/racecourse), a futuristic stadium with a grandstand bigger than most airport terminals. Spanning 1.6km, it has a solar- and titanium-panelled roof, can accommodate up to 60,000 spectators and integrates a five-star hotel. For the exact racing schedule and tickets, contact **Dubai Racing Club** (www.dubairacingclub.com). Even if you don't like horse racing, attending a race presents great people-watching opportunities.

CAMEL RACING

Traditionally, camels were raced by child jockeys, sometimes as young as six or seven years and weighing less than 20kg. They were often 'bought' from impoverished families in Pakistan or Bangladesh, trained in miserable conditions and kept deliberately underweight. International human-rights groups decried the practice and in 2005 the UAE issued a ban on the use of children. Human jockeys have since been replaced with robotic ones operated remotely by their owners, who race around the inside track in their SUVs, cheering on their camels. Trust us, it's a weird sight.

If you want to watch camel racing, head to the Al Marmoom Camel Racetrack, around 45 minutes from the city on the Dubai–Al-Ain E66 road. Races are held from October to March at 7am and 2pm, mainly at weekends. Call ahead on ☎04-832 6526 to confirm. Entrance is free.

MOTOR RACING

Motor sports are exceedingly popular with Emiratis. The **Emirates Motor Sports Federation** (EMSF; www.emsf.ae) holds events throughout the year, with the important ones scheduled to take place during the cooler months. A round of the FIA Cross-Country Rally World Cup, the **Abu Dhabi**

Desert Challenge (www.abudhabidesertchallenge.com) brings top rally drivers to the UAE from around the world in March. There are several smaller rallies in February and March, including the 1000 Dunes Rally and the Spring Desert Rally, which are both 4WD events. Visit EMSF's website for details.

UAE FOOTBALL

On winter weeknights, neighbourhood stadiums in Dubai are packed with up to 10,000 spectators – mostly young Emirati men – passionately barracking for their favourite football teams. Surprisingly, most foreigners (expats or visitors) hardly attend the matches. And they're rarely covered by the local English-language press. If you're a football fan, attend a match once and you may be hooked – the carnival atmosphere is electric. Fans dress up in colour-coordinated outfits, and a singer and band of drummers lead song and dance routines to inspire their teams.

Founded in 1973, the United Arab Emirates (UAE) football league was renamed UAE Premier Division for the 2009/10 season and consists of a dozen teams. Tempers may flare during matches between the old rivals: Al-Ahli, Sheikh Mohammed's red-and-white jersey team, and the purple-clad Al-Ain. Dubai-based Al-Ahli also represented the UAE in the 2009 FIFA Club World Cup, held in Abu Dhabi, losing 0-2 to Auckland City in their only game. In the 2010 FIFA club tournament, the Abu Dhabi–based Al-Wahda team represented the UAE.

If you would like to attend a football match, check the www.dubaifootball.com and www.football7s.com websites, which include schedules and venues of upcoming matches. You can purchase tickets via these sites or from the dedicated ticket agencies listed in the Need to Know section.

RUGBY

Dubai's rugby club, **Dubai Exiles Rugby Club** (www.dubaiexiles.com), has been headquartered at a slick new stadium called The Sevens, located about 30 minutes outside Dubai on the Al-Ain Rd. The Exiles are a founding member of the Arabian Gulf Rugby Football Union and put on one of Dubai's biggest sporting events, the **Dubai Rugby Sevens** (www.dubairugby7s.com), an annual three-day event featuring 16 international squads held in November or December.

Competition Sports Calendar

Dubai Marathon (www.dubaimarathon.org) Sweat it out in January with thousands of other runners or just cheer 'em on during this popular street race with a prize fund of a million dollars. In 2010, Haile Gebrselassie won the race for the third year in a row. Less-energetic types can enter a 10km run or a 3km 'fun run'.

Dubai Desert Classic (www.dubaidesertclassic.com) The golfing elite, including Rory McIlroy and Henrik Stenson, comes to town for this fine February event, held at the Emirates Golf Club (p116). There have been some thrilling finishes over the past couple of years – the 18th hole has become legendary on the PGA circuit.

Dubai Tennis Championships (www.dubaitennischampionships.com) Big-name players like Serena Williams and Novak Djokovic volley away at this two-week pro event in February at the Aviation Club (p62). The women play in the first week, men in the second. It's a big opportunity to see some great hitting in a relatively small stadium.

Dubai World Cup (www.dubaiworldcup.com) Racing season culminates in March with the world's richest horse race, now held at the Meydan Racecourse (p89). Prize money rings up at a record-holding US$10 million. While there's no betting, this is the city's biggest social event, with local society women sporting the silliest hats this side of Ascot. Godolphin, the stable owned by Dubai's royal family, tends to dominate proceedings on the racetrack.

Dubai Rugby Sevens (www.dubairugby7s.com) Held in November or December, this is the first round of the eight-leg International Rugby Board Sevens World Series. The three-day event features 16 international squads, various amateur teams and live entertainment. Up to 150,000 spectators make the pilgrimage to the spanking-new 'The Sevens' stadium, about 30 minutes south of Sheikh Zayed Rd on the Al-Ain Rd. Book well ahead.

Dubai World Championship Golf Tournament (www.dubaiworldchampionship.com) This major new golfing championship in November is the crowning tournament of the Race to Dubai. It pits the PGA European Tour's top players against each other in 49 tournaments in 26 destinations over the course of one year. Held since 2008/9, it replaced the European Tour Order of Merit and comes with a purse of US$7.5 million. It's played on the new Jumeirah Golf Estates, which will eventually consist of four courses designed by Greg Norman, Sergio Garcia, Vijay Singh and Pete Dye.

Explore Dubai & Abu Dhabi

Neighbourhoods at a Glance

❶ Deira (p50)

Deira feels like a cross between Cairo and Karachi. Dusty, crowded and chaotic, it's a world away from the slick and sanitised city piercing the clouds at the other end of town. At the Dhow Wharfage, colourful wooden boats arrive from Iran with boxes of cuddly toys, televisions and batteries to be sold at the nearby souqs. At these atmospheric ancestors to today's malls, you can sip sugary tea and haggle for bargains with traders whose families have tended the same shop for generations.

❷ Bur Dubai (p63)

Bustling Bur Dubai is home to the restored historical quarters of Bastakia and Shindagha, wonderful for late afternoon and evening strolls. Bur Dubai Souq is just as lively as the Deira souqs with the aesthetic plus of

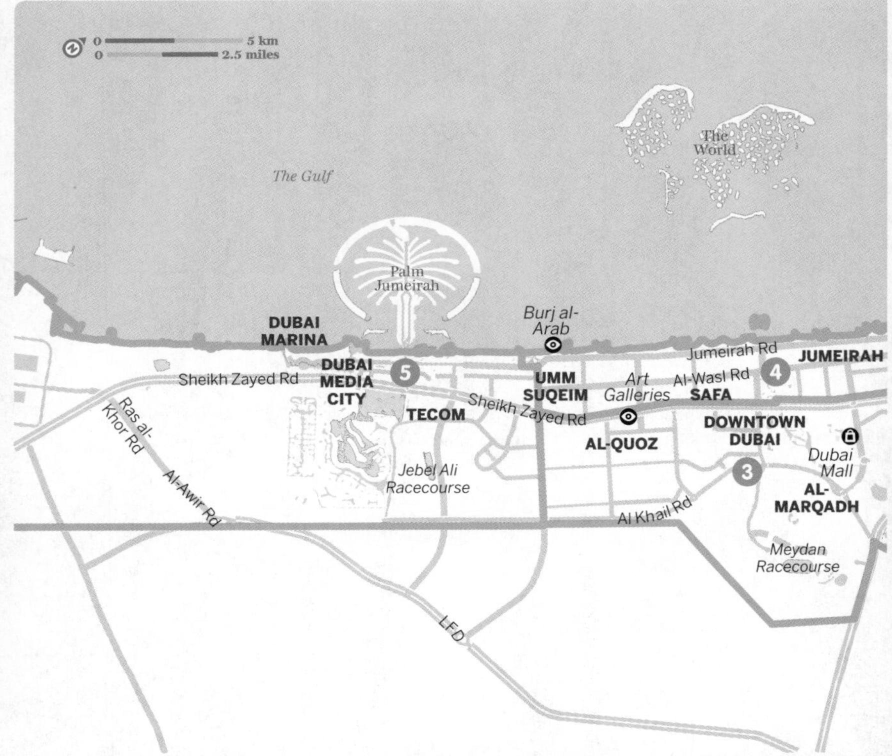

wooden arcades and a waterfront location. Little India, in the surrounding streets, with its textile and sari stores and Indian eateries, can easily absorb a couple of interesting hours. Past the concrete jungle of Golden Sands is Karama, home to a popular mall with cheap souvenir shops and counterfeit designer goods. The neighbourhood may be made up of dilapidated low-cost housing, but it has a real community spirit that can be hard to find elsewhere in Dubai.

3 Sheikh Zayed Road & Around (p77)

Dubai's main artery, Sheikh Zayed Rd is a super-busy highway that runs from the World Trade Centre Roundabout, on the edge of Bur Dubai, 55km south to Jebel Ali Port, halfway to Abu Dhabi. The road is flanked by a phalanx of skyscrapers, including the 828m-high Burj Khalifa. Overlooking a lake, the behemoth is the centrepiece of one of the most prestigious developments, known as Downtown Dubai, which encompasses the Dubai Mall, the Dubai Fountain, Souq al-Bahar and several of the city's most prestigious five-star hotels.

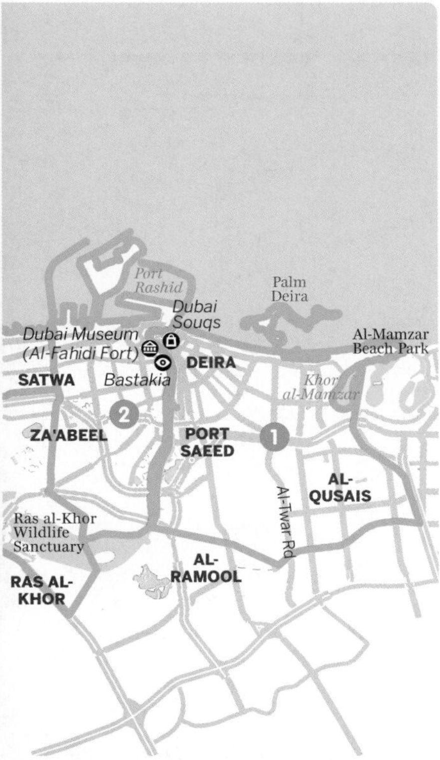

4 Jumeirah (p91)

Before there was Dubai Marina and the Palm Jumeirah, Jumeirah was the place where everybody went to realise their Dubai dreams. It's the emirate's answer to Bondi or Malibu, with excellent public beaches, boutique shopping, copious spas and health clubs, and a mix of Mercedes and expensive 4WDs in villa driveways. The actual boundaries can seem confusing as the name crops up all over the place, attached to hotels that are actually situated in Dubai Marina and to the famous Palm 'Jumeirah' Island. In reality, on its northern edge Jumeirah rubs up against vibrant Satwa, while to the south the neighbourhood encompasses Madinat Jumeirah before seamlessly shifting to New Dubai.

5 New Dubai (p104)

New Dubai consists of several different areas. In Dubai Marina you not only find bobbing yachts but also the group of buttercream-yellow towers known as the Jumeirah Beach Residence (aka JBR), which flank one of Dubai's most popular walking areas: The Walk at JBR. North of here, Al-Sufouh encompasses some of the most upmarket hotels in town, as well as the free zones of Dubai Internet City, an information technology park; and Dubai Media City, home to CNN, BBC World, Bloomberg and other outlets. Jutting into the Gulf is the Palm Jumeirah, the smallest of three planned artificial islands off the coast of Dubai but the only one to see fruition (and likely to stay that way).

Deira

Neighbourhood Top Five

❶ Taking in the **souqs** (p52): spicy aromas at the Spice Souq, glittering gold at the Gold Souq, pungent Arabian *attars* at the Perfume Souq and a glimpse of expat life at the Deira Covered Souq and the New Naif Market.

❷ Enjoying an intriguing look at the culture and lifestyle of old Dubai at the **Heritage House** (p52).

❸ Wondering at the timeless sight of loaded-up dhows at the **Dhow Wharfage** (p53).

❹ Checking out Dubai's first school, **Al-Ahmadiya** (p53), housed in an exquisite traditional building.

❺ Crossing the Creek in a traditional **abra** (p52), enjoying an atmospheric journey unchanged for decades.

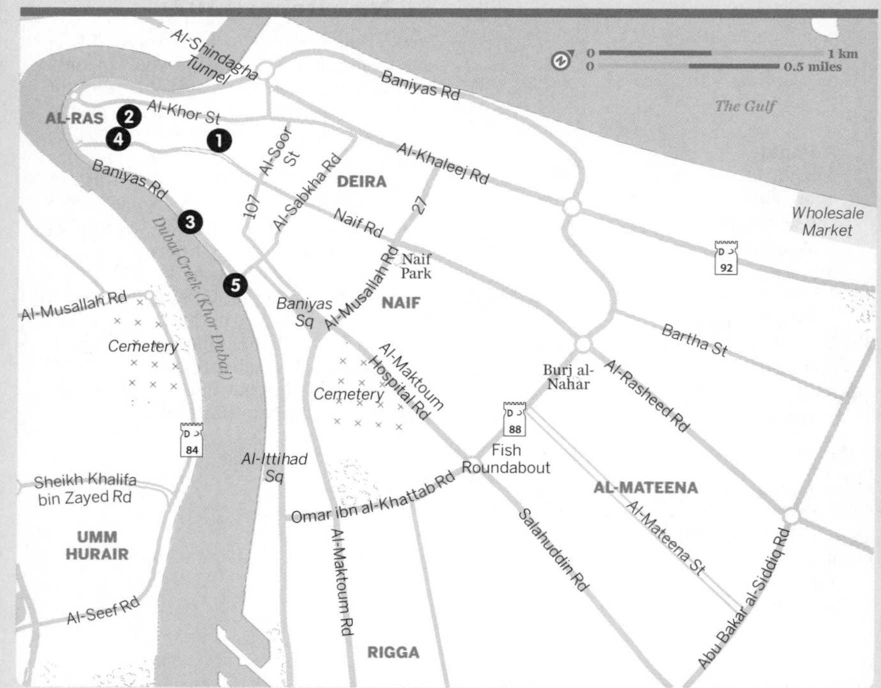

For more detail of this area, see Map p206 and p208

Explore Deira

The most-historic part of Deira is near the mouth of the Creek in an area called Al-Ras. This is the site of the souqs and markets, and it's where traditional dhows unload their goods. Plan to spend a whole morning exploring the souqs (most are under cover) or, if it is in the height of summer, hit the area in the early evening. Many stalls will close for a few hours in the afternoon for prayer, lunch and rest and don't open on Fridays until late afternoon.

The Deira area is fascinatingly multicultural. The signs on shop windows change every 50m, from Tamil to Sinhalese, Malayalam, Urdu, Pashto, Tagalog and Amharic. But don't worry: everybody speaks a little English. Adventurous foodies can lap up authentic fare in the Syrian, Ethiopian, Iraqi and Afghan sections of Deira. If you're there at night, you'll find Russian, Filipino, Lebanese, Indian and Pakistani nightclubs, often all on the same floor and typically featuring ear-rupturing house bands, overpriced beers and, yes, plenty of illicit and seedy goings-on. But these dives are not without their charms; some of the best live music is there for the taking if you keep your ears, eyes and mind open.

Away from the souqs, south of Al-Maktoum Bridge, is Port Saeed which has pockets of interest, most notably the Deira City Centre Mall, the Dubai Creek Golf & Yacht Club and the adjacent Park Hyatt hotel. Away from the Creek are Dubai International Airport and such exotic neighbourhoods as Al-Mateena and Naif.

Local Life

- **Haggle** Enjoy bartering in the souqs. It's a favourite pastime of the locals here and, as long as you don't mind a bit of lighthearted confrontation, is good fun and generally rewarding.
- **Traditional coffee** Kick-start your day by ducking into one of the tucked-away cafes and having a shot of Arabic coffee.
- **Ethnic meals** Dine at one of the ethnic restaurants located in the Al Ras area – just follow your instincts and the hungry diners.

Getting There & Away

- **Metro** There are several convenient metro stations that connect the rest of the city with Deira. On the Red Line, there's Al Rigga, Union (at Union Sq) and Deira City Centre. On the Green Line, there's Al Ras, Palm Deira and Baniyas Sq.
- **Boat** The area is served by *abra* and water bus from Bur Dubai's Abra & Water Bus Station.

Lonely Planet's Top Tip

One of the best buys at the Spice Souq is saffron, which is much cheaper here than in Europe or the USA. But do check the prices at several places as they can vary considerably. Also, don't forget that if you are making a purchase here, or at any of the souqs, you will probably have to pay in cash as credit cards are not widely accepted, so make sure you have plenty of small denomination notes and coins handy.

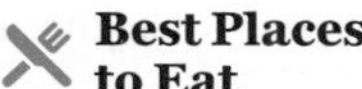

Best Places to Eat

- Traiteur (p54)
- Xiao Wei Yang (p54)
- Shabestan (p54)
- Miyako (p55)

For reviews, see p54

Best Places to Drink

- Issimo (p57)
- Terrace (p57)
- QD's (p57)

For reviews, see p57

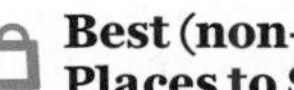

Best (non-souq) Places to Shop

- Deira City Centre (p58)
- Carrefour (p60)
- Al-Ghurair City (p58)
- Dubai Festival Centre (p61)
- Lush (p60)

For reviews, see p58

SIGHTS

The main sights of Deira are all within easy walking distance of each other around the atmospheric mouth of Dubai Creek.

DEIRA GOLD SOUQ SOUQ

Map p206 (Btwn Souq Deira & Old Baladiya Sts) All that glitters is gold (and occasionally silver) at this colourful market located on and around Sikkat al-Khail St. At any given time over 25 tonnes of gold is on display in jewellery-shop windows in Dubai. Even if you're not in the market for bling, a stroll through the covered arcades of the enormous Gold Souq is a must. Hundreds of stores overflow with every kind of jewellery imaginable, from tasteful diamond earrings to over-the-top golden Indian wedding necklaces. It's the largest gold market in the region, and one of the largest in the world.

Settle down on a wooden bench beneath the wooden-latticed arcades of the main thoroughfare (Sikkat al-Khail St) and enjoy the colourful street theatre of touts hawking knock-off watches, hard-working Afghan men dragging heavy carts of goods, African women in colourful kaftans and animated *abaya*-clad women out on a shopping spree.

DEIRA SPICE SOUQ SOUQ

Map p206 (Btwn Baniyas Rd, Al-Ras St & Al-Abra St) Just follow your nose to the best buys at this evocative souq. The guttural singsong of Arabic bounces around the lanes of this small covered market as stallholders try to sell you aromatic frankincense, dried lemons, chillies or exotic herbs and spices. While this can't compare to the Istanbul bazaar equivalent, it's still worth a half-hour of your time to take in the wonderfully restored wind towers and the pungent aromas from the jute sacks. Since this is a working souq, not a tourist attraction, the tiny shops also sell groceries, plastics and other household goods to locals and sailors from the dhows. Good buys include incense burners, saffron, rose water, henna kits and *sheesha* water pipes.

FREE HERITAGE HOUSE MUSEUM

Map p206 (Al-Ahmadiya St; ⌚8am-7.30pm Sat-Thu, 2.30-7.30pm Fri; 👪) This renovated 1890 courtyard house, just north of the Spice Souq, once belonged to Sheikh Ahmed bin Dalmouk, the founder of Al-Ahmadiya School; it offers a rare opportunity to peek inside a wealthy pearl merchant's residence. Built from coral and gypsum, the rooms wrap around a central courtyard flanked by verandahs to keep direct sunlight out. If you are feeling footsore you can sit back

CREEK CROSSING

Dubai Creek (the Creek) meanders for some 15km from Shindagha to the Ras al-Khor Wildlife Refuge, dividing Deira from Bur Dubai. Under the leadership of Maktoum bin Butti, members of the Bani Yas tribe first settled on its banks in 1833. Used for pearling and fishing expeditions in the early 20th century, the Creek was dredged in 1961 to allow larger commercial vessels to dock. The first bridge, Al-Maktoum Bridge, opened two years later.

To this day, many people have a mental barrier when it comes to crossing the Creek over to Deira. It's a bit like some Londoners' aversion to going 'south of the river' or Manhattanites' reticence to head across to Brooklyn. While it's true that traffic can be horrible during rush hour, congestion eased in 2007 with the opening of the 13-lane Business Bay Bridge near Dubai Festival City, and a six-lane Floating Bridge (open 6am to 10pm) near Creekside Park. A fourth bridge, Al-Garhoud Bridge, was widened to 13 lanes. There's also Al-Shindagha Tunnel near the mouth of the Creek, which is open for both vehicles and pedestrians.

Using public transport, you now have three options for crossing the Creek. The fastest and easiest is Dubai metro's Red Line, which runs underground, below the Creek between Union and Khalid bin al-Waleed stations. The most atmospheric way to get across, though is a Dh1 ride aboard a traditional *abra* (water taxi) that links the Bur Duba and Deira souqs in a quick five minutes. In summer, you might prefer the air-conditioned comfort of the water buses, which cost just a few dirhams more. For more on these options see p175.

on cushions under the central Bedouin-style tent and enjoy coffee and traditional snacks, such as loqmat (fried flour balls with rose water and honey) for just Dh3.

Most rooms have audiovisual displays and recreate traditional aspects of daily life, complete with dioramas. They include the *majlis* (meeting room), kitchen, marriage room (with a singularly gloomy-looking model bride and groom), traditional larder or 'store' (complete with sound effects), and a cattle pen. There is also an exhibition of rare photographs taken in Dubai between 1948 and 1953.

FREE AL-AHMADIYA SCHOOL MUSEUM

Map p206 (Al-Ahmadiya St, north of Spice Souq; ⏲8am-7.30pm Sat-Thu, 2.30-7.30pm Fri; 👪) Dubai's first school was founded by the pearl merchant Sheikh Ahmed bin Dalmouk and welcomed its first students, all boys, in 1912. You can see the original classroom where they squeezed behind wooden desks to learn the Holy Quran, grammar, Arabic calligraphy, mathematics, literature and astronomy, plus a recreation of an Al Muttawa home-schooling session. Exhibits are pretty basic, although teachers, in particular, may be interested in the more-informative videos about the development of education in the United Arab Emirates (UAE). The building is lovely: note the exquisite detail, especially the intricate carving within the courtyard arches, the heavy carved doors and the decorative gypsum panels outside the entrance. It remained in use as a school until the student body outgrew the premises in 1963.

DHOW WHARFAGE HARBOUR

Map p208 (Along Baniyas Rd) Dhows are long flat wooden vessels used in the Indian Ocean and Arabian Sea, and they've docked at the Creek since the 1830s when the Maktoums established a free-trade port, luring merchants away from Persia. Today's dhows trade with Iran, Iraq, Pakistan, Oman, India, Yemen, Somalia and Sudan, and you'll see them precariously loaded with everything from air-conditioners to chewing gum to car tyres, almost all of it re-exported after arriving by air or container ship from countries like China, South Korea and Singapore. Try to chat to the sailors if you can – if you find one who speaks English, you may learn that it takes a day to get to Iran by sea and seven days to Somalia, or that dhow captains earn as little as Dh400 a month. If your sailor friend is in a chatty mood, he may even regale you with real-life pirate stories. The gangs of thieves that stalk the waters off Yemen and Somalia sometimes make life very tough for Dubai's hard-working dhow sailors.

FISH MARKET MARKET

Map p206 (Al-Khaleej Rd) Shrimp (prawns) the size of bananas, metre-long kingfish and mountains of blue crabs are among the treasures of the sea being hawked at Dubai's largest and busiest fish market, which is near the Al-Shindagha Tunnel. The smell can be a bit overpowering but you'll get used to it after a while and it's great to watch, not just the wiggling wares, but the wild haggling between the blue-suited vendors and their customers. Come either early in the morning or in the evening, and wear sneakers or other waterproof shoes. If you're buying, ask to have the fish cleaned. The adjacent fruit and vegetable market isn't nearly as exciting but great for stocking up on anything fresh from pears to papayas, all neatly stacked and bargain-priced. Date lovers have a whole row of stands to peruse. Remember dates are packed full of minerals and vitamins and can contribute to that 'five a day' optimum daily intake.

DEIRA COVERED SOUQ SOUQ

Map p206 (Btwn Al-Sabkha Rd, 107 St & Naif Rd) Despite the name, Deira Covered Souq is only partly covered and really more a warren of small shops on narrow lanes spread across a few square blocks. Even if you're not keen on cheap textiles, knock-off Dior scarves, *kandouras* (casual shirt-dresses worn by men and women), large boxes of washing powder and cheap trainers, you're sure to be wowed by the high-energy street scene.

NEW NAIF MARKET SOUQ

Map p206 (Btwn Naif South St, 9a St & Deira St) The historic Naif Souq succumbed to a major blaze in 2008 and was replaced by this new-look version in the summer of 2010, when the 200-plus traders returned to the air-conditioned comfort of their new premises. Come here for Indian textiles, inexpensive fashion, souvenirs, accessories, shoes and perfumes. There are also restaurants, free wi-fi and parking. Although the traders provide a reassuring atmosphere of banter and barter, the charm of the former souq, one of the oldest in the city, is largely gone. Let's just hope the traders, who have had their rent doubled, do not follow suit.

EATING

Deira has a great street scene: snag a pavement table beneath flickering neon and soak up the local colour. This is where many immigrants live, and there's a wealth of restaurants here – Chinese, Arabic, African and especially Indian. With several notable exceptions, Deira lacks upmarket restaurants. For a white-tablecloth dinner with wine, head to Downtown Dubai or Dubai Marina. If you're on a budget, you can do well for under Dh20 (see the boxed text, p56).

TRAITEUR FRENCH $$$

Map p208 (☎04-317 2222; www.dubai.park.hyatt.com; Park Hyatt Dubai, mains Dh130-190; ⏰7pm-midnight) A meal at Traiteur is pure drama, both on the plate and in the striking 14m-high dining room with origami wall features and theatrical lighting. Watch a small army of chefs in the raised show kitchen toil over classic French brasserie fare. Ask the sommelier to help you choose from the 4200-bottle wine cellar, one of the largest in Dubai. Reservations essential.

XIAO WEI YANG CHINESE $

Map p206 (Baniyas Rd; hotpots from Dh26, ingredients from Dh10; ⏰noon-2am) For hotpot novices, this is how it works. Choose a herb-based or spicy hotpot base which bubbles happily on a hotplate on the table. Next, fill a small bowl with a delicious combination of satay, garlic, coriander, chilli and various spices. Then, choose around three ingredients such as raw fish balls, crab, tofu, shitake mushrooms, young spinach, spicy lamb and eggs, which you cook in the cauldron before dipping into your spicy concoction. Delicious! There's little atmosphere or English spoken: you're here for the food.

SHABESTAN PERSIAN $$$

Map p206 (☎04-205 7333; www.radissonblu.com; Radisson Blu Hotel, Baniyas Rd; mains Dh90-155) Shabestan is Dubai's top Persian restaurant. At dinner time, the window-lined dining room reveals a panorama of glittering lights over the Creek. Start with a smoky *mizra ghasemi* (aubergine dip with tomatoes and egg), move on to *fesenjan-ba morgh* (roast chicken in a pomegranate sauce) and save room for the vermicelli ice cream with saffron and rose water. Reservations essential.

GET LOST: DEIRA

Sometimes it pays to rip up the script and improvise. Some of the most fascinating parts of town aren't home to a single tourist attraction worth recommending, but are brimming with the soul the city is so frequently accused of lacking. Dubai is a safe city – there aren't any no-go areas and even the scariest-looking alleyways will be quite harmless. Be adventurous and spontaneous. Put away the maps and follow your instinct. But before you hurl this guidebook into the Creek, read our suggestions of the best areas in Deira in which to get hopelessly, joyously lost.

Naif (Map p206) The area between Naif Rd and Al-Khaleej Rd is a labyrinthine muddle of slim, cluttered streets, and one of the best places in town for urban photography. It's not always pretty, but here you'll find old men smoking *sheesha* and playing backgammon on the pavements; pockets of Ethiopia and Somalia; hilariously awful fake Rolexes; games consoles; heady perfumes; blindingly bright shop facades; and the occasional goat, walking nonchalantly down the centre of the street. You just don't get this on the Palm Jumeirah...

Al Mateena (Map p206) Despite its out-of-the-way location, Al-Mateena St is one of the most enticing walk streets in town, with wide pavements, palm trees and a narrow park-like strip running along its centre. In the Iraqi restaurants and cafes you'll see *masgouf* – a whole fish sliced in half, spicily seasoned and barbecued over an open flame. And the *sheesha* cafes have to be seen to be believed: check out the rock gardens, dangling fronds and artificial lakes. Nearby Al-Muraqqabat Rd brims with superb Syrian and Palestinian eateries.

MIYAKO JAPANESE **$$**

Map p206 (☎04-317 2222; www.dubai.regency.hyatt.com; Hyatt Regency Dubai; 3-course business lunches Dh75, mains from Dh90) The cool minimalist dining room of this excellent Japanese eatery feels very Tokyo, with sleek surfaces of stainless steel, shoji screens and an authentic tatami room. The sushi is stellar and the *shabu shabu* is superb, made with tender and tasty beef; the crumbed fried oysters and braised pork belly *(kakuni)* merit special attention, as well. Reservations essential.

AL MANSOUR DHOW ARABIC **$$**

Map p206 (☎04-205 7333; www.radissonblu.com; outside Radisson Blu Hotel, Deira; 2hr dinner cruise Dh185) For a traditional experience, book a table on this old wooden dhow cheerfully decorated with bands of twinkling lights and operated by the Radisson Blu Hotel. The international buffet is heavy on Middle Eastern and Indian choices and accompanied by an *oud* player. Afterwards, relax with a *sheesha* in the upper-deck lounge.

ASHIANA INDIAN **$$**

Map p206 (☎04-207 1733; www.starwoodhotels.com; Sheraton Dubai Creek Hotel & Towers, Baniyas Rd; mains Dh80-120; ⌚7.30pm-11.30pm daily, noon-3pm Fri; ☑) This oldie but goodie is still one of the city's top Indian restaurants. Presentations of the northern Indian fare are brilliant: *dum biryani* is cooked in a pot sealed with bread, elegantly perfuming the meat. Sophisticated, complex curries justify the prices, as do the solicitous service, atmospheric dining room and live sitar music. Good vegetarian food, too. Reservations essential.

SUMIBIYA JAPANESE **$$**

Map p206 (☎04-205 7333; www.radissonblu.com; Radisson Blu Hotel, Baniyas Rd; mains Dh70-145; 👪) At the first Japanese *yakiniku*-style restaurant in Dubai, every stone table has a recessed gas grill where you cook your own meat, then pair it with sauces and condiments. Though the Wagyu beef and seafood run high (from Dh125), the set menus are a relative bargain. There's nothing romantic about the narrow windowless room, but it's foodie fun for families or groups. Reservations recommended.

CHINA CLUB CHINESE **$$**

Map p206 (☎04-205 7333; www.radissonblu.com; Radisson Blu Hotel, Baniyas Rd; yum cha Dh95, mains Dh70-135) Lunchtime yum cha is a superb deal here. At dinner, the classics are also spot-on, including a standout Szechuan-style spicy boiled lamb and a crispy, delicious Peking duck carved and rolled tableside. Private dining rooms with plush red decor are ideal for a group, while the main dining space is a disappointing study in beige. Reservations recommended.

AL-DAWAAR INTERNATIONAL **$$**

Map p206 (Hyatt Regency Dubai; buffet lunches/dinners Dh165/230) In a city that likes to teeter on the cutting edge, this revolving restaurant on the 25th floor is as delightfully old school as a bag of gummi bears. Tacky you think? Not so. Actually, the decor is quite sophisticated, the buffet varied and bountiful, and the views of the city are a delight, especially at night.

SPICE ISLAND INTERNATIONAL **$$**

Map p206 (☎04-262 5555; Renaissance Dubai Hotel, near Salahuddin Rd; buffets with soft/house/premium drinks Dh169/219/289; ⌚6.30-11.30pm; 👪) With dishes from China, Japan, India, Italy, Mexico and Mongolia, plus seafood and loads of desserts, Spice Island is not just a visual feast, it's one of the best all-round buffets in town. Its recession-friendly prices give it an edge with young expat families; the kiddie play area with supervised activities like face painting doesn't hurt either. Friday brunch is busiest so be sure to reserve ahead of time.

GLASSHOUSE MEDITERRANEAN BRASSERIE INTERNATIONAL **$$**

Map p206 (☎04-212 7551; Hilton Dubai Creek, Baniyas Rd, Rigga; mains Dh95-110, brunches Dh220) Glasshouse is one of Dubai's most accomplished brasserie-style restaurants which, as the name suggests, has vast picture windows overlooking palms and the Creek beyond. The daily brunch and comfort-food menu offers fresh takes on classics, such as pea and broad bean risotto and a tiger prawn bruschetta with red chilli, garlic and lemon. Come on Monday and Wednesday and get drinks for just Dh1 when ordering two courses. Reservations recommended.

DEIRA'S BEST ETHNIC EATS

If you want to sample some of Dubai's cheapest and best ethnic cooking, hit the backstreets of Deira, and eat beside the working-class expat workers who've imported their culinary traditions to Dubai. The following recommendations are for adventurous travellers. At first glance, some might look scary – Westerners don't usually wander into these joints – but we've sampled all of them, and they're the real deal. In a city that embraces artificiality, it's refreshing to find authenticity. Best of all, you'll probably get change from your Dh50 note. No credit cards.

Ashwaq Cafeteria (Map p206; Sikkat al-Khail St) Located in a prime people-watching spot at the junction of Al-Soor and Sikkat al-Khail Sts, this is not much more than a kiosk with a few outside tables serving up excellent *shwarma*, washed down with a fresh mango juice.

Abesinian Restaurant (Map p206; Somali St, near 23 St junction; mains Dh12-35; ⏲10am-midnight) The staff are welcoming and warm at this homey Ethiopian restaurant, where the big platters of curry and stews are best sopped up with *injera,* spongy flatbread of native grain. Tricky to find but worth it.

Afghan Khorasan Kebab House (Map p206; behind Naif Mosque, off Deira St; mains Dh15-35; ⏲11am-1am) Big hunks of meat – lamb, beef, chicken – charred on foot-long skewers come served with rice and bread. Eat with your hands, but not if you opt for the Afghan curry. Tricky to find but locals can direct you.

Al-Baghdadi Home (Map p206; Al-Mateena St, opposite Dubai Palm Hotel; mains Dh30-60; ⏲noon-3am) In Little Iraq, on one of Dubai's best, lesser-known walking streets, Al-Baghdadi spit-roasts whole fish beside an open fire (the traditional preparation) in the restaurant's window, and serves it with bread and lentil salad. (Note: Don't order randomly – *patchaa* is sheep's head.)

Aroos Damascus (Map p206; Al-Muraqqabat Rd, at Al-Jazeira St; mains Dh10-30; ⏲7am-3am; 👪) Syrian food is similar to Lebanese, but uses more cumin in the *fattoosh* and spice in the kebabs. Our favourite dish is *arayees* (Syrian bread stuffed with ground lamb and grilled). The sweetness of the bread plays off the gamey flavour of the meat. Great tabouli, fantastic fresh-from-the-oven bread, huge outdoor patio and cool flickering neon.

Pinoy Grill (Map p206; Al-Rigga Rd, at Al-Jazeira St; dishes Dh15-30; ⏲noon-2am Sat-Thu, 1pm-2am Fri; 👪) A friendly and welcoming intro to the weird, wonderful world of Filipino cuisine, which borrows from Spanish, Indonesian and French, mixing pungent ingredients, such as garlic and chillies, in sweet and savoury combinations not always tastebud-friendly to foreigners. But the menu is in English, and the super-fun staff will guide you.

CAFE ARABESQUE MIDDLE EASTERN **$$**

Map p208 (☎04-317 2222; www.dubai.park.hyatt.com; Park Hyatt Dubai, next to Dubai Creek Golf & Yacht Club; mezze Dh35-70, kebabs Dh60-180, set menus from Dh150 Wed-Fri; 👪) Snag a table on the Creekside verandah, then dip into a pool of pleasurable dishes from Jordan, Syria, Lebanon and Turkey at this classy yet low-key eatery at the Park Hyatt. As well as a tantalising selection of mezze and salads, there are juicy kebabs prepared in the wood-burning oven and reasonably priced set menus. Reservations recommended.

THAI KITCHEN THAI **$$**

Map p208 (☎04-602 1234; www.dubai.park.hyatt.com; Park Hyatt Dubai, next to Dubai Creek Golf & Yacht Club; small dishes Dh28-60, set menus Dh210; ⏲7pm-midnight) The decor is decidedly un-Thai, with black-lacquer tables, a swooping wave-form ceiling and not a branch of bamboo. But the Thai chefs know their stuff: dishes are inspired by Bangkok street eats and served tapas-style, perfect for grazing and sharing. Standouts include chicken massaman curry, lobster tail and cashews, and green papaya salad. The Friday brunch here is excellent. Reservations recommended.

TABLE 9 INTERNATIONAL $$$

Map p206 (☎04-212 7551; Hilton Dubai Creek, Baniyas Rd; mains Dh100; ⏲6-11pm; ✎) Gordon Ramsay's famous Verre restaurant closed down here in late 2011, only to be resurrected, renamed and rebranded by his former star chefs Scott Price and Nick Alvis. Opened after this book was researched, Table 9's intent was to add an arty touch of informality to the place without compromising a soupçon on the quality of the food. Tasting menus include one fully vegetarian and a chef selection of starters and mains.

YUM! ASIAN $$

Map p206 (www.radissonblu.com; Radisson Blu Hotel, Baniyas Rd; mains Dh45-65; ⏲noon-1am; 👪) Though not as dynamic or sophisticated as some Asian restaurants, Yum! is a good pick for a quick bowl of noodles when you're wandering along the Creek – and you can be in and out in half an hour.

DRINKING & NIGHTLIFE

ISSIMO SPORTS BAR

Map p206 (Hilton Dubai Creek, Baniyas Rd; ⏲11am-2am) Illuminated blue flooring, black-leather sofas and sleek chrome finishing lend a James Bond look to this sports-and-martini bar. If you're not into sports – or TV – you may find the giant screens distracting. Good for drinks before dining at Table 9 or the Glasshouse Mediterranean Brasserie.

IRISH VILLAGE PUB

Map p208 (☎04-282 4750; Aviation Club, Al-Garhoud Rd; ⏲11am-1.30am) Better known as 'the IV', this always-buzzy pub, with its faux Irish-main-street facade, is popular with expats for its pondside 'beer garden'. No happy hour, but there's Guinness and Kilkenny on tap and plenty of cheap, cheerful and licensed restaurants nearby, plus regular live concerts.

TERRACE BAR

Map p208 (Park Hyatt Dubai, next to Dubai Creek Golf & Yacht Club; ⏲noon-1.30am) Specialising in French oysters, caviar, champagne and vodka, the Terrace is one of Dubai's smartest waterside lounge bars. Sit on the deck and watch the moored boats bobbing in the marina. There is live music Monday to Thursday, and every Saturday a barbecue brunch. Sunday is ladies' night and on Monday there are drink specials for all.

QD'S CLUB

Map p208 (Dubai Creek Golf & Yacht Club, Deira; ⏲6pm-2am) Watch the ballet of lighted dhows floating by while sipping cosmos at this always-fun outdoor Creekside lounge, shaped like a giant circle. The main action is on the (very public) raised centre ring, where Oriental carpets and cushions set an inviting mood. For privacy, retreat to the vast wooden deck jutting over the water, or book a cabana. Great for *sheesha,* but skip the food. The action moves to an air-conditioned tent in the summer.

KU-BU BAR

Map p206 (Radisson Blu Hotel, Baniyas Rd; ⏲6.30pm-2am) A DJ spins funky tunes at

EXPAT LABOUR

Deira and Bur Dubai are two neighbourhoods where you will be undoubtedly struck by the sheer numbers of Indians, Pakistanis and Asians and, concurrently, the lack of Emirati citizens on the streets. While the globalisation of the international labour market (read: cheap foreign labour) has made the phenomenal growth of Dubai so attainable, there is one hurdle in the economy that Dubai is seeking to overcome. Dubai is highly dependent upon this expat labour and, at the same time, its citizens are having trouble finding meaningful employment. While the government in the past had made some attempt to 'Emiratise' the economy by placing nationals in the public workforce and imposing local employee quotas on private companies, this hasn't been particularly successful. One of the problems is that private companies are reluctant to hire nationals, often due to the misguided notion that they are lazy. A more likely reason, though, is that nationals expect to start on a salary that's far above what the equivalent expat would receive. There is no doubt that Dubai will be dependent on foreign labour and expertise for a long time to come.

LOCAL KNOWLEDGE

TIME FOR A CUPPA

There isn't a home in India that doesn't start the day with a steaming cup of *kadak chai*, even in the height of summer. Pop into any of the Indian-run cafes or bars in Deira or Bur Dubai and treat yourself to a cup of this fragrant sweet tea with green cardamom, peppercorns and cinnamon.

this windowless, tattoo-themed bar with stools draped in cowhide and secluded nooks that are made even more private with plush draperies. A good choice for drinks before or after dinner at the Radisson Blu's terrific restaurants.

ENTERTAINMENT

JULES BAR LIVE MUSIC

Map p208 (Le Meridien Dubai, Al-Garhoud; cover incl 1 drink Tue, Wed, Fri & Sat Dh50, incl 2 drinks Thu Dh100; ⏲11am-3am) The six-piece Filipino house band kicks, twirls and belts out Top-40 hits, while an odd mix of oil workers, southeast Asians and European flight crews (especially on Fridays) grind shoulder-to-shoulder on the floor. Beer's a bargain at Sunday's Corona Beach Party, and on Tuesday women get admission and one drink for free. If you need nibbles, there's a decent Mexican menu.

SHOPPING

DEIRA CITY CENTRE SHOPPING MALL

Map p208 (www.deiracitycentre.com; Baniyas Rd; ⏲10am-10pm Sun-Wed, 10am-midnight Thu-Sat) Though other malls are bigger and flashier, Deira City Centre remains a stalwart for its logical layout and wide selection of shops, from big-name chain stores like H&M and Zara to independent shops carrying good-quality carpets, souvenirs and handicrafts. There's also a huge branch of the Carrefour supermarket, food courts, a textile court selling Indian and Middle Eastern clothes and fabrics, and a multiplex cinema.

AL-GHURAIR CITY SHOPPING MALL

Map p206 (cnr Al-Rigga & Omar ibn al-Khattab Rds; ⏲10am-10pm Sat-Thu, 2-10pm Fri) If seeing all those flowing robes has made you want your own checked *gutra* (white headcloth

WORTH A DETOUR

MIRDIF CITY CENTRE

Opened in March 2010, the Mirdif City Centre shopping mall has all the high-street favourites, plus some real gems:

Pottery Barn (www.potterybarn.com) First to open in the Middle East and an Aladdin's Cave of tasteful decor items.

United Designers (www.uniteddesigners.ae) Showcases local UAE-based fashion designers with the aim of supporting young emerging talent.

Apple Bottoms (www.applebottoms.com) Caters to fashion-conscious women of all those apple-and-pear shapes and sizes.

Balmain (www.balmain.com) Sophisticated stylish menswear from French fashion guru Cristophe Decarnin.

See by Chloe (www.chloe.com) The junior version of this well-known designer brand, aimed at a younger, more-informal fashionista.

Ajmal (www.ajmalperfume.com) A family-owned company since the 1950s, selling Middle Eastern oils and perfumes that are well priced and exquisitely bottled.

Another perk is that you can drop off the kids at the massive **Playnation** (www.playnation.com), which includes a waterpark, a skydiving simulator, bowling alley and amusement arcade.

To get here, head southeast of the airport on Airport Rd for around 10km. The mall is well signposted.

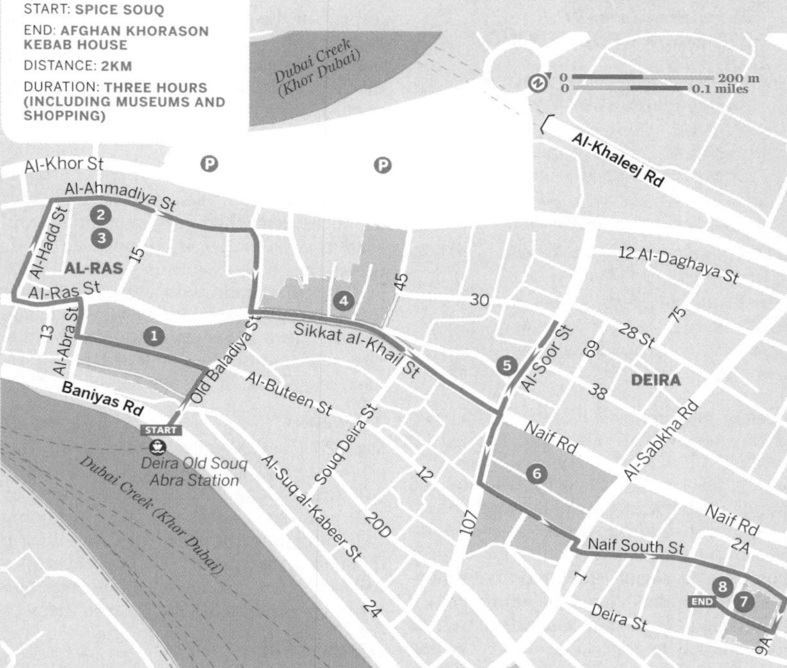

Neighbourhood Walk
Deira Souq Stroll

As soon as you step off the *abra* at Deira Old Souq Abra Station, the heady scents will lure you across to the 1 **Spice Souq**. Take some time to explore. Turn right as you exit on Al-Abra St, then left on Al-Ras St and right again on Al-Hadd St.

At the end of Al-Hadd St turn right and follow Al-Ahmadiya St to the beautifully restored 2 **Heritage House** for intriguing insights into Dubai's history and culture.

Behind Heritage House is Dubai's first school, 3 **Al-Ahmadiya School**. Look around, then continue along Al-Ahmadiya St, turning right into Old Baladiya St, where you'll find more wholesalers, this time trading in *gutras* (men's white headcloths), sandals and Chinese products.

Ahead, to the left, is the wooden latticed archway entrance to Dubai's famous 4 **Gold Souq**. Pop into the small shops to look at over-the-top gold pieces created for brides' dowries and duck into the narrow lanes to suss out tiny teashops, simple cafeterias, busy tailors and barber shops.

Exit the Gold Souq, follow Sikkat al-Khail St to Al-Soor St and turn left. This is the heart of the 5 **Perfume Souq**, a string of shops selling heady Arabian *attars* (perfumes) and *oud* (fragrant wood). Backtrack and continue straight on what is now 107 St, with hawkers selling cut-price clothes, Chinese-made shoes and kitschy souvenirs.

Tucked east of 107 St are the tiny alleys of the 6 **Deira Covered Souq**, a warren of little shops selling everything from textiles to *sheesha* pipes. Cross Al-Sabkha Rd, head into Naif South St and turn right into 9A St. Keep going until you arrive at the 7 **New Naif Market**, which has risen from the ashes of the historic Naif Souq.

If you've worked up an appetite, a carnivorous feast at 8 **Afghan Khorasan Kebab House** will keep you sated for ages. Find it by turning right into a little alley about half a block past the Naif Mosque.

BEST BOOKS FOR BUYING CARPETS

- *Oriental Rugs Today*, 2nd edition, by Emmett Eiland
- *Persian Rugs and Carpets: The Fabric of Life* by Essie Sakhai
- *Oriental Rugs, A Complete Guide* by Murray L Eiland
- *The Carpet: Origins, Art and History* by Enza Milanesi
- *Kilims: a Buyer's Guide* by Lee Allane
- *Tribal Rugs* by James Opie

worn by men in the Gulf States), grab yours at this ageing mall. The place to shop for national dress, it offers stylish *abayas* (full-length black robes worn by women) and *shaylas* (headscarves), quality leather sandals, and *dishdashas* (men's shirt-dresses) in browns and greys (popular for winter). There are also some contemporary fashion-conscious outlets here, including French Connection, Mexx and Guess, as well as some excellent specialty shops selling everything from Arabic jewellery to hand-woven rugs.

CARREFOUR SUPERMARKET

Map p208 (Deira City Centre, Baniyas Rd; ⌚9am-midnight Sat-Wed, 9am-1am Thu & Fri) This enormous French hypermarket draws big crowds of Emiratis and European expats for its off-the-jet-fresh seafood, foie gras, French cheeses, freshly baked bread and plump Arabian olives. It also stocks an excellent selection of well-priced mobile phones, digital cameras and electronics. Also in the Mall of the Emirates.

LUSH BEAUTY

Map p208 (Deira City Centre, Baniyas Rd) This is much more than just another natural soap and cosmetics shop, with all kinds of organic body-beautiful products, such as lip balms made with natural oils, foot lotion with ginger oil and cloves, lemon cuticle butter, coconut deodorant, vanilla puff talc and some wonderful perfumes; have a squirt of the orange blossom.

AL WASHIA ACCESSORIES

Map p208 (Deira City Centre, Baniyas Rd) Has all that bling got to you yet? If so, then you can glitter along with the best of them by picking up some accessories here, including twinkling tiaras, jewelled hairpins, dingle-dangle earrings, fancy clutch bags and a few surprises, such as cushion-cover embroidery sets with Middle Eastern themes.

MANGO TOUCH ACCESSORIES

Map p208 (Deira City Centre, Baniyas Rd) The stylish Spanish Mango chain has cleverly bagged a corner of the market with this boutique store which specialises in original, reasonably priced bags, mostly handmade with prices dangling at the Dh120 mark. There are a few leather numbers closer to the Dh600 tag.

HENNA

Henna body tattooing is a long-standing tradition dating back 6000 years, when central-Turkish women began painting their hands in homage to the Mother Goddess. The practice spread throughout the eastern Mediterranean, where the henna shrub grows wild. Today, Emirati women continue the tradition by decorating their hands, nails and feet for special events, particularly weddings. A few nights before the nuptials, brides-to-be are honoured with *layyat al-henna* (henna night). This is a women-only affair, part of a week of festivities leading up to the big day. The bride is depilated, anointed head-to-toe with perfumes and oils, and shampooed with henna, jasmine or perfume. Her hands, wrists, ankles and feet are then tattooed with intricate floral designs, which typically last around six weeks. Lore has it that the duration of the tattoos is an indication to the mother-in-law of what kind of wife the bride will become. If she's a hard worker – and thus a more desirable daughter-in-law – the henna will penetrate deeper and remain longer.

Want to give it a try? Henna tents are all over the city. Look for signs depicting henna-painted hands in Deira City Centre (Map p208), BurJuman Centre (Map p210), Souq Madinat Jumeirah (Map p218), Jumeirah Emirates Towers (Map p216) and hotel lobbies.

ZARA CLOTHING

Map p208 (Deira City Centre, Baniyas Rd) Stylish Spain-based Zara has stores all over Dubai, but this is the original branch, with a fabulous selection of smart-looking affordable clothes and accessories. It rarely strays from its black, white, beige and grey colour palette, but the cuts and styling feel very now and look expensive.

MIKYAJY BEAUTY

Map p208 (Deira City Centre, Baniyas Rd) You feel like you're walking into a chocolate gift-box at tiny Mikyajy, the Gulf's home-grown make-up brand. Developed to suit the colouring of Middle Eastern women, it's now also popular with foreigners who appreciate vibrant colours such as turquoise and tangerine.

GIFT VILLAGE DEPARTMENT STORE

Map p206 (Baniyas St) If you have spent all your money on Jimmy Choo shoes and at the Gold Souq and need a new inflight bag, this cut-price place has a great range, as well as stocking just about everything else, including cosmetics, shoes, clothing, toys, sports goods, jewellery and superbly kitsch souvenirs.

DAMAS JEWELLERY

Map p208 (Deira City Centre, Baniyas Rd; ⌚10am-10pm Sun-Wed, 10am-midnight Thu-Sat) Damas may not be the most innovative jeweller in Dubai, but with over 50 stores, it's the most trusted. Among the diamonds and gold, look for classic pieces and big-designer names such as Fabergé and Tiffany.

VIRGIN MEGASTORE MUSIC

Map p208 (Deira City Centre, Baniyas Rd; ⌚10am-10pm Sun-Wed, 10am-midnight Thu-Sat) The enthusiastic sales staff are great at suggesting Middle Eastern music to take back home, from traditional *oud* music to Oriental chill-out. The selection is huge. Also check out the Arabian and Iranian DVDs. The store in the Mall of the Emirates is bigger, but for Middle Eastern tunes, this one's best.

EARLY LEARNING CENTRE TOYS

Map p208 (Deira City Centre, Baniyas Rd) Parents: if you failed to pack enough toys to keep your little ones entertained, fret not. The Early Learning Centre stocks great games designed to get kids thinking and developing key learning skills. And because they're not always easy to figure out, they'll keep children busy for hours. There are additional branches around town, including at the Mall of the Emirates and Souq Madinat Jumeirah.

WORTH A DETOUR

DUBAI FESTIVAL CENTRE

Another of Dubai's newer shopping and entertainment centres, **Dubai Festival Centre** (off Map p208; www.dubaifestivalcentre.com) has all the standard shops, plus Ikea – probably not that useful unless you have hand luggage space for a flatpack. Its main plus is the picturesque Creekside location, which is lined with some 50 bars and some fine restaurants, including the UK celebrity chef Jamie Oliver's **Jamie's Italian** (☎04-232 9969; www.jamieoliver.com/italian/dubai; ⌚closed Sun). You can also take an *abra* ride here, ogle at the yachts at the luxurious Festival Marina or just enjoy a rare waterside stroll. The **Festival Concert Arena** (www.dubaifestivalcity.com) also stages some top acts, such as the late Amy Winehouse who appeared on stage here, albeit sadly worse for wear, in February 2011. The Dubai Festival Centre (part of the larger residential community Dubai Festival City) is located just southwest of the airport, near Business Bay Bridge.

WOMEN'S SECRET WOMEN'S CLOTHING

Map p208 (Deira City Centre, Baniyas Rd) This sassy Spanish label is popular for its global-pop-art-inspired underwear, swimwear and nightwear. Expect anything from cute Mexican cross-stitched bra-and-pants sets to Moroccan-style kaftan-like nightdresses.

SPORTS & ACTIVITIES

AMARA SPA

Map p208 (☎04-602 1234; www.dubai.park.hyatt.com; Park Hyatt Dubai; day pass weekdays/weekends Dh300/350) Dubai's top spa at the Park Hyatt has eight treatment suites, including three for couples, all with their own private walled gardens complete with outdoor rain showers. Nonguests can enjoy a day pass or choose one of the treatments that entitles you to daylong use of the steam bath, sauna and pool. Choose your own background music, then lean back for a luxurious footbath followed by your selected treatment. Tempting ones, especially if you just got off the plane, include the Spirit of Amara (Dh820) which includes a scrub down with Aleppo soap enriched with laurel oils followed by a rain shower and full-body massage using the spa's signature oil of frankincense, amber, myrrh and sandalwood. Best of all, afterwards you're not shoved out the door but are free to enjoy the tranquil garden over tea and dates. Treatments also entitle you to use the gym and relax by the palm-tree-shaded pool, so make a day of it. Reserve well ahead.

DUBAI CREEK GOLF & YACHT CLUB GOLF

Map p208 (☎04-295 6000; www.dubaigolf.com; near Deira side of Al-Garhoud Bridge; Sun-Wed Dh595, Thu-Sat Dh795) The one-time host course of the Dubai Desert Classic has been redesigned by a former winner of the tournament, Thomas Björn. The Creekside location is gorgeous, as is the landscaping, with meticulously groomed fairways lined by date and coconut palms and water hazards. The high-class Park Hyatt Dubai (p137) is within walking distance of the greens. Beginners can go wild on the par-three nine-hole course (Dh75).

BLISS RELAXOLOGY DAY SPA

Map p208 (☎04-286 9444; Shop 11, Emirates Blvd, G Block, Al-Garhoud; ⏲9am-midnight) It's not quite pampering fit for Queen Nefertiti, but if you're in bad need of working out the kinks without spending buckets of money, this relaxation station might just do the trick. Treatments range from a traditional Thai massage to foot reflexology, and start at Dh90 for 30 minutes. The spa is near the airport and next to Welcare Hospital.

AVIATION CLUB GYM

Map p208 (☎282 4122; www.aviationclub.ae; Dubai Tennis Stadium, Al-Garhoud Rd, Deira; day pass Dh250, not incl group fitness; ⏲6am-11pm) Packed after work and at weekends – and with good reason – the Aviation Club has body pump and spinning classes, and a big selection of weights and circuit training for a pre-cardio workout or before a lap-swim in the half-Olympic-size pool. This is where the Dubai Tennis Championships are held; the club's eight tennis courts are available only by reservation.

Bur Dubai

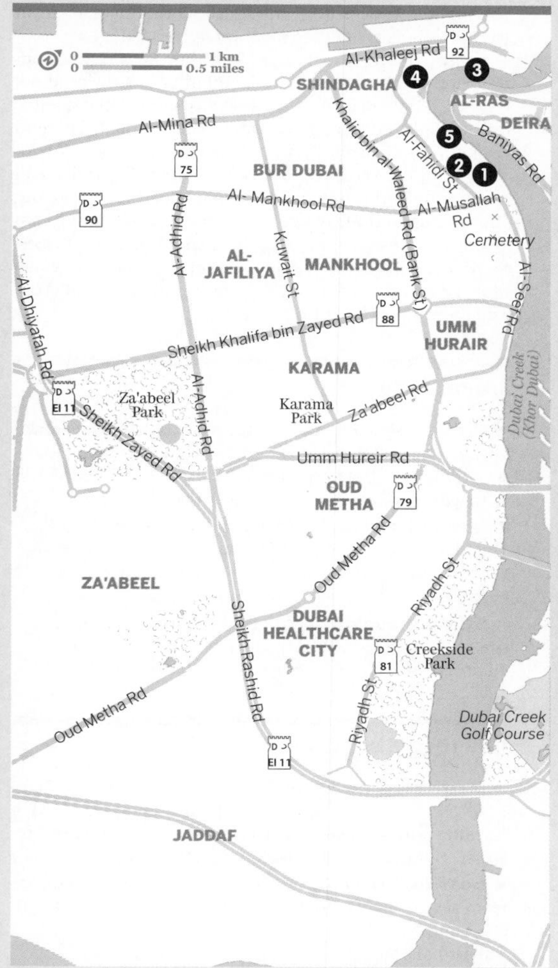

Neighbourhood Top Five

❶ Strolling through Dubai's atmospheric **Bastakia Quarter** (p65) old town, popping into the museums, galleries and souvenir shops and enjoying the traditional architecture, dazzling bougainvillea, narrow car-free lanes and air of tranquillity of bygone years.

❷ Visiting **Dubai Museum** (p65) for a speedy and entertaining introduction to the city.

❸ Exploring **Sheikh Saeed al-Maktoum House** (p66), with its rare collection of photos of early Dubai.

❹ Wandering along the waterfront **Shindagha Heritage Area** (p66) at sunset and enjoying a drink overlooking the Creek.

❺ Bartering for souvenirs at the lively **Bur Dubai Souq** (p66) before exploring the surrounding bustling streets.

For more detail of this area, see Map p210 and Map p214 ➡

Lonely Planet's Top Tip

Consider hiring an *abra* to do the same trip as the cruise companies – but you'll be at water level, with the wind in your hair and surrounded by swirling seagulls. It's a more-interesting experience, especially if the boat captain speaks a little English or you speak Urdu, Hindi or Arabic – you might learn a lot more about the Creek and those who work on it. *Abras* can be hired from *abra* stations along the Creek for around Dh100 an hour.

Best Places to Eat

- Peppercrab (p67)
- Asha's (p69)
- Awtar (p69)
- Lemongrass (p69)

For reviews, see p67

Best Places to Drink

- Cooz (p72)
- Old Vic (p72)
- Red Lounge (p72)

For reviews, see p72

Best Museums

- Dubai Museum (p65)
- Sheikh Saeed al-Maktoum House (p66)
- Traditional Architecture Museum (p66)

For reviews, see p65

Explore Bur Dubai

Bur Dubai was the first part of the city to be settled and, in many ways, is the antithesis of the shiny new high-rise areas with their sophisticated hotels and glitzy sights. The streets here bustle with life, activity and, above all, people.

The oldest areas along the waterfront are the most appealing. Near the mouth of the Creek, quiet Shindagha is filled with historic buildings and is great for a waterfront stroll. South of here is the vibrant Bur Dubai Souq district; it's also the place to catch *abras* (water taxis) and water buses to stops along the Creek. Further on are Dubai Museum and the charming, car-free Bastakia Quarter with its restored courtyard houses and wind towers. From here, Al-Seef Rd leads south along the waterfront to Umm Hurair, home to most foreign consulates.

Away from the Creek, Bur Dubai becomes rather nondescript, if not without its highlights. The Mankhool district is stacked with inexpensive hotel apartments, quirky nightlife, good restaurants and an upmarket mall (BurJuman Centre). South of the mall, across Sheikh Khalifa bin Zayed Rd, Karama is a hive of activity and has a real community feel due to its mostly Filipino and Indian population. It's great for bargain shopping and ethnic eateries serving princely meals at paupers' prices. South of Za'abeel Rd, sprawling Oud Metha is easily recognised by the eye-catching Egyptian-themed Wafi Mall and pyramid-shaped Raffles hotel.

Local Life

- **Creekside view** Sip a creamy avocado smoothie (laced with honey and milk) at one of the waterfront cafes and watch the traditional wooden *abras* crossing the Creek.
- **Vegetarian dining** Bur Dubai has the highest concentration of Indian vegetarian restaurants in Dubai, to cater to the large Indian population. Join them for lunch (many local restaurants are closed in the evening).
- **Ethnic shopping** Check out the traditional Punjabi dress of long tunics and baggy trousers in brightly coloured silk or cotton at the local clothing stores.

Getting There & Away

- **Metro** The most convenient metro stops are the Red Line's Khalid bin al-Waleed (for BurJuman Centre), Al Karama and Al Jafiliya. The Green Line travels south to Dubai Healthcare City and stops at Al Fahidi.
- **Boat** You can hop across the Creek to Deira via *abra* from several spots along the Creek, including the Dubai Old Souq Abra & Water Bus Station, just beyond the Bur Dubai Souq.

SIGHTS

BASTAKIA QUARTER — HISTORIC QUARTER

Map p210 Traffic noise fades to a quiet hum in the labyrinthine lanes of the historic Bastakia Quarter, Dubai's old town. Here you'll find restored wind-tower houses that were built nearly a century ago by wealthy pearl and textile merchants from Persia. Typical houses are two storeys high, with a central courtyard surrounded by rooms, and decorative arches featuring intricate carvings. Despite their comparatively plain facades, the houses have wonderful carved wooden doors, crenulations, carved grilles and stucco panels.

The Sheikh Mohammed Centre for Cultural Understanding (see boxed text, p67) operates guided Bastakia walking tours at 10am on Sunday and Thursday (Dh50, reservations advised). However, the compact area is also easily explored on an aimless wander, although you may go around in a few circles, but that's just part of the fun! There is a handful of galleries and craft shops here, as well as the admirable **Mawaheb from Beautiful People** (www.mawaheb-dubai.com), an art studio for people with special needs.

FREE AL-SERKAL CULTURAL FOUNDATION — GALLERY

Map p210 (Heritage House 79, Al-Fahidi Roundabout; ⌚9.30am-8pm Sat-Thu, closed Fri) Next door to the Orient Guest House, this rambling Bastakia Quarter courtyard building – with its labyrinth of galleries set around a vast central courtyard – provides a fitting setting for traditional and cutting-edge works by local and international artists. Exhibitions change monthly.

FREE MAJLIS GALLERY — GALLERY

Map p210 (www.themajlisgallery.com; Al-Fahidi Roundabout; ⌚9.30am-8pm Sat-Thu) In a fabulous old house in the Bastakia Quarter, Majlis Gallery is one of Dubai's oldest commercial galleries, established in 1989. Compared with the progressive galleries in Al-Quoz (p80), Majlis is much more traditional and gentle. It focuses on paintings and sculpture created by international artists, many of them based in – and inspired by – the region. The central courtyard surrounds a magnificent henna tree. The gallery also offers inexpensive two-day painting and drawing workshops.

DUBAI MUSEUM — MUSEUM

Map p210 (Al-Fahidi St; adult/child Dh3/1; ⌚8.30am-8.30pm Sat-Thu, 2.30-8.30pm Fri; 👪) Located opposite the Grand Mosque, this low-key museum explores Dubai's history, culture and traditions and, although the emphasis on cutesy dioramas seems more geared towards school trips, it's definitely worth a visit. The exhibits are housed in 1799 Al-Fahidi Fort, considered the oldest building in Dubai and once the seat of government and residence of Dubai's rulers.

Start with a quick spin around the courtyard, with its old-time fishing boats and traditional dwellings, including a *barasti* (a traditional palm-leaf house) that includes a wind tower and a frighteningly basic kitchen – essentially just a pot and a pile of kindling. Pop behind the heavy carved wooden doors to check out modest displays of instruments and handcrafted weapons before heading down a spiralling ramp to the main galleries.

In the first room a slick multimedia presentation charts Dubai's exponential growth from tiny trading post to megalopolis, although the timeline on the opposite wall goes into greater depth. Beyond here, a series of dioramas recreates old Dubai, including a souq, a school, and a desert camp. Other displays focus on the Bedu; desert flora and fauna; traditional costumes and jewellery; and pearling, fishing and dhow (traditional wooden boat) building.

The highlight for many will be the final archaeology section (which seems back to front, somehow...). It features detailed information about the local settlements, which are believed to have been established here from around 2000 BC to 1000 BC. Don't miss the large well-lit gallery opposite the gift shop, with its displays of unearthed artefacts from the numerous tombs that have been discovered in the area. At one tomb alone (Al Soufouh) 16 ceramic vessels were found. Comprehensive explanatory panelling is in English and Arabic.

'HINDI LANE' — STREET

Map p210 (off Ali bin Abi Talib St) Venturing behind the Grand Mosque you'll stumble upon two places of worship behind very modest exteriors – just keep an eye out for the piles of shoes at the bottom of stairways. One set of staircases leads to the Shri Nathje Jayate Temple, also known as the Krishna Mandir (*mandir* is Hindi for temple). Shri Nathje is the main deity of

Pushtimarg, a Hindu devotional sect based near Udaipur in Rajasthan, India. Just beyond this temple (heading towards the Creek) is a colourful alleyway that expats refer to as 'Hindi Lane'. Here, vendors sell religious paraphernalia and offerings to take to the temples: baskets of fruit, garlands of flowers, gold-embossed holy images, sacred ash, sandalwood paste and packets of *bindis* (the little pendants Hindu women stick to their foreheads). Tucked amid the bustle is a series of staircases leading up to the other house of worship, the Sikh Gurudaba.

FREE GRAND MOSQUE — MOSQUE

Map p210 (Ali bin Abi Talib St) Situated opposite Dubai Museum, Dubai's tallest minaret (70m high) lords over more than 50 small and large domes, giving this huge mosque its distinctive silhouette. It's much younger than it looks, dating back only to 1998, but is, in fact, a replica of the original one from 1900. As well as being the centre of Dubai's religious and cultural life, the original Grand Mosque was also home to the town's *kuttab* (Quranic school), where children learned to recite the Quran from memory. As with all Dubai mosques except Jumeirah Mosque (p93), it's off limits to non-Muslims.

BUR DUBAI SOUQ — SOUQ

Map p210 (btwn Bur Dubai waterfront & Ali bin Abi Talib St) The breezy renovated Bur Dubai Souq may not be old as the Deira souqs but it can be just as atmospheric – although be prepared for pushy vendors. Friday evenings here are especially lively, as it turns into a virtual crawling carnival with expat workers loading up on socks, pashminas, T-shirts and knock-off Calvins on their day off. (The souq is generally hectic at night, but peaceful in the morning.) There's an area known as the **Textile Souq** because it specialises in colourful bales of fancy fabrics, most of them from India and other Asian countries. The surrounding streets – crammed with tailors, sari stores and jewellery shops – may not be as pleasing to the eye but are still intriguing and worth exploring.

SHINDAGHA HERITAGE AREA — HISTORIC SITE

Map p210 The Shindagha waterfront, on the northern side of the Creek, is one of the most historic areas in Dubai, with origins in the 1860s. It significantly gained in importance in the late 19th century, when the ruling family relocated here. This old district has been under restoration since 1996 and many of the gorgeous residences and mosques sparkle with renewed splendour. A paved walkway dotted with a few restaurants and museums parallels the waterfront and is popular with strollers and joggers. The nicest time to visit is around sunset; there's plenty of seating overlooking the water.

FREE TRADITIONAL ARCHITECTURE MUSEUM — MUSEUM

Map p210 (Shindagha Heritage Area; 8am-8pm Mon-Sat, 8am-2.30pm Sun) This magnificent Shindagha courtyard house has seen stints as a residence, jail and police station. Today it houses a thorough exhibit on traditional Arab architecture. This is the place to learn how those wind towers really work and why there are different dwelling types along the coast, in the mountains and in the desert. Most galleries feature entertaining and informative videos, which the caretaker will be only too happy to start up.

SHEIKH SAEED AL-MAKTOUM HOUSE — MUSEUM

Map p210 (Shindagha Heritage Area; adult/child Dh2/1; 8am-8.30pm Sat-Thu, 3-9.30pm Fri) The grand courtyard house of Sheikh Saeed, the grandfather of current Dubai ruler Sheikh Mohammed, is the crown jewel of the restored Shindagha Heritage Area. Built in 1896, under Sheikh Maktoum bin Hasher al-Maktoum, the house was home to the ruling family until Sheikh Saeed's death in 1958. Aside from being an architectural marvel, the building is now a museum of pre-oil times, with an excellent collection of photographs of Dubai taken in the 1940s and '50s on the Creek, in the souqs and at traditional celebrations. Included are some striking colour photos of girls adorned for the *tawminah*, a festival that celebrates children's successful recitations of the Quran. Other rooms feature coins, stamps and documents dating back as far as 1791, as well as an interesting display on pearl diving.

FREE HERITAGE & DIVING VILLAGES — MUSEUMS

Map p210 (Shindagha Heritage Area; 8am-10pm Sat-Thu, 8-11am & 4-10pm Fri) Located towards the end of the Shindagha waterfront, the Heritage and Diving Villages are intended to acquaint tourists with the region's traditional arts, customs and architecture. This is where you can nibble on piping-hot *dosas* (paper-thin lentil-flour pancakes) made by burka-clad women, pose with a falconer, hop on a camel or browse around touristy stalls. The villages are usually pretty quiet year round, except during Eid celebrations and the Dubai Shopping Festival (p20), when unusual traditional activities such as rifle-throwing competitions bring in the curious.

CREEKSIDE PARK — PARK

Map p214 (off Riyadh St; admission Dh5; ⌚8am-11pm Sat-Wed, to 11.30pm Thu, Fri & public holidays; 👪) Located between Al-Garhoud and Al-Maktoum Bridges, the large and lovely Creekside Park has playgrounds for kids to romp around, gardens for relaxing, kiosks, restaurants and barbecue pits. It's hugely popular, especially on weekends. A 2.5km **cable-car ride** (adult/child Dh25/15) delivers fabulous vistas of the park and waterfront from 30m in the air.

CHILDREN'S CITY — INTERACTIVE MUSEUM

Map p214 (Creekside Park; www.childrencity.ae; adult/child Dh15/10; ⌚9am-8pm Sat-Thu, 3-9pm Fri; 👪) At the southern end of Creekside Park, you'll stumble across two places for entertaining the kiddies. Enter through Gate 1 for Children's City, a learning centre comprising colourful Lego-style buildings that are jam-packed with more than 50 interactive exhibits. These exhibits, geared for children between the ages of two and 15 years, playfully explain scientific concepts, the human body, space exploration and natural wonders. One of the most popular exhibits is a simulator where you try flying on a magic carpet or riding a camel. Computer luddites (of any age) may like to try their hand sending a message from the giant computer, while under-fives can retreat to a special play area.

DUBAI DOLPHINARIUM — DOLPHIN SHOW

Map p214 (www.dubaidolphinarium.ae; adult/child Dh100/50; ⌚shows 11am & 5pm Mon-Thu, 11am, 3pm & 6pm Fri & Sat; 👪) Since the Dolphinarium opened in 2008, the dolphins here have delighted audiences with their tricks and stunts. Private swimming sessions with Flipper's cousins are also available (Dh2100 for up to three people). Although now quite popular, the facility's opening generated criticism from animal-rights activists contending that dolphins should not be held in captivity.

> **OPEN DOORS, OPEN MINDS**
>
> Such is the enlightened motto of the **Sheikh Mohammed Centre for Cultural Understanding** (Map p210; ☎04-353 6666; www.culture.ae; near Al-Seef Roundabout, Bastakia), a unique institution founded by Sheikh Mohammed in 1995 to build bridges between cultures and to help visitors and expats understand the traditions and customs of the United Arab Emirates (UAE). In addition to conducting guided tours of the Bastakia Quarter and Jumeirah Mosque (p93), the centre also hosts a hugely popular **Cultural Breakfast** (per person Dh50; ⌚10am Mon) and **Cultural Lunch** (per person Dh60; ⌚1pm Sun), where you get a chance to meet, ask questions of and exchange ideas with nationals while tasting delicious homemade Emirati food. Make reservations as early as possible.

ZA'ABEEL PARK — PARK

Map p214 (cnr Sheikh Khalifa bin Zayed & Al-Qataiyat Rds; admission Dh5; ⌚8am-11pm Sun-Wed, to 11.30pm Thu-Sat; 👪) This park has gorgeous lakes, ponds, a jogging track, a skateboard park, a BMX track and retail and food facilities – not to mention fabulous views of the Sheikh Zayed Rd skyline. It is also home to Stargate theme park (p76).

EATING

This is possibly Dubai's most eclectic eating area: restaurants run the gamut from dirt-cheap curry joints to white-tablecloth restaurants worthy of a Michelin star.

PEPPERCRAB — ASIAN $$$

Map p214 (☎04-317 2222; Grand Hyatt Dubai, Al-Qataiyat Rd; mains Dh120-220; ⌚7-11.30pm Sat-Wed, to 1am Thu & Fri) If you've never had Singaporean food, Peppercrab is perfect for surrendering your culinary virginity. Prepare your palate with plump wonton and crunchy baby squid, then don an apron

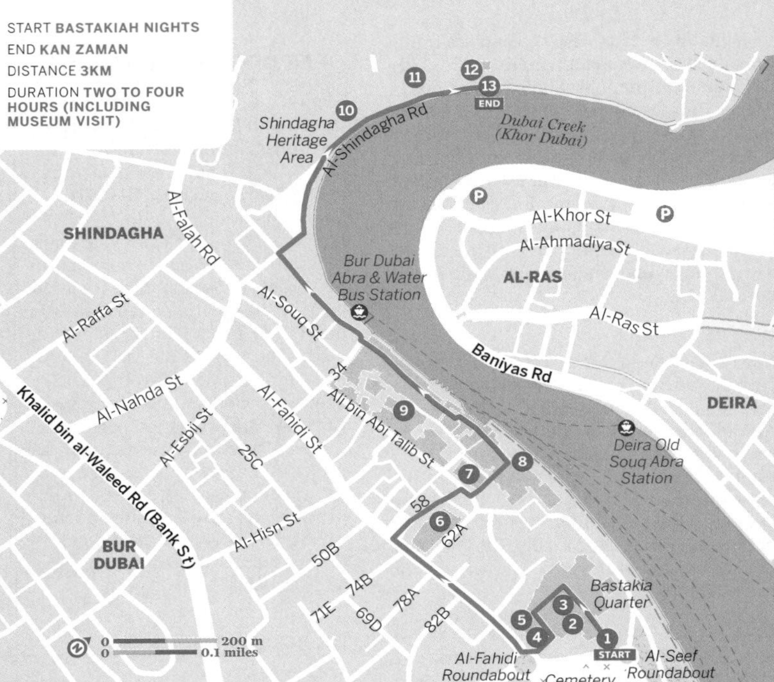

Neighbourhood Walk

Bur Dubai Waterside Walk

This waterside walk kicks off at romantic **1 Bastakiah Nights** restaurant, near Al-Seef Rd. Afterwards, spend time wandering the quarter's atmospheric narrow lanes. Savour the ambience of **2 XVA**, a cafe, gift shop and hotel in a superbly restored Bastakia courtyard residence.

Next door to the XVA Hotel, check out the latest exhibits at **3 Al-Serkal Cultural Foundation**, an art gallery and cultural centre within yet another charming courtyard building. Make three lefts as you exit Al-Serkal to inspect the exquisite paintings, sculpture and ceramics at **4 Majlis Gallery**. Grab a refreshing fruit cocktail or crisp salad at **5 Basta Art Cafe**, a charming walled garden surrounded by leafy trees and birdsong.

Head north along Al-Fahidi St to **6 Dubai Museum** for an hour, soaking up the history, heritage and development of this burgeoning city. Turn right as you exit the museum and make another right on 58 St for great views of the architectural details of the **7 Grand Mosque**. Take the lane to the mosque's right-hand side, and continue straight ahead for a few steps to get to **8 Hindi Lane**, a vibrant and colourful alley with tiny stores selling religious paraphernalia. Turn left into the alleyway.

Stroll beneath the wooden arcades of **9 Bur Dubai Souq**, and past colourful textile shops, pausing for freshly squeezed orange juice. When you reach Bur Dubai Abra Station, walk past boats along the waterfront to Shindagha Heritage Area, where fans of Arab architecture will love in-depth exhibits at handsomely restored **10 Traditional Architecture Museum**. Near the mouth of the Creek, splendid **11 Sheikh Saeed al-Maktoum House** is the key building in the area, displaying an intriguing collection of old photographs of Dubai. If you're visiting during Eid or the Dubai Shopping Festival, the **12 Heritage and Diving Villages** will be a hive of activity, providing an authentic glimpse into Emirati traditions. Finally, nab a waterfront table at **13 Kan Zaman** and enjoy a fresh juice or tasty, traditional Middle Eastern meal.

and get ready to do battle with the main event, the eponymous 'peppercrab' – a succulent, flaky, tender crustacean paired with a feisty, pepper-laced sauce that's a virtual flavour bomb. Reservations essential.

ASHA'S MODERN INDIAN **$$**

Map p214 (☎04-324 4100; Wafi Mall, Pyramids, Sheikh Rashid Rd; mains from Dh65; 👪) Namesake of Bollywood singer Asha Bhosle, Asha's packs a see-and-be-seen crowd of rich Indian expats into its sexy, low-light, tandoori-orange dining room, with ethnic-fusion dance music playing in the background. The menu focuses on contemporary northwest Indian fare, with palate-teasers such as spicy-ginger-garlic marinated prawns and white chicken curry (with almonds, chilli seeds and yogurt) – both being Asha's personal recipes. It's a fabulous place to party; if tots are tagging along, they've even got their own play area. Reservations recommended.

AWTAR LEBANESE **$$**

Map p214 (☎04-317 2222; Grand Hyatt Dubai, Al-Qataiyat Rd; mains from Dh65; ⏰7.30pm-3am Sun-Fri) Locals love the opulent Bedouin tent-like atmosphere and warm welcome of this formal Lebanese restaurant, complete with belly dancer and live band – it's common for women to stand up, clap and sway to the music. The menu lists the usual mezze and kebabs, as well as a full page of meat dishes, all served as mountainous portions. If you're loath to shout over the noise, book for 8pm. But for maximum fun, round up a posse and come at 10pm, when the scene gets rockin'. Request one of the swoop-backed booths for the best views. Reservations recommended.

LEMONGRASS THAI **$$**

Map p214 (mains Dh35-65; ⏰noon-11pm) Located just south of Lamcy Plaza in Oud Metha, Lemongrass' soothing mango-and-lime-coloured dining room is an ideal setting for brightly flavoured cooking and solicitous service. Pad thai is presented in an omelette wrapper – a nice touch – and curries have marvellous depth of flavour. If you like spicy, say so; the kitchen is shy with the heat. Cool down with the house favourite *lanna* dessert (*pandan*-flavoured ice cream with palm seeds, sweetcorn and red beans – *pandan* is a plant found in the Far East that has a similar flavour to vanilla).

BAIT AL WAKEEL MIDDLE EASTERN **$**

Map p210 (Textile Souq, Bur Dubai Souq; mains Dh35-50) In one of the city's most romantic settings – overlooking the Creek, with its view of bobbing boats – this restaurant has lots of history. The building, formerly a shipping office, is one of Dubai's oldest, dating back to 1935, and the dining deck was formerly a landing stage for boats. Stick to the Arabic dishes, rather than going Asian, and you won't be disappointed. The mezze plates are good, as are the lamb and *kofta* (spicy meatballs) and seafood. If there's a queue, follow the Creek for around 50m to **Blue Barjeel** and console yourself (and your wallet) with a dish of hummus with pita bread and a mango juice (Dh18).

SPECIAL OSTADI IRANIAN **$**

Map p210 (Al-Musallah Rd, Bur Dubai; mains Dh25; ⏰noon-4pm) This spit-'n'-sawdust authentic Iranian restaurant enjoys a prominent corner position and prominent place in the heart of its loyal kebab-loving clientele. Dating from 1978, it is one of Dubai's longest-standing restaurants.

SHIV GANYA INDIAN, VEGETARIAN **$**

Map p210 (Al Rolla Residence, Al Rolla Rd; mains Dh18-25) A vegetarian Indian restaurant where the daily Dh37 buffet should put a

BACCHANALIAN BOATING

A great way to experience the exotic magic of old Dubai is during a dinner cruise along the Creek. Feed tummy and soul as you gently cruise past historic waterfront houses, sparkling high-rises, jutting wind towers and dhows (traditional wooden boats) bound for India or Iran. Dining rooms are air-conditioned and alcohol is served. **Bateaux Dubai** (off Map p210; ☎04-399 4994; www.bateauxdubai.com; Al-Seef Rd, Bur Dubai Creek; per person 2½hr dinner cruise Dh350; ⏰8.30-11pm) is a good choice, especially if food is as important to you as ambience. Indulge in a four-course à la carte feast aboard this stylish contemporary boat with its floor-to-ceiling windows, linen-draped tables and live pianist-and-guitar duo. The price includes unlimited soft and alcoholic drinks. The other recommended dinner cruise is **Al Mansour Dhow** in Deira (see p55).

A QUESTION OF PORK

Pork is available for non-Muslims in a special room at some larger supermarkets. In many hotel restaurants, pork is a menu item and is usually clearly labelled as such. However, the 'beef bacon' and 'turkey ham' that are commonly available are nothing more than a reminder of how tasty the real thing is – unless you are a vegetarian, of course.

satisfied waddle in your step. Favourite dishes include traditional Mumbai *chaat* (savoury street snacks) and cubes of paneer (white cheese) with spinach, peas and lots of spices. There is a plenty of heat in the dishes; cool down with a masala mint-based tea. This is a popular restaurant with local Indian families and has comfortable seating and good service.

FIRE & ICE STEAKHOUSE **$$$**

Map p214 (☎04-341 9888; Raffles Dubai, Sheikh Rashid Rd; mains Dh95-190, steaks Dh135-420; ⏲7pm-11.30pm) With its floor-to-ceiling exposed brick walls, the Raffles steakhouse exudes a sleek, sophisticated New York vibe. Sip a martini while casually scanning the contented crowd and anticipating such menu stars as Angus prime sirloin, rack of lamb and the signature carrot cake. And whatever you order, get a serving of fries – you'll thank us. There's an award-winning list of 900 or so wines, which is especially strong on New World varietals. Reservations essential.

CHUTNEYS INDIAN **$$**

Map p214 (☎04-310 4340; Mövenpick Hotel Bur Dubai, 19 St; mains Dh60-80, thali Dh55-75) Chutneys provides a first-class culinary journey to northern India. The lunchtime-only thalis are superb and include a vegetarian option, or opt for juicy kebabs, fluffy birianis or the chicken-based *tawa murgh rayyan* – a chicken- and tomato-based curry that was voted the best in Dubai in a local publication. In the evening you can enjoy a truly romantic dinner for two by closing the curtains around your table while Ghazal singers croon smoothly in the background. Reservations are recommended.

OLIVE GOURMET LEBANESE **$**

Map p210 (BurJuman Centre, cnr Khalid bin al-Waleed & Sheikh Khalifa bin Zayed Rds; mains Dh35-48) Right across from the metro entrance, this restaurant may not be worth crossing town to seek out, but if you are in the BurJuman area, it offers reliably good and relatively inexpensive Lebanese food. Take a detour from the usual hummus and kebab route and order *foul medammas* (black fava beans with lemon juice, olive oil, tomatoes and garlic), *makanek* (charcoal-grilled sausages in a pomegranate sauce) or fried calamari with garlic and lemon, all served by congenial fezzed-up waiters.

KHAZANA INDIAN **$$**

Map p214 (☎04-336 0061; off 14 St; mains Dh40-80; ⏲noon-2.30pm & 7-11pm; 👪) Khazana means 'treasure' in Hindi and, certainly, the steady stream of regulars indicates that Khazana is one of the best Indian restaurants in town. Curries are sensitively spiced, the ingredients are the freshest available, and as this is Indian celebrity chef Sanjeer Kapoor's signature restaurant, the standard is indisputably high. Ample bamboo and rattan create a relaxed feel-good ambience, helped along by the friendly servers. It's located behind the American Hospital, and reservations are recommended.

KAN ZAMAN MIDDLE EASTERN **$**

Map p210 (Shindagha Heritage Area, mezze Dh12-20, mains Dh30-70; ⏲4.30pm-2.30am) Stop by this Creekside favourite to munch on mezze and grills (the tangy lamb *shwarma* is delish) or fresh *saj manakish* (Lebanese pastry topped with cheese, thyme and meat). At the very least, partake of an avocado smoothie with honey and milk: it's the best in town. During the cooler months, sit on the big outdoor patio and watch the passing parade of boats against the backdrop of historic Deira and Bur Dubai.

ANTIQUE BAZAAR INDIAN **$$**

Map p210 (☎04-397 7444; Four Points by Sheraton Bur Dubai, Khalid bin al-Waleed Rd; mains Dh40-50) This is not just any old curryhouse – resembling an exotic Mogul palace, the decor is sumptuously ornate with carved-wood seats, ivory-inset tables, swing chairs and richly patterned fabrics. There is a resident sitar player at lunchtime, with more of a show at dinner, which is when the place is most atmospheric.

Dishes are attractively presented and the most popular include a succulent *murgh tikka lababdar* (chicken in a spicy yogurt-based sauce) and birianis. Reservations recommended.

BASTA ART CAFE CAFE $

Map p210 (Al-Fahidi St, Bastakia Quarter; mains Dh30-45; 👪) A cool respite while exploring the Bastakia Quarter. Lounge back in a white-wicker sofa in this sun-dappled garden, surrounded by pots of crimson bougainvillea and colourful abstract art. It's great for breakfast or a light lunch, with an 18-plus salad choice, plus filled baked potatoes and similar cafe fare. Don't miss the small gift shop selling a variety of souvenirs, including locally made delicate jewellery inset with semiprecious stones. And don't miss the mint lemonade.

SARAVANAA BHAVAN INDIAN, VEGETARIAN $

Map p210 (4-5 Kahlifa bin Saeed Bldg; mains Dh13-15) Head a block back from the Bur Dubai Abra & Water Bus Station to find this superb no-frills place, one of the best Indian vegetarian restaurants in town. If you thought vegetarian was restrictive, think again. This vast menu includes wonderfully buttery paneer vegetarian dishes, rogan josh, birianis, *dosas* and a medley of side orders.

LEBANESE VILLAGE RESTAURANT LEBANESE $

Map p210 (Al-Mankhool Rd; mains Dh30-65) Everything tastes very fresh at this Lebanese restaurant, even though the menu is so lengthy that it reads like a book. For a start, there are 17 different salads, including a succulent parsley-laden tabouli. Sit under a shady umbrella on the street-side terrace, which is more appealing than the bright diner-style interior. Alternatively, you can order a takeaway, which is handy if you're staying in one of the numerous, surrounding hotel-apartment blocks.

PAUL FRENCH $

Map p214 (Wafi Mall, Sheikh Rashid Rd; sandwiches & salads Dh35-55, mains Dh70; 👪) This French cafe is an upmarket mall staple. It's packed with expats who come for the scrumptious croissants (especially the almond ones), ample-sized breakfasts and a small, but selective, choice of salads, sandwiches and mains. It's a bit pricey but a reliable standby. There are additional branches at several other malls.

XVA CAFE VEGETARIAN $

Map p210 (XVA Hotel, Bastakia Quarter; dishes Dh20-35; 📶) Escape Dubai's bustle at this artsy courtyard cafe in the historic Bastakia Quarter, located just off Al-Fahidi St. The menu eschews meat in favour of offerings such as aubergine burger, tuna salad and a vegetarian croque monsieur. Wash it down with intensely green mint-lemonade – a must-order.

CURRY LEAF SRI LANKAN $

Map p210 (Al-Mussalla Tower, Bank St; mains Dh15-30; ⏲11.30am-midnight; 👪) Hoppers (crispy rice-flour pancakes with fried egg) go well with the smoky-hot, spice-rich curries at this Sri Lankan place in an electronics mall food court. A few Dutch colonial dishes round out the menu; try the *lumpries* (spiced rice baked with meat, egg and aubergine). By the time you read this, the menu will have expanded to include some Thai and Indian dishes.

BASTAKIAH NIGHTS LEBANESE $$

Map p210 (☎04-353 7772; Bastakia Quarter; mains Dh50-75; ⏲11.30am-midnight) One of the city's most romantic restaurants, Bastakiah Nights occupies a restored courtyard with fabulous old Arabian-style atmosphere. The menu is mainly Lebanese but includes a few Emirati dishes. Although the food isn't the best in town, the atmosphere is terrific, especially for dinner when the courtyard is candlelit and the indigo night sky is overhead. Be wary of the overpriced set menu – you're better off ordering a couple of à la carte dishes. No alcohol. Reservations recommended.

NOBLE HOUSE CHINESE $$$

Map p214 (☎324 8888; Raffles Dubai, Sheikh Rashid Rd; mains Dh110-150; ⏲Tue-Sat 7pm-11.30pm) Marvel at the stunning skyline views from the 17th floor while you sample some of the finest and most original Szechuan and Cantonese dishes in Dubai. The decor is stylish and clubby with plush high-back tasselled chairs, and the waiting staff love to show off, especially pouring sauces from aloft with perfect aim into tiny glasses. Get into the mellow mood with a pre-dinner cocktail at the adjacent Red Lounge. Reservations recommended.

DRINKING & NIGHTLIFE

COOZ COCKTAIL BAR

Map p214 (www.dubai.grand.hyatt.com; Grand Hyatt Dubai, Al-Qataiyat Rd; 6pm-3am) Sip a martini at this dimly lit, super-stylish cocktail bar and enjoy some smooth live jazz – some of the most authentic sounds in Dubai, in fact – by the resident singer and pianist.

OLD VIC BAR

Map p210 (www.ramadadubai.com; Ramada Hotel, Al-Mankhool Rd; noon-1am) This is about as authentic as the English-style pubs get in Dubai and gets packed out with homesick Brits, here for the big-screen sports and ale on tap. The added perk is the nightly live entertainment, generally jazz with a singer, which adds a soupçon of sophistication.

RED LOUNGE BAR

Map p214 (www.dubai.raffles.com; Raffles Dubai, Sheikh Rashid Rd; 6pm-3am) Before you have even shelled out for a (costly) drink, this is a seriously heady setting. It's at the dizzy peak of Raffles' iconic pyramid building, with stunning panoramic views of the city skyline. The decor is red and plush. Dress to impress (this is a fashionista favourite). Move on to the People by Crystal nightclub next door if you feel like shifting into dance mode.

CHI CLUB

Map p214 (www.chinightclubdubai.com; 12A St, Oud Metha) The favourite of young expat party people, especially on Friday nights, Chi sometimes hosts live music, but the big draws are its DJs playing funk, house, disco, drum 'n' bass, and whatever else inspires. Located next to Al-Nasr Leisureland, there are four big spaces, including a Balinese-themed outdoor garden where you can chill in a cushioned lounge or VIP cabana.

PEOPLE BY CRYSTAL CLUB

Map p214 (www.dubai.raffles.com; Raffles Dubai, Sheikh Rashid Rd; 10pm-3am) Another of the see-and-be-seen breed of sophisticated nightclub with stylish decor, sultry lighting, world-class DJs and incredible views from the top of Raffles' famous pyramid.

SUBMARINE CLUB

Map p210 (Dhow Palace Hotel, Kuwait St; 6pm-3am) Dive into the basement of this hotel to arrive at a compact, industrial bar that's popular with a refreshingly unpretentious crowd. There's often a band to kick things into gear, along with DJs that shower beat junkies with a heady mix of deep house to trance, funk to R&B. Casual dress is just fine.

ROCK BOTTOM CAFÉ CLUB

Map p214 (www.regentpalacehotel.co.uk/Dubai.asp; Regent Palace Hotel, Sheikh Khalifa bin Zayed Rd; noon-3am) Fittingly located next to Casanova (a barber), this place has a '70s-era American roadhouse feel, with a cover band blaring out Top-40 hits and a DJ filling in the breaks with gusto. It's a regular pub by day, but with a mob of friends and a bottle of tequila gone, it's the quintessential ending to a rollickin' night on the town. There's another branch in the **Ramee Rose Hotel** (www.rameehotels.com) in Dubai Internet City.

SHOPPING

WAFI MALL MALL

Map p214 (www.wafi.com; Sheikh Rashid Rd) Westerners mistakenly bypass palatial Wafi in favour of the behemoth shopping malls, which explains why it's so quiet. It's their loss. It may have once resembled a third-rate airport terminal, but the newer wing's stained-glass pyramids are stunning and the entire complex, encompassing the superb Pharaohs' Club, is a pure Egyptian-cum-Las-Vegas-style extravaganza with sphinxes, pharaohs, and columns decorated with mock hieroglyphics. While Emirati women love Wafi's fancy French stores like Chanel and Givenchy, you may well prefer sussing out lesser-known regional boutiques or stocking up on underwear at M&S (the best view of the stained glass is from just outside the main entrance of M&S).

Duck into the mall's basement to browse around Souq Khan Murjan, which also has stunning decor with a stained-glass ceiling and plenty of decorative wood. Although there is a good, if pricey, selection of crafts and goods from around the Arabian world here, alas, it too is practically deserted. Refuelling stops include Asha's and Noble House at the adjacent Raffles hotel.

BURJUMAN CENTRE MALL

Map p210 (www.burjuman.com; cnr Khalid bin al-Waleed & Sheikh Khalifa bin Zayed Rds)

DUBAI'S SHOPPING FESTIVALS

Every year from mid-January to mid-February, the month-long **Dubai Shopping Festival** (www.dubaishoppingfestival.com) draws hordes of bargain-hunting tourists from around the world. This is a good time to visit Dubai: in addition to the huge discounts in the souqs and malls, the weather is usually gorgeous and the city is abuzz. Outdoor souqs, amusement rides and food stalls are set up in many neighbourhoods, with the best on the Bur Dubai waterfront across from the British Embassy. There are traditional performances and displays at the Heritage and Diving Villages, family entertainment across the city, concerts and events in the parks, and nightly fireworks, best viewed from Creekside Park. **Dubai Summer Surprises**, a related event, is held during the unbearably hot months of July and August; it mainly attracts visitors from other Gulf countries. NB: For the best bargains at either festival, come during the last week, when retailers slash prices even further to clear out their inventory.

The carnival-like **Global Village** (☎04-362 4114; www.globalvillage.ae; off Hwy E311; admission Dh10; ⏰4pm-midnight Sun-Wed, to 1am Thu & Fri) runs from late November to late February, about 13km south of Sheikh Zayed Rd. Think of it as a sort of 'world fair' for shoppers. Each of the 30-something pavilions showcases a specific nation's culture and – of course – products. Some favourites: the Afghanistan pavilion for fretwork-bordered stone pendants and beaded-silver earrings; Palestine for traditional cross-stitch *kandouras* (casual shirt-dresses worn by men and women) and ever-popular cushion covers; Yemen for its authentic *khanjars* (traditional curved daggers); India for spangled fabrics and slippers; and Kenya for its kitsch bottle-top handbags. Check out the earnest entertainment, from Chinese opera to Turkish whirling dervishes.

BurJuman has a huge concentration of high-end labels and an easy-to-navigate floor plan. There are wide expanses of shiny marble studded with white leather sofas for resting weary feet. Max out your credit card at over 320 top purveyors, including Saks Fifth Avenue, Dolce & Gabbana, Donna Karan, Kenzo, Calvin Klein, Christian Lacroix, Cartier and Tiffany. There's a cheap and chowable food court on the 3rd floor, as well as some classier choices, like Paul and Olive Gourmet. The mall is also a stop on the Big Bus Company (p176) route.

FIVE GREEN — FASHION

Map p214 (Garden Home, Oud Metha Rd, Oud Metha) You may get lost trying to find one of the city's leading indie boutiques and concept stores, but it's worth it to meet the cool kids of Dubai's retail scene. In addition to its art installations, international magazines and music by Jazzanova and Soot, Five Green carries cool unisex labels such as Teenage Millionaire, Paul Frank, Paper Denim & Cloth and Upper Playground.

AHMED EISA KAMALI — SHEESHA

Map p214 (Lamcy Plaza) This modest store has some fine *sheeshas* (water pipes used to smoke tobacco), ranging from Dh30 to Dh350 and from bejewelled and colourful to the more mainstream version. There's an endless range of flavoured tobaccos, including strawberry and coffee. In fact, there's just about every flavour you can think of, except for plain tobacco.

AL-OROOBA ORIENTAL — CARPETS

Map p210 (BurJuman Centre; cnr Khalid bin al-Waleed & Sheikh Khalifa bin Zayed Rds) You'll have to decide whether to enjoy the ritual of unfurling fine carpets or combing over the cool collection of Bedouin jewellery, Kashmiri shawls, prayer beads, ceramics and *khanjars*. You won't have time for both: this is high-quality stuff that merits careful attention.

GALAXY PIANO — PIANOS

Map p210 (www.galaxypiano.com; BurJuman Centre; cnr Khalid bin al-Waleed & Sheikh Khalifa bin Zayed Rds) OK, we know you're unlikely to buy a piano while on your hols, but this showroom would even make Elton John swoon. Acrylic glass uprights and grands include a little gold number and a scarlet-and-silver show-stopper. Fabulous!

LOCAL KNOWLEDGE

TAILOR-MADE FASHION

The backstreets of Bur Dubai are filled with talented Indian tailors who will run up a dress or suit for you in a couple of days. Some also sell material, although you'd be better off paying a visit to the nearby Textile Souq (within the main Bur Dubai Souq), where you can ponder over endless swatches of wonderful fabrics. The best street for choice is Al-Hisn (off Al Fahidi St, near the Dubai Museum), where reliable tailors include poetically named Dream Girls and Hollywood Tailors. Expect to pay about Dh150 for a dress and allow at least three days for your garment to be sewn up.

FACES BEAUTY

Map p210 (BurJuman Centre; cnr Khalid bin al-Waleed & Sheikh Khalifa bin Zayed Rds) There's an entire global menu of make-up, fragrances and skincare potions here to help you get prettified and smelling good. As well as the usual glamour brands (Armani to Chanel), Faces also stocks products by Benefil San Francisco, Dr Brandt from Florida, London's Molton Brown and other harder-to-source beauty purveyors.

BATEEL FOOD

Map p210 (www.bateel.com; BurJuman Centre; cnr Khalid bin al-Waleed & Sheikh Khalifa bin Zayed Rds; ⌚10am-10pm Sat-Wed, to 11pm Thu & Fri) Old-style traditional Arabian hospitality meant dates and camel milk. Now Emiratis offer their guests Bateel's scrumptious date chocolates and truffles, made using European chocolate-making techniques. Staff are happy to give you a sample before you buy. Check the website for additional branches, and if you fancy a date cake or pastry, check out Cafe Bateel on the same level. For more about Bateel, see p40.

AL-AIN CENTRE ELECTRONICS

Map p210 (Al-Mankhool Rd; ⌚10am-10pm) Jam-packed with small shops selling every kind of software, hardware and accessory for PCs, this computer and electronics mall also has a good range of digital cameras and mobile phones. (The ground floor has a couple of fast-food outlets and an ice cream counter.)

SHOPPERS DEPARTMENT STORE DEPARTMENT STORE

Map p210 (Al-Musallah Rd) Head upstairs in this Pakistani-run department store for a fine array of colourful and traditional Punjabi tunic tops. These look great with jeans or leggings and cost from just Dh50. The mega-bling babywear for girls is also pretty eye-catching, with enough taffeta and frills to blow their little socks off. Located just before the Al-Fahidi roundabout, note that Al-Mankhool Rd has plenty of similar Indian-run businesses and shops. Look for such old-fashioned shopfront gems as Karana Typing, up from here on your right (just in case you forgot to bring your laptop).

OHM RECORDS MUSIC

Map p214 (Al Kifaf Bldg, Trade Centre Rd; ⌚noon-9pm) DJs dig Ohm, the first Dubai shop to carry vinyl. Located a half-block south of Sheikh Khalifa bin Zayed Rd, opposite BurJuman Centre, there's a discerning selection of house, trance, progressive, trip-hop and drum 'n' bass, as well as DJ equipment and accessories.

AJMAL PERFUME

Map p210 (www.ajmalperfume.com; BurJuman Centre; cnr Khalid bin al-Waleed & Sheikh Khalifa bin Zayed Rds) The place for traditional Arabian *attars* (perfumes), Ajmal custom-blends its earthy scents and pours them into fancy gold or jewel-encrusted bottles. These aren't fancy French colognes – they're woody and pungent perfumes. Ask for the signature scent 'Ajmal', based on white musk and jasmine (Dh300). Other branches are in Deira City Centre, Mall of the Emirates and Dubai Mall.

KARAMA SHOPPING CENTRE SHOPPING CENTRE

Map p214 (Kuwait St, Karama) A visually unappealing concrete souq, Karama's bustling backstreet shopping area is crammed with stores selling handicrafts and souvenirs, 'genuine fake' watches and knock-off designer clothing. Check out the freakish mannequins that front most of the stores. Since much of the clothing is produced in Asian countries, sizes are often small. In other words, if you normally wear a size S and now need XL, it's probably not because you overindulged at those brunches. Prices are low, but bargaining lowers them further – be adamant. Listen for the cries of hucksters hawking pirated movies. The municipality seems to look the other way.

ROYAL SAFFRON SPICES

Map p210 (Bastakia Souq) This place is easy to find, just around the corner from Majlis Gallery – or follow the wafting smell of burning *bachoor* (incense). This tiny shop is crammed full of fresh spices like cloves, cardamom and cinnamon, plus fragrant oils, dried fruits and nuts, frankincense from Somalia and Oman, henna hair dye – and quirky salt and pepper sheikh and sheikhas.

SILK WONDERS SOUVENIRS

Map p210 (Atheryat Mall, Al-Fahidi St) Located across from the Dubai Museum, this is just one of a pick 'n' mix selection of stores on the mall's ground level that sells inexpensive clothes, shawls, accessories and dust collectors – including ornaments from India and Iranian carved boxes. It's also good for cheap T-shirts for family back home, and for sequinned bedspreads and woven silk-and-wool rugs to blitz your hand luggage allowance.

BANG & OLUFSEN ELECTRONICS

Map p210 (www.bang-olufsen.com; BurJuman Centre; cnr Khalid bin al-Waleed & Sheikh Khalifa bin Zayed Rds) State-of-the-art and sophisticated electronics with sleek unobtrusive designs that work equally well in a minimalist New York penthouse as in a full-on family-sized villa.

SPORTS & ACTIVITIES

PHARAOHS' CLUB GYM

Map p214 (04-324 0000; www.wafi.com; Wafi Mall, Sheikh Rashid Rd; classes Dh38-62, gym per day Dh200, pool per day Dh130; 6.30am-10.15pm Sat-Thu, 9am-9pm Fri) This is the closest you'll find to an LA-style club, with some serious weight-lifting equipment (including 100lb dumb-bells), a superb climbing wall (the highest in the region at a dizzy 13.5m) and various fitness classes. The best amenity is the enormous, free-form 'lazy-river' rooftop swimming pool, which is available for one-day drop-ins and is great for kids.

FITNESS FIRST GYM

Map p210 (www.fitnessfirstme.com; BurJuman Centre, cnr Khalid bin al-Waleed & Sheikh Khalifa bin Zayed Rds; day pass Dh100; 6am-11pm) This huge global chain has eight massive branches in Dubai with state-of-the-art cardio equipment, a great line-up of classes from Body Pump and Spinning to Pilates and kick-boxing, and a full complement of free weights. Some also have swimming pools and gender-segregated sauna and steam rooms. On-site trainers help you tone your muscles. Aside from the BurJuman Centre, handy branches are at Dubai Festival City (p61), Dubai International Financial Centre (Map p216) and Ibn Battuta Mall (p106).

CRICKET CRAZY

The enormous Indian and Pakistani communities in Dubai l-o-v-e cricket. You'll see them playing on sandy lots between buildings during their lunch breaks, in parks on their days off, and late at night in empty car parks. In contrast, you won't see Emiratis playing: cricket in Dubai belongs to the subcontinental nationalities. If you want to get under the skin of the game, talk to taxi drivers – you can be sure most of them have posters of their favourite players taped to their bedroom walls. But first ask where your driver is from – there's disdain between Pakistanis and Indians. Each will tell you that his country's team is the best, and then explain at length why. (Some drivers need a bit of cajoling; show enthusiasm and you'll get the whole story.) When Pakistan plays India, the city lights up. Remember: these two nationalities account for about 45% of Dubai's population, far outnumbering Emiratis. Because most of them can't afford the price of satellite TV, they meet up outside their local eateries in Deira or Bur Dubai to watch the match. Throngs of riveted fans swarm the pavements beneath the crackling neon – it's a sight to behold. Football is the Emirati's game (for more information, see p45).

SAVING FACE IN DUBAI

Dubai does a roaring trade in plastic surgery, rivalling Los Angeles for rhinoplasty, liposuction and breast augmentation. It makes sense, when you think about it. Geographically speaking, although Dubai seems to be in the middle of nowhere, it's halfway between London and Singapore, and most of the world's airlines fly here. Londoners and Russians can jet here in a few hours and remain totally anonymous while they get their faces done, a world away from their normal social circles. And all that high-end shopping means they can also build new wardrobes to match their new noses, with zero fear of running into anyone they know.

If you're staying at a five-star beach resort – one of the self-contained compounds that guests need never leave before flying back home – keep an eye out for folks hiding behind oversized black sunglasses. Chances are there are a couple of big fat shiners turning purple beneath those Gucci frames.

GRAND HYATT GYM GYM

Map p214 (☎04-317 1234; www.hyatt.com; Grand Hyatt Dubai, Al-Qataiyat Rd; day pass Sun-Thu Dh250, Fri & Sat Dh300; ⏲6am-11pm; 👪) The top-notch equipment here includes Smith racks, cable-crossover racks and full circuit-training equipment. The gym also offers aerobics, yoga and on-site trainers to guide your workout. Justify the price by spending the afternoon inside with a treatment at the glittering spa or outside by Dubai's biggest swimming pool. Also outdoors you'll find a meandering 450m running track beneath tall palms, and four tennis courts. Children have their own pool.

WONDER BUS TOURS BOAT TOUR

Map p210 (☎04-359 5656; www.wonderbustours.net; BurJuman Centre, cnr Khalid bin al-Waleed & Sheikh Khalifa bin Zayed Rds; tours adult/child Dh140/95; 👪) Twice a day (actual times depend on the tide) this amphibious bus drives down to the Creek, plunges into the water, cruises for an hour and then drives back onto land and returns to the BurJuman Centre. It's a fun tour with a multilingual guide who is both entertaining and informative.

STARGATE THEME PARK

Map p214 (www.stargatedubai.com; admission Dh2; ⏲10am-10pm Sat-Wed, to midnight Thu & Fri; 👪) This space-themed amusement park is aimed at children aged four to 14. It consists of five domed buildings (named Earth, Moon, Saturn, Mars and UFO) where they can race go-karts, ride a roller coaster, take a spin on a small ice rink or watch 3-D movies. To reach Stargate, enter through Gate 4 of Za'abeel Park. Note that rides are not covered in the admission price, but various packages are available.

AL-NASR LEISURELAND ICE SKATING

Map p214 (www.alnasrll.com; 12A St; adult/child incl boot hire Dh10/5; ⏲2hr sessions 10am, 1pm, 4pm & 7.30pm; 👪) Open since 1979, Leisureland is definitely long in the tooth, but it's got a bit of character and lots of facilities under one roof, including a gym, tennis and squash courts, a bowling alley and an ice rink. Sure, it's not as snazzy as the Dubai Ice Rink, but it's bigger than the one at the Hyatt Regency Dubai. Of the several eateries, Viva Goa (Indian restaurant) is the best pick.

Sheikh Zayed Road & Around

DOWNTOWN DUBAI | AL-QUOZ | FINANCIAL DISTRICT

Neighbourhood Top Five

❶ Gazing skywards at the extraordinary, elegantly tapered **Burj Khalifa** (p79), Dubai's most famous landmark. Soaring upwards for a staggering 828m, it's the world's tallest man-made structure – take the elevator to the top for incredible panoramic views.

❷ Shopping at the mother of all malls: **Dubai Mall** (p79), with a record-breaking 1200 shops.

❸ Checking out the superb Middle Eastern artwork at **Gate Village** in the Financial Centre (p82).

❹ Spotting flocks of migratory birds at **Ras al-Khor Wildlife Sanctuary** (p80).

❺ Wondering at beautifully choreographed dancing fountains at **Dubai Fountain** (p79), from a restaurant vantage point.

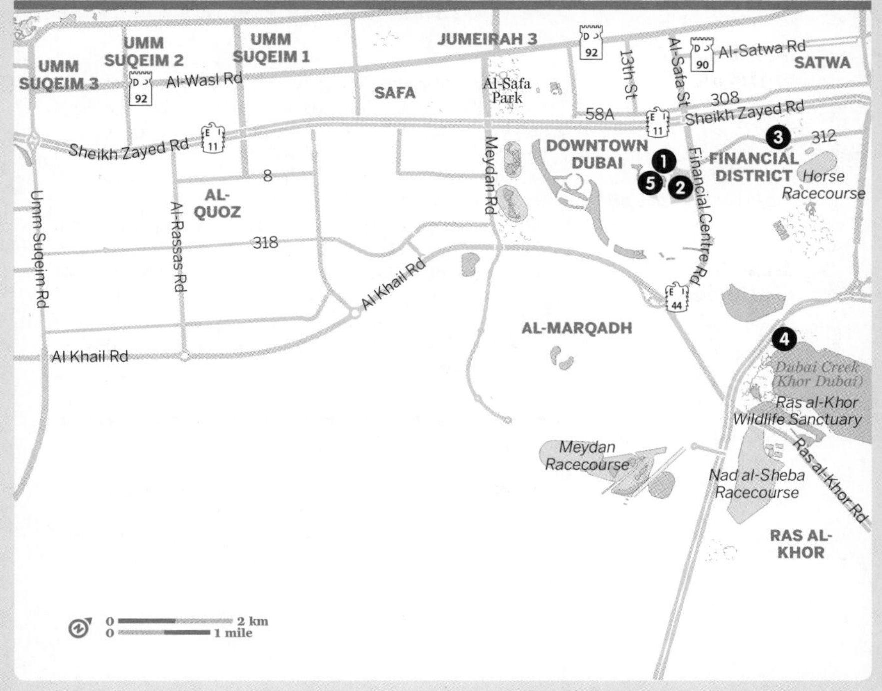

For more detail of this area, see Map p216

Lonely Planet's Top Tip

If you're driving to Dubai Mall, be sure to collect a free ticket at the entrance. The ticket states on which level you are parked, making it easier to find your way back to your car. However, in a worst-case scenario (weighed down with shopping, screaming toddler in tow and dying for the loo), never fear – there are cameras above every parking space, so attendants should be able to help you find your car.

Best Places to Eat

- Asado (p83)
- Baker & Spice (p83)
- Ivy (p84)

For reviews, see p83

Best Places to Drink

- Calabar (p86)
- Ikandy (p86)
- Neos (p86)

For reviews, see p86

Best Art Galleries

- Gallery Isabelle Van Den Eynde (p80)
- Third Line (p81)
- Cuadro (p82)

For reviews, see p79

Explore Sheikh Zayed Road & Around

'Who wants to explore a vast 10-lane highway?', you may ask. And, certainly, the name 'Sheikh Zayed Rd' hardly has an appealing ring to it. Yet this road lies at the very heart of Dubai's extraordinary meteoric development, and is flanked by gleaming modern skyscrapers, including several of the city's iconic modern landmarks. The pinnacle is the Burj Khalifa, the tallest structure in the world, and it's at the epicentre of Downtown Dubai's most tantalising tourist sights – Dubai Mall,Dubai Fountain and Souq al-Bahar. Plan your Burj Khalifa visit to coincide with the dancing fountain display from 7pm each night.

North of here, the Financial District is anchored by the Dubai International Financial Centre (DIFC), which also doesn't instantly shout out 'tourism'. However, as well as being home to the stock exchange and banks, this is where you'll find Gate Village, with its excellent world-class art galleries and several fine restaurants. Other notable buildings include the World Trade Centre (a 1979 building that looks prehistoric alongside its futuristic cohorts) and the strikingly beautiful Jumeirah Emirates Towers.

South of Downtown Dubai, Sheikh Zayed Rd bisects gritty, industrial-flavoured Al-Quoz, which has some of the city's most exciting cutting-edge galleries. Art aficionados should definitely explore this area, but head here before mid-morning heat sets in, and plan your route because there's precious little shade.

Local Life

- **Friday shopping** You may occasionally wonder where all the local Emiratis are, particularly if you're staying in Bur Dubai, Deira, or at a tourist complex or beach hotel. But you'll see hundreds of local families at Dubai Mall on a Friday evening (the later the better – it's open to midnight).
- **Business lunch** Head for the DIFC around lunchtime and take your pick of several excellent restaurants, dining among Emirati businessmen, fiercely fashionable corporate staff and fresh-faced financial whiz kids.
- **Art event** Don the smock-and-beret look and head for one of the Gate Village Art Nights, a hip monthly event attracting who's who in the local art world.

Getting There & Away

- **Metro** The Dubai metro Red Line conveniently runs along the entire length of Sheikh Zayed Rd. Major stations are World Trade Centre, Financial Centre, Burj Khalifa/Dubai Mall, Al-Quoz and First Gulf Bank.

SIGHTS

Downtown Dubai

It's easy to spend an entire day taking in the sights of this newly developed area, which has positioned itself as the vibrant and urban centrepiece of Dubai. The nearest metro stop is Burj Khalifa/Dubai Mall.

BURJ KHALIFA ICONIC BUILDING

Map p216 (04-888 8124, toll free 800 2884 3867; www.burjkhalifa.ae; entrance ground fl, Dubai Mall, Financial Centre Rd; reserved admission adult or child over 13yr Dh100, child 4-12yr Dh75, instant admission Dh400; 10am-10pm Sun-Wed, 10am-midnight Thu-Sat;) Call it impressive or call it preposterous, there's no denying that the Burj Khalifa is a groundbreaking feat of architecture and engineering. The world's tallest building pierces the sky at 828m (seven times the height of Big Ben) and opened on 4 January 2010, only six years after excavations began. Up to 13,000 workers toiled day and night, at times putting up a new floor in as little as three days. Inside Dubai's own 'Tower of Babel' is a mix of offices and apartments; the building is also home to Armani Hotel (p140) – the world's first hotel to be designed and developed by Giorgio Armani.

For visitors, the main attraction is the observation deck on the 124th floor. From such lofty heights you can easily pinpoint the offshore developments and other landmarks. Getting to the deck means passing various multimedia exhibits until a double-decker lift whisks you up at 10m per second. When you reach level 124, you're a lofty 442m in the air. Reserved time-stamped tickets are available at the ticket office and online; ponying up Dh400 lets you go straight through.

FREE **DUBAI FOUNTAIN** FOUNTAIN

Map p216 (Burj Khalifa Lake; shows every 20min 7-10pm Sun-Wed, 7-11pm Thu-Sat;) Against the backdrop of the Burj Khalifa in the midst of a massive artificial lake, these choreographed dancing fountains are the antithesis of what you'd expect to find in the desert. Water undulates as gracefully as a belly dancer, arcs like a dolphin and surges as high as 150m to stirring soundtracks gathered from around the world. There are plenty of great vantage points, including from some of the restaurants at Souq al-Bahar, the bridge linking Souq al-Bahar with Dubai Mall, and the Dubai Mall terrace.

DUBAI MALL MALL

Map p216 (www.thedubaimall.com; Financial Centre Rd; 10am-10pm Sun-Wed, 10am-midnight Thu-Sat;) The world's largest shopping centre, Dubai Mall is much more than the sum of its 1200 stores: it's a veritable family entertainment centre. Check out Dubai Aquarium & Underwater Zoo, Sega Republic indoor amusement park, KidZania and Olympic-sized Dubai Ice Rink.

There's also a four-storey waterfall that's gorgeously lit at night. The Gold Souq at the centre of the mall is dominated by the beautiful Treasury Dome, a 25m by 13m atrium-cum-projection-ceiling with multimedia shows, which is pathetically undervisited.

Dubai Mall has its own glossy monthly magazine, the *Dubai Mall,* and free wi-fi access, but you need a United Arab Emirates (UAE) mobile-phone number to register for the service (see p178 for details on how to obtain one), although this may soon change. For more on the mall, see p88.

SOUQ AL-BAHAR MALL

Map p216 (www.soukalbahar.ae; Old Town Island, next to Dubai Mall; 10am-10pm Sat-Thu, 2-10pm Fri) Designed in contemporary Arabic style, this attractive mall is Downtown Dubai's answer to Madinat Jumeirah (p93). Meaning 'Market of the Sailor', it features natural-stone walkways, high arches and front-row seats overlooking Dubai Fountain from several of its restaurants and bars, including Baker & Spice (p83), Left Bank and Karma Kafe (p84). It's located next to Dubai Mall.

DUBAI AQUARIUM & UNDERWATER ZOO AQUARIUM

Map p216 (www.thedubaiaquarium.com; Dubai Mall, Financial Centre Rd; aquarium tunnel & underwater zoo Dh50; 10am-10pm Sun-Wed, 10am-midnight Thu-Sat;) Dubai Mall's most mesmerising sight is this gargantuan aquarium where 33,000 beasties flit and dart amid artificial coral and behind the 'world's largest acrylic viewing panel' (as recorded in the *Guinness World Records*). Sharks and rays are top attractions, but other crowd-pleasers include a sumo-sized giant grouper and massive schools of pelagic fish. You can view quite a lot for free

BIRD SANCTUARY

Right in the heart of the city, **Ras al-Khor Wildlife Sanctuary** (Map p216; Sheikh Zayed Rd; ☎04-338 2324; www.wildlife.ae; admission free; ⏰9am-4pm Sat-Thu; 👪) is an amazing nature preserve that narrowly escaped becoming an area of massive development (complete with artificial islands, shopping malls and hotels) in a project which, as of 2012, has been indefinitely suspended.

Pretty pink flamingos steal the show in winter but, in fact, avid birdwatchers can spot more than 250 species in this pastiche of salt flats, mudflats, mangroves and lagoons spread over an area of around 6.2 sq km (2.4 sq miles). At the mouth of Dubai Creek, the sanctuary is an important stopover on the east African–west Asian flyway, as well as being home to innumerable native plant species. There are three hides (platforms) with fantastically sharp binoculars for who want close-ups of the birds without disturbing them. The flamingo roost is off the junction of Al-Wasl and Oud Metha Rds. Groups of five or over must apply to the Environment Department at the Municipality for a permit at least two days before planning to visit. You can download an application form from www.wildlife.ae.

from the outside, or pay for access to the walk-through tunnel. A highlight here is a darkened cave where you can go nose-to-nose with dozens of toothy sharks. If that's not close enough, don a wetsuit and join a dive instructor on a shark dive (Dh625 to Dh1025, depending on whether you're a licenced diver). Don't worry: all sharks are kept on a closely monitored feeding schedule to keep their predatory behaviour in check. If that's too thrilling, hop on a glass-bottomed boat for a glacial float (Dh25).

Upstairs, the very worthwhile Underwater Zoo journeys through three eco-zones: rainforest, rocky shore and living ocean, and a total of 38 aquatic displays. There are lots of rare and interesting denizens here, including air-breathing African lungfish, cheeky archerfish that catch insects by shooting water, spooky giant spider crabs and otherworldly sea dragons.

Budget at least 30 minutes each for the tunnel and the zoo.

KIDZANIA THEME PARK

Map p216 (www.kidzania.com; 2nd fl, Dubai Mall, Financial Centre Rd; child 1-4yr Dh95, child 4-16yr Dh130, adult Dh90, Zuper Package incl food & shopping voucher Dh199; ⏰10am-10pm Sun-Wed, 10am-midnight Thu-Sat; 👪) A real winner with the kiddies, this interactive miniature city has offices, a school, a racetrack, a fire station, a hospital and a bank, and other real-world places. Children dress up and slip into adult roles to playfully explore what it's like to be a firefighter, doctor, mechanic, pilot or other professional; there are 70 roles to choose from. They even earn a salary (in a currency called Kidzos, no less) with which they buy goods and services, thus learning the value of money. There is also a toddlers' section for activities with accompanying parents. For older kids, you can just drop them off while you shop. What bliss!

Al-Quoz

The most cutting-edge galleries within Dubai's growing art scene are in this industrial area south of Sheikh Zayed Rd, between Downtown Dubai and Mall of the Emirates. However, don't picture yourself strolling from gallery to gallery as though you were in London's Soho: most are tucked away in nondescript buildings or anonymous warehouses and are hard to find. And don't count on your taxi driver knowing the way. Most galleries have location maps on their websites – and be sure to pick up a copy of the ArtMap publication, which is invaluable because it includes maps of all galleries (www.artinthecity.com). The closest metro station is Al-Quoz.

GALLERY ISABELLE VAN DEN EYNDE GALLERY

Map p216 (☎04-340 3965; www.ivde.net; off Sheikh Zayed Rd, btwn Interchange Nos 3 & 4; ⏰10am-7pm Sat-Thu) Previously known as B21, this innovative gallery has lifted some of the Middle East's most promising talent from obscurity into the spotlight. The mythology-laced installations, videos and collages of Cairo-based Lara Baladi and the distorted photography of Iranian-born

Ramin Haerizadeh are among the works that have attracted collectors and the curious since the space's opening in 2005.

THIRD LINE GALLERY

Map p216 (☎04-341 1367; www.thethirdline.com; off Sheikh Zayed Rd; ⏲11am-8pm Sat-Thu) Located between Interchange Nos 3 and 4, Third Line is run by a couple of talented young curators (Sunny Rahbar and Claudia Cellini) and is one of the city's more exciting spaces for contemporary Middle Eastern art. Artists represented often transcend the rules of traditional styles to create fresh new forms. The gallery regularly exhibits at international art fairs, including the Frieze Art Fair (London), Artissima (Turin, Italy) and Art Beat Istanbul. It represents emerging Emirati artists as well as famous names like Iranian artist Farhad Moshiri, and controversial Iraqi artist Hayv Kahraman with her depictions of honour killings, gender and war.

1X1 CONTEMPORARY ART GALLERY

Map p216 (☎04-341 1287; www.1x1artgallery.com; Al-Quoz Industrial 1, no 4, off Sheikh Zayed Rd; ⏲11am-8pm Sat-Thu) Moved from its Jumeirah home and occupying a converted warehouse, this gallery has emerged as a key place for sourcing Indian art. This is in part because of the efforts of Malini Gulrajani, whose mission is to showcase the best in contemporary works from the subcontinent. With shows featuring painters Shibu Natesan and Chittrovanu Mazumdar, and N N Rimzon (famed for his energised sculptures), this grand and elegant gallery has a fixed spot on the radar of avid collectors.

GREEN ART GALLERY GALLERY

Map p216 (☎04-346 9305; www.gagallery.com; 8 St, Al-Serkal Ave, off Sheikh Zayed Rd; ⏲10am-6pm Sat-Thu) This gallery dates back to 1995 and was a key player in the promotion of local artists in the region. In 2010 the gallery moved to Al-Quoz, where a 280-sq-metre warehouse provides the perfect setting for renowned and emerging Middle Eastern artists, photographers and sculptors. Typical exhibitions include a solo show of recent works by renowned Turkish photographer Nazif Topcuoglu, and a seven-channel video installation entitled *Balloons on the Sea* by Turkish artist Hale Tenger, which was voted one of the best international shows of 2011 by leading contemporary art magazine *Artforum*.

JAMJAR GALLERY

Map p216 (☎04-341 7303; www.thejamjardubai.com; 17A St, exit 39 off Sheikh Zayed Rd; ⏲10am-8pm Mon-Thu & Sat, 2-8pm Fri) JamJar is more than just another gallery exhibiting contemporary art by emerging local and international talent. It's a DIY painting studio, too, so if you're feeling the creative urge, you can hire an easel, a canvas and all the paint and paper you require to create your own masterpiece. Located behind Dubai Garden Centre.

MEEM GALLERY GALLERY

Map p216 (☎04-347 7883; www.meem.ae; Umm Suqeim Rd, off Interchange No 4; ⏲10am-7pm Sat-Thu) An ambitious co-venture by two Emirati business tycoons and British art dealer Charlie Pocock, this blue-chip gallery is dedicated to presenting the masters of modern Arab art. As such, it usually exhibits some pretty big names, such as Libyan calligrapher Ali Omar Ermes, the pop art of

JUMANA – SECRET OF THE DESERT

Don't miss the dazzling theatrical show at **Al Sahra Desert Resort** (☎04-362 7011; www.alsahra.com; Dubailand; adult/child Dh230/115; ⏲9pm Tue-Sat; 👪). It's a no-expenses spared production featuring the knee-trembling voice of Omar Sharif as the storyteller. The pyrotechnics were designed by the guys responsible for the opening of the Athens Olympics in 2004, the composer is Jean Musy, and the massive stage is comparable to Milan's La Scala (only surrounded by water). The visual effects are extraordinary, including three 35mm-wide by 18m-high water screens that create a backdrop to the stage. Celebrating the culture and history of Arabia, the cast includes acrobats, dancers, horses and camels and the result is truly entertaining. To get here take Sheikh Zayed Rd towards Abu Dhabi. Exit towards the Green Community and turn right onto Emirates Rd. At the next roundabout turn left towards Al-Ain and continue 30km until you reach the well-signposted resort.

Jordan's Jamal Abdul Rahim or paintings by modern Arab art pioneer Dia Al-Azzawi from Iraq.

CARBON 12 GALLERY

Map p216 (☎050-464 4392; www.carbon12dubai.com; Warehouse D37, St 8, Al-Serkal Ave, off Sheikh Zayed Rd; ⏲11.30am-7pm Sat-Thu) This edgy gallery represents paintings, sculpture, photographs and media created by newly discovered (as well as internationally established) artists, all of them handpicked. The clear lines and minimalist vibe of the white-cube space offers a perfect setting for both large-scale and smaller pieces.

COURTYARD GALLERY

Map p216 (☎04-347 5050; www.courtyard-uae.com; off Sheikh Zayed Rd, btwn Interchange Nos 3 & 4; ⏲10am-6pm Sat-Thu) This cultural complex wraps around its eponymous courtyard, flanked by an eccentric hodgepodge of buildings that makes it look like a miniature movie-studio backdrop: here an Arab fort, there a Moorish facade or an Egyptian tomb. It's the brainchild of Iranian expat artist Dariush Zandi, who also runs the bilevel gallery Total Arts at The Courtyard, specialising in Middle Eastern art. Other spaces are occupied by a cafe, artists' studios and various creative businesses.

CARTOON ART GALLERY GALLERY

Map p216 (☎04-346 6467; www.cartoonartgallery.org; 4B St, off Sheikh Zayed Rd; ⏲10am-6pm Sat-Thu) Located a couple of doors away from Courtyard (and a branch of Lime Tree Cafe), this is the first gallery in the Middle East that's dedicated to cartoons. Typical temporary exhibitions are artwork and posters illustrating the world of Tintin, as well as animated cartoons by such illustrious names as Japanese Hayao Miyazaki.

Financial District

Anchored by the iconic twin Jumeirah Emirates Towers, the Financial District is largely the domain of the business brigade. If you're into art, however, there are several important galleries you need to check out in Gate Village, which is a modernist cluster of 10 mid-rise stone-clad towers built around walkways and small piazzas and linked to Dubai International Financial Centre by two wooden bridges. If possible, try to attend one of Gate Village's monthly Art Nights with food, drink, entertainment and speakers from the art world. Check www.difc.ae for dates. If you're riding the metro, get off at Emirates Towers.

CUADRO GALLERY

Map p216 (☎04-425 0400; www.cuadroart.com; Bldg 10, Gate Village; ⏲noon-6pm Sat, 10am-9pm Sun-Thu) In a fabulous space taking up the entire ground floor of Gate Village's Bldg 10, this highly regarded gallery presents exciting contemporary artists and sculptors from both the West and Middle East, as well as screening art-house films and organising workshops.

OPERA GALLERY GALLERY

Map p216 (☎04-323 0820; www.operagallery.com; Bldg 3, Gate Village; ⏲10am-8pm Sun-Thu) For big spenders, this gallery has a small 'black room' with works by such masters as Picasso, Miró and Chagall. Otherwise the work is typically large canvases by Middle Eastern contemporary artists, as well as sculptures, furniture and photography. It also organises major art events such as a Salvador Dalí exhibition of sculptures (which took place in Dubai Mall in November 2011).

ART SAWA GALLERY

Map p216 (☎04-340 8660; www.artsawa.com; Bldg 8, Gate Village; ⏲9am-8pm Sat-Thu, 3-9pm Fri) This is one of the Village's smaller galleries, and typically has cutting-edge installations and exhibitions by celebrated contemporary artists of the Middle Eastern and Arab worlds.

EMPTY QUARTER GALLERY

Map p216 (☎04-323 1210; www.theemptyquarter.com; Bldg 2, Gate Village; ⏲9am-10pm Sat-Thu, 3-10pm Fri) This sleek gallery is devoted exclusively to fine-art photography, generally with an evocative or political theme; recent themes include a focus on urban overcrowding, with some harrowing photos of the homeless.

XVA GALLERY

Map p216 (☎04-358 5117; www.xvagallery.com; Bldg 7, Gate Village) This gallery exhibits a diverse selection of work, with an emphasis on Iran and the Arab world. Formerly located in the XVA Hotel (p139), the large airy gallery is overseen by curator Mona Hauser, who established the Bastakia Art

Fair (2007–2010). Unfortunately, the fair has been suspended (at least temporarily).

AYYAM GALLERY GALLERY

Map p216 (☎04-439 2390; www.ayyamgallery.com; Bldg 3, Gate Village) Another exciting new gallery showcasing primarily local artists from the UAE and Middle East. Exhibitions typically change bi-monthly – check the website for an update.

EATING

The tower hotels lining the Sheikh Zayed Rd strip are the representative core of contemporary Dubai. Dinner here positions you well to travel elsewhere afterwards, but with so many nearby hotels, bars and nightclubs, you may as well stick around. But good luck crossing the road: there's only one pedestrian overpass. Take a taxi, instead.

Downtown Dubai

ASADO ARGENTINIAN $$$

Map p216 (☎04-428 7971; Palace – The Old Town, Emaar Blvd; mains Dh110-290; ⌚7pm-midnight) Meat lovers will be in bovine heaven at this cheerful, lusty steakhouse. Choose your quality cut of tenderloin, veal chop, rib eye or sirloin from a tray brought to your table by servers clad gaucho-style. While it's being cooked to order, sit back and savour the delicious bread, the views of the Burj Khalifa (sit on the terrace) and the sultry tunes from the live band. All meats are served with a selection of delicious sauces, salts and mustards. A sommelier stands by to help you pick the perfect bottle from what is purportedly the most extensive selection of Argentinian wines in the Middle East. Reservations recommended.

BAKER & SPICE INTERNATIONAL $$

Map p216 (www.bakerandspiceme.com; Souq al-Bahar, Sheikh Zayed Rd; mains Dh48-85, salad bar Dh54) Chunky wood furniture, a warm ochre-and-pale-green colour scheme, rows of white orchids and a novel fruit and veg display over the bar set the scene for one of the best healthy-eating options in the city. The menu reflects what is in season and incorporates organic local produce, whenever possible. The salad bar, one of the best in town, has a set price choice of four dishes. Typical mains are wild prawns and mushroom linguine, and scallops with a beetroot and orange salad and pomegranate dressing. You can also buy jarred organic goodies, including preserves.

RIVINGTON GRILL BRITISH $$

Map p216 (☎04-423 0903; www.rivingtongrill.ae; Souq al-Bahar, Sheikh Zayed Rd; mains Dh85-140) If you're planning a dinner here, call ahead to snag a table on the candle-lit terrace overlooking the fountains. The grub is deliciously upmarket Brit: beef Wellington, smoked haddock fishcakes, Lancashire hotpot and bubble and squeak together with poshed-up mushy peas. There is also a classic (Sunday) roast served on Saturday. Reservations recommended.

HOI AN VIETNAMESE $$$

Map p216 (☎04-343 8888; Shangri-La Hotel, Sheikh Zayed Rd; mains Dh100-140; ⌚7pm-midnight) Teak latticework, plantation shutters and spinning wooden ceiling fans evoke a *très civilisé* colonial-era Vietnam at this upmarket restaurant, where the flavours are lively and bright. Start with the crispy crab rolls, then move on to the signatures: lotus-leaf-wrapped sea bass with ginger-lemon sauce, or a spicy chicken and lemongrass stir-fry. A great date spot, thanks to deliciously low lighting and genteel service. Reservations recommended.

THIPTARA THAI $$$

Map p216 (☎04-428 7961; Palace – The Old Town, Emaar Blvd; mains Dh90-190, set menus from Dh250; ⌚7pm-midnight) Thiptara wows with its romantic setting in a lakeside pagoda, with front-row views of the Burj Khalifa and Dubai Fountain. The food's just as impressive, with elegant interpretations of classic Thai dishes, although portions are small and the final bill can be quite steep. The chef grows his own herbs, which perk up such dishes as green-papaya salad and beef in spicy brown sauce with on-the-vine peppercorns. Alas, the interior is too austere (sit on the deck), but exceptional cooking and solicitous service by the all-Thai staff make up for it. Reservations essential.

HUKAMA CHINESE $$$

Map p216 (☎04-436 8888; Address Downtown Dubai, Emaar Blvd; mains Dh80-160; ⌚6-11pm) A dramatic high-ceilinged dining room, complexion-friendly lighting, sweeping views of the Burj Khalifa and wonderful Chinese fare are all woven together like a fine tapestry at this elegant restaurant. The menu is loaded with interesting items such as wasabi-coated king prawns or foie gras terrine with hawthorn jelly and sugar-cured dates. Service can be a tad overbearing, however. Reservations essential.

NA3NA3 MIDDLE EASTERN **$$**

Map p216 (☎04-438 8888; Address Dubai Mall, Emaar Blvd; lunch/dinner Dh120/140; ⌚6.30am-1am; 👪) If you're new to Middle Eastern food, the bountiful and beautifully displayed buffet in this bright and airy restaurant would be a good place to start a culinary investigation. You may be tempted to make an entire meal from the mezze alone, but that would mean missing the hot dishes and freshly baked breads emerging nonstop from the open kitchen. The curious name means 'mint' in Arabic and is pronounced 'na-na'. Reservations recommended.

FAZARIS INTERNATIONAL **$$$**

Map p216 (Address Downtown Dubai, Emaar Blvd; mains Dh75-160, Fri brunches without/with alcohol Dh290/390; ⌚6.30-11am, noon-3.30pm & 6.30-11pm) Named for an 8th-century Persian philosopher, this all-day restaurant lets you hopscotch from Japan (sushi) to India (chicken tikka) to Italy (penne arrabiata) without leaving your table. The white chocolate *sabayon* (Italian-style custard dessert) paired with marinated berries and pepper-strawberry ice cream is the perfect finale.

KARMA KAFE ASIAN **$$$**

Map p216 (☎04-423 0909; Souq al-Bahar, Sheikh Zayed Rd; mains Dh75-150; ⌚4pm-2am Sat-Wed, to 3am Thu & Fri) This gorgeous space is another Midas-touch venture by the people behind Buddha Bar. As with the mothership, a large Buddha oversees the dining room, which in this case is intimate and drenched in sensuous crimson. The food caters for adventurous palates: salmon marinated in cherries, and sashimi tacos are typically experimental flavour combinations that work surprisingly well. The terrace has stunning fountain views. Reservations essential.

MARRAKECH MOROCCAN **$$**

Map p216 (☎04-405 2703; Shangri-La Hotel, Sheikh Zayed Rd; mains Dh60-100; ⌚7pm-midnight Mon-Sat) Keyhole doorways, North African wall tiles and flickering candle lanterns casting moody shadows: Marrakech hits all the classic Moroccan design buttons yet manages to feel light, elegant and contemporary. The kitchen embraces a similar approach by dishing up modern spins on such signature dishes as *pastilla* (pigeon pie), couscous royale and tagine without sacrificing the cuisine's traditional earthiness. The best tables are in view of the soulful musician or, for privacy, in an arched alcove. Reservations recommended.

EMPORIO ARMANI CAFFÉ INTERNATIONAL **$$**

Map p216 (ground fl, Dubai Mall, Financial Centre Rd; mains Dh55-160) This outpost of the Armani empire offers the best example of Dubai's mall food revolution, and is fittingly surrounded by designer stores. The coffee is superb, the food is stylishly presented and the Italian flavours are so good that we wish it had a liquor licence so we could top off the meal with a limoncello.

MORE INTERNATIONAL **$**

Map p216 (ground fl, Dubai Mall, Financial Centre Rd; mains Dh30-70; ⌚8am-11pm; 📶👪) This jazzy, industrial-flavoured space in Dubai Mall draws a congenial mix of locals, expats and tourists. The menu hops around the world – from Thai curries and Italian pastas to Spanish paella and fat burgers. The execution is OK, but if it sounds too experimental, skip it. Breakfast is served all day. The restaurant has mushroomed to eight branches over the last couple of years.

Financial District

IVY BRITISH **$$$**

Map p216 (☎04-319 8767; www.theivy.ae; Jumeirah Emirates Towers hotel, Sheikh Zayed Rd; mains Dh95-120, business lunch Dh150) The former US-style bar that was here has done a 360-degree flip and the venue is now home to a branch of one of London's best-loved restaurants. Dark oak panelling, soft green leather upholstery and stunning chandeliers set the retro-chic scene for a dining experience that includes classic British dishes like shepherd's pie and nostalgic sweet treats such as sticky toffee pudding. The business lunch is a great deal and, overall, the Ivy is not as pricey as its celeb-clientele packaging may suggest. Reservations essential.

ZUMA JAPANESE $$$

Map p216 (☎04-425 5660; set lunches Dh 120, mains Dh75-120) This dramatic bi-level restaurant attracts power-lunching execs and the sexy crowd for low-light dinners. There's a sushi counter and a robata grill and an immensely popular Friday brunch.

LA PETITE MAISON FRENCH $$

Map p216 (☎04-439 0505; www.lpmdubai.ae; Bldg 8, Gate Village, Sheikh Zayed Rd; mains Dh75-95) It has been said that France's famed *cuisine Niçoise* (cuisine of Nice) is so hard to master because it's essentially so simple, relying mainly on the freshness and seasonality of the ingredients. A relative newcomer on Dubai's continental dining scene, La Petite Maison has got it right and has fast become one of the most talked-about new restaurants. It serves exquisite classic dishes like onion tart and pasta with beef ragout and mushrooms. Don't miss it. Reservations essential.

EXCHANGE GRILL STEAKHOUSE $$$

Map p216 (☎04-311 8316; Fairmont Hotel, Sheikh Zayed Rd; steaks Dh185-245; ⏲12.30-3.30pm Sun-Thu & 7pm-midnight daily) One of Dubai's premier steakhouses, Exchange Grill has a clubby feel, with oversized leather armchairs orbiting linen-draped tables and big-picture windows overlooking the glittering strip. You'll have a fine time spiking your cholesterol level with trendy Wagyu beef or the less pricey but actually more-flavoursome aged Angus prime. Seafood rounds out the menu, but beef is definitely the big draw. There's a respectable wine list, too. Reservations recommended.

VU'S FUSION $$$

Map p216 (☎04-319 8088; 50th fl, Boulevard at Jumeirah Emirates Towers, Sheikh Zayed Rd; 3-course business lunch Dh165, dinner mains Dh150-230) The highest restaurant in town, with stellar views. The formal, white-linen-tablecloth dining room is popular with the Rolex crowd celebrating the inking of a deal. The menu changes fairly frequently but the dishes cut no corners, with super-fresh ingredients and an assured range of dishes: Irish organic salmon, milk-fed veal chop, 'line caught' sea bass... you get the picture. Pricey wines. Reservations essential.

SPECTRUM ON ONE INTERNATIONAL $$$

Map p216 (☎04-311 8316; Fairmont Hotel, Sheikh Zayed Rd; mains Dh100-245, 3-course menus Dh190; ⏲6.30pm-1am; 👪) Spectrum competes for top honours as Dubai's best live-action buffet. The food is solidly good and a visual feast, with no disappointments from its eight kitchens cooking up six distinct cuisines from around the world: Arabian, Indian, Thai, European, Japanese and Chinese. It's also great for kids. Signature dishes include sliced mixed teppanyaki, black-pepper beef, yogurt-marinated chicken and warm molten chocolate cake. There's also a fantastic Friday brunch (see boxed text, p110). Reservations recommended.

RIB ROOM STEAKHOUSE $$$

Map p216 (☎04-319 8088; Boulevard at Jumeirah Emirates Towers, Sheikh Zayed Rd; mains Dh115-160; ⏲12.30-3pm Sat-Thu, 7pm-midnight daily) Surrender to your inner carnivore at this power-player hangout where the air is practically perfumed with testosterone. The yummy cuts of aged steaks, juicy prime rib and chateaubriand speak for themselves, but even more-complicated dishes like braised Wagyu beef cheeks in port wine arrive without needless flights of fancy. Reservations essential.

AL-NAFOORAH LEBANESE $$$

Map p216 (Boulevard at Jumeirah Emirates Towers, Sheikh Zayed Rd; mezze Dh35-70, mains Dh100-120; ⏲12.30-3pm & 8pm-midnight) Tucked away in the base of Emirates Towers, Al-Nafoorah's clubby, wood-panelled dining room feels like a Wall Street power-lunch spot. The mezze stand out – try the *kibbeh* (meat-filled, cracked-wheat croquettes) – more than the kebabs on the classic Lebanese menu, but really, the kitchen does everything quite well. It's quieter and more formal than most Lebanese restaurants, making this a great choice for a dressy-casual night out without the noisy fanfare of the big Lebanese party places.

NOODLE HOUSE ASIAN $

Map p216 (Lower level, Boulevard at Jumeirah Emirates Towers, Sheikh Zayed Rd; mains Dh30-66; ⏲noon-midnight; 👪) The concept at this reliably good, always-packed pan-Asian joint is simple: sit down at long wooden communal tables and order by ticking dishes on a tear-off menu pad. There's great variety – laksa (coconut-based curry) to pad thai to roast duck – to please disparate tastes. Some dishes even come in small and large sizes to match hunger levels. Wines by the glass and several Asian beers, including Tiger on tap, are available. If there's a wait, leave your mobile number and head next door to Agency for pre-dinner drinks. There are now four other branches around town, including in Souq Madinat Jumeirah and Dubai Mall.

GOURMET BURGER KITCHEN BURGERS $

Map p216 (Level B1, Dubai International Financial Centre; burgers Dh28-34; ⏲9am-10pm Sat-Wed, to 11pm Thu & Fri; 👪) This patty-and-bun UK import stacks its burgers so high you risk dislocating your jaw when trying to bite into one. Go classic or try one of the more adventurous choices, like the Kiwi Burger with beetroot, egg, pineapple and cheddar, inspired by the founders' New Zealand origins.

ZAATAR W ZEIT LEBANESE $

Map p216 (near Shangri-La Hotel, Sheikh Zayed Rd; dishes Dh7-33; ⏲24hr; 👪) In the wee hours, this Lebanese fast-food joint is full of night owls hoping to restore balance to the brain with *manaeesh* – flat bread topped with cheese, tomatoes, minced meats or *zaatar* (thyme, sesame, marjoram and oregano). Think Lebanese pizza. *Laban taza* (a salted yogurt drink), not cola, goes best with them. Other branches are in Dubai Mall, Mall of the Emirates and on The Walk at JBR.

DRINKING & NIGHTLIFE

CALABAR BAR

Map p216 (ground fl, Address Downtown Dubai, Emaar Blvd; ⏲6pm-2am) You'll have plenty of time to study the space-age Burj Khalifa, the eye-candy crowd and the sexy cocktail bar setting while you're waiting...and waiting... for your pricey but potent cocktail at this Latino-themed bar. A winner the moment it opened, it's the kind of place that may very well stay cool long after it's done being hot.

IKANDY BAR

Map p216 (Shangri-La Hotel, Sheikh Zayed Rd; ⏲6pm-2am Oct-Mar) Wear white to Ikandy and your clothes will glow in the diffuse hot-pink light reflecting off the diaphanous fabric hanging from the palm trees. The vibe is chilled, almost mellow, helped along by the rooftop poolside setting, the ambient sounds and the inventive cocktails (try the Thai martini made with lemongrass and basil). Stellar views of the Burj Khalifa.

NEOS BAR

Map p216 (Address Downtown Dubai, Emaar Blvd; ⏲6pm-2am) At this glamour vixen, you can swirl your cosmo with the posh set 63 floors above Dubai Fountain. It takes two lifts to get to what is currently the highest bar in town, an urban den of shiny metal, carpeted floors and killer views. The dress code has relaxed a lot since opening: we even spotted sneaker-wearers – yikes!

CIN CIN BAR

Map p216 (Fairmont Hotel, Sheikh Zayed Rd; ⏲6pm-2am) You'd be hard-pressed to find a more impressive wine-and-spirits list than the one at this sleek wine bar. Cin Cin is styled with blue light, deep leather club chairs and changing-colour ice buckets. The drinks list is dizzying, with over 400 wines – 55 by the glass – 50 vodkas and 26 scotches. Prices skew high, but you'll find good French vintages in the Dh300 range. Shine your shoes.

AGENCY BAR

Map p216 (Boulevard at Jumeirah Emirates Towers, Sheikh Zayed Rd; ⏲noon-midnight Sun-Thu) This is a decent spot for pre-dinner unwinding, even though it's in the basement of an office tower and feels like it. Women receive the first two drinks for free on Tuesday. Also in Souq Madinat Jumeirah.

HARRY GHATTO'S BAR

Map p216 (Boulevard at Jumeirah Emirates Towers, Sheikh Zayed Rd; ⏲8pm-3am) Knock back a couple of drinks if you need to loosen your nerves before belting out your best J-Lo or Justin at this beloved karaoke bar, which is in the same tower as Sheikh Mohammed's office. Drinks are expensive and service only so-so, but we love the odd mix of people drawn here, including the occasional *dishdasha*-clad local (a *dishdasha* is a man's shirt-dress).

VU'S BAR BAR

Map p216 (Jumeirah Emirates Towers hotel, Sheikh Zayed Rd; ⏲6pm-3am) Until Neos opened, Vu's was *the* Dubai bar with a view. The panorama from the 51st floor is still breathtaking, but the soft red- and black-leather chairs feel dated and are now filled largely with a moneyed salt-and-pepper crowd grateful for the dim lighting. Still, it's an atmospheric spot for cocktails and quiet conversation. Look sharp.

HIVE
WINE BAR

Map p216 (Souq al-Bahar, Sheikh Zayed Rd; ⏲10am-late) At this good-looking party den, local and visiting lovelies heat up the dance floor or drape themselves over brown leather sofas on the terrace. Alas, there's no view of Dubai Fountain. Special deals (such as ladies' night Tuesday, and two-for-one-pizza Sunday) help draw in the punters.

DOUBLE DECKER
PUB

Map p216 (Al-Murooj Rotana Hotel, Al-Saffa St; ⏲noon-3am) You'll feel quite Piccadilly at this boozy, boisterous bi-level pub that's decked out in a London transport theme. Drinks promotions, quiz nights, English premiership football and better-than-average (by far) pub grub attract an expat crowd.

FIBBER MAGEE'S
PUB

Map p216 (www.fibbersdubai.com; Sheikh Zayed Rd; ⏲7pm-3am) This scruffy boozer, found behind Crowne Plaza Hotel, isn't about seeing and being seen – quite frankly, it's a bit too dark for that. It's Dubai's most authentic Irish pub, with great ales, stouts and fat fish and chips to sop it all up. Tuesday is quiz night (arrive by 8pm). Great fun on match nights.

NEZESAUSSI
SPORTS BAR

Map p216 (Al-Manzil Hotel, Burj Khalifa Blvd; ⏲6pm-2am Sun-Thu, noon-2am Fri & Sat) Throw back pints with your mates at this high-end sports bar with wall-to-wall TVs and great food. The name is an amalgam of New Zealand, South Africa and Australia, and the bar snacks selection plays on those countries' classics. Standouts include *boerewors* (spicy sausage) and grilled New Zealand lamb. The rugby-ball-shaped bar is surrounded by sports paraphernalia donated by famous players. During the 2011 Rugby World Cup final, queues to the bar virtually stretched from the hotel's reception.

CAVALLI CLUB
CLUB

Map p216 (www.cavalliclubdubai.com; Fairmont Hotel, Sheikh Zayed Rd; ⏲7pm-2am) Roberto Cavalli, Italian fashion designer of over-the-top glam, rock and animal-print fame, has his own nightclub where the rich and beautiful keep the champagne flowing amid a virtual Aladdin's cave of black quartz and Swarovski crystals. Girls, wear your little black dress or risk feeling frumpy. Boys, shine your shoes. Enter from the back of the hotel.

ZINC
CLUB

Map p216 (www.ichotelsgroup.com; Crowne Plaza Hotel, Sheikh Zayed Rd; ⏲10pm-3am) This reliable standby has a killer sound system and plays R&B, popular tunes and house for a crowd that likes to have fun without the pretence, including lots of cabin crew. We like it here because people don't seem to care who you are; they're here to dance and drink, not show off. Bar service is quick – well, for Dubai. Men pay cover (Dh50 to Dh100); women don't.

ZYARA
CAFE

Map p216 (Union Tower, Sheikh Zayed Rd; ⏲8am-1am) Puff away in the shadow of giant skyscrapers at this convivial boho-cool Lebanese cafe. The colourful doll-house-like interior is great for booze-free socialising over a game of cards or backgammon. The *sheesha* (water pipe used to smoke tobacco) is outdoors, where you sit at living-room-like clusters of cushy sofas on a palm-lined patio while gazing up at the impossibly tall towers. It's located behind the National Bank of Abu Dhabi.

☆ ENTERTAINMENT

BLUE BAR
LIVE MUSIC

Map p216 (Novotel World Trade Centre, 312th Rd, off Sheikh Zayed Rd; ⏲2pm-2am) Cool cats of all ages gather in this relaxed joint for some of the finest live jazz and blues in town. It's tucked away in a ho-hum business hotel but once inside, all is forgiven. The mostly local talent starts performing at 10pm (Wednesday to Friday only), so get here early to snag a table and quaff a cold one from the standout selection of Belgian draught beers. When there's no band, it's just another bar.

REEL CINEMAS
CINEMA

Map p216 (☎04-449 1988; www.reelcinemas.ae; 2nd fl, Dubai Mall, Financial Centre Rd; tickets Dh30, 3-D films Dh40) Pre-assigned seats, THX sound and a staggering 22 screens make Reel one of the top flick-magnets in town. The fare is mostly Hollywood blockbusters, except in the Picturehouse, purportedly the UAE's first dedicated art-house cinema. If you don't want to sit with the hoi polloi, shell out Dh110 for a reclining leather chair in a 32-seat platinum movie suite.

SHOPPING

DUBAI MALL MALL

Map p216 (www.thedubaimall.com; Sheikh Zayed Rd; ⌚10am-10pm Sun-Wed, 10am-midnight Thu-Sat; 📶) With around 1200 stores, this is not merely a mall – it's a small city unto itself, with an Olympic-sized ice rink, a huge aquarium, indoor theme parks and 160 food outlets. There's a strong European label presence here, along with branches of Galeries Lafayette department store from France, Hamley's toy store from the UK and the first Bloomingdale's outside the United States. It's a ginormous, day-lit mall with wide aisles and lots of open spaces, atriums and even a fashion catwalk. The four floors are divided into 'precincts' with clusters of product categories: search for high-end designers on Fashion Ave (which has marble floors and silver resting divans), high-street fashions on the ground floor and active-wear next to the ice rink.

SOUQ AL-BAHAR SHOPPING CENTRE

Map p216 (www.soukalbahar.ae; Old Town Island, next to Dubai Mall; ⌚10am-10pm Sun-Thu, 2-10pm Fri) Souq al-Bahar is Downtown Dubai's answer to Souq Madinat Jumeirah, although it's much smaller and less flashy. Unfortunately several stores have shifted over to Dubai Mall so it's generally quieter than in former years. Overall, shops are geared to the tourist market; there's an Arthur Murray Dance School and you can also get henna body tattoos here. The basement Spinneys supermarket is a great place to stock up on foodie treats.

ORGANIC FOODS & CAFE FOOD

Map p216 (ground fl, Dubai Mall, Financial Centre Rd) Despite the massive amounts of jet fuel required to ship them in, the fruits and vegies are 100% organic at Dubai's first natural supermarket. This provides a refreshing, much-needed alternative to the flavourless produce sold elsewhere. And that's not all; this shop is vast with an extensive selection of organic packaged goodies, as well as freshly baked bread, a cheese section, a butcher and even a 'pork room'. You can buy passable pizza by the slice for just Dh10 but, overall, the restaurant fare is disappointing. For a healthy lunch hightail it to Baker & Spice instead (p83). Environmentally friendly kiddie wear made by Bornsage (www.dubaibabies.com) is also available here.

MARAMI ACCESSORIES

Map p216 (Dubai Mall, Financial Centre Rd) Every girl knows that you can pep up any bland outfit with the right accessory. And so does Salama Alabbar, who stocks ultrachic jewellery, handbags, scarves and hair accessories in her elegant boutique near the aquarium in Dubai Mall. Look for brands like Lebanese bag designer Sandra J, Ambrosia from Paris and Assya from the UK, as well as a line custom designed by local creatives.

KINOKUNIYA BOOKS

Map p216 (2nd fl, Dubai Mall, Financial Centre Rd) If you forgot to pack your iPad or your Kindle, never fear; this massive 6300-sq-metre bookstore stocks over half a million books and 1000 magazines in English, Arabic, Japanese, French, German and Chinese. It is also home to a pleasant cafe with superb fountain views.

CANDYLICIOUS FOOD

Map p216 (ground fl, Dubai Mall, Financial Centre Rd) Stand under the lollipop tree, guzzle a root-beer float at the soda fountain or soak up the tempting aroma of Garretts' gourmet popcorn at this colourful candy emporium. The 1000th store to open in Dubai Mall, it's stocked to the rafters with everything from humble jelly beans to gourmet chocolate from France and Switzerland. Pure bliss. Just don't tell your dentist. You'll find it next to Dubai Aquarium.

AN ICE-COLD TREAT

Dubai Mall is home to some of the best ice cream in town. Elbow your way to any of the following for some gelato time out (see Map p216).

- **Cold Stone Creamery** Some wonderful fruity flavours, plus one-offs like peanut-butter cup.
- **Frozen Yoghurt Factory** Go healthy (sort of) with one of these creamy choices.
- **Milano** The Italians have got it right. Delicious gelato with lots of flavours.
- **Morelli's Gelato** Another sure-fire Italian place with the same creamy fab flavours.

ARMANI JUNIOR CHILDREN

Map p216; (1st fl; Dubai Mall, Financial Centre Rd) This iconic designer name has introduced a fabulous range for children with classic tea dresses, timeless knits, stylish formal wear for tots and some funky fun swimwear as well.

TAHARAN PERSIAN CARPETS & ANTIQUES GIFTS

Map p216 (www.pch.ae; 1st fl, Souq al-Bahar, Old Town Island, next to Dubai Mall) The name is misleading, because although it sells carpets and a handful of antiques, there are also some superb Iranian decorative items including delicately carved boxes made from gorgeous peacock-coloured turquoise, as well as blue decorative plates, fancy stained-glass lamps and plenty of colourful silver jewellery and trinkets.

GOLD & DIAMOND PARK JEWELLERY

(Sheikh Zayed Rd; ⏲10am-10pm Sat-Thu, 4-10pm Fri) A cooler alternative to the Deira Gold Souq in the summer months, air-conditioned Gold & Diamond Park, located near Interchange No 4 and the First Gulf Bank metro stop, houses some 90 retailers in an Arabian-style building. Don't forget to bargain.

BOULEVARD AT JUMEIRAH EMIRATES TOWERS MALL

Map p216 (www.boulevarddubai.com; Sheikh Zayed Rd; ⏲10am-10pm Sat-Thu, 2-10pm Fri) If you feel as though you're being watched, you probably are. Emirates Towers is the location of Sheikh Mohammed's offices, and the secret police are everywhere. Dress appropriately and keep your voice down as you nose around exclusive designer boutiques like Bulgari, Cartier and Zegna. At day's end, sip chardonnay at Agency, sing karaoke at Harry Ghatto's or dine on stylish British grub at the Ivy.

HOW TO 'DO' DUBAI MALL

Dubai Mall is a shopper's Shangri-La but it's so huge that it's all rather bewildering. Don't be intimidated: make your first order of business to pick up a map from one of 18 information desks strategically positioned near entrances and throughout the four floors. These are also staffed with friendly, English-speaking folk who are happy to point you in the right direction. Alternatively, you can use the interactive electronic store finders to show you the way to a particular store. Like many malls, Dubai Mall is busiest on Thursday night and Friday after 4pm, so avoid these times if you don't like crowds. There's a free shuttle service and newer San Francisco–style trolley bus that run to select area hotels – pick up a timetable at an information desk. Wi-fi is free as well, but for now you need a United Arab Emirates (UAE) mobile-phone number to register for the service.

SPORTS & ACTIVITIES

MEYDAN RACECOURSE HORSE RACING

Off Map p216 (☎04-327 0077; www.meydan.ae/racecourse; Al-Marqadh) A passionate love of Arabian thoroughbreds courses through the blood of Emiratis, and Dubai-based **Godolphin** (www.godolphin.com) stables are well known to horse-racing enthusiasts worldwide. Racing season starts in November with the 10-week Winter Racing Challenge, but doesn't heat up until January, when Dubai International Racing Carnival gets under way. It culminates in late March with the elite **Dubai World Cup**, the world's richest horse race, with prize money of a dizzying US$10 million.

Dubai racing's new home is spectacular **Meydan Racecourse**, located about 5km southwest of Sheikh Zayed Rd. It has a futuristic stadium with a grandstand bigger than most airport terminals. Spanning 1.6km, it has a solar- and titanium-panelled roof, can accommodate up to 60,000 spectators and integrates a five-star hotel, the Sky Bubble 360° vista restaurant and an IMAX theatre. There's a free-admission area where dress is casual. For the grandstand you'll need tickets and should dress to the nines. For the exact racing schedule and tickets, check the website of **Dubai Racing Club** (www.dubairacingclub.com). Even if you don't like horse racing, attending a race presents great people-watching opportunities.

To get here, take the 2nd interchange from Sheikh Zayed Rd, turn left onto Al-Meydan Rd and follow the signs.

DUBAI ICE RINK ICE SKATING

Map p216 (☎04-437 3111; www.dubaiicerink.com; ground fl, Dubai Mall, Financial Centre Rd; per session incl skates Dh50, disco sessions Dh75; ⏲2hr sessions 10am, 12.15pm, 2.30pm, 5.45pm & 8pm daily, plus 9.45pm Thu-Sat) This state-of-the-art Olympic-sized ice rink is ringed with cafes and restaurants and can even be converted into a concert arena. Sign up for a private or group class if you're a little wobbly in the knees. There are also disco sessions for the braver shakers and movers.

SPA AT THE PALACE – THE OLD TOWN DAY SPA

Map p216 (☎04-428 7888; www.thepalace-dubai.com; Palace – The Old Town, Emaar Blvd; ⏲9am-10pm) Surrender to the magic of Arabia in this intimate, sensuously lit spa where treatments incorporate Asian products and techniques. A favourite is the One Desert Journey (Dh685), where you choose from a selection of traditional essences such as jasmine, musk, orange blossom or verbena, depending on your mood. The 'trip' starts with a rose-petal footbath, followed by a revitalising sand and salt scrub. At the next stop you'll be drenched in an oil masque before submitting to a restorative massage using an 'oussada' cushion filled with three types of dried mint from Morocco. Finally, drift into semiconscious bliss with a cup of tea in the relaxation room. There are only four treatment rooms for women and two for men, each with their own private shower and toilet. As a hotel guest, you're free to wallow in the gorgeously appointed spa with Jacuzzi, sauna and steam, even without booking a treatment.

SEGA REPUBLIC THEME PARK

Map p216 (www.segarepublic.com; 2nd fl, Dubai Mall, Financial Centre Rd; per ride Dh15-30; ⏲10am-10pm Sun-Wed, 10am-midnight Thu-Sat; 👪) Dubai Mall's indoor amusement park is packed with thrills. Five zones of entertainment include such must-rides as Spin Gear, a rotating roller coaster that shoots you through complete darkness; the Wild Wing and Wild Jungle motion-simulators that take you on an Indiana Jones–style adventure; and Storm G, a high-speed bobsled ride that twists and turns 360 degrees. There's also marginally tamer karaoke singing. Some rides have height restrictions. Pay either per ride or get a Power Pass (Dh140) for unlimited trips. The Platinum Power Pass (Dh220) includes unlimited rides plus Dh200 credit for arcade games.

GEMS OF YOGA YOGA

Map p216 (☎04-331 5161/1328; www.gemsofyogadubai.com; 17th fl above KFC, btwn Fairmont & Crowne Plaza hotels, Sheikh Zayed Rd; introductory class Dh75-100, unlimited weekly classes Dh400-450; ⏲6.30am-10pm Sat-Thu, 10am-8pm Fri) These guys are serious about their yoga. There are plenty of specialised programmes, from Desktop Yoga for stress relief to Power Yoga (a combination of aerobics and yoga). Call ahead or check the website for schedules.

1847 SALON

Map p216 (☎04-330 1847; www.thegroomingcompany.ae; Boulevard at Jumeirah Emirates Towers, Sheikh Zayed Rd; traditional shave Dh100; ⏲9am-9pm Sat-Thu, 1-9pm Fri) Men: if you're lucky enough to be able to grow a good-looking beard, we highly recommend you do so while in Dubai. Locals will approve and be ever-so-slightly more accepting of you. However, many expats prefer to keep a hairless visage; the dandies among them indulge in an old-fashioned straight-razor shave – complete with hot towels beforehand – at the clubby men-only 'grooming salon' 1847. Ask about packages, including body scrubs, mani-pedis and massages. Good haircuts, too. There are four other branches in town; check the website.

TALISE DAY SPA

Map p216 (☎04-319 8181; www.jumeirah.com/talise; Jumeirah Emirates Towers, Sheikh Zayed Rd; ⏲9am-11pm) Finally, a spa squarely aimed at stressed and jet-lagged executives who are badly in need of – but have little time for – revitalisation. There's the usual range of massages and spa treatments, plus a few esoteric ones. How about kick-starting your capillaries in the Oxygen Lounge (per 15/30/60 minutes Dh85/165/330) or tricking your body into believing it got eight hours of sleep by spending only one in a flotation pool (Dh330)? There is another branch in Jumeirah (p103).

DUBAI CREEK STRIDERS RUNNING

Map p216 (☎04-321 1999; www.dubaicreekstriders.com) The Striders meet for weekly training runs on Friday mornings at 7am, on the road opposite the Novotel (319 St), near the convention halls of the World Trade Centre. The run's length varies depending on the season, but it's generally at least 10km. Contact the club to register before turning up.

Jumeirah

JUMEIRAH | UMM SUQEIM

Neighbourhood Top Five

❶ Stepping into a quasi-Arabian souq at **Madinat Jumeirah** (p93) with its sumptuous architecture and surrounding network of Venetian-style canals, subtropical vegetation and Burj al-Arab backdrop. Plan to stay a while, as the restaurants are top-notch.

❷ Sipping a cuppa in the lavish surroundings of the **Burj al-Arab** (p94) when you book an afternoon-tea slot.

❸ Wondering at the intricately detailed **Jumeirah Mosque** (p93) on a guided tour.

❹ Feeding the ducks with the kids at **Al-Safa Park** (p93), a rare green space.

❺ Kicking back on **Jumeirah Open Beach** (p94) before exploring the surrounding shopping malls.

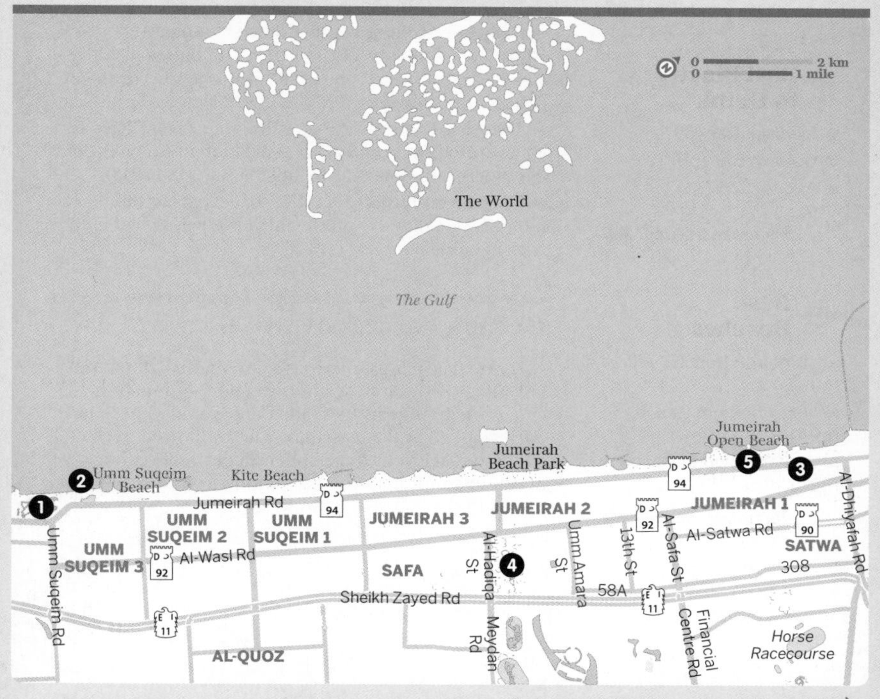

For more detail of this area, see Map p218

Lonely Planet's Top Tip

It's not well publicised, but the Burj al-Arab has a strict dress code for its Skyview Bar. Fashionable or not, collarless shirts won't get guys past the doormen and jeans have to be elegant (eek, we think that means an ironed crease!). Of course, trainers are a definite no-no, however much they cost. Women have more flexibility – as long as they look sufficiently dressed up they should be able to pass scrutiny.

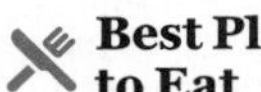

Best Places to Eat

- Al-Mahara (p95)
- Zheng He's (p95)
- Pierchic (p95)

For reviews, see p95

Best Places to Drink

- Skyview Bar (p97)
- Uptown Bar (p97)
- Agency (p97)

For reviews, see p97

Best Beaches

- Jumeirah Beach Park (p94)
- Umm Suqeim Beach (p94)
- Jumeirah Open Beach (p94)

For reviews, see p94

Explore Jumeirah

The most interesting stretch of Jumeirah is along Jumeirah Rd, just south of Jumeirah Mosque. This is where you'll find indie boutiques like S*uce (p99), fancy spas like Sensasia (p103), and expat cafes such as the wonderful Lime Tree Cafe (p95). Stop here for a slice of carrot cake and organically sourced coffee. If you feel like doing more shopping, there are some reasonable malls around, such as the Mercato Mall (p102), as well as some modest-sized commercial centres (for a change) around the Jumeirah Open Beach.

Further on, Jumeirah Beach Park is the most popular public beach in town. Head here if you fancy flaking out on the beach; you can rent sunbeds and parasols for just Dh15. Take note of the cautionary signs though. The sea here is famous for its riptides and there have been accidents – and worse.

Jumeirah has been officially subdivided into sections 1, 2 and 3 as it stretches for many kilometres. For the photo of the Burj al-Arab, head for the romantically evocative Madinat Jumeirah (beyond Jumeirah 3) where you can also explore the souq, high-end hotels and fancy restaurants and clubs.

Local Life

- **People-watching** Wander down bustling Al-Dhiyafah Rd in Satwa (Map p218), stopping for a *shwarma* or drink at one of the atmospheric cheap-eat restaurants or cafes.
- **Tailoring** Got your eye on a designer dress? Then do what the locals do and get it copied for a pittance at one of numerous tailors on Al-Huidaba Rd (Map p218).
- **Bargain shopping** Join the local expats at the monthly flea market (p100) which is always piled high with genuine bargains.

Getting There & Away

- **Metro** The closest metro stop to Madinat Jumeirah is Mall of the Emirates; to Satwa and the Jumeirah Open Beach, stop at the Trade Centre; and to Al-Safa Park, hop out at Business Bay. You'll still need to catch a taxi to reach your final Jumeirah destination but, depending on where you are coming from, combining a taxi with the metro may work out cheaper, overall.

SIGHTS

FREE JUMEIRAH MOSQUE — MOSQUE

Map p218 (Jumeirah Rd, Jumeirah 1; tours 10am Sat, Sun, Tue & Thu) If you want to learn about Islamic religion and culture, beat a fast track to this splendid, intricately detailed mosque (stunningly lit at night). It's the only one in Dubai that's open to non-Muslims, but only during the one-hour guided tours operated by the Sheikh Mohammed Centre for Cultural Understanding (see the boxed text, p67), which wrap up with a Q&A session. There's no need to pre-book; just register at the mosque before the tour. Show up dressed modestly (no shorts, back and arms should be covered and women need to wear a headscarf) and remove your shoes before entering. Cameras are allowed.

AL-SAFA PARK — PARK

Map p218 (Jumeirah 2; admission Dh3; 8am-11pm;) Bordered by Sheikh Zayed and Al-Wasl roads, this pretty and popular park is a pastiche of lawn, gardens and waterfalls, a ladies' garden, children's playgrounds and even a lake where you can feed the ducks or take your sweetie for a spin in a rowing or paddle boat. Sporty types can use the jogging track or play volleyball, basketball, football or tennis. After dark the rides (near Al-Wasl Rd) get busy. Tuesday is women and children only. The Dubai Flea Market (p100) is held here once a month.

MAJLIS GHORFAT UM-AL-SHEEF — HISTORIC BUILDING

Map p218 (Jumeirah 3; admission Dh1; 8.30am-8.30pm Sat-Thu, 3.30-8.30pm Fri) Located south of Jumeirah Rd, behind Citibank, this traditional building has been well restored and is worth a stop if you are in the area. The two-storey structure was built in 1955 as a summer residence of the late Sheikh Rashid bin Saeed al-Maktoum. Made of gypsum and coral rock with a palm frond roof and a wind tower, it provided a cool retreat from the heat. The palm tree garden features a traditional *falaj* irrigation system. The actual *majlis* (meeting room) upstairs is decorated with cushions, rugs, a coffee pot, pottery and food platters, and is pretty close to the way it would have looked in Sheikh Rashid's day.

FREE PRO ART GALLERY — ART GALLERY

Map p218 (www.proartuae.com; Palm Strip Mall, Jumeirah 1; 10am-10pm Sat-Thu) Based on an extraordinary donated private collection, this gallery is more like an art museum with original paintings, lithographs and sculptures by such smock-and-beret masters as Chagall, Dufy, Damien Hirst, Arman, Le Corbusier (yes, he was an artist too…) and Picasso. These days the gallery concentrates on street art – there are a couple of original Banksys here – with a vibrant program of regular exhibitions.

Umm Suqeim

Popular with families, residential Umm Suqeim (also divided into sections 1, 2 and 3) is flanked by fabulous beaches and a clutch of high-end resorts, including Jumeirah Beach Hotel and the Burj al-Arab. It is punctuated by the Disneyesque but still evocative Madinat Jumeirah, with its souq, high-end hotels and fancy restaurants and party spots. This beach is particularly popular with the surfing crowd. Note that there are no facilities.

MADINAT JUMEIRAH — HOTEL COMPLEX

Map p218 (Al-Sufouh Rd, Umm Suqeim 3) A city within a city, the Madinat Jumeirah is a Dubai must-see. There's plenty to do at this fanciful hotel, shopping and entertainment complex with the Burj al-Arab in the background. Explore the Arabian-style architecture, snoop around the splendid Al-Qsar and Mina A' Salam hotels, or get lost in the labyrinth of the souvenir-saturated souq. There are some exquisite details throughout, so if you see some stairs, take them – they might lead you to a hidden terrace with a mesmerising vista of the sprawling complex. If you're a hotel guest, or have a restaurant reservation, you can catch the silent *abras* (water taxis) cruising along the 4km-long network of Venetian-style canals for free. Otherwise, the cost is Dh50 for a guest tour. Billowing bougainvillea, bushy banana trees and soaring palms characterise the enchanting grounds, which are scrupulously maintained by a small army of gardeners. Sure, there's an undeniable 'Disney does Arabia' artifice about the whole place, but it's all done tastefully and, not surprisingly, it's one of Dubai's most popular spots.

PUBLIC EXPOSURE

If you're not staying at a beachfront five-star place but want to swim in the Gulf, you've got two options: either head to one of Dubai's free public beaches or pay for a day at a beach club.

Dipping without Dirhams

Dubai's free beaches...

Jumeirah Open Beach (Map p218; next to Dubai Marine Beach Resort & Spa, Jumeirah 1) Also known as Russian Beach because of its popularity with Russian tourists, this stretch of white sand is paralleled by a paved path popular with strollers, joggers, skaters and cyclists. Alas, on Fridays it teems with off-duty male guest workers keen on ogling bikini beauties. Although you probably won't get physically accosted, women may feel more comfortable further south at Jumeirah Beach Park. Showers, toilets and kiosks are available.

Kite Beach (Map p218) Also known as Wollongong Beach, this long pristine stretch of sand is quiet and a great place for relaxed sunbathing but it has zero facilities. It's about 3km north of the Burj al-Arab, past Umm Suqeim Hospital, Umm Suqeim 1.

Umm Suqeim Beach (Map p218; btwn Jumeirah Beach Hotel & Kite Beach) This white sandy beach, with fabulous views of the Burj al-Arab, has showers and shelter and is popular with Jumeirah families and Western expatriates.

Jumeirah Beach Residence Open Beach (Map p220; Jumeirah Beach Residence, Dubai Marina) This is a lovely wide beach paralleling The Walk at JBR. There are no facilities here.

Beaches for Bucks

The ones that cost...

Jumeirah Beach Park (Map p218; per person/car Dh5/20; ⏲7am-10.30pm Sun-Wed, 7am-11pm Thu-Sat) It's a real treat to take a walk on the grass at this verdant park, as it's a couple of degrees cooler than the beach. Fronting onto a long stretch of sand, the park has lifeguards on duty, children's play area, barbecues, picnic tables, walkways and kiosks. Monday is women and children only.

Al-Mamzar Beach Park (Al-Mamzar Creek, Deira; per person/car Dh5/30; ⏲8am-11pm) One of Dubai's hidden gems, this large, landscaped park on a small headland in Deira has lovely white sandy beaches, barbecues and kiosks. Kids have plenty of open space and play areas for romping around, plus three pools with waterslides for cooling off. Friday is busy, but during the week you can have the place to yourself. Wednesday is women and children only. Catch a cab to get here.

Le Meridien Mina Seyahi Beach Resort & Marina (p145; adult/child Sun-Thu Dh175/100, Fri-Sat Dh250/150) The calm beach, wonderful pools including a 150m-long winding lagoon, and a water sports centre offering everything from banana boat rides to windsurfing make this resort a family favourite.

Mina A'Salam & Al-Qsar (p142) The Dh750 tab buys you access to a dreamy beach and fabulous pools and includes a Dh250 food voucher. Buy tickets at the Health Club.

BURJ AL-ARAB HOTEL

Map p218 (www.burj-al-arab.com; Jumeirah Rd, Umm Suqeim 3) We're suckers for trivia, so let's kick off by telling you that the lobby of the Burj al-Arab is so high, the Statue of Liberty would fit quite nicely into it. Or that the sail-shaped building tops out at 321m, just a few metres shorter than the Eiffel Tower. And here's one more: 1600 sq metres in the hotel are sheathed in gold leaf.

In its first decade since opening, the Burj al-Arab has been more than just the iconic symbol of a booming city in the sand; it has challenged preconceived ideas of what an Arab country in the Middle East can achieve. It's built on an artificial island 280m offshore from the Jumeirah Beach Hotel, to which it is linked by a causeway. This five-star hotel (it's best to ignore the nonsense about seven stars) is worth visiting, if only to gawk at an interior that's every bit as gaudy as the exterior is gorgeous. If you're not staying, you need a restaurant reservation to get past lobby security. Don't expect any bargains: Friday brunch is Dh525 and afternoon tea will set you back between Dh275 and Dh425 with several options available, including Asian. Settings include the Skyview Bar, some 200m above the waves. Check the website for details. If you don't want tea, you can come here for cocktails (between 8pm and 1am), accompanied by live jazz. But, again, you must reserve in advance.

EATING

The restaurants in Dubai's low-rise, high-rent district draw wealthy locals and tourists on holiday. Though the beach is never far away, it's barely visible from some of the eateries reviewed here; for ocean views, head to New Dubai or Madinat Jumeirah. The restaurants at Madinat Jumeirah generally have good-quality food and are the most scenic – though they tend to be touristy and overpriced. Note that Al-Dhiyafah Rd in Satwa is the best walking street in the city and is tops for a late-night *shwarma*.

AL-MAHARA SEAFOOD **$$$**

Map p218 (☎04-301 7600; www.jumeirah.com; Burj al-Arab, Jumeirah Rd, Umm Suqeim 3; mains Dh250-300; ⏰12.30-3pm & 7-11.30pm) A lift posing as a submarine deposits you at a gold-leaf-clad tunnel leading you to Dubai's most unique restaurant. Diners sit around a huge circular aquarium where clownfish flit and baby sharks dart as their sea bass and halibut cousins are being...devoured. Surreal yes, but at least the quality measures up to the hype. Try the Maine lobster starter and bring that platinum card. Reservations essential.

ZHENG HE'S CHINESE **$$**

Map p218 (☎04-366 6730; www.jumeirah.com; Mina A'Salam, Madinat Jumeirah, Al-Sufouh Rd, Umm Suqeim 3; mains Dh75-240) An army of 20 clatters pans and fires woks behind the glass of the open kitchen at spectacular Zheng He's, famed for its fresh, light dim sum and stellar seafood specials (many diners go for the live tank, but others prefer the wasabi prawns with black pepper). The Sino-chic room is gorgeous, with a pagoda-style ceiling. No children under four years old. Reservations essential.

LIME TREE CAFE INTERNATIONAL **$**

Map p218 (Jumeirah Rd, Jumeirah 1; mains Dh20-40; ⏰7.30am-6pm; 👪) The salads, quiches, focaccias and wraps are innovative and the smoothies lip-smackingly creamy (try the blueberry) at this expat favourite on the Jumeirah strip. Other assets are its use of fresh ingredients (including organic coffee) and the wholesome cooking (just how the yoga mammas, power shoppers and health nuts like it). Portions are generous, prices good, and the carrot cake is the best in town. Located near the Jumeirah Mosque.

PIERCHIC SEAFOOD **$$$**

Map p218 (☎04-366 6730; www.madinatjumeirah.com; Al-Qasr, Madinat Jumeirah, Al-Sufouh Rd, Umm Suqeim 3; mains Dh100-240; ⏰noon-3pm & 7pm-midnight) Looking for a place to drop an engagement ring into a glass of champagne? Make reservations for this stunning seafood house at the end of a long pier jutting out to sea. The best tables line the outdoor decks and provide gorgeous vistas of the Burj al-Arab and Madinat Jumeirah. The food is solidly good, but the overambitious menu can get a little heavy-handed with its ingredient combinations; keep your order simple and you'll fare better. Note that sitting inside defeats the purpose of coming here. Reservations essential.

SMILING BKK THAI **$**

Map p218 (☎04-349 6677; off Al-Wasl Rd, Jumeirah 1; mains Dh25-50; ⏰11am-midnight; 👪)

DID YOU KNOW?

The white metal crosspieces at the top of the Burj al-Arab form what is said to be the largest cross in the Middle East – but it's only visible from the sea. Some say the Western architect did it on purpose. Regardless, by the time it was discovered, it was too late to redesign the tower, even if its owner Sheikh Mohammed had wanted to – the hotel has already put Dubai on the map and become the icon for the city. What do you think? Go see it on a boat charter and decide for yourself. The scale of it is amazing.

LOCAL KNOWLEDGE

RAMADAN LIFE

For visitors interested in Islam or religion in general, Ramadan is a fascinating time to visit Dubai. If you walk the backstreets of Jumeirah areas such as Satwa, you'll see mosques with mats and carpets laid out with food ready for mosque attendees, and witness the streets come to life – well into the wee hours.

Locals will kill us for including this indie hole-in-the-wall Thai gem (located near Jumeirah Post Office), but it's too good not to share. The walls of the cheek-by-jowl space are covered with hipster mishmash (think Van Gogh paint-by-numbers postcards), and there's scratchy rock-and-roll blaring through big speakers (sit outside for quiet conversation). A Thai national cooks your dinner. The food is good, sometimes very good, but what's even better is the adventure of finding this underground boho hangout. (Hint: look for the mustachioed neon Mona Lisa, just west of the Jumeirah Post Office.)

THE MEAT COMPANY STEAKHOUSE $$

Map p218 (☎04 368 6040; Madinat Jumeirah, Al-Sufouh Rd, Umm Suqeim 3; mains Dh85-120; ⌚7pm-11.30pm) Overlooking the canals at Madinat Jumeirah with the Burj Khalifa backdrop, this place takes its meat seriously and gives you a beefy choice ranging from an Australian grain-fed Angus to a Brazilian grass-fed beast. Other options include a hanging skewer of marinated lamb and there are several veggie side dishes such as wild mushrooms. This is a popular celeb place judging by the signed plates on the wall. Reservations recommended.

PAI THAI THAI $$

Map p218 (☎04-366 6730; Al-Qasr, Madinat Jumeirah, Al-Sufouh Rd, Umm Suqeim 3; mains Dh55-180; ⌚6.30-11.30pm) A boat ride, a waterside table and candlelight are the hallmarks of a romantic night out and this enchanting spot at the Al-Qasr sparks on all cylinders. If your date doesn't make you swoon, then the beautifully crafted Thai dishes should still ensure an unforgettable evening. Or come for Friday brunch (with/without alcohol Dh240/190). Reservations recommended.

PARS IRANIAN KITCHEN IRANIAN $

Map p218 (Satwa Roundabout, Satwa; mezze Dh15-20, mains Dh35-55; ⌚6pm-1am; 👪) Enjoy hot wheels of bread made daily in the outside brick oven along with such classics as creamy *muttabal* (purée of aubergine mixed with tahini, lemon and olive oil), hummus, and juicy Iranian-style spicy kebabs paired with buttery saffron rice. You'll feel like a pasha lounging amid the fat pillows on a carpeted platform surrounded by twinkle-lit hedges. Too authentic? Opt for a traditional table. Alas, the lack of indoor seating makes Pars a poor choice in summer. There's a daytime traditional Iranian bakery here, as well.

JAPENGO CAFE INTERNATIONAL $

Map p218 (Palm Strip Mall, Jumeirah Rd, Jumeirah 1; mains Dh30-50; 👪) Grab a window or terrace seat for great views of the Jumeirah Mosque. Decorated with plenty of rattan contrasting with shiny black, the menu is vast and varied, featuring dishes from east to west. Opt for the east or, more specifically the Indonesian-style *nasi goreng istimewa* (fried rice with sausages, eggs and prawns), sushi, sashimi, tempura dishes or a delicately spiced curry. The children's menu includes some nostalgic favourites, such as lightly boiled eggs with toast soldiers for dipping. This is the original branch of a successful small local chain.

THE ONE INTERNATIONAL $

Map p218 (Jumeirah Rd, near Jumeirah Mosque, Jumeirah 1; dishes Dh20-45; ⌚9am-9pm) Deli dabblers will be in salad and sandwich heaven at this stylish outpost upstairs at THE One home design store. All food is freshly prepared and calibrated to health- and waist-watchers without sacrificing a lick to the taste gods. Reliable choices include the smoked salmon wrap and the Arabic chicken salad. A good alternative if Lime Tree Cafe is full.

RAVI PAKISTANI $

Map p218 (Al-Satwa Rd, Satwa; mains Dh15-20; ⌚24hr) Everyone from cabbies to five-star chefs flock to this legendary Pakistani eatery (dating from 1978) where you eat like a prince and pay like a pauper. Loosen that belt for helpings of spicy curries, succulent grilled meats, creamy dahl (lentils) and fresh, buttery naan. Be prepared for the no-frills dining room or, better still, wait for an outside table to watch Satwa on parade.

BELLA DONNA ITALIAN $

Map p218 (Mercato Mall, Jumeirah Rd, Jumeirah 1; pizzas & pastas Dh35-55; ⌚11am-11pm; 👪) Ponder the beauty of Marilyn, Audrey and other classic Hollywood stars as you sit in this art-deco-inspired dining room and munch on tender-crusted thin pizzas and house-made pastas. The strong coffee will jack you up for shopping in the adjoining Mercato Mall. Sit on the terrace for glimpses of the azure Gulf.

NOODLE BOWL CHINESE $

Map p218 (Dune Center, Al Diyafa St, Satwa; mains Dh30-45; 🖉) Noodles are prepared here in every style imaginable – and none involve a microwave. Braised, tossed, fried and added to soups, accompaniments include seafood, beef, chicken, duck and tofu for the vegetarians. The dim sum also gets a star rating, served steamed or deep fried – or even as a dessert, deep fried and filled with creamy custard. The dining space is Asian-inspired with light colours and the occasional ornamental Buddha.

DRINKING & NIGHTLIFE

SKYVIEW BAR COCKTAIL BAR

Map p218 (☎04-301 7600; www.burjalarab.com; Burj al-Arab, off Jumeirah Rd, Umm Suqeim 3; ⌚noon-2am) Despite the stratospheric tab, cocktails (Dh275 minimum) or afternoon tea (from Dh275) on the 27th floor of the Burj al-Arab ranks high on tourists' must-do lists. And with good reason: the views are simply breathtaking. Do arrive before sunset or don't bother. And *do* book ahead. As for the Liberace-meets-*Star Trek* interiors, all we can say is: 'Welcome to the Burj'.

UPTOWN BAR COCKTAIL BAR

Map p218 (www.jumeirah.com; 25th fl, Jumeirah Beach Hotel, Jumeirah Rd, Umm Suqeim 3; ⌚9pm-3am Mon-Fri) This place has a beautifully calibrated seductive feel with fiery mood lighting, low-slung couches and stunning views from the hotel's 25th floor. There's a lot of SM (standing and modelling, that is) going on as this is another popular venue for Dubai's beautiful crowd.

AGENCY WINE BAR

Map p218 (www.madinatjumeirah.com; Souq Madinat Jumeirah, Al-Sufouh Rd, Umm Suqeim 3; ⌚noon-1am) A convivial wine bar frequented by khaki-clad tourists and expats, Agency is a civilised spot for a pre-dinner drink. As at its sister branch at Jumeirah Emirates Towers, the wine list includes unusual varietals (skip the New World wines in favour of better French labels), but here there's a terrace overlooking the Madinat canals and with glimpses of the Burj al-Arab. Satisfying bar snacks include fried calamari and cheese fondue with truffle oil. Good luck snagging a table at peak times.

BAHRI BAR COCKTAIL BAR

Map p218 (www.jumeirah.com; Mina A'Salam, Madinat Jumeirah, Umm Suqeim 3; ⌚4pm-2am Sat-Wed, to 3am Thu & Fri) A great choice in winter, Bahri has a fabulous verandah laid with Persian carpets and big cane sofas where you can take in gorgeous views of the Burj al-Arab. The vibe is very grown-up – just the kind of place you take your parents for sunset drinks. For a fun treat, order the camel-milk mocktail.

LEGENDS SPORTS BAR

Map p218 (www.rydges.com; Rydges Plaza, Al-Dhiyafah Rd, Satwa) This Australian sports bar, on the ground floor of this handsome hotel, is packed during rugby matches, on Thursdays with its live band and on Fridays when there is a good-humoured jam session. Others may just be here for the beer – Crown Lager or Victoria Bitter keep the local Aussie expats happy.

LEFT BANK COCKTAIL BAR

Map p218 (www.madinatjumeirah.com; Souq Madinat Jumeirah, Al-Sufouh Rd, Umm Suqeim 3; ⌚noon-2am) We love the waterside tables, with *abras* floating past, but the real party is inside the dark bar, where moody lighting, giant mirrors, leather club chairs and chill beats create a dynamic lounge scene. Ladies' night is Wednesday with five mixed drinks for Dh5. Also at Souq al-Bahar.

MALECON BAR

Map p218 (www.dxbmarine.com; Dubai Marine Beach Resort & Spa, Jumeirah Rd, Jumeirah 1; ⌚7pm-3am) Tequila is the essential drink at Malecon, an important stopover for the party crowd after 10pm or so (come here earlier for tasty Cuban food). Tipping its hat to Havana's graffiti-walled Bodeguita del Medio, this Latino-inspired bar is the place to hit late, do shots and twirl with a Cuban heel. Look sharp; though unpretentious, the crowd appreciates nice gear.

BAR ZAR COCKTAIL BAR

Map p218 (www.madinatjumeirah.com; Souq Madinat Jumeirah, Al-Sufouh Rd, Umm Suqeim 3; ⏲5pm-2am Sat-Wed, 5pm-3am Thu, 4pm-3am Fri) Bar Zar is a bit of a pick-up joint, but it's good for pre-club cocktails. Skip the glorified sports bar upstairs and report straight to the waterfront terrace to sip cold beers and killer cosmos. There are different nightly promotions, including ladies' night on Monday.

360° CLUB

Map p218 (www.jumeirah.com; Jumeirah Beach Hotel, Jumeirah Rd, Umm Suqeim 3; ⏲6pm-2am Tue-Thu, 4pm-2am Fri & Sat) Capping a long, curved pier, 360° delivers magical views of the Burj al-Arab, especially when the sun slips seaward. Lined with plush sink-into sofas, all are welcome here, although expect to pay around Dh50 for a drink. At weekends there are top-notch DJs and lots of shiny happy souls. This club was voted one of the top 60 clubs in the world a few years back. We agree.

TRILOGY CLUB

Map p218 (www.madinatjumeirah.com; Souq Madinat Jumeirah, Al-Sufouh Rd, Umm Suqeim 3; ⏲9pm-late) With three floors of Moroccan-inspired decor and a sumptuous gold-and-silver colour scheme, this is another place that brings in the best on the international DJ circuit. It's located at the entrance to the souq so thankfully it's easy to find.

BOUDOIR CLUB

Map p218 (www.myboudoir.com; Dubai Marine Beach Resort & Spa, Jumeirah Rd, Jumeirah 1; ⏲7.30pm-3am) Though snooty expats don't tend to mix with the Lebanese crowd at Boudoir, we love the look of the place. Tufted red-velvet booths, beaded curtains and tasselled draperies lend a super-model vibe – indeed, you may spot one among the wannabes – and the circular layout is perfect for twirling away from the occasional unwanted advance by a Lothario. This place is high on the chic-o-meter, so look sharp or be ostracised.

KOUBBA CLUB

Map p218 (www.madinatjumeirah.com; Al-Qasr Hotel, Souq Madinat Jumeirah, Al-Sufouh Rd, Umm Suqeim 3; ⏲6pm-2am) Score a candle-lit table on the terrace overlooking the Madinat canals and illuminated Burj, and you'll instantly know you've found one of the most tranquil and romantic spots in all Dubai. The interior is nearly as compelling, with plush red velvet and Oriental cushions for you to lie against as you chill out to live Arabian-lounge music.

SHO CHO CLUB

Map p218 (www.dxbmarine.com; Dubai Marine Beach Resort & Spa, Jumeirah Rd, Jumeirah 1; ⏲7pm-3am) The cool minimalist interior, with its blue lights and wall-mounted fish tanks, may draw you in, but the beachside deck is the place to be. Take in the laid-back vibe as the cool ocean breezes blow and the DJ's soundtrack competes with the crashing waves.

ENTERTAINMENT

FRIDGE LIVE MUSIC

(www.thefridgedubai.com; Warehouse 5, 26 St, near Al-Rassas Rd, Umm Suqeim 3) This music promoter also presents the occasional concert in its funky warehouse venue in the industrial Al-Quoz district. It's big on local talent who are still below the radar, and features an eclectic line-up that may include a Japanese shakuhachi flute player, a Filipino choir or an Irish harpist. To reach here, head south on Al-Rassas Rd and due east on 26 St; after around 1km, the club is located on your right.

JAMBASE LIVE MUSIC

Map p218 (www.jumeirah.com; Souq Madinat Jumeirah, Al-Sufouh Rd, Umm Suqeim 3; ⏲7pm-2am Mon-Sat) If you enjoy dining, drinking and dancing without changing location, this moody basement supper club should fit the bill. The ambience gets increasingly lively as blood alcohol levels rise and a jazz quintet moves on from mellow jazz to soul, R&B, Motown and other high-energy sounds. The food's billed as US-style (think prime rib, roast chicken; mains Dh90 to Dh160) and hearty, if nothing out of the ordinary.

LOCAL KNOWLEDGE

YASMINE BEHNAM: FASHION INNOVATOR

Yasmine Behnam is Managing Partner of **A Boutique Society** (www.facebook.com/aboutiquesociety), a pop-up store that takes places for three days in varying venues and showcases emerging brands and labels that cannot be found elsewhere in the Middle East.

Where do you like to shop for fashion in Dubai? Aside from my own pop-up store, I really enjoy If, a gorgeous boutique in a villa in the Umm Suqeim area which sells fantastic conceptual Japanese/Belgian type of brands such as Comme Des Garcons, Rick Owens and Haider Ackermann. I also like shopping for vintage, second-hand designer wear at Garderobe on the Jumeirah Beach Rd.

What do you like to do on your day off? I try and avoid beaches, pools or anywhere with crowds. I prefer to take a boat ride on the Marina or head out to the Bab al-Shams Desert Resort & Spa (p144) to enjoy a mint tea or mezze meal on the roof terrace. It is particularly magical at sunset.

Your secret place in Dubai? I love poking around for Middle Eastern inspiration at O' de Rose (p99), which is in a homey villa and sells crafts, clothing, art and accessories by local artisans.

FIRST GROUP THEATRE AT MADINAT THEATRE

Map p218 (www.madinattheatre.com; Souq Madinat Jumeirah, Al-Sufouh Rd, Umm Suqueim 3) An eclectic program of crowd-pleasing entertainment ranging from the Sound of Music to Russian ballet and comedy shows feeds the cravings of Dubai's culture-starved residents. Performances take place in a gorgeous 442-seat theatre.

SHOPPING

O' DE ROSE HANDICRAFTS

Map p218 (www.o-derose.com; 999 Al-Wasl Rd, Umm Suqueim 2) The antithesis of the cookie-cutter malls, this delightful boutique is set in a homey residential villa. Run by Lebanese-born fashion designer Mimi Shakhashir, O' de Rose sells all sorts of ethno-chic creations, ranging from hand-painted ceramics to hand-blown Syrian vases. Customers are greeted with a glass of refreshing O' de Rose (roseflower drink); set aside plenty of time to browse.

IF FASHION

Map p218 (Umm Al Sheif St, Umm Suqeim 1) Already a smash hit in Beirut and New York, this boutique is a fashion pioneer selling refreshing lesser-known designer labels such as Johnny Farah and Marc Le Bihan that combine avant-garde haute couture with classic lines and fantastic accessories.

S*UCE FASHION

Map p218 (Village Mall, Jumeirah Rd, Jumeirah 1; ⌚10am-9pm Sat-Thu, 4.30-10pm Fri) This is the original store of women-owned S*uce (pronounced 'sauce'), a pioneer on Dubai's growing indie fashion boutique scene. Join the style brigade searching for top-tier denim, flirty frocks, sassy accessories, sexy sandals and deluxe tees. Look for such key contemporary designers as Karta, Tsumori Chisato, Vanessa Bruno, Isabella Cappeto, Alice McCall and Philip Lim, as well as local labels such as Essa, Bil Arabi and Sugar Vintage. There's another branch in Dubai Mall.

S*UCE LIGHT FASHION

Map p218 (1st fl, Jumeirah Centre, Jumeirah Rd, Jumeirah 1; ⌚10am-9pm Sat-Thu, 4.30-10pm Fri) Not flush enough to drop Dh1500 for a pair of jeans at S*uce? Just pop across the street to its outlet, where a limited selection and a less-glam ambience translate into items at 50% to 70% off.

YASMINE FASHION

(Map p218; Souq Madinat Jumeirah, Al-Sufouh Rd, Al-Sufouh 2) This house of ladies' *jalabiyas* (traditional garment native to the Gulf) includes some exquisite handwoven designs made from fine woven pashmina or cashmere. If you find the *jalabiyas* a tad too dressy for wafting around the house, then go for one of the equally decorative scarves or shawls.

LOCAL KNOWLEDGE

PASHMINA: TELLING REAL FROM FAKE

Women around the world adore pashminas, those feather-light cashmere shawls worn by the Middle East's best-dressed ladies. If you're shopping for a girlfriend or your mother, you can never go wrong with a pashmina. They come in hundreds of colours and styles, some beaded and embroidered, others with pompom edging – you'll have no trouble finding one you like. But aside from setting it alight to make sure it doesn't melt (as polyester does), how can you be sure it's real? Here's the trick. Hold the fabric at its corner. Loop your index finger around it and squeeze hard. Now pull the fabric through. If it's polyester, it won't budge. If it's cashmere, it'll pull through – though the friction may give you a mild case of rope burn. Try it at home with a thin piece of polyester before you hit the shops; then try it with cashmere. You'll never be fooled again.

SHOWCASE ANTIQUES, ART & FRAMES — ANTIQUES

Map p218 (Villa 679, Jumeirah Rd, Umm Suqeim) Browse this three-storey Jumeirah villa for antique *khanjars,* firearms, Arabian coffee pots, Bedouin jewellery and costumes. It's one of few places in Dubai to carry quality collectables and antiques, with certificates of authenticity to back them up. It's across from Dubai Municipality Building, near the corner of Al-Manara St.

GARDEROBE — VINTAGE FASHION

Map p218 (www.garderobevintage.com; Jumeirah Rd, Jumeirah 3) This is the place to come to snag a one-off vintage item at an affordable price. The secondhand designerwear and accessories are in tip-top condition and typically include items by Chanel, Hermes, Alexander Wang and Gucci. It's a concept that has proved a big hit here, particularly among the expatriate community.

HOUSE OF PROSE — BOOKS

Map p218 (Jumeirah Plaza, Jumeirah Rd, Jumeirah 1; ⌚9am-8pm Sat-Thu, 5-8pm Fri) This comfortably worn-round-the-edges bookstore overflows with secondhand English-language books, from classic literature to obscure biographies and travel guides. After you've read your book, you can bring it back for 50% credit towards your next purchase. There's another branch in Ibn Battuta Mall.

BLUE CACTUS — FASHION

Map p218 (Jumeirah Centre, Jumeirah Rd, Jumeirah 1; ⌚10am-9pm Sat-Thu, 4.30-9pm Fri) The buyer at this upstairs boutique is from Mexico, hence the Frida Kahlo emphasis in the decor and brilliant colours and patterns in the fashions and accessories. There are sleek long dresses, sassy separates and some Ascot-worthy hats, as well as a cool collection of Mexican silver jewellery.

FLEURT — FASHION

Map p218 (www.mercatoshoppingmall.com; Mercato Mall, Jumeirah Rd, Jumeirah 1) This small boutique keeps trend-hungry stylistas looking good in funky-smart fashions by Betsey Johnson and Soul Revival, among other progressives. The collection is refreshingly offbeat, with spangles and sequins, curve-hugging lines and cheeky party frocks. If you're into classic design, go elsewhere.

LUXECOUTURE — FASHION

Map p218 (Souq Madinat Jumeirah, Al-Sufouh Rd, Al-Sufouh) Alejandra Tokoph-Cox is a Dubai style-maker who often travels to New York to ferret out the latest design trends and import them to Dubai. Her sleek boutiques stock all the hot labels you see on Lindsay, Cameron and Paris, including NYC, Yumi Kim, Shoshana and Tracy Watts, plus jewellery by Dogeared and Nadri. Find the boutique next to Segreto Italian restaurant.

ARTS & CRAFTS — GIFTS

Map p218 (www.mercatoshoppingmall.com; Mercato Mall, Jumeirah Centre, Jumeirah Rd, Jumeirah 1) A great place to pick up that original pashmina shawl or an exquisitely hand-sequined sari or tunic. Owner Tahir imports everything from India, including quality hand-knotted rugs, intricately carved rosewood boxes, and similar.

DUBAI FLEA MARKET — FLEA MARKET

Map p218 (www.dubai-fleamarket.com; Gate 5, Al-Wasl Rd, Al-Safa Park; admission Dh3; ⌚8am-

3pm every 1st Sat Oct-May) Flea markets are like urban archaeology: you'll need plenty of patience and luck when sifting through other people's trash and detritus, but oh, the thrill when finally unearthing a piece of treasure! So trade malls for stalls and look for bargains amid the piles of pre-loved clothing, furniture, toys, home appliances, electronics, art, books and other stuff that's spilled out of local closets.

TOPSHOP CLOTHING

Map p218 (www.mercatoshoppingmall.com; Mercato Mall, Jumeirah Rd, Jumeirah 1) The jewel in the crown of British high-street fashion.

CARPET BUYING 101

Due diligence is essential for prospective carpet buyers. Though you may only want a piece to match your curtains, you'll save a lot of time and money if you do a little homework. Your first order of business: read *Oriental Rugs Today* by Emmett Eiland, an excellent primer on buying new Oriental rugs.

In the early 1900s, rug makers started using fast-acting chemicals and machines to streamline the arduous processes of carding, washing, dying and spinning wool into thread, leaving only the actual weaving to be done by hand. One hundred years later, traditional cultures have been decimated, and the market flooded with bad rugs destined to depreciate in value.

A rug's quality depends entirely on how the wool was processed. It doesn't matter if the rug was hand-knotted if the wool is lousy. The best comes from sheep at high altitudes, which produce impenetrably thick, long-staple fleece, heavy with lanolin. No acids should ever be applied; otherwise the lanolin washes away. Lanolin yields naturally stain-resistant, lustrous fibre that doesn't shed. The dye should be vegetal-based pigment. This guarantees saturated, rich colour tones with a depth and vibrancy unattainable with chemicals.

The dyed wool is hand-spun into thread, which by nature has occasional lumps and challenges the craftsmanship of the weavers, forcing them to compensate for the lumps by occasionally changing the shape, size or position of a knot. These subtle variations in a finished carpet's pattern – visible only upon close inspection – give the carpet its character, and actually make the rug more valuable.

Dealers will hype knot density, weave quality and country of origin, but really, they don't matter. The crucial thing to find out is how the wool was treated. A rug made with acid-treated wool will never look as good as it did the day you bought it. Conversely, a properly made rug will grow more lustrous in colour over time and will last centuries.

Here's a quick test. Stand on top of the rug with rubber-soled shoes and do the twist. Grind the fibres underfoot. If they shed, it's lousy wool. You can also spill water onto the rug. See how fast it absorbs. Ideally it should puddle for an instant, indicating a high presence of lanolin. Best of all, red wine will not stain lanolin-rich wool.

We've endeavoured to list good dealers, but you'll be taking your chances in Dubai if you're looking for an investment piece. However, if you just want a gorgeous pattern that will look great in your living room, pack a few fabric swatches from your sofa and curtains, and go for it. Patterns range from simple four-colour tribal designs in wool to wildly ornate, lustrous, multicoloured silk carpets that shimmer under the light. Look through books before you leave home to get a sense of what you like. Once in the stores, plan to linger a long time with dealers, slowly sipping tea while they unfurl dozens of carpets. The process is great fun. Just don't get too enthusiastic or the dealer won't bargain as readily.

If you're serious about becoming a collector, hold off. Read Emmett Eiland's book; Google 'DOBAG', a Turkish-rug-making cultural-survival project; and check out www.yayla.com for other reliable background info. Follow links to nonprofit organisations (such as DOBAG) that not only help reconstruct rug-making cultures threatened by modernisation, but also help to educate, house and feed the people of these cultures, giving them a voice in an age of industrial domination. And you'll get a fantastic carpet to boot.

Topshop's diverse selection runs from denim and jumpers to inexpensive jazzy accessories, such as handbags and colourful earrings. Also in Deira City Centre, Ibn Battuta Shopping Mall and Wafi Mall.

CAMEL COMPANY SOUVENIRS

Map p218 (Souq Madinat Jumeirah, Al-Sufouh Rd, Al-Sufouh 2; ⌚10am-11pm) If you can slap a camel on it, Camel Company has it. This hands-down best spot for camel souvenirs carries plush stuffed camels that sing when you squeeze them, camels in Hawaiian shirts, on T-shirts, coffee cups, mouse-pads, notebooks, greeting cards and fridge magnets.

MERCATO MALL SHOPPING MALL

Map p218 (www.mercatoshoppingmall.com; Jumeirah Rd, Jumeirah 1; ⌚10am-10pm) One of the most attractive malls in Dubai, Mercato blends the grandeur of a European train station with the playfulness of an Italian palazzo. Think soaring murals and an arched glass ceiling. It's fun to wander among the brick colonnades, and the compact size makes shopping here less overwhelming than at other malls. There are a few stylish boutiques like Fleurt, a small Topshop, a Virgin Megastore, and some interesting carpet and curio shops.

SOUQ MADINAT JUMEIRAH SHOPPING CENTRE

Map p218 (Madinat Jumeirah, Al-Sufouh 2; ⌚10am-11pm) More a themed shopping mall than a traditional Arabian market, the souq is a bit of a tourist trap, with prices that are considerably higher than they are in real souqs. Still, it's an attractive spot for a wander and worth visiting if only to see how the enormous Madinat Jumeirah complex fits together. Outside, *abras* float by on man-made canals, and dozens of al fresco bars and restaurants overlook the scene. The floor plan is intentionally confusing: officials say that it's meant to mimic a real souq but others think it's to keep you trapped and lure you into emptying your wallet.

CAMEL CRAZY

Our favourite camel gifts:

- Stuffed camels that play Arabic music when cuddled
- Camelspotting CD – cool Middle Eastern music
- Sabine Moser's Camel-O-Shy children's books
- Intricate camel-patterned cushion covers

LATA'S SOUVENIRS

Map p218 (Souq Madinat Jumeirah, Al-Sufouh Rd, Al-Sufouh 2; ⌚10am-11pm) This is our favourite one-stop shop for Arabian and Middle Eastern souvenirs, such as Moroccan lamps, brass coffee tables, *khanjars* (see the boxed text, p103) and silver prayer holders. It also stocks some fabulous silver jewellery, and some not-so-fabulous costume pieces. Tell the staff what you're after, and they'll steer you right to it.

SPORTS & ACTIVITIES

WILD WADI WATERPARK WATERPARK

Map p218 (www.wildwadi.com; Jumeirah Rd, Umm Suqeim 3; admission over/under 110cm Dh205/165; ⌚10am-6pm Nov-Feb, 10am-7pm Mar-May & Sep-Oct, 10am-8pm Jun-Aug; 👪) When the kids grow weary of the beach and hotel pool, you'll score big-time by bringing them to Wild Wadi. More than a dozen ingeniously interconnected rides follow a vague theme about an Arabian adventurer named Juha and his friend Sinbad the sailor, who get shipwrecked together. There are plenty of gentle rides for tots, plus a big-wave pool, a white-water rapids 'river' and a 33m-high Jumeirah Sceirah slide that drops you at a speed of 80km/h (hold on to your trunks, guys!). Thrill-seekers can also test their bodyboarding mettle on Wipeout, a permanent wave. Children must be at least 110cm tall for some of the scarier rides. Check the website for discounts. From April to October Wild Wadi is open for women and children only on Thursday evenings (over/under 110cm Dh165/135; open 8pm to midnight April, May, September and October, and 9pm to 1am June to August).

AL BOOM DIVING DIVING

Map p218 (www.alboomdiving.com; cnr Al-Wasl Rd & 33 St, Jumeirah 1; bubblemaker course Dh275; 👪) Al Boom is the largest dive operation in the United Arab Emirates (UAE) and leads daily guided dive trips off Dubai and to the East Coast and the Musandam Peninsula. The experienced staff offer the gamut of courses, from Discover Scuba Diving to Instructor

LOCAL KNOWLEDGE

KHANJARS

Visit the Al-Ain camel market (p129) or the bullfights at Fujairah (p131) and you'll see old Emirati men wearing *khanjars* (traditional curved daggers) over their *dishdashas* (men's shirt-dresses). Traditionally, *khanjar* handles were made from rhino horn; today, they are often made of wood. Regular *khanjar*s have two rings where the belt is attached, and their scabbards are decorated with thin silver wire. The intricacy of the wire-thread pattern and its workmanship determine value. Sayidi *khanjar*s have five rings and are often covered entirely in silver sheet, with little or no wire, and their quality is assessed by weight and craftsmanship. A *khanjar* ought to feel heavy when you pick it up. Don't believe anyone who tells you a specific *khanjar* is 'very old' – few will be more than 30 to 40 years old. If you're in the market for one, there's an especially good selection at two Jumeirah based stores: Lata's (p102) and Showcase Antiques, Art & Frames (p100).

level. They also offer PADI Bubblemaker courses for children from the age of eight (provided they can swim). Youngsters can then advance to PADI Seal Team or Master Seal Team programs where they learn basic techniques including environmental awareness. When they reach 12 years old, children can go on open-water dives.

PAVILION DIVE CENTRE DIVING

Map p218 (www.thepaviliondivecentre.com; Jumeirah Beach Hotel, Jumeirah Rd, Umm Suqeim 3; beginner's dive Dh325, Bubblemaker Dh275; 👪) Pavilion runs the entire program of classes including diving for beginners and those necessary for PADI certification; they also rent equipment to experienced divers, lead two-dive trips off the Musandam Peninsula and organise bubblemaker classes for children from the age of eight.

DUBAI ROAD RUNNERS RUNNING

Map p218 (www.dubai-road-runners.com; Al-Safa Park, Jumeirah; per adult Dh5; ⏲6.30pm Sat; 👪) The club welcomes runners of all ages and abilities to run one or two laps of the park (3.4km per lap). Runners predict how long it will take them to run the course; the one closest wins a prize. It's fun and communal. Just show up in the car park of Gate 4 (off 55 St). There are 10km runs on Fridays; check the website for details. It's good for older, active teens, as well.

SKILLZ GYM

Map p218 (☎050-556 1751; www.skillz.ae; Madinat Jumeirah, Al-Sufouh Rd, Umm Suqeim 3; day pass Dh75; ⏲6am-10.30pm; 👪) This kiddie-gym has a good range of equipment and also includes access to the adjacent Quay Health Club's rock-climbing wall. Children aged from seven to 17 are eligible.

SENSASIA URBAN SPA SPA

Map p218 (☎04-349 8850; www.sensasiaspas.com; Village Mall, Jumeirah Rd, Jumeirah 1; ⏲10am-10pm) Detox treatments, facials and massage from Bali, Japan and Thailand are the specialities at this women's indie day spa done in sensuous Far East–meets–Middle East style. The menu includes such highly original options as warm cocoa-butter stone therapy, chocolate body buff, fennel colon cleanse (!) and pro-collagen quartz lift. For the ultimate indulgence, become 'Queen for a Day' (Dh1500).

TALISE SPA

Map p218 (☎04-366 6818; www.madinatjumeirah.com/spa; Madinat Jumeirah, Al-Sufouh Rd, Umm Suqeim 3; ⏲9am-10pm) Arrive by *abra* at this Arabian-themed spa, which has 28 gorgeous free-standing temple-like treatment rooms complete with altars laden with quartz crystal – they're like the inside of a genie's bottle. The only problem is, once your treatment is over, you can't enjoy the sumptuous surroundings because you're hustled out the door to make room for the next appointment. Still, the treatments are top-notch – a blend of Eastern and Western, from Ayurvedic cupping to Swedish massage – and convenient if you're staying at the Madinat. There's another branch in Jumeirah Emirates Towers (p140).

DUBAI INTERNATIONAL ART CENTRE ART COURSE

Map p218 (☎04-344 4398; www.artdubai.com; Villa 27, Street 75B, near Mercato Mall, Jumeirah Rd, Jumeirah 1) Offers a plethora of art-related courses, but it's the Arabic calligraphy lessons that are most appealing. Classes cost Dh190 per three-hour session.

New Dubai

Neighbourhood Top Five

❶ Strolling along **The Walk at JBR** (p106) provides a rare opportunity in this city to stretch your legs in the open air. This attractive pedestrian walkway has a Mediterranean-holiday feel with its cosmopolitan restaurants, cafes and boutiques.

❷ Skiing at **Ski Dubai** (p113) is a real novelty and a great way to cool off.

❸ Taking a monorail trip to the fascinating attractions of **Atlantis** (p106) at the Palm Jumeirah.

❹ Enjoying a waterfront lunch and gorgeous views at one of the restaurants at **Dubai Marina** (p107).

❺ Indulging in some of Dubai's best shopping, entertainment and restaurants at the **Mall of the Emirates** (p106).

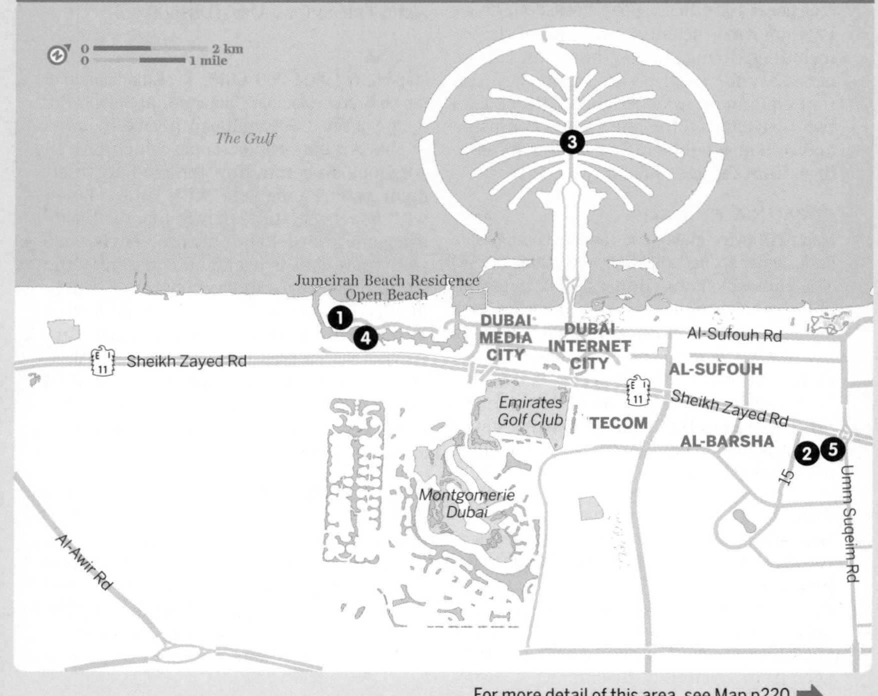

For more detail of this area, see Map p220

Explore New Dubai

New Dubai is well named and most dramatically reflects the city's ability to reinvent itself, creating artificial islands out at sea and constructing a lofty thicket of skyscrapers in the middle of the desert. Although the best view of the Palm Jumeirah is from above (from a plane or Google Earth!), it's worth hopping on the monorail to the major landmark, the Atlantis luxury resort, with its unabashed over-the-top decor, superb nightlife and elaborate family-friendly aqua attractions.

Dubai Marina has some fine restaurants and bars as well. Try and grab a waterfront table at dusk to enjoy an illuminated skyscraper landscape, or take a morning boat ride from the marina and head to Marina Mall, a mini mall that packs a serious retail punch. You can stride out at The Walk at JBR or the waterfront Marina Walk, which both have plenty of places to stop for refreshments and some suitably impressive, if neck-craning, views.

As you travel south of Jumeirah, remember that there was nothing here except a few hotels fronting a pristine beach only a few years ago. Then the construction boom arrived with a vengeance, giving birth to hundreds of apartment buildings, office towers and even more hotels. There's no sightseeing in the traditional sense here, and much of the architecture is... well... uninspired, but the plethora of upmarket restaurants, bars and clubs, plus the lovely beach, will probably bring you here at some point in your trip.

New Dubai also covers the inland neighbourhood of Al-Barsha, which is bisected by the remaining stretch of Sheikh Zayed Rd linking the Mall of the Emirates with Jebel Ali via the Ibn Battuta Mall; both shopping malls are well worth a visit.

Local Life

- **Barasti time!** Barasti (p111) is the local expats' favourite place to party. It's loud, welcoming and refreshingly informal.
- **Sheesha** Get puffing on a *sheesha* pipe at one of the bars or cafes on Marina Walk.
- **Red-carpet viewing** Splash out on an Emirati favourite: the Gold Class screening room at the Vox Mall of the Emirates cinema (p112).

Getting There & Away

- **Metro** Dubai metro's Red Line stops include Mall of the Emirates, Dubai Marina and Ibn Battuta shopping mall. For the Mall of the Emirates, hop on the F09 feeder bus at the metro station.

Lonely Planet's Top Tip

If you are visiting Dubai just after the two big shopping festivals (either at the end of August or March), then you may well find that there are still some seriously slashed prices in the shops, particularly at the Mall of the Emirates. The sales racks will probably be concealed at the back of the shop, so do ask – it's well worth it as you could save up to 80% on the price tag.

Best Places to Eat

- Rhodes Mezzanine (p107)
- Eauzone (p107)
- Indego (p107)

For reviews, see p107

Best Places to Drink

- Rooftop Bar (p109)
- BiCE Sky Bar (p110)
- Buddha Bar (p111)

For reviews, see p109

Best Views

- Bar 44 (p111)
- Jumeirah Beach Residence Open Beach (p106)
- Dubai Marina (p106)

SIGHTS

THE WALK AT JBR — OUTDOORS

Map p220 (Dubai Marina; most outlets 10am-10pm Sat-Thu, 3.30-10pm Fri;) Located in front of the Jumeirah Beach Residence, the city's first outdoor shopping and dining promenade was built in 2008 to meet the needs of the 20,000 people living in the Jumeirah Beach Residence development. But right from the start, The Walk's attractive mix of more than 300 largely family-friendly restaurants, cafes, shops, supermarkets and boutiques has also drawn scores of tourists and residents from other neighbourhoods. They come to stroll down the 1.7km Walk, watch the world on parade from a pavement cafe or to browse for knick-knacks at the Covent Garden Market (p113). On Thursday and Friday nights, traffic slows to a crawl, letting you get a good look at all those shiny Ferraris, Maseratis and other fancy cars rumbling along here. If you fancy dipping your toes in the ocean, head to the Jumeirah Beach Residence Open Beach, fronting the Hilton Dubai Jumeirah, with its views of the Palm Jumeirah.

MALL OF THE EMIRATES — SHOPPING MALL

Map p220 (www.malloftheemirates.com; Sheikh Zayed Rd, Interchange No 4, Al-Barsha; 10am-10pm Sun-Wed, 10am-midnight Thu-Sat) Dubai's most popular mall (and the second biggest after Dubai Mall) sprawls with acres of polished white marble. The curiosity of Ski Dubai (p113) is a major draw, as are the remarkably good food court and comfortable multiplex with its Gold Class screening room. The downside is the relatively narrow walkways and the lack of daylight, making it feel a tad claustrophobic at peak periods.

USEFUL MAPS

The free *Dubai at a Glance* map is available from the Department of Tourism & Commerce Marketing (DTCM) welcome desks (including the airport) and hotel concierges. Bookshops, petrol stations, supermarkets and hotel shops also stock maps. The most accurate maps are published by Explorer; its *Dubai Mini Map* (Dh18) provides a large fold-out overview map with detailed maps of key areas. For more detail, invest in the *Dubai Map* (Dh45) or the comprehensive *Dubai Street Atlas* (Dh145).

IBN BATTUTA MALL — SHOPPING MALL

Map p220 (www.ibnbattutamall.com; Sheikh Zayed Rd; 10am-10pm Sun-Wed, 10am-midnight Thu-Sat) The shopping here is only so-so, but this mall is still well worth a visit for its stunning architecture and design, which traces the way stations of 14th-century Arab scholar and traveller, Ibn Battuta. It's divided into six sections, each reflecting a region he visited, including Tunisia, Andalucía and Egypt. The most stunning is the Persian Court, crowned by a beautiful handpainted dome. The centrepiece of the China Court is a full-size Chinese junk, while in the India Court you can pose with an 8m-high elephant. Surprisingly, there's nothing kitsch or 'Disney' about this place – the craftsmanship and attention to detail are simply stunning. There's also an exhibit about Ibn Battuta and his accomplishments. The Mall is situated between Interchange numbers 5 and 6.

LOST CHAMBERS — AQUARIUM

Map p220 (www.atlantisthepalm.com; Atlantis – The Palm, Palm Jumeirah; adult/child under 12yr Dh100/70, ray feeding Dh175, tour Dh75, combo ticket incl Aquaventure adult/child Dh250/200; 10am-10pm;) This fantastic labyrinth of underwater halls, passageways and fish-tanks recreates the legend of the lost city of Atlantis. Some 65,000 exotic marine creatures inhabit 20 aquariums, where rays flutter and jellyfish dance, moray eels lurk, and pretty-but-poisonous lionfish float. The centrepiece is the 11-million-litre Ambassador Lagoon. You can feed the rays or go on a guided tour, but if you choose to do none of the above, at least wander to the entrance where you can see one of the largest aquariums for free.

DUBAI FERRY — BOAT TOUR

Map p220 (Water Transport Station, Marina Mall, Dubai Marina; ticket Dh75; 11am-9pm) This one-hour boat trip departs at 11am, 5pm, 7pm and 9pm from Marina Mall and takes in several of the city's major sights, including Jumeirah Beach Park and Heritage Village. Tickets can be bought on board. The ferry leaves from one of the most scenic parts of Dubai Marina so don't worry if you get here early as you can enjoy the views of the water flanked by a show-stopping selection of shimmering towers.

PALM JUMEIRAH: PITFALLS IN PARADISE

Even in a city known for its outlandish megaprojects, the Palm Jumeirah stands out: an artificial island in the shape of a palm tree made from 1 billion cubic metres of dredged sand and stone. Built to increase Dubai's beachfront, it consists of a 2km trunk and 16-frond crown, which are kept in place by an 11km-long crescent-shaped breakwater. An elevated driverless monorail whisks passengers from the Gateway Towers station at the bottom of the trunk to the Atlantis – The Palm Hotel. Eventually, it may be linked to the Dubai metro's Red Line.

'May' seems to be the operative word when it comes to the Palm Jumeirah. When construction began in 2001, developers envisioned the island to be a mix of five-star hotels, luxurious beachfront villas, high-rise apartment buildings, marinas and malls. But it soon became clear that not all was going according to plan. The completion date kept getting pushed back, construction density was higher and building quality lower than advertised. After innumerable delays, at least one more hotel has opened: One&Only The Palm (p143). However, others (including the Trump International Hotel & Tower) have been officially cancelled (as of February 2011). The QE2, which was purchased by developers for use as a floating hotel, will now relocate to Cape Town. Apparently, the amount of asbestos that was used in the original building of the luxury liner was potentially hazardous and a major factor in this decision.

The environmental impact of the Palm Jumeirah has been significant. Dredging had an adverse effect on local marine life and the breakwater inhibited tidal movement, leading to stagnant water, excessive algae growth and smelly beaches. On a more positive note, the problem has since been somewhat alleviated by cutting gaps into the breakwater. Furthermore, well-publicised *New York Times* reports in 2009 stating that the Palm was sinking by a clip of 5mm per year, have been categorically refuted by developers Nakheel who say that there have been no reports of any structural problems on any of the buildings.

EATING

The city's sprawling beach resorts, with their many top-end restaurants, happening bars and popular nightclubs, dominate New Dubai. If you're not staying at a resort, spend an evening at one. They are far from the chaos of inner Dubai, and you won't have to hail a taxi until it's time to go home. This section also includes several restaurants in the Mall of the Emirates.

TOP CHOICE RHODES MEZZANINE — MODERN BRITISH $$$

Map p220 (☎04-317 6000; Grosvenor House, Al-Sufouh Rd, Dubai Marina; mains Dh180-240; ⏰7.30pm-11.30pm Mon-Sat) Celebrity chef Gary Rhodes is famous for bringing British cuisine into the 21st century and has a Michelin star to prove it. Here, the emphasis is squarely on quality ingredients prepared in fresh, surprising ways. There's fish on the menu but it's meat lovers who will discover culinary nirvana in the finest fillet steak, rack of lamb or slow-roasted pork belly. In August 2010 Rhodes opened his second restaurant, a dedicated steakhouse: **Rhodes Twenty 10** (Map p220; Le Royal Meridien Beach Resort & Spa; cnr Murjan Ave & Dhow St, off Al-Sufouh Rd, Al-Sufouh, Dubai Marina). Reservations are essential for both restaurants.

EAUZONE — FUSION $$$

Map p220 (☎04-399 9999; Arabian Court, One&Only Royal Mirage, Al-Sufouh Rd, Al-Sufouh; mains Dh115-225) This jewel of a restaurant is an inspired port of call drawing friends, romancing couples and fashionable families. The poolside setting is sublime, with decks jutting out over illuminated blue water like little islands, while the menu is a winning fusion of European cooking techniques and Pacific Rim flavours. This is smart cooking; you won't be disappointed. Reservations essential.

INDEGO — INDIAN $$$

Map p220 (☎04-317 6000; Grosvenor House, Al-Sufouh Rd, Dubai Marina; mains Dh110-240; ⏰7.30pm-midnight Sun-Fri, to 1am Thu) Michelin-starred Vineet Bhatia is the consulting chef at this gracious Indian restaurant with an intimate dining room, lorded over by big brass Natraj sculptures. Recommended dishes include the house-smoked tandoori salmon, wild mushroom biryani and the chocolate samosas. Note that, unlike most Indian cooking, plates here are delicately composed and not designed for sharing. Reservations essential.

TIFFINBITES INDIAN $$

Map p220 (The Walk at JBR, Dubai Marina; mains Dh30-60, tiffins Dh49) Despite the name, a tiffin is considerably more satisfying than a mere bite; it is an entire meal comprising three separate bowls containing a curry, a vegetable dish and rice. Choices include butter chicken, *palak paneer* (with cheese), *chana masala* (with chickpeas) and lamb *rogan*. This place pushes the 'we serve real Indian food' tagline and it seems spot on. Prices are fair and the quantities generous. The decor? Best described as a cross between a Bollywood set and an ice cream parlour, but it somehow works. There is also terrace seating.

MAYA MEXICAN $$$

Map p220 (04-316 5550; www.richardsandoval.com; Le Royal Meridien Beach Resort & Spa, cnr Murjan Ave & Dhow St, off Al-Sufouh Rd, Al-Sufouh, Dubai Marina; mains Dh110-235; 7.30pm-midnight Mon-Sat) Richard Sandoval, the man who introduced modern Mexican food to America, is behind the menu at this sophisticated restaurant where you'll be treated to a piñata of flavours. Start out with creamy guacamole, prepared tableside of course, before moving on to such authentic mains as *mole poblano,* salmon azteca or finger-lickin' *costillas ahumadas* (smokey short ribs, that is). The rooftop bar is a delight, as well. Sandoval's second Dubai venture, **Toro Toro** (Map p220; Grosvenor House, Al-Sufouh Rd, Dubai Marina), opened in late 2011 with a similarly enticing menu. Reservations essential.

NINA INDIAN $$

Map p220 (04-399 9999; Arabian Court, One&Only Royal Mirage, Al-Sufouh Rd, Al-Sufouh; mains Dh60-145; 7-11.30pm Mon-Sat) Follow the locals to this lush den where the floor-to-ceiling purple fabric, red-orange light and beaded curtains set a seductive backdrop for the dynamic cooking on offer. The chef combines Indian with a touch of Thai and tempers it with European techniques. The results will perk up even the most passive proboscis: rich spices means flavours develop slowly on the palate with an elegant complexity that demands savouring. Choose the chef's selection of starters and curries for a sense of his broad repertoire. Reservations essential.

BUDDHA BAR ASIAN $$$

Map p220 (04-317 6000; Grosvenor House, Al-Sufouh Rd, Dubai Marina; mains Dh155-295; 8pm-2am Sat-Wed, 8pm-3am Thu & Fri) At last a restaurant that knows the power of good lighting. So what if the pounding music requires you to shout over the table? You're in the shadow of a giant Buddha, rubbing shoulders with Dubai's beautiful crowd, and you look fabulous in that new outfit. Oh, the food? It (nearly) measures up to the room – a mishmash of Thai and Japanese with a dash of Chinese. But really, who cares – unless you forgot to bring your platinum card, that is. Make reservations several days ahead, even during the week.

BICE ITALIAN $$$

Map p220 (04-399 1111; Hilton Dubai Jumeirah, The Walk at JBR, Dubai Marina; pastas Dh80-210, pizzas Dh70-90, mains Dh150-220; noon-3pm & 7pm-midnight;) With a reputation for being one of the best Italian restaurants in town, BiCE's elegant, continental dining room is often fully packed, so reservations are essential. Head chef Cosimo continues to add his creative touch to traditional dishes by using just a few top-quality ingredients and letting them shine. Beef carpaccio, veal Milanese, house-made pasta, wild-mushroom risotto, linguini with seafood... There are few real surprises on the menu, but no one is complaining – particularly about the tiramisu, reputed to be the best in town.

SPLENDIDO ITALIAN $$$

Map p220 (04-399 4000; Ritz-Carlton Hotel, The Walk at JBR, Dubai Marina; pastas Dh80-120, mains Dh140-220) Tall palms sway in the breeze around the outdoor patio at the Ritz-Carlton's northern Italian restaurant, creating the perfect atmosphere for romantics. It's also not as formal as you'd expect, given the setting and pricing. In fact, the cooking is more upmarket trattoria style; it's earthy and rich as in the *ravioli alle noci* (walnut-and-mascarpone ravioli) and *agnello arrosto* (pan-roasted lamb loin). Reservations essential.

AQUARA SEAFOOD $$$

Map p220 (04-362 7900; Dubai Marina Yacht Club, Marina Walk, Dubai Marina; mains Dh100-190; 7.30pm-10.30pm Sat-Thu, noon-3pm Fri)

The views of fancy yachts and a forest of sleek high-rises impress almost as much as the Asian-infused fare at this chic seafood shrine that's always packed to the gills thanks to dock-fresh ingredients and flawlessly crafted plates. The Friday brunch is hugely popular and, again, concentrates on seafood. Reservations essential.

MAZINA BUFFET **$$$**

Map p220 (☎04-436 7777; The Address Dubai Marina, Dubai Marina; buffets with alcohol Dh250, breakfast buffet Dh150, family buffet Dh195; ⏰6.30am-10.30am, noon-3pm & 6.30-11pm; 👪) Like Las Vegas, Dubai is buffet city, so it's hard to stand out from the pack. But Mazina does get a few things right: the sushi, for instance, and the Thai red and green curries. The clincher, though, is what's called the Teppanyaki Ice Cream station, where premium ice cream gets mixed up with your choice of ingredients: everything from nuts to M&Ms and gummi bears. Friday is for the ladies-who-breakfast with a special buffet, while Saturday is family brunch with face painting and other kiddie-geared distractions. Reservations recommended.

AL-KHAIMA MIDDLE EASTERN **$$**

Map p220 (☎04-316 5550; Le Royal Meridien Beach Resort & Spa, cnr Murjan Ave & Dhow St, off Al-Sufouh Rd, Al-Sufouh, Dubai Marina; mains Dh85-200; ⏰7pm-midnight) In the cooler months there are few places more romantic than the *majlis*-style tents in the garden of the relaxed Meridien resort. Classic mezze such as *baba ghanooj,* hummus and *fattoosh* are orchestrated into culinary symphonies, and the enormous platters of charcoal-grilled kebabs are just as delicious. Wind down the evening pasha-style while languidly puffing on the *sheesha*. Reservations recommended.

TAGINE MOROCCAN **$$**

Map p220 (☎04-399 9999; The Palace, One&Only Royal Mirage, Al-Sufouh Rd, Al-Sufouh; mains Dh75-170; ⏰7pm-11.30pm Tue-Sun; 🍷) Get cosy between throw pillows at a low-slung table in the dim dining room, then take your tastebuds on a magic-carpet ride while tapping your toes to the live Moroccan band. Fez-capped waiters serve big platters of tagine and couscous with all the extras and a vegetarian choice. This is the real deal. Book ahead and request a table near the band.

TRIBES AFRICAN **$$**

Map p220 (Mall of the Emirates, Al-Barsha; mains Dh40-60; 👪) At last, a restaurant in a mall with muted lighting. All the better for appreciating the bush decor with its shields, spears and faux fur throws. The food is generally meaty plus some alternatives, including Mozambique prawns and Ugandan fish croquettes. There are steaks, beef ribs, curries and various pies, as well as nine styles of burgers, including spicy salmon. Tribal drumming is a regular floor show that contributes to the *Out of Africa* experience.

FRANKIE'S ITALIAN BAR & GRILL ITALIAN **$$**

Map p220 (☎04-396 7222; Oasis Beach Tower, The Walk at JBR, Dubai Marina; pasta Dh80-130, pizza Dh45-60) Look for the neon-lit movie-style sign with super-chef Marco Pierre White and horse-racing legend Frankie Dettori as the star billing. Considering the celeb connections, this Italian bar and grill is comfortingly down-to-earth with its cosy russet tones, parquet flooring and nightly easy-listening pianist. There is nothing nouveau about the huge portions either with gnocchi, tagliatelle and lasagne dishes and an exceptional spinach and ricotta ravioli on a mushroom cheese fondue. The traditional oven churns out decent pizzas, as well. Reservations recommended.

SEZZAM INTERNATIONAL **$$**

Map p220 (Mall of the Emirates, Al-Barsha; mains Dh50-70; 👪) A great choice for fussy families or a diverse group of friends, the giant food court here has several stations that dish up everything from freshly made sushi to burgers, pasta and pizza (including a saucy little choice topped with chicken tikka). A great venue for Friday brunch (see the boxed text, p110) and also notable for its setting overlooking the adjacent Ski Dubai winter wonderland.

DRINKING & NIGHTLIFE

TOP CHOICE ROOFTOP BAR COCKTAIL BAR

Map p220 (Arabian Court, One&Only Royal Mirage, Al-Sufouh Rd, Al-Sufouh; ⏰5pm-1am) The fabric-draped nooks, cushioned banquettes, Moroccan lanterns and Oriental carpets make this candlelit rooftop bar one of Dubai's most sublime spots. Come at

LET'S DO BRUNCH...

The working week in Dubai runs from Sunday to Thursday, which means (nearly) everyone is off on Friday. An expat institution, Friday brunch is a major element of the Dubai social scene – particularly among bacchanalian revellers – and every hotel-restaurant in town sets up an all-you-can-eat buffet with an option for unlimited champagne or wine. Some smaller, independent restaurants also serve brunch, but without alcohol, making them popular with local families. Here's our shortlist for top brunches in town.

Al-Qasr (Map p218; ☎04-366 6730; Al-Qasr, Madinat Jumeirah; without/with drinks Dh425/525; ⏰12.30-4pm Fri) Come here hungry to enjoy this unbelievable cornucopia of delectables – meats, sushi, seafood, foie gras, beautiful salads, mezze, all sorts of hot dishes, etc. It's one of the more expensive brunch feasts in town but the quality and range justifies the price tag.

Aquara (p108; with soft/house/premium drinks Dh220/290/350; ⏰12.30-3.30pm Fri) Seafood lovers rejoice over this fishy bonanza of sushi, sashimi, crabs, oysters, clams and cooked-to-order lobster, all artistically presented. Don't forget to hit the dessert room. This brunch is extremely good value.

Iranian Club (Map p214; ☎04-336 7700; Oud Metha Rd; brunches Dh79; ⏰1-4pm Fri) Feast at this Persian-cuisine showcase owned by the Iranian government. Start by rolling cheese and mint in hot bread, then sample soups and marinated salads, followed by tender kebabs and stews from an enormous buffet. Pace yourself. Women must wear headscarves, men long trousers, and there's no alcohol, but it's worth altering your habits for a culturally rich afternoon.

Sezzam (p109; without alcohol Dh150; ⏰12.30-3pm Fri; 👪) This giant food court has superb views of the ski slopes, children's entertainment, including a bouncy castle, and several food stations with plenty of choice.

Spectrum on One (p85; with soft/house/premium drinks Dh295/395/550; ⏰noon-3pm Fri) This top brunch pick features free-flowing champagne, eight buffets with six different cuisines and an entire room full of port and cheeses.

Spice Island (p55; with soft/house/premium drinks Dh159/209/279; ⏰noon-3pm Fri; 👪) The oldest brunch buffet in town, Spice Island offers seven cuisines and six live cooking stations. Great value and especially popular with families.

Splendido (p108; with alcohol Dh375; ⏰12.30-3pm Fri) This Friday champagne brunch has a constant league of fans with its ample choice, including a sushi bar, Middle Eastern dishes and lavish cheese board, plus desserts.

Thai Kitchen (p56; with soft drinks/beer & wine Dh195/245; ⏰noon-4pm Fri) Sample an enormous repertoire of Thai cooking, served tapas-style. Mellow scene, good for nondrinkers.

Yalumba (Map p208; ☎04-217 0000; Le Meridien Dubai, Airport Rd; champagne brunches Dh499; ⏰12.30-3.30pm Fri) One of the few to offer an à la carte menu so you won't have to schlep plates. Great roasts. Go the whole hog with vintage Bollinger champagne. The raucous atmosphere gives it an edge with party people.

sunset to watch the sky change colour – but not earlier; the bar doesn't pick up until later. There's a good menu of mezze in case you're feeling peckish. Views of the Palm Jumeirah, and the romantic vibe, make this an ideal spot for couples.

BICE SKY BAR — BAR

Map p220 (Hilton Dubai Jumeirah, The Walk at JBR, Dubai Marina; ⏰6.15pm-2.30am) It may not be as much on the hipster radar as Neos or Bar 44 but, when it comes to glorious views, this quiet, chic lounge on the 10th floor of the beachfront Hilton can definitely compete. In this case, it's the sparkling Palm Jumeirah and glistening Gulf waters that will make you want to order that second cocktail. Soft piano music and comfy leather chairs help create a relaxed, romantic mood.

BUDDHA BAR
BAR

Map p220 (☎04-399 8888; Grosvenor House, Al-Sufouh Rd, Dubai Marina; ⏰8pm-2am Sat-Wed, 8pm-3am Thu & Fri) If there are celebs in town, they'll show up at Buddha Bar, where the dramatic Asian-inspired interiors are decked out with gorgeous chandeliers, a wall of reflective sheer glass, and an enormous Buddha lording over the heathens. The bartenders put on quite a show with their impressive shakes. Arrive early or prepare to queue; otherwise book dinner for guaranteed admission.

1897
COCKTAIL BAR

Map p220 (Kempinski Hotel, Mall of the Emirates, Al-Barsha; ⏰2pm-2am) Channel your inner Cary Grant and head to the bar at this grown-up, moodily lit drinks' parlour at the Kempinksi. Don't bother if you're a beer lover – you'd be wasting the bar staff's considerable talents. Decorated in plush purple and polished wood, this place lures chatty sophisticates; ladies get two free bubbly drinks on Wednesdays.

SAMUVAR
CAFE

Map p220 (Iris Blue Tower, Dubai Marina; ⏰9am-midnight) Wedged happily between Grosvenor House and the Dusit Hotel, this dedicated smoking tea lounge has comfortable seats sprawled out on the vast terrace by the water with the Manhattan-style skyscape beyond. If you fancy a cuppa along with your smoke, there are 31 different teas, plus fruit juices, coffees and a selection of sweet treats.

BAR 44
BAR

Map p220 (Grosvenor House, Al-Sufouh Rd, Dubai Marina; ⏰6pm-2am) Service is slow, cocktails are wimpy and prices are high, but the views really are worth the trip up to this swanky bar on the 44th floor of the Grosvenor House hotel. Done in a retro-'70s chic, with high-backed tufted-velvet banquettes and buttery-soft leather tub chairs, this is the spot to kick up your (high) heels and take in the sweeping panorama of the marina and Palm Jumeirah. Good backup if Buddha Bar is full.

BLENDS
BAR

Map p220 (Address Dubai Marina Mall, Dubai Marina) The name is very appropriate because Blends indeed folds three distinct libation stations into its 4th-floor space. Channel Ernest Hemingway in the clubby cigar room, complete with leather sofa, dark woods and a coffered ceiling. For date night, the sultry, candlelit champagne bar, with its floor-to-ceiling windows, provides a suitable setting for quiet conversation. And, finally, there's the trendy cocktail lounge. Ladies get free selected drinks here on Tuesday from 8pm to 11pm.

LOCAL KNOWLEDGE

VIP AREAS

Many nightclubs have VIP areas with extras such as private hostess table service, free valet parking, tailor-made menu, private bar, total privacy, fully controllable sound and light system, specially tailored packages, complimentary limo and, generally, the best views in the venue. Expect to pay around Dh3000 for the privilege(s).

LIBRARY BAR
BAR

Map p220 (Ritz-Carlton Hotel, The Walk at JBR, Dubai Marina; ⏰3pm-1.30am) This hushed and classic bar feels like a retreat from Dubai's in-your-face modernity. Polished wood, muted lighting, leather sofas and rich carpets combine to create a timeless colonial-style atmosphere. The bar menu has some interesting nibbles, but this is really more the kind of place to steer your luxury sedan for a post-dinner Glenfiddich or port.

MAYA
COCKTAIL BAR

Map p220 (Le Royal Meridien Beach Resort & Spa, Murjan Ave & Dhow St, Dubai Marina; ⏰6pm-2am Mon-Sat) Arrive an hour before sunset to snag one of the Gulf-view tables on the rooftop bar of this upmarket Mexican restaurant at the Royal Meridien and swill top-shelf tequila-spiked margaritas as the sun slowly slips into the sea. A plate of succulent duck enchiladas sure beats the nachos as the perfect booze accompaniment.

BARASTI
CLUB

Map p220 (Le Meridien Mina Seyahi Beach Resort & Marina, Al-Sufouh Rd, Al-Sufouh; ⏰11am-2am) Seaside Barasti is the locals' favourite (especially expat Brits) for laid-back sundowners. Attracting all ages, this is a casual place. There's no need to dress up – you can head straight here after a day at the beach – but don't come unless you like crowds. At weekends, the place can be crammed with 4000 or more shiny happy people. DJs play indoors, but it's generally better to sit outside within earshot of the sea. There is occasional live music and Monday is ladies' night with one free drink and half-price deals all evening.

NASIMI BEACH CLUB

Map p220 (www.atlantisthepalm.com; Atlantis – The Palm, Palm Jumeirah; ⏲1pm-1am) The Atlantis' spin on Barasti has benefitted from a sophisticated overhaul in 2011 and draws a more upmarket crowd to its fantastic beachside setting. Plop down on a beach bag and chill to soulful house, funk, electro and Chicago house. Friday nights are buzziest, when international DJs hit the decks. Try and catch one of their full-moon parties with circus performers and dancers or their annual Chill Out Festival in April. There's also a daily happy hour from 4pm to 6pm and free bubbly for the gals on Tuesdays from 8pm to 10pm.

N'DULGE CLUB

Map p220 (www.atlantisthepalm.com; Atlantis – The Palm, Palm Jumeirah; ⏲9.30pm-3am) Formerly the Sanctuary and located at the iconic Atlantis resort, this sexy nightclub has three areas, including the N'Dulge Arena with its circular suspended catwalk used to showcase circus performers as well as magicians, mimes, dancers and stilt walkers. There's also an al fresco terrace and a restaurant serving sushi and similar with a community table option. Theme nights, fashion shows and guest DJs are also on offer with an average Dh100 admission, although ladies generally have free entrance before 11pm.

CATWALK CLUB CLUB

Map p220 (Golden Tulip, Sheikh Zayed Rd, Al-Barsha; ⏲9pm-3am) Yes, there really is a catwalk here where you can strut your stuff in between looking lively to the DJs spinning the discs. Space can get tight, but this is a spirited fun option and, if you turn up too early, you can always head to the Locker Room sports bar upstairs for a pint of ale and some big-screen footy.

SHEESHA COURTYARD SHEESHA

Map p220 (One&Only Royal Mirage, Al-Sufouh Rd, Al-Sufouh; ⏲7pm-1am) The Royal Mirage sure gets it right. Reclining on beaded cushions and thick carpets in an Arabian palm courtyard is the ultimate way to enjoy a *sheesha,* along with a drink. Although it would take a connoisseur to appreciate the 20 different flavours on offer, you can't go wrong with the sweet aroma of apple.

ENTERTAINMENT

VOX MALL OF THE EMIRATES CINEMA

Map p220 (www.voxcinemas.com; Mall of the Emirates, Sheikh Zayed Rd, Al-Barsha; tickets Dh30, Gold Class Dh110) Vox would be just another multiplex were it not for its Gold Class screening rooms, where seats are enormous recliners and servers bring you blankets, popcorn in silver bowls and drinks in glass goblets. This is adult movie watching: no one under 18 years old is allowed and everyone actually pays attention to the film. Buy tickets in advance via the website.

DUBAI COMMUNITY THEATRE & ARTS CENTRE LIVE MUSIC

Map p220 (☎04-341 4777; www.ductac.org; 2nd fl, Mall of the Emirates, Sheikh Zayed Rd, Al-Barsha) DUCTAC, as it's known, is a thriving performance venue at the Mall of the Emirates that puts on all sorts of diversions, from classical concerts to Bollywood retrospectives, Arabic folklore to large-scale mural projects. Much support is given to Emirati talent, making this a good place to plug into the local scene. The entrance is in the Orange Car Park, between rows S and T.

PALLADIUM LIVE MUSIC

Map p220 (☎04 367 6520; www.palladiumdubai.com; tickets through www.boxofficeme.com; Dubai Media City, Dubai Marina) Dubai's main performance venue can seat up to 15,000 people and comes with all the high-tech trappings, plus one of the largest stages in the UAE. Recent foot-tapping talent include the Duke Wellington tribute band.

SHOPPING

MALL OF THE EMIRATES SHOPPING MALL

Map p220 (www.malloftheemirates.com; Sheikh Zayed Rd, Interchange No 4, Al-Barsha; ⏲10am-10pm Sun-Wed, 10am-midnight Thu-Sat) The Mall of the Emirates is (another) of Dubai's massive shopping malls with a terrific range of retail options. Along with the usual brands, there's a Harvey Nichols and a big Borders with an awesome selection of

SKI DUBAI

Skiing in the desert? Where else but in Dubai? The city's most incongruous attraction, **Ski Dubai** (Map p220; ☎04-409 4000; www.skidxb.com; Mall of the Emirates, Al-Barsha; Snow Park admission adult/child Dh120/110, Ski Slope per 2hr Dh180/150, all day Dh300/275, lessons per hr from Dh140; ⏲10am-11pm Sun-Wed, 10am-midnight Thu, 9am-midnight Fri, 9am-11pm Sat; 👪) is a faux winter wonderland built right into the gargantuan Mall of the Emirates. It comes complete with ice sculptures, a tiny sledding hill, five ski runs (the longest being 400m) and a Freestyle Zone with jumps and rails. Gulf Arabs especially are fascinated by this snowy display, but they typically restrict themselves to the walk-through Snow Park, passing through a colour-lit igloo filled with carved-ice penguins and dragons, then sledding down a little hill in plastic toboggans. Skiers and boarders are kept separate from the Snow Park and instead whiz down a forking slope – one side for beginners, one for intermediates. The 60m (196ft) vertical drop is an ant hill when compared with a real ski mountain, but if you've never skied or boarded before, it's a good place to learn the basics. Advanced skiers quickly grow weary of the too-short runs (think 30 seconds at a good clip) but generally everybody is pleasantly surprised by the velvety snow. Conditions are ideal: at night, the interior is chilled to -8°C, and snow guns blow feather-light powder. During opening hours it warms to a perfect -1°C. Though weekends are more crowded, Ski Dubai operates a faster-moving secondary lift and a rope tow that significantly shortens the ride uphill, giving you more runs per hour than you can get riding the chair. Pretty much everything is provided, including socks and skis, although gloves and hats are not (for hygiene reasons). Bring your own or buy some in the adjoining ski shop; gloves start at around Dh10, and hats at Dh30. If you bring your own equipment and/or clothing you'll get a 5% discount on each.

travel books (ask nicely and they may show you the banned book list).

IBN BATTUTA MALL — SHOPPING MALL

Map p220 (www.ibnbattutamall.com; Sheikh Zayed Rd, btwn Interchanges No 5 & No 6; ⏲10am-10pm Sun-Wed, 10am-midnight Thu-Sat) The 14th-century Arab scholar Ibn Battuta travelled 120,000km over 30 years. You'll have a better idea of how he felt after trekking from one end of this behemoth mall to the other. It's divided into six sections, each decorated in the style of a country he visited – Andalucía, Tunisia, Egypt, Persia, India and China. Though the shopping is not nearly as special as the decoration, worthwhile stops include Ginger & Lace and the Bauhaus lifestyle store. If you're too exhausted to walk back, hop on the golf-cart shuttle (Dh5).

COVENT GARDEN MARKET — MARKET

Map p220 (www.coventgardenmarket.ae; The Walk at JBR, Rimal Sector; ⏲5pm-midnight Wed & Thu, 10am-9pm Fri & Sat) If you're not into shopping, grab a latte and send the others out to peruse the lacy scarves, fancy necklaces, designer T-shirts and pretty purses at this bustling arts and crafts market. Bring the kids: clowns, bands and balloon-animal makers provide the entertainment. Easy to find, near the entrance to the Hilton Hotel.

MARINA MALL — SHOPPING MALL

Map p220 (Dubai Marina, www.dubaimarinamall.com; ⏲10am-10pm Sun-Wed, 10am-midnight Thu-Sat) It makes a change. A mall with around 160 stores, where you won't get lost quite so readily as you will in the mega-size variety, yet the shops are just as good. Here you can find such great stores as H&M, Reebok, Mango, Boots, Mothercare, Monsoon, Miss Sixty, the Early Learning Centre and the upmarket UK supermarket chain Waitrose, as well as plenty of restaurants and cafes.

GINGER & LACE — FASHION

Map p220 (Ibn Battuta Mall, Sheikh Zayed Rd) Ginger & Lace stocks an eclectic selection of colourful, whimsical fashion by high-spirited New York designers Anna Sui and Betsey Johnson, London-based bag maven Zufi Alexander and Spanish illustrator-turned-fashion designer Jordi Labanda. There's another store in Wafi Mall.

AIZONE — FASHION

Map p220 (Mall of the Emirates, Sheikh Zayed Rd, Al-Barsha) Lose yourself for hours in this

CONCERT & SPORTS VENUES

Several sports stadiums double as crowd-pulling concert venues. One of the largest is **Yas Arena** (www.yasisland.ae) home to Formula One, in Abu Dhabi. Dubai's **Meydan Racecourse** (www.meydan.ae) is another popular venue, along with **The Sevens** (www.dubairugby7s.com), a purpose-built rugby sevens stadium on the Dubai–Al Ain Rd. Check the websites for upcoming concert info and don't hang around if you are planning to attend. Big-name acts such as Paul McCartney, Elton John and Tom Jones have recently appeared at these venues.

enormous Lebanese fashion emporium, with hard-to-find labels and snappy fashions for twirling on the dance floor. Look for the latest from Bibelot, Juicy Couture, Spy and Lotus. Prices are high, but the collection is special.

BAUHAUS FASHION

Map p220 (India Court, Ibn Battuta Mall, Sheikh Zayed Rd) High-energy tunes keep girls and boys flipping fast through Evisu denim, Bulzeye tees and Drifter hoodies at this hip lifestyle boutique specialising in non-mainstream fashion, art and music. The store design was inspired by the revolutionary 1920s Bauhaus design movement and mixes all sorts of materials, from acrylic to wood, leather to metal and bricks.

BOUTIQUE 1 FASHION

Map p220 (The Walk at JBR, Dubai Marina; ⏲10am-11pm) Ground zero for prêt-à-porter straight off the runways of Paris and Milan, Boutique 1 is the pinnacle of Dubai's fashion scene, with designers like Missoni and Yves St Laurent represented. Its gorgeous three-storey store on The Walk stocks not only fashionable frocks but also home accessories, beauty products, furniture and even books.

AMINIAN PERSIAN CARPETS CARPETS

Map p220 (Mall of the Emirates, Sheikh Zayed Rd, Al-Barsha) This trusted rug trader offers great service and stocks a wide selection of classic Persian carpets and colourful tribal kilims. Plan to linger a while: the collection is far more extensive than it first appears.

G-1 ARTS & CRAFTS

Map p220 (The Walk at JBR, Dubai Marina) If you're not too confident behind the camera lens you can pick up a masterful print of Dubai here, as well as highly decorative canvases by well-known Middle Eastern artists such as Syrian Helen Abbas. More straightforward stationery and cards are also available.

TAPE À L'OEIL CHILDREN

Map p220 (Mall of the Emirates, Sheikh Zayed Rd, Al-Barsha) A refreshing alternative to Gap Kids, this French brand carries fun kids' clothes that look like miniature adult wear. Denim features prominently, as do skirts and sweaters that look best on kids who keep their hair combed.

FOREVER 21 CLOTHING

Map p220 (Mall of the Emirates, Sheikh Zayed Rd, Al-Barsha) Cutting in on H&M for affordable style and selection, this is one of Dubai's largest stores, with an extensive range of youthful, affordable fashion and accessories, although most are in teeny teen sizes.

FONO ELECTRONICS

Map p220 (Mall of the Emirates, Sheikh Zayed Rd, Al-Barsha) This is a good place to come for phones, whether you are looking for the bog standard pay-as-you-go variety or the all-out, gem-encrusted bling kind.

THE TOY STORE TOYS

Map p220 (Mall of the Emirates, Sheikh Zayed Rd, Al-Barsha) A Hamleys-style mega toy store with everything you need to entertain the wee ones, ranging from life-size stuffed giraffes to Fisher Price telephones (mobiles, that is). Find it near the entrance to Ski Dubai.

JUMBO ELECTRONICS ELECTRONICS

Map p220 (Mall of the Emirates, Sheikh Zayed Rd, Al-Barsha) The mother of Dubai's electronics stores, this place stocks all the latest computers, cameras, mobile phones, games and gadgets under one giant roof. There are 15 more outlets located across town, including one in Deira City Centre and another in Wafi Mall.

RECTANGLE JAUNE CLOTHING

Map p220 (Mall of the Emirates, Sheikh Zayed Rd, Al-Barsha) A great store for men, with a terrific selection of dress shirts in snappy stripes and bold patterns by a team of fashion-savvy Lebanese designers. There's another branch in Deira City Centre.

SPORTS & ACTIVITIES

AQUAVENTURE

WATERPARK

Map p220 (www.atlantisthepalm.com; Atlantis – The Palm, Palm Jumeirah; over/under 1.2m Dh200/165, combo ticket incl Lost Chambers Dh250/200; ⏲10am-sunset; 👪) Adrenalin rushes are guaranteed at this waterpark at the Atlantis hotel. The centrepiece is the 27.5m-high Ziggurat (great views!), the launch pad for seven slides, including the most wicked of them all: Leap of Faith, a near-vertical plunge into a shark-infested lagoon, albeit protected by a transparent tunnel. There's also more than 2km of nonstop river action with cascades, tidal waves and rapids. Unfortunately, long lines between attractions tend to interrupt your momentum. Little ones can keep cool in an enormous water playground where climbing structures and rope bridges lead to myriad slides. Tickets also include access to a private beach, although the water is quite murky and the sand filled with sharp coral pieces.

DOLPHIN BAY

DOLPHIN PARK

Map p220 (www.atlantisthepalm.com; Atlantis – The Palm, Palm Jumeirah; shallow-/deep-water interaction Dh790/975, incl same day access to Aquaventure & private beach, observer pass Dh300; 👪) Dolphin Bay is the place to make friends with those sociable mammals known for their playfulness and intelligence. Touch, hug or kiss them in a shallow pool or catch a piggyback ride to the deeper waters of the lagoon.

Animal welfare activists believe that human interaction exacerbates the dolphins' stress already caused by captivity, but people sure seem to be thrilled by the experience. Learn more about this contentious subject from the **Whale and Dolphin Conservation Society** (WDCS; www.wdcs.com.org).

ARTHUR MURRAY DANCE SCHOOL

DANCE

Map p220 (☎04-448 6458; www.arthurmurraydubai.com; 201 Reef Tower, Jumeirah Lakes Towers; sample class Dh100; ⏲9am-9pm) This well-known name in the world of dance has exploded onto the scene, especially since the popularity of TV dance contests such as *Strictly Come Dancing*. Instructors teach a wide range of dances, including ballroom, like the Viennese Waltz; Latin, including the Merengue, Samba and Mambo; Country Western (think Texas Two-Step); and speciality dances, including the Nightclub Two-Step to wow them on the dance floor (and the classic Polka, which probably won't). If you are short on time you can enrol for a sample class where you will learn a range of steps from several different dances.

ONE&ONLY SPA

DAY SPA

Map p220 (☎04-399 9999; www.oneandonlyresorts.com; One&Only Royal Mirage, Al-Sufouh Rd, Al-Sufouh; ⏲9.30am-9pm) Do you want to unwind, restore or elevate? These are the magic words at this exclusive spa with a dozen treatment rooms where massages, wraps, scrubs and facials are calibrated to achieve your chosen goal. A Swedish massage is just the way to melt away the strains of the day, although for the most unique experience, sign up for a treatment in the Oriental Hammam (see the boxed text, below).

SOFTTOUCH SPA

DAY SPA

Map p220 (☎04-341 0000; www.kempinski-dubai.com; Kempinski Hotel, Mall of the Emirates,

THE ROYAL TREATMENT

In a city built on facsimiles and gimmicks, the not-to-be-missed Oriental Hammam at the One&Only Spa stands out as the hands-down best re-creation of another country's cultural institution: a Moroccan bathhouse. Moroccan-born attendants walk you into a giant, echoey, steamy marble room lit by stained-glass lanterns, where they wrap you in muslin, bathe you on a marble bench from a running hot-water fountain, then lay you down on an enormous, heated marble cube – head-to-toe with three other men or women (depending on the day) – and scrub your entire body with exfoliating coarse gloves. Next, they bathe you again, then lead you to a steam room where you relax before receiving an invigorating mud body mask and honey facial, a brief massage and your final rinse. Afterwards, you're wrapped in dry muslin and escorted to a meditative relaxation room, where you drift to sleep beneath a blanket and awaken to hot mint tea and dates – just like in Morocco. Pure bliss!

Sheikh Zayed Rd, Al-Barsha) Conveniently located for a post–Ski Dubai rubdown, Softtouch specialises in Ayurvedic oil-drip treatments as well as massages. The sumptuous Asian look – slate floors, Thai-silk walls, orange hanging lamps – is conducive to relaxation. An initial consultation is followed by a tailored treatment performed with you lying down on a special teak table imported from India.

THE PALACE WATER SPORTS WATER SPORTS

Map p220 (☎04-399 9999; www.oneandonlyresorts.com; One&Only Royal Mirage, Al-Sufouh Rd, Al-Sufouh; ⏰10am-7pm) Although these folks operate from an office at the hotel, they are independent and arrange an impressive number of water sports, including waterskiing (Dh140 for 15 minutes), speed boat ride (Dh325 for 30 minutes), kayaking (Dh40 for 30 minutes) and windsurfing (Dh150 for 50 minutes).

FAVOURITE THINGS ACTIVITY CENTRE

Map p220 (www.favouritethings.com; Marina Mall; ⏰9am-9pm) These guys have it all covered. They offer several areas and activities for children, including a jungle gym, art and cooking classes, a sand room and a soft play area for tots. They have puppet shows and story time at weekends and don't forget the parents with a cafe and shop selling all kinds of trendy and practical kiddie-geared wear and products. There is also a dance studio with classes for children and adults, ranging from classical ballet to hip hop.

EMIRATES GOLF CLUB GOLF

Map p220 (☎04-380 1555; www.dubaigolf.com; Interchange No 5, Sheikh Zayed Rd; Majlis/Faldo course Dh995/695) The first grass championship course in the Middle East is home to the **Dubai Desert Classic** (www.dubaidesertclassic.com), a major tournament on the PGA European Tour circuit. There are two 18-hole courses: the Faldo course, designed by Nick Faldo; and the Majlis course, which recently got the nod from US magazine *Golf Digest* as being one of the best courses outside the USA. The nearest Red Line metro stop is Nakheel.

MONTGOMERIE DUBAI GOLF

Map p220 (☎04-390 5600; www.themontgomerie.com; Emirates Hills; course Dh795) Fans of Scottish links will enjoy this world-class course designed by Colin Montgomerie, which has 14 lakes and 81 bunkers. The par-three 13th hole is on an island shaped like the UAE and is purportedly the largest single green in the world: 5400 sq metres, or the size of nine normal greens combined. To reach here, take the Interchange No 5 exit off Sheikh Zayed Rd.

JUMEIRAH GOLF ESTATES GOLF

(☎04-375 9999; www.jumeirahgolfestates.com) Located off Sheikh Zayed Rd, this is Dubai's newest golf club (and residential complex) and is home to the Dubai World Championship Golf Tournament (p45). Take Interchange No 7 in the direction of Abu Dhabi; the club is located at the intersection with Emirates Rd.

Abu Dhabi

Sheikh Zayed bin Sultan al-Nahyan Mosque p119

This fabulous mosque – also known as the Grand Mosque – is a vast building with fairytale domes, lofty minarets and spectacular Islamic detail, including handcrafted panels, richly carved surfaces and massive twinkling chandeliers.

Falcon Hospital p120

Take a flight of fancy to the fascinating (and unusual) Falcon Hospital.

Emirates Palace Hotel p119

Wonder at the sheer opulence and lashings of gold leaf at the extraordinary Emirates Palace Hotel.

Abu Dhabi Heritage Village p119

Watch the craftsmen at the Abu Dhabi Heritage Village with its re-creation of a Bedouin encampment.

Ferrari World Abu Dhabi p119

Scream as loud as you can when riding the fastest rollercoaster in the world at Ferrari World Abu Dhabi.

Explore

The emirate of Abu Dhabi has recently invested heavily in culture, education and environmental innovation. Slowly, almost stealthily, the largest – and wealthiest – emirate is emerging from the shadow of its glamorous northern neighbour. In other words, if you haven't visited for a while, you'll be in for a surprise.

One of the most welcome recent developments is the expansion and extension of the waterfront Corniche, with its white sandy beaches and wide Mediterranean-style promenade. You can rent a sunbed and beach umbrella here; remember, Fridays are busiest.

Like its flashier neighbour, Abu Dhabi also has some futuristic buildings. Don't miss the extraordinary disc-shaped HQ or the Leaning Tower of Pisa–style Gate Tower. And be sure to visit the stunning main mosque, whose snowy white marble domes seem to hover above the city like a mirage. And nearby, on Yas Island, looms the glass grid shell of the spectacular Yas Hotel, which has the city's Formula One racetrack roaring through it.

Abu Dhabi is by far the largest emirate, comprising almost 87% of the country's total area. Looking at the impressive skyline, you may find it hard to imagine that only 50 years ago Abu Dhabi was little more than a fishing village with a fort, a few coral buildings and a smattering of *barasti* huts.

The emirate is reasonably straightforward to navigate as it is planned along a classic American grid system. The Corniche Rd is bookended by the *mina* (port) to the east and the Emirates Palace to the west. The main confusion you will encounter regards streets that, perplexingly, often have multiple names, as well as numbers. Pass the Sat Nav someone...!

LOCAL LIFE

- **Sheesha time** *Sheesha* cafes are spread across the grassy verge next to the Corniche and are great for soaking up some local ambience.
- **Quran reciting** Approaching the Grand Mosque, you pass by the tomb of Sheikh Zayed where attendants recite the Quran 24/7 over the beloved ruler's grave.
- **Fruit & vegetables** Watch the vendors haggle with customers at this colourful fruit and vegetable souq at the port.

Best Places to Eat

- Finz (p121)
- Jones the Grocer (p120)
- Sho Cho (p121)

Best Places to Drink

- Cristal (p122)
- Belgian Café (p122)
- Etoiles (p123)

Best Shopping

- Central Market (p123)
- Marina Mall (p123)
- Abu Dhabi Mall (p123)

Top Tip

Unlike many other mosques, Abu Dhabi's magnificent Grand Mosque allows non-Muslims to visit on their own. However, for a more in-depth experience we recommend that you join one of the free 60- to 90-minute guided tours (in English) that conclude with a Q&A session.

Getting There & Away

Bus Buses to Abu Dhabi leave from Dubai's Al-Ghubaiba station every 40 minutes (single Dh20, return Dh40). The trip takes two hours.

Car Abu Dhabi is approximately 1½ hour's drive from Dubai. Follow the Sheikh Zayed Rd (E11 highway) southwards and follow the signs.

Taxi A private taxi will cost in the range of Dh250, although a shared taxi will reduce the price to around Dh50. **Al-Ghazal** (☎02-444 9300; ghazal@adnh.com) takes advance bookings.

Need to Know

- **Area Code** 02
- **Location** 150km south of Dubai
- **Tourist Office** ☎02-444 0444; www.visitabudhabi.ae, www.abudhabitourism.ae; Al-Salam St

SIGHTS

Abu Dhabi's sights are not neatly sectioned off in one part of town, so be prepared to use a taxi to get around. Alternatively, consider the hop-on, hop-off option of the **Big Bus Company** (tollfree ☎800 244 287; www.bigbustours.com), which takes in most of the iconic sights and is particularly convenient if you are short on time.

TOP CHOICE **SHEIKH ZAYED BIN SULTAN AL-NAHYAN MOSQUE** MOSQUE
(Airport Rd & 5th St; ⌚9am-noon Sat-Thu, tours 10am Sun-Thu) Also known as the Grand Mosque, this snow-white house of worship is Abu Dhabi's stunning landmark, easily visible from afar and impressive inside and out. Conceived by the late Sheikh Zayed, it can accommodate up to 40,000 worshippers in its central courtyard and main prayer hall. The grand-yet-delicate composition of marble, gold, semiprecious stones, crystals and ceramics takes design cues from Morocco, Turkey and even India's Taj Mahal. The main prayer hall features the world's largest Persian carpet, which took 2000 craftsmen two years to complete, while seven gold-plated crystal chandeliers hang majestically from the ceiling. The mosque is 13km south of the centre of Abu Dhabi.

EMIRATES PALACE HOTEL
(☎02-690 9000; www.emiratespalace.com; Corniche Rd West) You don't have to check in to check out this truly luxurious hotel. It is colossal: nearly 400 rooms and suites, 114 domes, a 1.3km private beach, a luxury spa and a lavish use of marble, gold and crystal throughout (including Swarovski crystal chandeliers). Consider indulging in the classic English afternoon tea (including scones and clotted cream, crumpets, traditional fruitcake and raspberry tart) for Dh205 or, at the very least, have a good wander around the lobby with its abundance of gold leaf and the only vending machine in the world that sells solid gold bars.

PEDAL POWER

Cruise along the Corniche via bicycle. **Funride** (Corniche Rd West & Khalid bin Abdel Aziz St), on the seafront, rents out bikes for just Dh30/20 per hour per adult/child.

FREE **ABU DHABI HERITAGE VILLAGE** MUSEUM
(Breakwater; ⌚9am-1pm Sat-Thu, 5-9pm daily) Offers a glimpse of life in the pre-oil days with a re-creation of a souq, a traditional mosque, a Bedouin encampment with goat-hair tents and a typical *barasti* desert house. Watch craftsmen make pots, blow glass, beat brass and weave on traditional looms. Don't miss the small museum here.

FERRARI WORLD ABU DHABI THEME PARK
(www.ferrariworldabudhabi.com; Yas Island; adult/child Dh225/165; 11am-8pm Tue-Sun; 👪) A must-do for Ferrari fans or anyone who fancies a ride on the world's fastest rollercoaster (top speed: 200km/h). Other attractions include

THE CULTURAL CAPITAL

One of the most ambitious cultural projects the world has seen is taking shape on Saadiyat Island off the coast of the capital. An international cast of five Pritzker Prize winners (the 'Oscar' of architecture) has created the blueprints for four museums and a performing-arts centre. Collectively known as the Cultural District, they are likely to become a spectacular showcase of 21st-century architecture, arts and culture.

Although the project has been fraught with delays, as of early 2012 the estimated completion dates are 2013 for the Louvre Abu Dhabi and 2014 for the Guggenheim Abu Dhabi. The Louvre is, perhaps, the most anticipated building, and will feature a white dome perforated by lacy window patterns that allow diffused light to filter into its interior. Galleries will exhibit paintings and artwork drawn from the Paris Louvre's priceless collection. The Guggenheim Abu Dhabi promises to be a similarly exciting building: a cacophonous composition of geometric shapes designed by Frank Gehry that will showcase international contemporary art.

Later phases will see the construction of the Sheikh Zayed National Museum, a Maritime Museum and a Performing Arts Centre. For more information, check the www.saadiyat.ae website.

Abu Dhabi

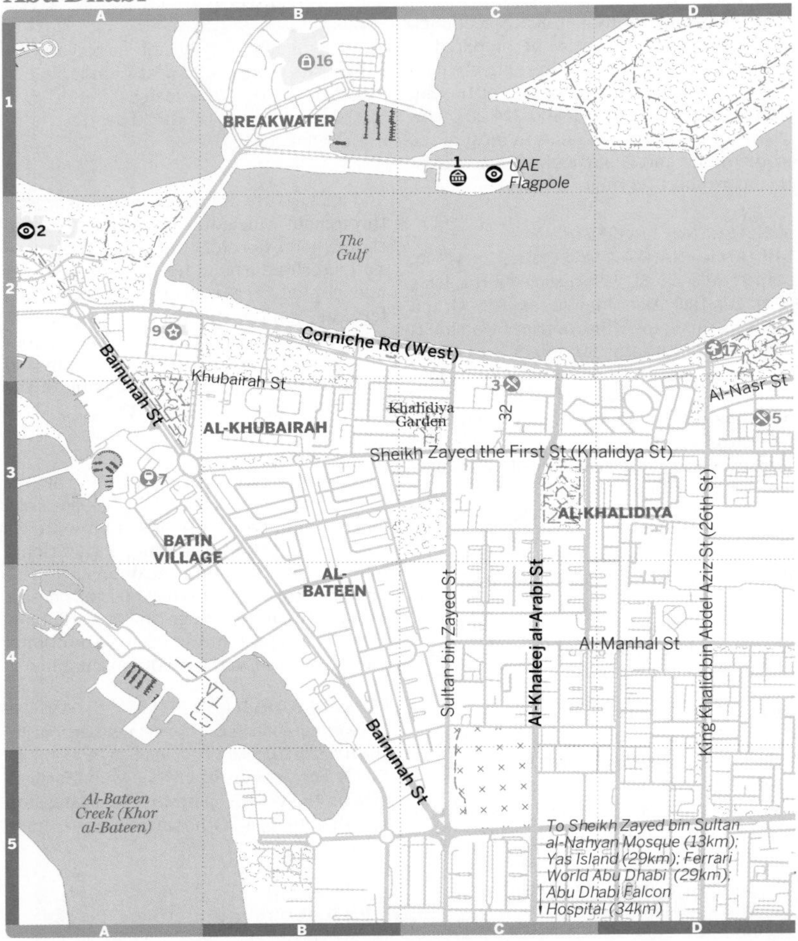

A B C D
1 2 3 4 5
16
BREAKWATER
1 UAE Flagpole
2
The Gulf
9
Corniche Rd (West)
17
Bainunah St
Khubairah St
3
Al-Nasr St
Khalidiya Garden
32
5
AL-KHUBAIRAH
Sheikh Zayed the First St (Khalidya St)
7
AL-KHALIDIYA
BATIN VILLAGE
AL-BATEEN
Sultan bin Zayed St
Al-Khaleej al-Arabi St
King Khalid bin Abdel Aziz St (26th St)
Al-Manhal St
Bainunah St
Al-Bateen Creek (Khor al-Bateen)
To Sheikh Zayed bin Sultan al-Nahyan Mosque (13km); Yas Island (29km); Ferrari World Abu Dhabi (29km); Abu Dhabi Falcon Hospital (34km)

a Ferrari carousel for tots, a 4D movie and an exhibition about the history of Ferrari. Yas Island is located around 29km from the centre of Abu Dhabi. Take the E10 highway north towards Dubai and follow the signs.

ABU DHABI FALCON HOSPITAL WILDLIFE

(www.falconhospital.com; Madinat Khalifa A; adult/child Dh170/60, with lunch Dh 220/80; ⏲10am-2pm Sun-Thu; 👪) The largest falcon hospital in the world with 'patients' arriving from all over the United Arab Emirates (UAE), this working veterinary clinic provides fascinating tours (with and without lunch). See free-flying falcons and learn just about everything you could possibly want to know about these intriguing birds, which are so symbolic and feature so widely throughout the UAE. The hospital is around 34km south of the centre of Abu Dhabi.

EATING

JONES THE GROCER INTERNATIONAL **$$**

(www.jonesthegrocer.com; Ground fl, Pearl Plaza Tower, 32nd St; mains Dh50-62) This Australian chain has just the right ingredients for Abu Dhabi's urban chic clientele. The atmosphere

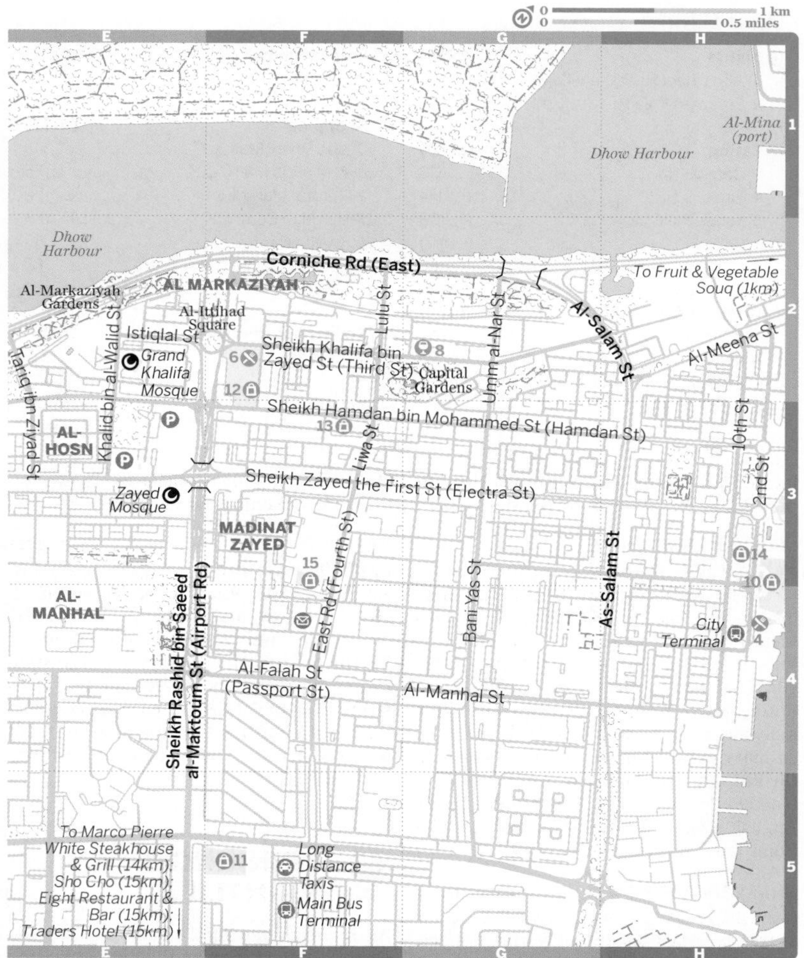

is up-to-the-minute with open-plan kitchens overlooking the dining area, with glistening stainless steel and an earthy wood colour scheme. Talking points include a chilled cheese room with samples to taste, and an eclectic menu with plenty of organic goodies.

FINZ SEAFOOD **$$**

(☎02-644 3000; Beach Rotana Hotel & Towers; mains Dh50-100) Amble down the jetty to snag a table at this wooden A-frame with terraces above the azure sea, then order a cocktail and prepare for some of the finest seafood in town. Whether grilled, wok-cooked, baked, cooked in a copper pan or prepared in the tandoor oven, the results are invariably delicious. Reservations are recommended.

SHO CHO JAPANESE **$$$**

(☎02-558 1117; www.sho-cho.com; Souq Qaryat Al Beri, Bain Al Jessrain; mains Dh100-210; 🍸) A stylish Japanese restaurant with appropriate minimalist decor in shades of blue and cream. Dishes are delicious, if also a tad minimalist. Don't miss the red snapper crisps starter or the delicate and decorative *maki* sushi rolls. The vegetarian sushi special should put a smile on the face of the non-carnivores. DJs add to the action at weekends. The Souq Qaryat Al Beri is

Abu Dhabi

located 15km from the centre via the Airport Rd. Reservations are essential.

MARCO PIERRE WHITE STEAKHOUSE & GRILL STEAKHOUSE $$$
(☎02-654 3333; Fairmont Bab al-Bhar, btwn the bridges; mains Dh200-250; ⏲7pm-1am) Meat lovers will be in heaven at this well-known restaurant established by British star chef Marco Pierre White. The swish dining room gets theatrical flourish from a dramatic 'flame wall' but fortunately the culinary pyrotechnics are kept in check in the kitchen. The emphasis is firmly on red-blooded quality cuts, prepared in classic English style and innovative grilled variations. Reservations are essential.

SHAKESPEARE & CO INTERNATIONAL $
(www.shakespeareandco.ae; Ground fl, Central Market; breakfast Dh48) Enjoy the wonderfully kitsch Victoriana decor, coupled with the best breakfast in town. Opt for the full English, filled crepes, Lebanese style or lightweight and healthy. There are bumper sandwiches and salads, too. Afterwards you can explore the surrounding boho-souq-style shops of the tastefully renovated Central Market.

CAFÉ DU ROI FRENCH $
(Corniche Rd West, Al-Khalidiya; mains Dh15-35; ⏲7am-midnight) This is one of a couple of superb French-style cafes in this neighbourhood. With superb coffee and delicious pastries, croissants and sandwiches, plus seven choices of fluffy filled omelettes, it's the perfect spot for some leisurely lingering.

SAYAD SEAFOOD $$$
(☎02-690 9000; www.emiratespalace.com; Emirates Palace Hotel, Ras Al Akhdar; mains Dh150-200) If you are looking for a combination of elegance and superb seafood, head for Sayad, one of Abu Dhabi's finest restaurants, appropriately located in the city's swankiest hotel. Dishes are fresh and imaginative, such as the Canadian lobster salad with watermelon and mango. Reservations are essential.

DRINKING & NIGHTLIFE

As in neighbouring Dubai, most of Abu Dhabi's hottest bars and clubs are located in those hotels that have a liquor licence.

CRISTAL COCKTAIL BAR
(Millennium Hotel, Khalifa; ⏲noon-2.30am) Dressed in polished mahogany and illuminated by candlelight and a fireplace, this slick place is a haven for a testosterone-fuelled crowd. Whisky and cigars are de rigueur for men, while ladies sip on French champagne. For sophistication on the cheap, come during happy hour (5pm to 8pm).

BELGIAN CAFÉ BAR
(Intercontinental Hotel, Khor Al Bateen; ⏲5pm-1am) Join the local expat crowd and enjoy a wide choice of imported draughts and

bottled beers. And don't forget that perfect accompaniment, a plate of perfectly fried *pommes frites* (served with the obligatory side of mayo).

ETOILES BAR

(Emirates Palace Hotel, Ras Al Akhdar; ⏲10pm-3.30am Mon-Wed, 11pm-3.30am Thu-Fri) Don those killer heels, gals, slick back the hair, chaps, and join the super-chic crowd at this achingly stylish and swish late-night bar. It's perfect for post-dinner drinks.

EIGHT RESTAURANT & BAR BAR

(Souq Qaryat Al Beri, Bain Al Jessrain; ⏲5pm-1am) Popular with cabin crews, this bar features regular theme nights, drink promotions and some really hot DJs from the international circuit. Great views.

ENTERTAINMENT

JAZZ BAR LIVE MUSIC

(☎02-681 1900; Hilton Abu Dhabi, Corniche Rd West; ⏲7am-2am Sun-Fri) Cool cats flock to this sophisticated supper club that serves contemporary fusion cuisine in a modern art deco–style setting, all against the backdrop of an excellent live band.

SLEEPING IN ABU DHABI

Traders Hotel (☎02-510 8880; www.tradershotel.com; Qaryat al Beri, Bain Al Jessrain; r Dh500; @≋)This is good value, especially given its illustrious neighbours, such as the Shangri-La Hotel. Look beyond the lurid fruit-coloured furniture in the lobby (pea green and shocking pink figure largely) as the rooms are modern and spacious. A private beach, landscaped gardens and a pool feature, and some of the city's best restaurants are within a short stroll.

Emirates Palace (☎02-690 9000; www.emiratespalace.com; Corniche Rd West; r from Dh1650; @≋) At this iconic luxurious hotel, managed by the Kempinski chain, the rooms are appropriately plush, if very traditional, with warm gold-coloured furnishings. Views overlook the lush landscaping or the Arabian Sea. Facilities include a gorgeous spa with a whole host of treatments.

LOCAL KNOWLEDGE

CONCERT TIME

As well as being home to Ferrari World, Yas Island is the venue for the Abu Dhabi Formula One Grand Prix, as well as being a major UAE concert venue with recent global acts such as Paul McCartney and Sade hitting the stage. Check www.yasisland.ae for the upcoming line-up.

SHOPPING

CENTRAL MARKET SHOPPING MALL

(www.centralmarket.ae; Hamdan St; ⏲10am-10pm Sun-Thu, 10am-11pm Fri & Sat) An inviting small mall pleasingly designed with warm lattice woodwork on the site of the original main souq. There are plenty of enticing stores here, including the Persian Carpet House & Antiques, Kashmir Cottage and the Chocolate Factory, plus restaurants and bars for that all-important pitstop.

MARINA MALL SHOPPING MALL

(⏲10am-10pm Sun-Thu, 10am-11pm Fri & Sat) For locals, the main draw of this large mall on the Breakwater seems to be Ikea, but fortunately there are over 400 other shops here in case you don't have room in your hand luggage for a flatpack. Entertainment options include **Fun City** (www.funcity.ae), a huge activity centre for children that includes a (relatively tame) roller coaster and dodgem cars.

ABU DHABI MALL SHOPPING MALL

(⏲10am-10pm Sun-Thu, 10am-11pm Fri & Sat) This elegant mall near the Beach Rotana has 220 outlets, including boutiques, designer stores and international chains, a six-screen multiplex, 40 restaurants, a children's entertainment area and a huge supermarket.

KALIFA CENTRE SHOPPING MALL SHOPPING MALL

(⏲10am-1pm & 4-10pm Sat-Thu, 4-10pm Fri) Located across the road from Abu Dhabi Mall, Khalifa Centre has a dozen stores selling handicrafts and carpets.

HAMDAN CENTRE SHOPPING MALL

(Hamdan St; ⏲10am-1.30pm & 5-10.30pm) Definitely more cheap than chic, this small, locally adored mall is the place to stock up on luggage, cheap fashions, leather goods and souvenirs.

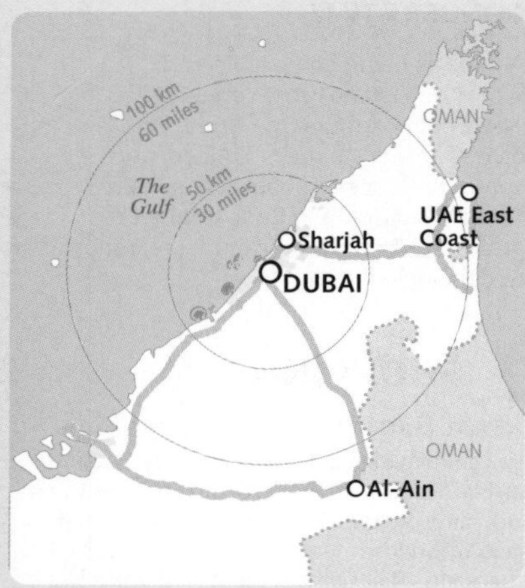

Day Trips from Dubai

Sharjah p125

Dubai's northern emirate neighbour, Sharjah doesn't dazzle with glitz but with culture, particularly around the restored central Heritage and Arts Area, among the most interesting neighbourhoods in the United Arab Emirates (UAE).

Al-Ain p128

Visit markets, forts, museums and a famous date-palm oasis in laid-back Al-Ain, a breath of fresh air after the frantic pace of Dubai.

UAE East Coast p130

Sleepy fishing villages, rugged mountains, desert dunes, museums and the oldest mosque in the UAE... this region has plenty to explore and is an easy getaway destination from Dubai.

Sharjah

Explore

Long before Abu Dhabi began improving its cultural credentials, Sharjah was declared the Unesco Cultural Capital of the Arab World – and deservedly so. Once you have penetrated the confusing outskirts of town, the historic old town, located north across Sharjah Bridge, is easy to navigate on foot. Plan on setting aside several hours to explore its Heritage and Arts Area, as well as the souqs and excellent museums.

One caveat: Sharjah takes its decency laws very seriously, so do dress modestly. That means no exposed knees, backs or bellies – and that goes for both men and women. It's also the only emirate that is 'dry' (ie no alcohol is available anywhere).

The Best...

- **Sight** Sharjah Museum of Islamic Civilisation (p125)
- **Place to Eat** Sadaf (p127)
- **Place to Shop** Central Souq (p127)

Top Tip

If you're visiting more than one museum in Sharjah, a 'Multi-Museum Ticket' will save you some dirhams. These cost Dh15 for individuals and Dh20 for families and are good for admission to several museums, as well as a few smaller venues. You can pick them up at any of the museums or the tourist office.

Getting there & Away

Bus Buses to Sharjah's Al-Jubail station near the Central Souq and Heritage and Arts Area depart every 10 minutes from Al-Ittihad station (Map p206) in Deira and from Al-Ghubaiba station in Bur Dubai (Map p210). The ride takes about 40 to 60 minutes and costs Dh5.

Car From the World Trade Centre roundabout, take the E11 (Sheikh Zayed Rd) north to Sharjah where it's called Al-Ittihad Rd. Traffic can be horrible, especially during rush hours, so it's best to travel in the late morning and late evening. The drive can take from 30 minutes to two hours, depending on traffic.

Taxi A taxi from Dubai starts at about Dh50, Dh20 of which is a tax that the taxi driver has to pay to the Sharjah authorities.

Need to Know

- **Area Code** ☎06
- **Location** 15km north of Dubai
- **Tourist Office** ☎06-556 6777; www.sharjah-welcome.com; 9th fl, Crescent Tower, Buheirah Corniche, Al Majaz; ⏲7.30am-2.30pm Sat-Thu

SIGHTS

SHARJAH MUSEUM OF ISLAMIC CIVILISATION MUSEUM

(www.islamicmuseum.ae; cnr Corniche & Gulf Rd; admission Dh5; ⏲8am-8pm Sat-Thu, 4-8pm Fri) A short stroll north of the centre is the fantastic Sharjah Museum of Islamic Civilisation. The collection covers various aspects of the Islamic faith, scientific accomplishments in the Arab world and 1400 years of Islamic art – and without one diorama in sight! Don't miss heading up to the cafeteria for a peek at the central dome with its striking deep-blue zodiac mosaic. The building, formerly a traditional souq, is stunning in its ornamentation and design.

BAIT AL-NABOODAH HISTORIC BUILDING

(www.sharjahmuseums.ae; Heritage & Arts Area, Al Sheyoukh; admission Dh5; ⏲8am-8pm Sat-Thu, 4-8pm Fri) In the 19th century, Sharjah's 'Who's Who' lived just inland from the Corniche, between Burj Ave and Al-Maraija Rd, today's Heritage and Arts Area. Many of the beautiful residences have been authentically restored using traditional materials such as sea rock, coral and gypsum. Wander through this labyrinthine quarter to come upon Bait al-Naboodah, a former prominent pearl trader's home. The house was renowned as a meeting place for merchants, sea captains and pearl divers, hence the large separate *majlis* (meeting room). The original part of the house dates back to 1845.

FREE **SHARJAH ART MUSEUM** MUSEUM

(www.sharjahmuseums.ae; ⏲8am-8pm Sat-Thu, 4-8pm Fri) Anchoring the Heritage and Arts

Area, Sharjah Art Museum is one of the UAE's largest and most impressive galleries. Its permanent exhibition includes 18th- and 19th-century oil paintings, watercolours and lithographs from the ruling family's collection. Curators also mount changing shows of local and international contemporary talent.

SHARJAH DESERT PARK PARK

(www.sharjahtourism.fi-demo.com; adult/child Dh15/free; ⏲9am-5.30pm Sun-Mon, 2-5.30pm Fri, 11am-5.30pm Sat; 👪) Located 26km east of Sharjah the park packs four venues into a 1-sq-km package: an Arabian Wildlife Centre, a Children's Farm, and two natural history museums. Well worth a trip.

AL-QASBA & AL MAJAZ MULTI-PURPOSE DEVELOPMENTS

(www.qaq.ae; Al Khan; 👪) South of the Khalid Lagoon, popular Al-Qasba is an attractively landscaped and lively mix of restaurants, cafes and entertainment venues along a canal. Diversions include a Ferris wheel, *abra* rides on the lagoon, and a superb contemporary art gallery, the Maraya Art Centre, which opened in 2011. Next door is the emirate's latest waterfront project, Al Majaz, another family-friendly development with fountains, playgrounds, jogging paths and green spaces.

SHARJAH AQUARIUM AQUARIUM

(www.sharjahaquarium.ae; off Al-Meena St; adult/child Dh20/free; ⏲8am-8pm Mon-Thu, 4-9pm Fri, 8am-9pm Sat; 👪) Ethereal sea horses, charming clownfish, spooky moray eels, prowling reef sharks and 250 or so other underwater species never fail to amuse, enlighten and entertain at the aquarium, located next to the Sharjah Maritime Museum.

SHARJAH MARITIME MUSEUM MUSEUM

(www.sharjahmuseums.ae; Al Khan; adult/child Dh8/4; ⏲8am-8pm Sat-Thu, 4-8pm Fri; 👪) At the Sharjah Maritime Museum, next to the aquarium, wooden dhows, fishing tools, devices used in pearl diving and historic photographs of grizzled old sea captains

DESERT SAFARIS

It may be one of the most urbanised countries in the world, but the United Arab Emirates (UAE) is extremely proud of its Bedouin heritage, and its people retain a strong affinity for the desert.

In the pre-oil age, life was harsh for Bedouin tribes in what was then the Trucial States. Food and water were scarce, and the simple living conditions were uncomfortable at the height of summer. Bedu would live in tents made from goat or camel hair, dig for water, and use falcons to hunt for birds and hares to supplement their basic diet of dates and camel milk. Those living on settlements had to pool their resources in order to survive, and a sense of community spirit imbued Bedu with the qualities of hospitality and generosity. Soon after the discovery of oil, the government built modern houses, roads, schools and hospitals for Dubai's desert dwellers, but the traditions and culture of life in the desert – from falconry to song and dance – remain intact.

A trip to the desert is an essential part of any Dubai holiday. If you can get some distance from the main road, the emptiness, vastness and tranquillity of the landscape can be breathtaking, with the ochre and orange dunes rippling gently in the wind and undulating as far as the eye can see. The country's biggest sand dune, Moreeb Hill, is in the Liwa desert, on the edge of the vast expanse known as Rub' al-Khali, the Empty Quarter. If you've read *Arabian Sands,* Sir Wilfred Thesiger's mesmerising account of his journeys across the Empty Quarter and experiences living with nomadic Bedu, a trip to Liwa will bring the book to life. That middle-of-nowhere satisfaction is harder to come by when you're close to Dubai, although there are plenty of quiet spots alongside the road to Hatta.

A plethora of tour companies also offer day and overnight trips to the desert. One of the most reputable is **Arabian Adventures** (www.arabian-adventures.com), which also offers a range of other tours throughout the UAE. For a more comprehensive list, see p176.

THE FRAGILE DESERT

An unfortunate consequence of the rapid growth of Dubai's tourism industry is damage to the desert. It is an extremely fragile ecosystem and home to hundreds of species, but in the parts of the desert where topsoil has been damaged by 4WDs, very little lives or grows. The Bedouin people have always had a huge amount of respect for the environment, but the desert is becoming more scarce as the development of Dubai continues apace. The biggest problem is pollution. Hundreds of camels die every year due to eating plastic bags carelessly dumped in the desert; the lumps of calcified plastic frequently found in the stomachs of dead camels can weigh up to 60kg.

By supporting the **Dubai Desert Conservation Reserve** (see the boxed text, p128) and limiting the area in which desert safari companies can operate to the environs of Al-Awir, the government is taking important steps to protect the environment. To do your bit, stick to tracks wherever possible when driving off-road and avoid damaging vegetation. Don't drive in wadis: these are important sources of drinking water and can be polluted by oil and grease from cars. Finally, take your rubbish home with you.

pay tribute to the key role the sea has played in the emirate's heritage.

EATING

SADAF PERSIAN $$

(☎06-569 3344; Al-Mina Rd; mains Dh30-45; ⊙lunch & dinner) Popular with Emirati families, who dine in private booths, Sadaf serves excellent authentic Persian cuisine. The spicy, moist kebabs are particularly good, and the 'Zereshk Polo Meat' (rice with Iranian red barberries and chicken or meat) is another star pick. Located opposite the Radisson Blu Hotel. Reservations are recommended for dinner.

SHABABEEK LEBANESE $$

(☎06-554 0444; Al-Qasba; mezze Dh12-18, mains Dh40-60; ⊙noon-midnight Sat-Wed, to 1am Thu & Fri) With its deep-purple walls, black furniture and Arabic design flourishes, this upmarket Lebanese restaurant channels Dubai trendiness but without the attitude – or the alcohol. Portions are not huge but flavours are delicately paired and enhanced by chef Ezzat Zubian's 'secret spices'. Reservations are recommended.

STEFANO'S ITALIAN $$

(Al-Qasba; mains Dh46-50; ⊙lunch & dinner) It may not be quite as mama makes, but this friendly Italian restaurant does a reasonable job on the familiar mainstays, including pizza, lasagne, ravioli, gnocchi and plenty of other pasta and saucy choices.

SHOPPING

CENTRAL SOUQ MARKET

(⊙9am-1pm & 4-11pm Sat-Thu, 9am-noon & 4-11pm Fri) Also called the Blue Souq, the Central Souq is a beautiful two-part building designed in ornate Arabic style. The ground floor is primarily a gold souq, while the small stores upstairs sell pashminas, rugs and curios from such far-flung places as Afghanistan and Rajasthan. If possible, come in the evenings – only tourists shop here during the day.

FREE **SOUQ AL-ARSA** MARKET

(⊙9am-1pm & 4-9pm Sat-Thu, 4-9pm Fri) The atmospheric Souq al-Arsa is the oldest souq in the UAE. Head for the central courtyard for the best stores, which sell everything from Indian pashminas to Yemeni daggers and at bargain prices – especially compared to Dubai. Seek out the traditional coffeehouse, a great stop for a reviving mint tea and plate of dates.

SLEEPING IN SHARJAH

Marbella Resort (☎06-574 1111; www.marbellaresort.com; Buheirah Corniche; 1-/2-bed ste Dh600/1000, villas Dh1500; @ ≋) Looking like a village transplanted from southern Spain, this oldie but goodie has 50 private villas set in lush tropical gardens, making it perfect for families. Facilities include two pools, a gym and tennis and squash courts to get you off that lounge chair, and a free daily shuttle to Dubai.

Al-Ain

Explore

With markets, forts, museums and a famous date-palm oasis, Al-Ain is a breath of fresh air after the frantic pace of Dubai. On the border with Oman, about a 90-minute drive out of town, the birthplace of Sheikh Zayed has greatly benefited from his patronage and passion for greening the desert; it's even nicknamed 'Garden City'. But the desert is never far away: simply driving the serpentine road up Jebel Hafeet will treat you to sweeping views of the arid splendour that is the Empty Quarter. Al-Ain itself is an increasingly dynamic place with a couple of excellent museums, an archaeological park, a superb zoo and an overall abundance of greenery, at least compared to its southerly neighbour.

Al-Ain is quite tough to navigate thanks to a bewildering abundance of roundabouts. Brown signs directing visitors to the major tourist attractions are helpful, but a few more wouldn't hurt.

Top Tip

The Al-Ain Wildlife Park is undergoing an impressive expansion to include a desert garden, an African village and the Sheikh Zayed Desert Learning Centre. They are also working in cooperation with several worldwide zoos, including the San Diego Zoo in the USA. The completion date is projected to be 2013; check the www.awpr.ae website for an update.

The Best...

- ➡ **Sight** Sheikh Zayed Palace Museum (p129)
- ➡ **Place to Eat** Makani (p130)
- ➡ **Place to Drink** Trader Vic's (p130)

Getting there & Away

Car From the World Trade Centre roundabout, head south on E11 (Sheikh Zayed Rd), then take exit 56 to Oud Metha Rd (E66) and follow it all the way to Al-Ain. The trip will take around 90 minutes.

Public transport Al-Ghazal runs minibuses between Al-Ain (Dh20, 1½ hours) and the Al-Ghubaiba bus station (Map p210) in Dubai every hour from 6.30am to 11.30pm. Al-Ain's bus station is off the Al-Murabba roundabout opposite the Lulu Centre. A taxi to or from Dubai will cost around Dh150.

Need to Know

- ➡ **Area Code** ☎03
- ➡ **Location** 160km southeast of Dubai
- ➡ **Tourist Office** (☎03-784 3996; Al-Jahili Fort, Hazah St; ⏰9am-5pm Sat, Sun & Tue-Thu, 3-5pm Fri)

DUBAI DESERT CONSERVATION RESERVE

The largest environmental project in Dubai to date, at least in terms of square kilometres, is one we hear practically nothing about. At 225 sq km, the **Dubai Desert Conservation Reserve** (www.ddcr.org) accounts for 5% of the emirate's total land. It's a national park, where the primary goal is to protect the desert's biodiversity, and it's located on the outskirts of Sharjah.

Dubai's approach to environmentalism is characteristically commercial. The DDCR is managed and funded by an airline and its super-luxurious resort inside the reserve. But Emirates Airlines, who initiated the project, has done a good job on the DDCR and now other countries are studying **Al Maha Desert Resort & Spa** (p144) as a model for luxury-sector ecotourism. Since its establishment in 1999, the reserve has reintroduced mountain gazelles and sand gazelles to Dubai's desert, as well as the Arabian oryx, which had almost completely disappeared a few decades ago.

The DDCR is divided into four zones. In the first zone, all human activity is prohibited, and in the second only very limited operations are allowed to take place. The third zone is only open to resort guests and the fourth is open to a small number of desert tour operators, including **Arabian Adventures** (www.arabian-adventures.com). If you can't afford a villa at Al Maha, going on a tour with this company is the only way you'll get in.

SIGHTS

FREE SHEIKH ZAYED PALACE MUSEUM MUSEUM

(www.adach.ae; cnr Al-Ain & Zayed ibn Sultan Sts; ⌚8.30am-7.30pm Sat-Thu, 3-7.30pm Fri) Sheikh Zayed's residence from 1937 to 1966 has been reinvented as the Sheikh Zayed Palace Museum. It is a beautiful adobe-coloured traditional building set around several courtyards with beds of cacti, magnolia trees and lofty palms. You can step inside the *majlis* (meeting room) where the ruler received visitors, see the curtained canopied bed where his wife slept (ever humble, he apparently preferred to sleep on the floor), and snap a photo of the Land Rover he used to visit the desert Bedu. There is also a gallery of portraits of the royal family, a Quran room, a kitchen and a replica of a grand court tent in the grounds, representing the iconic link with Bedouin life.

AL-AIN WILDLIFE PARK ZOO

(www.awpr.ae; adult/child Dh15/5; ⌚9am-8pm, last admission 1hr before closing; 👪) Al-Ain is also the home of the region's largest and arguably best zoo, with spacious enclosures inhabited by grazing Arabian oryx, prancing gazelles, lazy crocodiles and hundreds of other species, including the rare white tiger. Tots will enjoy the Elezba Petting Zoo, opened in 2011, plus camel rides and various animal encounters, including giraffe feeding. A zoo shuttle service takes visitors on a tour with hop-on and hop-off options at the main exhibits. This zoo gets the thumbs-up for its successful conservation and breeding program.

CAMEL MARKET CAMEL MARKET

(Mezyad Rd, just before Bawadi Mall; ⌚7am-sunset; 👪) Dusty, noisy, pungent and chaotic, this famous camel market is a wonderful immersion into the ancient Arabic culture that's so hard to find in the UAE today. All sorts of camels are holed up in pens, from babies that might grow up to be racers to studs kept for breeding. The intense haggling is fun to watch, but you'll also quickly realise that you're as much an attraction to the traders as they are to you (especially if you're a woman!). Some may try to make you pay for a tour but you're free to walk around on your own. If you take photos of the animals or their owners (always ask first, of course) it's nice to give a small tip. Note that the trading takes place in the morning but it's usually possible to see the corralled animals throughout the day. Afterwards you can wander around the adjacent covered (and a tad soulless) new souq. The camel market is located approximately 35km south of the centre of Al-Ain, on Mezyad Rd.

WORTH A DETOUR

JEBEL HAFEET

Don't leave Al-Ain without driving up Jebel Hafeet. This majestic, jagged, 1240m limestone mountain rears out of the plain south of Al-Ain. A new and extremely curvy road snakes its way up to the top, past evocatively eroded formations and shrubs eking out a living between the rocks. The area is home to red foxes, feral cats and the rock hyrax, which resembles a large rabbit.

The top of Jebel Hafeet is about 30km from central Al-Ain, including the 12km stretch of mountain road. From the town centre, head west on Khalifa bin Zayed St towards the airport, then follow the brown signs.

AL-AIN OASIS GARDENS

Linking the museums is the 3000-acre Al-Ain Oasis. A marked route leads through this atmospheric labyrinth of shaded cultivated plots irrigated by a traditional *falaj* (underground system of tunnels). There are nearly 150,000 date palms here, along with mango, almond, banana and fig trees.

AL-AIN NATIONAL MUSEUM MUSEUM

(www.aam.gov.ae; Zayed ibn Sultan St; admission Dh3; ⌚8.30am-7.30pm Sat-Thu, 3-7.30pm Fri) The charmingly old-fashioned Al-Ain National Museum is perfect for boning up on the ancient past of Al-Ain and surrounding region. Highlights include archaeological displays and artefacts from the tombs at nearby Hili and Umm an-Nar, which date to the 3rd millennium BC. The ethnography galleries contain beautiful silver Bedouin jewellery, traditional costumes and a harrowing display of primitive surgical instruments with lots of sharp points and hooks – ouch!

FREE AL-JAHILI FORT HISTORIC BUILDING

(www.adach.ae; Hazah St; ⌚9am-5pm Sat, Sun & Tue-Thu, 3-5pm Fri) In freshly restored glory, Al-Jahili is one of the largest forts in the UAE. Built in the 1890s as a royal summer residence, it now houses a visitor

SLEEPING IN AL-AIN

Danat Al-Ain Resort (03-768 6686; www.danathotels.com; cnr Khalid ibn Sultan & Al-Salam Sts; r Dh360-450;) Surrounded by lush gardens, this resort is good for families, with a great pool area and dedicated children's activities. Rooms are fairly bland but the restaurant choice is impressive, specialising in cuisines from East to West. The atmospheric Nawafeer Tent Lebanese restaurant has live music every night.

Al-Ain Rotana Hotel (03-754 5111; www.rotana.com; Zayed bin Sultan St; d Dh450-650;) This central hotel, with its soaring atrium, is a top choice. It has plush, spacious rooms in various sizes, all sporting the full range of mod cons.

information centre with an excellent selection of brochures on the UAE. You can also enjoy complimentary Arabic coffee and dates and check out the permanent exhibition devoted to the British explorer and author Sir Wilfred Thesiger.

FREE HILI ARCHAEOLOGICAL PARK ARCHAEOLOGICAL SITE

(Hili, close to Oman border; 10am-1pm) Use the knowledge you've gained at Al-Ain National Museum to make better sense of the remains in the landscaped gardens of Hili Archaeological Park. This is the largest Bronze Age complex in the UAE, dating back some 4000 years. In addition to what you see here there are other remains, including tombs and an Iron Age falaj, located in a protected area nearby. On view are the foundations of a tower and mud-brick buildings, as well as the restored circular Grand Tomb with its decorative carvings.

EATING

MAKANI LEBANESE $$

(Hilton Al-Ain Mall; mains from Dh55; 6pm-1am) Meaning 'my place' in Arabic, the al fresco atmosphere is a delight with plenty of palms and comfortable rattan-style furniture. Indulge in traditional Lebanese and Arabic specialities, many of which are prepared at your table. Live Arabic music creates a fitting accompaniment, as does the selection of Lebanese wines.

SHAHRYAR IRANIAN $

(Al-Ain Mall; dishes from Dh15) Located in the Bawadi Mall, near the camel market and souq (around 35km north of the centre), this simple, spotless eatery serves reliable Iranian staples, including kebabs, rice dishes and a tasty salad combo with tabouleh, hummus and fattoosh (with strips of bread), along with fresh-from-the-oven traditional Iranian bread.

AL-DIWAN RESTAURANT LEBANESE $

(Khalifa St; mains Dh30-80; 8am-2am;) Lebanese *shish tawooq* (marinated chicken grilled on skewers), pizza margarita, Mexican steak, Iranian yogurt chicken – this big, bright eatery with floor-to-ceiling windows certainly covers all the bases. Judging by what's on the plates of diners, though, it's the grilled kebabs that give this place local-fave status.

DRINKING

TRADER VIC'S BAR

(03-754 5111; Al-Ain Rotana Hotel, Zayed bin Sultan St; 12.30-3.30pm & 7.30-11.30pm) Sip exotic rum concoctions while taking in the trippy tiki decor and enjoying a wide choice of tasty bar snacks. Still hungry? Then consider booking a table for dinner when a live Cuban band will get your toes tapping between courses.

UAE East Coast

Explore

Dubai's relentless drive to create the tallest, longest, biggest and best versions of just about everything has made it the pin-up boy of 21st-century urban development. But while the mad developers of the city get ever closer to complete domination of the *Guinness World Records*, some of the villages and towns on the East Coast (about 130km east of Dubai) resemble the dioramas of yesteryear at the Dubai Museum. Tiny roadside mosques, date palms burdened with fruit, camels wandering down the middle of highways, and pristine white-sand beaches with barely a hotel in sight can still be found here.

Plan an early start if you're going just for the day and want some time to relax on the beach. If you do this excursion on a Friday you can catch the bull-butting in Fujairah (see the boxed text) on the way home, although downsides include heavy traffic and more-crowded beaches.

The Best...

- **Sight** Badiyah Mosque (p132)
- **Place to Eat** Al-Meshwar (p133)
- **Place to Shop** Friday Market (p132)

Top Tip

Although many of the beaches in the UAE look calm, they often have dangerous rip tides. If you are swimming at any of the beaches on the East Coast (or elsewhere in the UAE), be very careful as most are unpatrolled and there are regular reports of people drowning.

Getting There & Away

Distance from Dubai 130km

Direction East

Travel time 90 minutes

Car Take the E11 towards Sharjah and then head in the direction of Al-Dhaid, on the E88. At Masafi you can take the E89 road heading north to Dibba or south to Fujairah; we recommend going north first to Dibba and then driving south along the coast.

Public transport Minibuses to Fujairah leave from Al-Ittihad station (Map p206; cnr of Omar ibn al-Khattab & Al-Rigga Rds) in Deira every 45 minutes and cost Dh25. It will cost just over Dh200 if you go by taxi. A taxi from Fujairah to Al-Aqah beach costs around Dh75. Unfortunately there's no public transport from Fujairah to Dubai, so you will have to return by taxi.

BEATING THE DRUM

Here's an environmentally friendly, social and entertaining way to see the desert: join a drum circle. **Dubai Drums** (www.dubaidrums.com) hosts regular full-moon drum circles (adult/child Dh190/85) in desert camps. Sessions usually last several hours and occasionally until the early hours of the morning. Watch for the near-legendary all-nighter events. Drums and a barbecue dinner are provided.

Need to Know

- **Area Code** ☎09
- **Location** 130km east of Dubai
- **Tourist Office** (☎09 223 1436; www.fujairah.ae; 9th fl, Fujairah Trade Centre Bldg, Hamad bin Abdullah Rd; ⏰8am-1pm Sat-Wed)

FUJAIRAH

Fujairah is the only emirate on the Indian Ocean. The main city, also called Fujairah, is a port town. For a peek into its past, drop by the dusty **Fujairah Museum** (cnr Al-Nakheel & Al-Salam Rds; adult/child Dh5/free; ⏰8.30am-1.30pm & 4.30-6.30pm Sun-Thu, 2-6.30pm Fri) or the impressive 17th-century **fort**, which is spectacularly floodlit at night and surrounded by low-lying traditional walls and houses, which are gradually being restored. Nature lovers should shoot down to the idyllic mangrove lagoon at **Khor Kalba**, a paradise for birdwatchers. Explore on your own or book a guided canoe safari with Dubai-based **Desert Rangers** (☎04-357 2233; www.desertrangers.com; adult/child Dh300/210; 👪).

If possible, visit Fujairah on a Friday when the ancient sport of **bull-butting** (btwn Corniche & Coast Rd; ⏰4-7pm Fri Oct-May) takes place in a dusty dirt patch on the southern outskirts of town (before Al-Rughailat Bridge). The practice was introduced centuries ago by the Portuguese, and today's contests see bulls brought here from all over the UAE to lock horns and test their strength against each other. The goal is for a competing bull to push its opponent out of a circle, which usually takes only a couple of minutes. Traditionally, the fighting took place in an open field, but since angry bulls would occasionally charge spectators, a new wire fence has been built to keep them enclosed.

SLEEPING ON THE UAE COAST

If you decide that one day is not enough on the East Coast, consider staying overnight at one of the following places:

Sandy Beach Hotel & Resort (09-244 5555; www.sandybm.com; d Dh500, ocean-view d Dh625, 1-/2-bedroom chalet Dh700/900, apt Dh1200;) At this expat favourite near the Badiyah Mosque, lodging ranges from basic ocean-view rooms to small cabins with private barbecues to a newer wing with sparkling, modern apartments with balconies. On the downside the lunchtime buffet is overpriced and poor. Beach access passes for nonguests cost Dh75.

Hotel JAL Fujairah Resort & Spa (04-204 3111; www.jalfujairahresort.ae; 6km south of Dibba; d from Dh700; @) Zen minimalism meets Arabian hospitality at this sprawling Japanese-owned outpost where you can open up the balcony door of your oversized room to let in the ocean breezes.

Le Meridien al-Aqah Beach Resort (09-244 9000; www.lemeridien-alaqah.com; d from Dh850; @) Just north of the Sandy Beach Hotel, this upmarket resort does everything to put you in the mood for a beach vacation. The balconied rooms give you plenty of elbow space and overlook the lush gardens, private beach and ocean. Dive, waterski, play volleyball or spend lazy days by the pool.

SIGHTS

BADIYAH MOSQUE — MOSQUE

(Badiyah; 7am-10pm) Located in the small village of Badiyah (also spelt Bidyah and Bidiya), around 20km south of Dibba on the E99, this tiny mosque is thought to be the oldest in the UAE (possibly dating back to the early 15th century). It's a simple structure, adorned with four pointed domes and resting on an internal pillar. A sign says that non-Muslims are not allowed to enter, but the resident imam will not take offence if you do catch a peek, as long as you are modestly dressed; take off your shoes and cover your head (women only). Behind the mosque, up on a hill, is a pair of ruined **watchtowers**. Walk up for superb 360-degree views of the Hajar Mountains, the gloriously blue ocean and a lush date-palm plantation.

FRIDAY MARKET — MARKET

(Masafi; 8am-10pm) The road from Dubai towards the coast is strangely desolate, a dune landscape punctuated only by power poles. However, a popular roadside attraction is Masafi's Friday Market. Contrary to its name, this strip of nearly identical stalls is actually open daily. It's a good place to stock up on fresh fruit, particularly locally grown bananas and mangoes; the wares on sale are mainly restricted to rugs, pottery and household goods.

DIBBA — VILLAGE

From Masafi, point the compass north and cut through the dramatically rugged Hajar Mountains to the sleepy fishing village of Dibba. This is the northernmost point of the 65km scenic East Coast highway to Fujairah, hemmed in by the Hajars, shimmering beaches and the turquoise expanse of the Gulf of Oman. The diving and snorkelling are still good here, despite the damaging effects of a prolonged red tide.

Dibba is unique in that its territory is shared by two emirates and the Sultanate of Oman. The most interesting section is the harbour in the Omani section – take your passport if you want to cross the border. Here you can watch grizzled fishermen haul in their catch, visit the fish and fresh produce market and take a dhow trip to unspoilt dive sites along the remote eastern coast of the Musandam Peninsula.

KHOR FAKKAN CORNICHE — BEACH

(Khor Fakkan;) Continuing south you'll soon arrive in Khor Fakkan, home to a super busy container port. Still, the town is not without its charms, especially along the corniche, which extends for several kilometres and is flanked by palm trees, gardens, kiosks and a playground, making it popular with families for picnics and waterfront strolls.

EATING

AL-MESHWAR LEBANESE

(Hamad bin Abdullah Rd, Fujairah; mezze Dh6-45, mains Dh25-115; cafe 9am-midnight, dining rooms 11.30am-2.30pm & 7-10pm;) For sustenance, steer towards Al-Meshwar, which serves up the gamut of Lebanese tummy temptations in a *Flintstones*-inspired building. Share a hot or cold appetiser platter to start with, then do battle with the mixed grill or go meat-free with the spinach and cheese fatayer (pastries). The downstairs *sheesha* cafe has free wi-fi and is a lot livelier than the two more formal upper floors.

IRANIAN PARS RESTAURANT PERSIAN

(Cnr Corniche Rd & Sheikh Khalid bin Mohammed al Qassini St, Khor Fakkan; mains Dh30) Approaching from the north, this restaurant is located at the far end of the corniche, just beyond the mosque and a long strip of banks. Locals give it the thumbs up for its generous portions of traditional Persian cuisine – try the tasty chelo kebab served with an enormous plateful of delicious rice. Note that since Khor Fakkan is part of the Sharjah emirate, it's alcohol-free.

SPORTS & ACTIVITIES

The beautiful stretch of beach south of Dibba is increasingly being snapped up by hotels and resorts and is one of the UAE's most popular diving sites.

AL BOOM DIVING DIVING

(04-342 2993; www. alboomdiving.com; Golden Tulip Hotel, Dibba; dives from Dh300, dhow trip w/ lunch Dh300;) Covering most of the UAE, Al Boom is an excellent diving operation with several dive sites in the Musandam. They also offer dhow cruises, which include lunch.

AL-MARSA DIVING

(06-544 1232; www.almarsamusandam.com; Dibba; dives from Dh400, sunset cruise Dh150) Based at Dibba harbour (with their main office in Sharjah), this reliable local diving operator offers a wide range of courses, including scuba diving, advanced diving courses, rescue and dive-master courses. Al-Marsa also offers dhow trips, including a sunset cruise.

FREESTYLE DIVERS DIVING

(04-244 5756; www.freestyledivers.com; Royal Beach Hotel, Dibba; dives from Dh450, 9am-5pm;) Another good choice, this outfit rents out gear and offers dive trips, PADI courses and Musandam excursions, as well as introductory pool diving courses for children (Dh250).

ABSOLUTE ADVENTURE CENTRE ADVENTURE SPORTS

(04-345 9900; www.adventure.ae; Dibba; kayaking from Dh495, treks from Dh350) Located near the Golden Tulip Hotel, this well-named outfit organises all sorts of outdoor adventures, including kayaking tours around the Musandam Peninsula, as well as trekking, mountain-biking and camping through the Hajar Mountains.

Sleeping

Although Dubai remains primarily a luxury travel destination, there is still a choice of places to unpack your suitcase, ranging from budget hotels and hotel apartments to international chain hotels and outrageously luxurious resorts such as the Burj al-Arab. There are more than 50,000 beds in Dubai – and not a Bedouin tent in sight.

Accommodation Options

There are essentially two types of hotel in Dubai: the beach resort and the city hotel. Beach resorts are generally five stars with private beaches (and waiter service), acres of marble, chandeliers and those pinch-yourself-extras such as private whirlpools and Armani pencil sharpeners. The number of midrange options is increasing and encompasses the business market. More tourist-orientated hotels in this price bracket may have five-star standard facilities generally coupled with an out-of-the-way location (ie away from the beach) and, all too often, little character. Budget hotels vary considerably, so always ask to check out the room before you check in.

Accommodation Websites

➡ **www.hotels.lonelyplanet.com** Lonely Planet's online booking service with insider lowdown on the best places to stay.

➡ **www.hrs.com** Emphasis on budget hotels and hotel apartments.

➡ **www.definitelydubai.com** Run by the official tourist authority with a solid choice of mainly midrange to top-end hotels.

Longer-Term Rentals

The Bur Dubai area is full of longer-term rentals; many hotels throughout the city also rent out furnished apartments with kitchens and washing machines. Prices start at around Dh350 for a studio in one of the midrange hotel apartments in Bur Dubai and often drop for stays longer than a week. At top-end apartments, rates are stratospheric.

Boutique Hotels & B&Bs

Boutique hotels are seemingly the antithesis of the biggest-is-best hotel scene in Dubai. But the idea is catching on (slowly) and there are several superb, characterful choices. There is also a small but growing number of B&Bs, usually set up by expats in private homes in residential areas. Staying in one of these won't give you much privacy or a wide range of top-end amenities but it will give you easy access to personal perspectives on life in Dubai.

Room Rates & Amenities

Room rates fluctuate enormously. At any given time most hotels will have some offer or another, ranging from a complimentary upgrade to discounted half-board. Overall, midrange and top-end hotels have superb facilities. Look for an indoor or outdoor swimming pool, diving centre, children's club, babysitting service, spa and gym, shuttle bus to beaches and malls, in-room wi-fi, dedicated taxi service, tennis courts, and restaurants and bars.

Single or Sharing

In theory, unmarried men and women should not share a room. In practice, hotels turn a blind eye. Having two different names is no tip-off, as most married Arab women keep their name. Two men sharing is acceptable, while single women may sometimes raise eyebrows due to the large number of 'working girls' in town.

Lonely Planet's Top Choices

XVA Hotel (p139) Atmospheric small guesthouse with a wealth of seductive details.

One&Only Royal Mirage (p143) Sumptuous hotel with lavish Arabian-style architecture and expansive gardens.

Burj al-Arab (p142) For sheer bling – and boasting – you can't beat it.

Park Hyatt Dubai (p137) Surrounded by lush green landscaping with superb facilities.

Raffles Dubai (p138) Slick, chic decor with water features and rooftop bar.

Best by Budget

$

Golden Sands Apartments (p139)

Centro Barsha (p146)

Ibis Mall of the Emirates (p146)

$$

Riviera Hotel (p137)

Orient Guest House (p139)

Ramada Hotel (p139)

Rydges Plaza (p143)

$$$

One&Only Royal Mirage (p143)

Al-Qasr, Madinat Jumeirah (p142)

Mina A' Salam, Madinat Jumeirah (p142)

Jumeirah Emirates Towers (p140)

Best for Views

Al-Qasr, Madinat Jumeirah (p142)

Burj al-Arab (p142)

Sheraton Dubai Creek Hotel & Towers (p137)

Jumeirah Beach Hotel (p142)

Shangri-La (p141)

Address Downtown Dubai (p141)

Best for Shopping

Coral Beach Boutique Hotel Apartments (p145)

Kempinski (p145)

Palace – The Old Town (p141)

Address Dubai Mall (p141)

Best for Romance

Al-Qasr, Madinat Jumeirah (p142)

Desert Palm (see the boxed text, p144)

One&Only Royal Mirage (p143)

Al Maha Desert Resort & Spa (see the boxed text, p144)

Raffles Dubai (p138)

Address Dubai Mall (p141)

Best for Hotel Dining

Al-Qasr, Madinat Jumeirah (p142)

One&Only Royal Mirage (p143)

Palace – The Old Town (p141)

Radisson Blu Hotel (p137)

Shangri-La (p141)

Best for Pools

Grand Hyatt Dubai (p139)

Le Royal Meridien Beach Resort & Spa (p143)

One&Only Royal Mirage (p143)

Ritz-Carlton Dubai (p144)

Address Downtown Dubai (p141)

Westin Dubai Mina Seyahi (p145)

NEED TO KNOW

Price Ranges

The prices in each category are for a standard double room with private bathroom in high season (October to April).

$	under Dh500
$$	Dh500–1000
$$$	over Dh1000

Check-In & Check-Out

Flights arrive in Dubai at all hours, so be sure to confirm your check-in time with the hotel prior to arrival. Check-in is generally at 2pm or 3pm, although it's sometimes possible to have access to your room earlier. Checkout is 11am or noon unless you arrange for a late checkout, which is often granted free.

Reservations

Most major hotel chains have online booking engines, saving you expensive telephone calls. Smaller hotels sometimes offer online booking, but they don't always use a secure server; verify the site's security certificate before sending your credit card number.

Listings

Please note that the hotel listings in this book are ordered by author preference.

Where to Stay

Neighbourhood	For	Against
Deira	Atmospheric area near the Creek and souqs. Inexpensive hotels.	Noisy, chaotic. Budget choices can be brothels, so always check carefully. Heavy traffic and nightmare parking during busy times of the day.
Bur Dubai	Inexpensive hotel apartments which are well serviced with supermarkets. Plenty of restaurant choices. The Bastakia Quarter has some of the best boutique options in the city.	Can be soulless away from the souq area, lacking the atmosphere of Deira and the glitz of modern Dubai.
Sheikh Zayed Road & Around	Excellent location at the city's geographic centre. Some superb luxury hotels. Handy to metro.	Horrendous rush-hour traffic, some distance from the sea.
Jumeirah	Good for beachfront hotels and Burj al-Arab views.	Creekside heritage sites are a good 20 minutes away. Shortage of budget options.
New Dubai	Home to the ritziest beach hotels around Dubai Marina, many with views of the Palm Jumeirah.	Can seem anonymous with an atmosphere and style of hotel that could be at any top international resort. No metro stop nearby.

Deira

TOP CHOICE PARK HYATT DUBAI LUXURY HOTEL $$$
Map p208 (04-602 1234; www.dubai.park.hyatt.com; next to Dubai Creek Golf & Yacht Club; r from Dh1275; @) The mile-long driveway through a lush date-palm grove is the first hint that the Park Hyatt is no ordinary hotel – an impression quickly confirmed the moment you step into the domed and pillared lobby. Tiptoeing between hip and haute, Park is Hyatt's luxury brand, and it's evident in the details: the light-flooded rooms are artfully styled in natural tones, tactile textiles and subdued arabesque flourishes. Count the dhows from your Creek-view balcony, rinse off the jetlag in the rain shower or huge oval tub and luxuriate in the multiple award-winning Amara Spa.

RADISSON BLU HOTEL HOTEL $$
Map p206 (04-222 7171; www.radissonblu.com; Baniyas Rd; r from Dh675; @) This Creekside stalwart was the city's first five-star hotel when it opened in 1975. As such it's old-fashioned but fits as comfortably as your favourite jeans. Rooms are snug but have been fast-forwarded into the 21st century, boasting a good range of business-class amenities and small, furnished balconies. Other trump cards include a location close to the souqs and dhow wharves and, best of all, the restaurants: Sumibiya (p55) for Japanese, China Club (p55) for yum cha, Shabestan (p54) for Persian and Yum! (p57) for noodles. The 24-hour gym has a separate work-out area for women.

HILTON DUBAI CREEK HOTEL $$
Map p206 (04-227 1111; www.hilton.com; Baniyas Rd, Rigga; r from Dh850; @) In a building designed by Bastille Opera architect, Carlos Ott, this sexy glass-and-chrome hotel offers a smart alternative to the conservative white-marble opulence of Dubai's other high-calibre establishments. After a day of turf-pounding you can retreat to rooms with wood-panelled walls, leather-padded headboards, grey-granite baths, and fabulous beds with feather-light duvets. Your flatscreen TV may have a gazillion channels, but you'll probably prefer the Creek views.

VILLA 47 B&B $
Map p208 (04-268 8239, 050 634 1286; www.villa47.com; cnr 19 & 47 Sts, Al-Garhoud; r incl breakfast Dh300; @) A superb find if you don't need buckets of privacy, this B&B is just two rooms in a bougainvillea-draped private home on a quiet street, yet close to the airport. Your outgoing hosts Ancy and Thomas make a mean Indian or English-style breakfast and will happily help you plan your day. The Irish Village pub (p57) and restaurants are close by.

RIVIERA HOTEL HOTEL $$
Map p206 (04-222 2131; www.rivierahotel-dubai.com; Baniyas Rd; r from Dh600; @) Next to the Carlton Tower Hotel, the Riviera has updated all their rooms, which are now a delight with soothing colour schemes, plush carpeting and classy slate-grey-and-cream bathrooms. The front rooms have Creekside views – make sure you request one when you book. No alcohol.

SHERATON DUBAI CREEK HOTEL & TOWERS LUXURY HOTEL $$$
Map p206 (04-228 1111; www.starwoodhotels.com; Baniyas Rd; r from Dh1050; @) Floor-to-ceiling windows provide mesmerising Creek vistas at this classic business-class property. Rooms don't get kudos for creative design, but amenities such as flatscreen TVs, DVD players, cushy bed linen and marble baths provide extra comfort. There's a well-equipped gym and unusual triangular pool. The Club Class provides 24-hour private butler service.

LANDMARK HOTEL HOTEL $$
Map p206 (04-228 6666; www.landmarkhotels.net; Baniyas Sq; r from Dh600; @) Just off Baniyas Sq, this is one of the better hotels in a hyper-busy Indian business district. Rooms are furnished in mass-market blond wood, but they're clean, have satellite TV and enough room to feel comfortable, if not to do cartwheels. The tiny rooftop pool provides an atmospheric panorama of Deira, especially during the call to prayer when mosques' loudspeakers compete in a blaring cacophony.

AL-BUSTAN ROTANA HOTEL $$
Map p208 (04-282 0000; www.rotana.com; Casablanca St, Al-Garhoud; r from Dh800; @) Everything works like a well-oiled machine at this warm and welcoming five-star hotel near the airport that mainly

caters for a business clientele. Rooms are dressed in tactile fabrics, thick carpets and warm earth colours, while wall-mounted flatscreen TVs, large desks, good mattresses and an oversized pool are additional comforts. Squash and tennis courts are handy for burning off those calorific deal-clinching lunches.

SHERATON DEIRA HOTEL **$$**

Map p206 (☎04-268 8888; www.starwoodhotels.com; Al-Mateena St; r from Dh650; @📶🏊) Rates are reasonable at this off-the-beaten-path five-star in Little Iraq. Standard rooms skimp on size if not on amenities, which include flatscreen TV and a coffeemaker. Go for the junior suites if you can score a good rate; they're extra-spacious, with large marble bathrooms and giant tubs.

Bur Dubai

TOP CHOICE RAFFLES DUBAI LUXURY HOTEL **$$$**

Map p214 (☎04-324 8888; www.dubai.raffles.com; Sheikh Rashid Rd, near Wafi Mall, Oud Metha; r from Dh1095; @📶🏊) Here's a luxury hotel that lives up to the moniker. Built in the shape of a pyramid, Raffles is a high-octane hot spot with magnificent oversized rooms (with balconies) done in the colours of a Moroccan kilim – deep blue, burgundy red and sandy taupe. Bathrooms are of limestone and sandstone imported from Egypt, with giant sunken tubs and rainfall showerheads. Zeitgeist-capturing in-room touches include Lavazza espresso machines, lighting controlled from a bedside console, iPod docking stations and free wi-fi.

THE CALL TO PRAYER

If you're staying in the older areas of Deira or Bur Dubai you might be woken around 4.30am by the inimitable wailing of the *azan* (the Muslim call to prayer) through speakers positioned on the minarets of nearby mosques. It's jarring, to be sure, but there's a haunting beauty to the sound, one that you'll only hear in Islamic countries.

Muslims pray five times a day: at dawn; when the sun is directly overhead; when the sun is in the position that creates shadows the same length as the object shadowed; at the beginning of sunset; and at twilight, when the last light of the sun disappears over the horizon. The exact times are printed in the daily newspapers and on websites. Once the call has been made, Muslims have half an hour to pray. An exception is made at dawn: after the call they have about 80 minutes in which to wake up, wash and pray before the sun has risen.

Muslims needn't be near a mosque to pray; they need only face Mecca. If devotees cannot get to a mosque, they'll stop wherever they are and drop to their knees. If you see someone praying, be as unobtrusive as possible, and avoid walking in front of the person. All public buildings, including government departments, libraries, shopping centres and airports, have designated prayer rooms. In every hotel room arrows on the ceiling, desk or bedside table indicate the direction of Mecca. Better hotels provide prayer rugs, sometimes with a built-in compass.

When you hear the call to prayer, listen for the phrasing. First comes *'Allah-u-akbar'*, which means 'God is Great'. This is repeated four times. Next comes *'Ashhadu an la illallah ha-illaah'* (I testify there is no god but God). This is repeated twice, as is the next line, *'Asshadu anna muhammadan rasuulu-ilaah'* (I testify that Mohammed is His messenger). Then come two shorter lines, also sung twice: *'Hayya ala as-salaah'* (Come to prayer) and *'Hayya ala al-falaah'* (Come to salvation). *'Allah-u-akbar'* is repeated twice more, before the closing line, *'Laa ilaah illa allah'* (There is no god but God).

The only variation on this standard format is at the dawn call. In this azan, after the exhortation to come to salvation, comes the gently nudging, repeated line *'As-salaatu khayrun min al nawn'*, which translates as 'It is better to pray than to sleep'.

If you're not in a hotel where you can hear the call to prayer, stop by the souqs in Deira and pick up a mosque alarm clock – it's the perfect souvenir to take home to friends.

TOP CHOICE XVA HOTEL BOUTIQUE HOTEL $$
Map p210 (☎04-353 5383; www.xvagallery.com; Bastakia Quarter; r from Dh600;) This chic boutique hotel occupies a century-old villa, complete with wind towers, in the heart of the historic Bastakia Quarter. Rooms open onto a courtyard doubling as a cafe and are decked out with local artwork, arabesque flourishes and rich colours. Ask for Room 1 with its large private terrace. The only downside is the lack of natural light in some rooms. Don't miss the gift shop and superb XVA gallery in the Financial District's Gate Village (p82).

ORIENT GUEST HOUSE BOUTIQUE HOTEL $$
Map p210 (☎04-351 9111; www.orientguesthouse.com; Bastakia Quarter; r Dh1000) Located close to the XVA Hotel, this romantic boutique hotel captures the feeling of old Dubai. Rooms in this former home surround a central courtyard; each is styled with carved wooden headboards, some with canopies, plus delicate chandeliers and velvety-soft jewel-tone fabrics. The overall atmosphere is pure tranquillity.

GRAND HYATT DUBAI LUXURY HOTEL $$$
Map p214 (☎04-317 1234; www.dubai.grand.hyatt.com; Al-Qataiyat Rd, Oud Metha; r from Dh1050; @) The vast white-marble lobby at this hulking resort re-creates a tropical rainforest, with dhow hulls hanging from the ceiling. Rooms are dressed in sophisticated shades of taupe, peach and auburn, and exude a timeless elegance with their thick carpets, picture windows and tasselled draperies. Bathrooms have separate tub and shower combinations. Facilities are impressive and include Dubai's biggest swimming pool, extensive palm-tree-studded gardens, a kids club, tennis courts, a fantastic gym and several excellent restaurants. Bonus points for the solar-panelled roof that cools the pools (or heats them in winter).

GOLDEN SANDS HOTEL APARTMENTS HOTEL APARTMENTS $
Map p210 (☎04-355 5553; www.goldensandsdubai.com; Mankhool; studio apt from Dh325; @) Golden Sands gets kudos for being a pioneer of the hotel apartment concept in Dubai and remains one of the best-value stays. The 750 studios, one- and two-bedroom apartments are spread over 12 stand-alone boxy buildings off Al-Mankhool Rd. They all include spacious living and sleeping spaces, although the bathrooms are small and showing their age. Furnishings are good and the efficient kitchenettes include a washing machine. There is a daily shuttle to Jumeirah Beach.

MÖVENPICK HOTEL BUR DUBAI HOTEL $$
Map p214 (☎04-336 6000; www.movenpick-hotels.com; 19 St, Oud Metha; r from Dh750; @) Tastefully revamped lobby decorated in shades of charcoal and cream lead to a Gone with the Wind sweeping staircase. The hotel takes its art seriously with regular exhibitions and some superb artworks throughout. The rooms' decor plays it safe in a midrange business kind of way, but crisp white quilts, feather pillows and spacious bathrooms more than compensate.

DAR AL SONDOS HOTEL APARTMENTS BY LE MERIDIEN HOTEL APARTMENTS $
Map p210 (☎04-393 8000; www.starwoodhotels.com; Rolla St; r from Dh360; @) In the heart of historic Dubai, these roomy digs put you within walking distance of a lot of major sights, including the Bastakia Quarter. You could even catch an *abra* (water taxi) to Deira and pick up some goodies at the markets, then whip up a delicious meal back in your kitchen. Wind down the day looking out over the sparkling city while splashing around in the rooftop pool.

RAMADA HOTEL HOTEL $$
Map p210 (☎04-351 9999; www.ramadadubai.com; Al-Mankhool Rd; r from Dh660;) The most attention-grabbing feature of this longstanding hotel is its cathedral-like stained glass feature that stretches 10 storeys up in the atrium and, fittingly for Dubai, is the world's tallest such artwork. Otherwise, the rooms get the thumbs up for their split-level spaciousness at 48 sq metres, although the decor is a little too heavy on the beige. Feel like a pint? Check out the hotel's Old Vic pub (p72).

FOUR POINTS BY SHERATON BUR DUBAI HOTEL $
Map p210 (☎04-397 7444; www.starwoodhotels.com; Khalid bin al-Waleed Rd, Mankhool; r from Dh425; @) Despite the gritty pavement scene out front, this Four Points (one of three in Dubai) is a reliable choice. The carpeted rooms are decked out in soothing soft yellows and cream, and has exceptionally

AIRPORT OPTIONS

Premier Inn (☎04-885 0999; www.premierinn.com; Airport Rd; r from Dh475; @ 📶 🏊) If your plane lands late or leaves early, this surprisingly stylish place just outside Terminal 3 is a convenient place to check in. The third Dubai property of this huge UK-based budget hotel chain delivers modern yet pocket-sized digs appealingly accented with the company's trademark purple. Plane-spotters can indulge their obsession while floating in the rooftop pool.

Dubai Youth Hostel (☎04-298 8151/61; www.uaeyha.com; 39 Al-Nahda Rd, Al-Qusais, btwn Lulu Hypermarket & Al Bustan Centre; dm/s/d/tr HI members Dh90/170/200/270, nonmembers Dh100/190/230/300; @ 🏊) Dubai's only hostel has facilities more typical of a hotel, including a pool, gym, sauna, Jacuzzi, tennis court, coffee shop and laundry. However, being located north of the airport, towards Sharjah, makes it a less than convenient base for extensive city exploring. Private rooms in the newer wing (Hostel A) come with TV, refrigerator and bathrooms, but the dorms in the older wings (Hostels B and C) are more basic. To get to the hostel from the airport take bus 34 from the Terminal 1 departure level; it runs every 30 minutes between 7.45am and 10.15pm (15 minutes, Dh3). A taxi should cost about Dh35 to Dh40. Check-in time is 2pm.

good bed linen, including marshmallow-soft feather pillows. You'll find an adequate gym, a small pool, a hot tub and restaurants, including the excellent Antique Bazaar Indian restaurant (see p70).

ARABIAN COURTYARD HOTEL & SPA HOTEL **$**

Map p210 (☎04-351 9111; www.arabiancourtyard.com; Al-Fahidi St; r from Dh500; @ 🏊) Located opposite the Dubai Museum, this hotel is an excellent launch pad for city explorers. The Arabian theme extends from the turbaned lobby staff to the design flourishes in the rooms, which are decent-sized (although the bathrooms are on the small side). Ask for a room overlooking the Creek. Overall, a good-value pick in a central location.

FOUR POINTS BY SHERATON DOWNTOWN DUBAI HOTEL **$**

Map p210 (☎04-354 3333; www.starwoodhotels.com; 4C St, off Al-Mankhool Rd, Mankhool; r from Dh475; @ 📶 🏊) The stark-white chrome-and-marble lobby can't quite decide what it's trying to be – contemporary Italian or 1970s disco – but rooms at this midrange hotel are spacious enough for a small family. The location is a bit nondescript, but extras such as comfy mattresses, big flatscreen TVs, and rooftop gym and pool compensate.

DUBAI NOVA HOTEL **$**

Map p210 (☎04-355 9000; www.dubainovahotel.com; Al-Fahidi St; r from Dh450; @) This modern block won't win any awards for decor or design, but the rooms are spacious, squeaky clean and simply decorated in red and white with pine furnishings. A couple of minutes from the Dubai Museum and close to the souqs, *abra* rides and plenty of restaurants, Nova is popular with Indian families and businessmen.

Sheikh Zayed Road & Around

TOP CHOICE JUMEIRAH EMIRATES TOWERS LUXURY HOTEL **$$**

Map p216 (☎04-330 0000; www.jumeirah.com; Sheikh Zayed Rd, Financial District; d from Dh950; @ 📶 🏊) Housed in one of Dubai's soaring steel-and-glass buildings, this is one of the Middle East's top business hotels. Glide up to your room in the panoramic lift for incredible views. Throughout the 52-floor hotel, the black-and-grey aesthetic is ultra-masculine and heavy on angular lines while the room layout is sleek and busy-exec-orientated. Solo women travellers should book the Chopard ladies' floor, where pink replaces grey and in-bath fridges let you chill your caviar face creams. Service here is among Dubai's best.

ARMANI HOTEL LUXURY HOTEL **$$$**

Map p216 (☎04-888 3888; www.dubai.armanihotels.com; Burj Khalifa, Downtown Dubai; r from Dh1700; @ 📶 🏊) The first hotel to carry the Armani name, the decor here is the antithesis of the other Burj. It's all understated elegance with a colour scheme of cream, chocolate brown, grey, black and the occasional splash of scarlet coupled with satin-covered walls. The sophistication is further emphasised by Armani-branded everything, from the sugar cubes to the shampoo.

ADDRESS DOWNTOWN DUBAI LUXURY HOTEL **$$$**

Map p216 (☎04-436 8888; www.theaddress.com; Emaar Blvd, Downtown Dubai; r from Dh1400; @☎≋) This hotel embodies everything Dubai has to offer: beauty, style, glamour and ambition. Since its opening, the Address has drawn the cognoscenti in droves, not only to its rooms but also to its edgy restaurants and buzzy bars. If you do stay, you'll find oversized rooms dressed in rich woods and tactile fabrics, endowed with killer views and the latest communication devices. If that's not enough, the 24-hour gym and five-tiered infinity pool beckon.

PALACE – THE OLD TOWN LUXURY HOTEL **$$$**

Map p216 (☎04-428 7888; www.thepalace-dubai.com; Emaar Blvd, The Old Town Island, Downtown Dubai; r from Dh1200; @☎≋) City explorers with a romantic streak will be utterly enchanted by this luxe contender in the shadow of the Burj Khalifa. A successful blend of Old World class and Arabic aesthetics, the Palace appeals to those with refined tastes. Rooms are chic and understated, styled in soothing earth tones, with balconies overlooking Dubai Fountain. Personal attention is key, from the personal check-in desk to the intimate spa and fabulous restaurants.

ADDRESS DUBAI MALL LUXURY HOTEL **$$$**

Map p216 (☎04-438 8888; www.theaddress.com; Emaar Blvd, Downtown Dubai; r from Dh1200; @☎≋) A modern interpretation of Arabic design traditions, this fashionable hotel is directly connected to Dubai Mall and thus tailor-made for shopaholics. Lug your loot to spacious rooms where sensuous materials – leather, wood and velvet – provide a soothing antidote to shopping exhaustion, as do the ultracomfy beds draped in fluffy pillows and cloud-soft Egyptian cotton. Rooms include huge flatscreen TVs, iPod docking stations and espresso machines. Wi-fi is free throughout and the gym and business lounge are both open around the clock.

QAMARDEEN HOTEL HOTEL **$$**

Map p216 (☎04-428 6888; www.qamardeenhotel.com; Burj Khalifa Blvd, Downtown Dubai; r from Dh805; @☎≋) Sister to the Al-Manzil, the Qamardeen manages to be hip but not overbearing, with bold splashes of colour in its soaring lobby and large rooms. The look appeals to the lifestyle crowd, thanks at least in part to fresh, ultrasuede upholstery, bright-white linen and uncluttered rooms. The palm-lined, blue-tiled pool is at the centre of a classic courtyard but doesn't get much sun. There is a small gym.

FAIRMONT LUXURY HOTEL **$$$**

Map p216 (☎04-332 5555; www.fairmont.com; Sheikh Zayed Rd, Financial District; r from Dh1200; @☎≋) The Fairmont is a distinctive sight at night when its four-poster towers are illuminated by coloured lights. Beyond the flash entrance portals, it also packs plenty of design features in its public areas and rooms with their firm, extra-comfy mattresses, high padded headboards and large desks. There are two rooftop pools and the restaurants are exceptional. Don't miss the fashionable king of bling's Cavalli Club nightclub.

SHANGRI-LA LUXURY HOTEL **$$$**

Map p216 (☎04-343 8888; www.shangri-la.com; Sheikh Zayed Rd, Downtown Dubai; r from Dh1200; @☎≋) Shangri-La is the mythical paradise first described in James Hilton's 1933 novel *Lost Horizon*. In Dubai, it's a business hotel imbued with an understatedly sexy vibe. Rooms are a winner in the looks department, with their blond woods, soft leather headboards and free-standing tubs. The range of first-rate restaurants is superb, as is the sizzling Ikandy rooftop bar (p86).

IBIS WORLD TRADE CENTRE HOTEL **$**

Map p216 (☎04-332 4444, reservations 04-318 7000; www.ibishotel.com; behind World Trade Centre, Sheikh Zayed Rd, Financial District; r Dh350-500; @) Of several Dubai branches of this good-value chain, this one near the World Trade Centre is the most central (the cheapest is in Deira). After the airy feel and modern design in the public areas, the ship's-cabin-sized rooms are a bit of a letdown, but at this price it's hard to find a hotel that's cleaner or more comfortable.

BABY SHARKS

A lone zebra shark that lives in the Burj al-Arab's aquarium prompted scientific interest in January 2012 after laying eggs for the fourth year in a row. Zebedee has never had access to a male shark but that has not stopped her producing numerous live offspring...

AL-MANZIL HOTEL HOTEL **$$**

Map p216 (04-428 5888; www.southernsun.com; Burj Khalifa Blvd, Downtown Dubai; r from Dh759;) Arabesque meets mid-century modern at Al-Manzil, where rooms whip vanilla, chocolate and orange hues into a sophisticated style sorbet. The open-plan rooms may not be for the ultramodest, but the giant rainfall showerheads and free-standing tubs are tempting, nonetheless. Dubai Mall is close by, and if you're jetting in on a late flight, the 24-hour pool and business centre might come in handy. Guests also have free access to the nearby Hayya gym.

DUSIT THANI DUBAI HOTEL **$$**

Map p216 (04-343 3333; www.dusit.com; Sheikh Zayed Rd, next to Interchange No 1; r from Dh795;) Shaped like an upside-down tuning fork, this is one of Dubai's most architecturally dramatic towers. A Thai chain whose target market is the business traveller, the Dusit Thani has rooms with big desks and oversized leather chairs, and the usual high-end amenities, such as featherlight down pillows. Upper-floor views are stellar. The rooftop pool is good for laps (though overhead trusses partially block the sun).

Jumeirah

TOP CHOICE AL-QASR, MADINAT JUMEIRAH LUXURY HOTEL **$$$**

Map p218 (04-366 8888; www.madinatjumeirah.com; Al-Sufouh Rd, Umm Suqeim 3; d from Dh3050;) If cookie-cutter hotels don't do it for you, this is your kind of place. Sister to Mina A' Salam, the 292-room Al-Qasr was styled after an Arabian summer palace. Details are extraordinary, such as the lobby's Austrian-crystal chandeliers reflecting rainbows on to mirror-polished inlaid-marble floors. Rooms sport heavy arabesque flourishes, rich colours and cushy furnishings, including sumptuous beds and his-and-hers bathroom amenities. The side-by-side balconies overlook the grand display of Madinat Jumeirah. Excellent service, great beach.

BURJ AL-ARAB LUXURY HOTEL **$$$**

Map p218 (04-301 7777; www.burj-al-arab.com; Jumeirah Rd, Umm Suqeim 3; ste from Dh6500;) This sail-shaped hotel is one of *the* iconic landmarks in Dubai. Decorated in Sheikh Mohammed's favourite colours – gold, royal blue and carmine red – it regularly hosts pop stars, royalty, billionaire Russians and the merely moneyed. Beyond the striking lobby with its attention-grabbing fountain lie 202 suites with more trimmings than a Christmas turkey. Even the smallest measure 170 sq metres and spread over two floors, making them bigger than most apartments. The decor is l-u-s-h, with moiré silk walls, mirrored ceilings over the beds, curlicue high-backed velvet chairs, and inlaid bathroom tiles displaying scenes of Venice. And all that gold? Yes, it's the real thing, covering a boggling 1590 sq metres of 25-carat gold leaf. Staying here means being whisked through customs at the airport and travelling to the hotel by Rolls Royce or helicopter.

JUMEIRAH BEACH HOTEL RESORT **$$$**

Map p218 (04-348 0000; www.jumeirah.com; Jumeirah Rd, Umm Suqeim 3; r from Dh2000;) The most family-friendly Jumeirah Group hotel is shaped like a giant wave and many rooms have stellar Burj al-Arab views. The beach is huge (nearly 1km long), but the decor looks very dated. Thankfully, at the time of research, the rooms were gradually being refurbished. It's a great resort for active types, with plenty of water sports, a superb health club, a climbing wall and tennis and squash courts. Little ones can make new friends in Sinbad's Kids Club; admission to the adjoining Wild Wadi Waterpark (p102) is also free for guests.

MINA A' SALAM, MADINAT JUMEIRAH RESORT **$$$**

Map p218 (04-366 8888; www.jumeirah.com; Al-Sufouh Rd, Umm Suqeim 3; r from Dh2500;) Meaning 'harbour of peace', the Mina A' Salam has few false notes. The striking lobby is a mere overture to the full symphony of luxury awaiting in huge, amenity-laden rooms with balconies overlooking the romantic jumble that is Madinat Jumeirah or the striking Burj al-Arab. Guests have the entire run of the place and adjacent sister property Al-Qasr, including the pools, the private beach and the kids club. Rates include free admission to Wild Wadi Waterpark (p102).

DUBAI MARINE BEACH RESORT & SPA RESORT **$$$**

Map p218 (04-346 1111; www.dxbmarine.com; Jumeirah Rd, Jumeirah 1; r from Dh1200;) You'll forgive the vintage-1980s condo-box architecture when you consider the convenience of staying a frisbee-toss from the paved Jumeirah Beach path (great for jogging or cycling), within earshot of the Jumeirah Mosque and close to eclectic shopping on Jumeirah Rd. Dubai Marine is a compact beachside resort with accommodation in low-level villas set among meandering lush tropical gardens complete with tumbling waterfalls. The resort is home to an awesome total of 15 terrific restaurants, bars and nightclubs, three pools, a well-equipped gym, kids club and a small sandy beach. Rooms are comfy enough but it's the facilities that stand out.

RYDGES PLAZA HOTEL **$$**

Map p218 (04-398 2222; www.rydges.com; Al-Dhiyafah Rd, Satwa; r Dh450-700;) In the heart of polyethnic Satwa, the Rydges has a clubby English-style decor with classic-designed wallpaper, plush carpeting and shiny dark-wood furniture. There are tubs plus big showers. The Australian-themed sports bar (p97) is justifiably popular and the health club has great circuit-training machines while the pool is good for laps. Jumeirah Beach and Deira are close and taxis are plentiful.

HOLIDAY INN EXPRESS HOTEL **$**

Map p218 (04-407 1777; www.hiexpress.com; cnr Jumeirah Rd & 60 St; r from Dh299;) This contemporary property would be more attractive if it didn't overlook Port Rashid, but at least you'll be close to the beach and Jumeirah. The overall look is clean and contemporary, starting in the Bauhaus-meets-Arabia lobby and transitioning nicely to the rooms kitted out in ebony and apricot hues. There's no pool but there is a free beach shuttle.

New Dubai

TOP CHOICE **ONE&ONLY ROYAL MIRAGE** RESORT **$$$**

Map p220 (04-399 9999; www.oneandonlyresorts.com; Al-Sufouh Rd, Al-Sufouh; Palace/Arabian Court r Dh2240-3740, Residence & Spa r Dh3540-5320;) A class act all around, the Royal Mirage consists of three parts: the Moorish-style Palace, the romantic Arabian Court, and the Residence & Spa, with its majestic spa and hammam (bathhouse). All rooms face the sea, are tastefully furnished and shine with thoughtful feel-at-home touches such as supremely comfortable beds. The gardens are a cross between Granada's Alhambra and an English garden, with bubbling fountains and croquet-quality lawns. Loll around the giant lagoon-style pools, or kick back on the 1km private beach. The bars and restaurants here are among Dubai's best. You can also hop on the complimentary water taxi to the sister hotel One&Only The Palm, which opened in 2011 and boasts similar luxurious facilities.

LE ROYAL MERIDIEN BEACH RESORT & SPA RESORT **$$$**

Map p220 (04-399 5555; www.leroyalmeridien-dubai.com; cnr Murjan Ave & Dhow St, off Al-Sufouh Rd, Al-Sufouh, Dubai Marina; r from Dh2050;) An urge to splurge would be well directed towards this 500-room resort flanking a gorgeous beach and extensive gardens. While rooms in the main building are the most family-friendly (some

TAXI SIR?

Many four- and five-star hotels in Dubai offer guests a dedicated taxi service in chauffeur-driven sedans under contract with the hotel. These 'limos' have no signage, though they do have meters (if not, don't get in) and generally cost about Dh5 more than a regular taxi. But when you're stuck in heavy traffic, the meter ticks fast; expect to pay nearly double the fee of a regular cab. If you object to paying more, tell the bell captain you want a regular taxi (you might have to insist). But if you are pressed for time – and there are no other cabs available – you'll be grateful for the wheels.

DESERT DREAMS

Just a short drive from the traffic jams, construction sites and megamalls are three stellar desert resorts. If you crave a little peace and quiet, and are prepared to spend some serious money, these hotels will show you a calmer, less-hurried side of Dubai.

Desert Palm (☎04-323 8888; www.desertpalm.ae; Hatta/Oman Rd; ste incl breakfast Dh1800-2500, villa Dh4500-6250;) Feel the stresses nibbling at your psyche evaporate the moment you step inside this luxe boutique retreat a short drive south of town and set on a private polo estate. You can opt either for a palm suite with floor-to-ceiling windows overlooking the polo field (plus Bang & Olufsen surround system and Apple iPod), or go for total privacy in one of the villas with private pool. Either way, you'll feel quite blissed out amid earth-toned decor, fancy linens and vast green landscapes. There's also an infinity pool, an on-site spa and a gourmet deli for picking up tasty treats to enjoy on the terrace or as a desert picnic.

Bab al-Shams Desert Resort & Spa (☎04-832 6699; www.meydanhotels.com; near Endurance Villlage; r incl breakfast from Dh1060; @) Resembling an Arabian fort and effortlessly blending into the desertscape, Bab al-Shams is a tonic for tourists seeking to indulge their *One Thousand and One Nights* fantasies. Its labyrinthine layout displays both Arabic and Moorish influences; rooms are gorgeous, spacious and evocatively earthy, with pillars, lanterns, paintings of desert landscapes and prettily patterned Bedouin-style pillows. While this is the perfect place to curl up with a book or meditate in the dunes, the stimuli-deprived will find plenty to do. A wonderful infinity pool beckons, as do the luscious Satori Spa and an archery range. Children under 12 years of age can let off steam in Sinbad's Club. Off-site activities include desert tours and horse and camel rides. Bab al-Shams is about 40 minutes south of Dubai.

Al Maha Desert Resort & Spa (☎04-303 4222; www.al-maha.com; off the Dubai to Al-Ain Rd; ste weekday/weekend incl all meals from Dh5430;) It may only be 65km southeast of Dubai (on the Dubai to Al-Ain Rd), but Al Maha feels like an entirely different universe. Gone are the traffic, the skyscrapers and the go-go attitude. At this remote desert eco-resort it's all about getting back to some elemental discoveries about yourself and where you fit into nature's grand design. Part of the Dubai Desert Conservation Reserve (DDCR), Al Maha is one of the most exclusive hotels in the Emirates and named for the endangered Arabian oryx, which are bred as part of DDCR's conservation program. The resort's 42 luxurious suites are all stand-alone, canvas-roofed bungalows with private plunge pools. Each one has its own patio with stunning vistas of the beautiful desert landscape and peach-coloured dunes, punctuated by mountains and grazing white oryx and gazelles. Rates include two daily activities such as a desert wildlife drive or a camel trek. Private vehicles, visitors and children under 12 years of age are not allowed, and taking meals at your suite rather than in the dining room is a popular choice. Save 30% by reserving a month or more in advance.

have connecting doors), discerning couples may be more charmed by the elegant, classically furnished retreats in the Tower Building. All have sea-view balconies. With three pools, a top-notch gym, a full menu of water sports and lots of activities for kids and teens, no one will get bored.

RITZ-CARLTON DUBAI LUXURY HOTEL **$$$**
Map p220 (☎04-399 4000; www.ritzcarlton.com; The Walk at JBR, Dubai Marina; r Dh2100; @) The Ritz-Carlton exudes an aura of timeless elegance. When it first opened in 1998, Dubai Marina was still the middle of nowhere. Now high-rises loom above, but the mature gardens and tall palms create a visual berm. The Mediterranean-villa-style resort is typical of the chain's restrained and elegant European style – conservative, but cushy – with plush fabrics, marble foyers and colonial-style hardwood furniture. All 138 rooms face the gardens and sea

beyond. Spend the day by one of three pools or on the expansive beach. An extension with 163 rooms was under construction when we visited.

WESTIN DUBAI MINA SEYAHI RESORT **$$$**

Map p220 (☎04-399 4141; www.westinminaseyahi.com; Al-Sufouh Rd, Al-Sufouh; r from Dh1700; @ 🛜 🏊 👪) The top choice for water sports enthusiasts, this sophisticated beach resort sits next to the yacht harbour and aesthetically is a cross between a sheikh's summer palace and an Italian palazzo. With their classic furniture and vanilla and chocolate hues, the oversized rooms look sharp yet homey. Ask for a sea view. The three pools include a 150m-long lagoon-like winding pool for lazing (the others are for kiddies and for swimming laps). The hotel shares facilities, including a water sports centre, with the neighbouring Le Meridien Mina Seyahi.

KEMPINSKI LUXURY HOTEL **$$$**

Map p220 (☎04-341 0000; www.kempinski-dubai.com; Mall of the Emirates, Al-Barsha; r from Dh1375; @ 🛜 🏊) Adjoining the Mall of the Emirates, the Kempinski is perfect for a shopping holiday. The monumental marble lobby contrasts with the rooms, which are warmly decorated in silver, burgundy and white, and have polished wooden floors and subtle Arabic design accents. Some of the bathrooms sport enormous tubs and travertine, sit-down shower stalls with rainfall showerheads. Spot the Burj al-Arab through floor-to-ceiling windows facing Sheikh Zayed Rd. The Kempinksi is also home to unique 'Ski Chalets', enormous Alpine-style apartments overlooking Ski Dubai.

LE MERIDIEN MINA SEYAHI BEACH RESORT & MARINA RESORT **$$$**

Map p220 (☎04-399 3333, www.lemeridien-minaseyahi.com; Al-Sufouh Rd, Al-Sufouh; r from Dh1350; @ 🛜 🏊 👪) Twinned with the Westin, this beachfront hotel is nirvana for active types, offering a plethora of water sports (from waterskiing to kayaking), tennis courts and an enormous gym with state-of-the-art equipment and courses in everything from Thai boxing to Pilates. The giant freeform pool is as lovely as the meandering palm-tree-lined gardens and calm beach. The resort's 210 rooms were renovated in 2011.

GROSVENOR HOUSE LUXURY HOTEL **$$$**

Map p220 (☎04-399 8888; www.grosvenorhouse.lemeridien.com; Al-Sufouh Rd, Dubai Marina; r from Dh1150; @ 🛜 🏊) Grosvenor House was the first hotel to open among the jumble of the Marina's sky-punching towers. The public areas are sleek, grown-up and angular, but rooms feel warm and homey with their cream and brown hues brightened by red accents. Beds have gazillion-thread-count linens and even come with a 'pillow menu'. Downstairs is the famous Buddha Bar (p111). Staying at the Grosvenor entitles you to full access to pool and beach facilities at the nearby sister hotel, Le Royal Meridien, served by a shuttle bus.

ADDRESS DUBAI MARINA LUXURY HOTEL **$$$**

Map p220 (☎436 7777; www.theaddress.com; Dubai Marina; r from Dh1000; @ 🛜 🏊) This place has the sophistication of a city hotel, but its location close to the beach, the Dubai Marina Mall and The Walk at JBR makes it popular with leisure lovers. Rooms are spacious with a fresh contemporary flair, as well as the gamut of amenities. The huge infinity pool on the 4th floor has heady views of the Marina yachts and high-rises.

NAJD HOTEL APARTMENTS HOTEL APARTMENTS **$$**

Map p220 (☎04-361 9007; www.najdhotelapartments.com; btwn 6A & 15 Sts, Al-Barsha; 1-/2-bedroom apt Dh950/1450; @ 🛜 🏊) One of the nicer of the hotel apartments mushrooming around the Mall of the Emirates, Najd is a welcoming host. The tiled-floor apartments make maximum use of space, packing a living room, bedroom, kitchen, full bathroom and guest bathroom into a relatively compact frame. Ask for a room overlooking Ski Dubai. Discounts are often available.

CORAL BEACH BOUTIQUE HOTEL APARTMENTS HOTEL APARTMENTS **$$**

Map p220 (☎04-340 9040; cnr 21 & 2 Sts, Al-Barsha; 1-/2-/3-bedroom apt Dh600/1200/1600; 🛜 🏊) You'll have plenty of space to stretch out in these stylish apartments that feature flatscreen TVs, tiled floors and natural stone bathrooms, and are within walking distance of the Mall of the Emirates. The rooftop pool is great for post-shopping relaxation, while additional perks include a good buffet breakfast, regular shuttle to the mall and free wi-fi.

IBIS MALL OF THE EMIRATES HOTEL $

Map p220 (☎04-382 3000; www.ibis.com; 2A St, Al-Barsha; r from Dh320; @ 📶) Classic Ibis: a good deal with few frills but sparkling clean rooms. If you'd rather drop your cash in the adjacent mall than loll by the pool or nosh on pillow treats, this is not a bad place to hang your hat. Just remember that you can't hang much more than that in the ship's-cabin-sized rooms.

CENTRO BARSHA HOTEL $

Map p220 (☎04-704 0000; www.rotana.com; Al Barsha 1; r from Dh500; @ 📶 🏊) An easy 10-minute walk from the Mall of the Emirates, this latest Rotana Centro hotel has small, contemporary rooms furnished in soft yellows, creams and browns, and features desks, flat screen TVs and abstract art on the walls. There's a comfy cocktail bar, a couple of acceptable restaurants and a fitness centre, plus outdoor pool.

Understand Dubai & Abu Dhabi

Dubai & Abu Dhabi Today

Most visitors to Dubai and Abu Dhabi won't notice anything amiss – and so they shouldn't. Although the global credit crunch hit developers hard, and some questionable new projects have been quietly shelved, this has not dulled the shine of the glossy shopping malls and iconic skyscrapers. Both emirates continue to be a global example of modern Arab cities that remain friendly with the West, something that is particularly meaningful these days, given their location in one of the most volatile regions in the world.

Best on Film

Mission Impossible Ghost Protocol (2011) Tom Cruise scales the Burj Khalifa in this latest 'Mission' thriller.

Syriana (2005) This political thriller starring George Clooney and Matt Damon was partly shot in Dubai.

Duplicity (2009) Spy-themed comedy features exterior shots of Dubai.

Naqaab (2007) Bollywood suspense thriller largely shot in and around Jumeirah Beach.

Best in Print

Arabia (Jonathan Raban; 1979) Fascinating author's travels through recently independent emirates.

Dubai: the Story of the World's Fastest City (Jim Krane; 2009) Balanced look at Dubai's rags-to-riches story.

Dubai: The Vulnerability of Success (Christopher M Davidson; 2008) An in-depth study of Dubai's post-oil development.

Dubai: Gilded Cage (Syed Ali; 2010) Scholarly and critical examination of Dubai's turbo-speed metamorphosis.

Windtower: Houses of the Bastaki (Anne Coles and Peter Jackson; 2011) Stunning coffee-table book about old Dubai.

Tourism versus Tradition

Tiny but turbocharged, Dubai continues to be a highly developed tourism destination offering superb shopping, lodging, eating, sports and relaxation beneath nearly year-round sunny skies. Crime is rare, almost everyone speaks English and tourists are unlikely to be hassled or ripped off. Having said that, Dubai and Abu Dhabi are still conservative by Western standards, and behaviour such as kissing in public, drunkenness or swearing is not tolerated. The most recent figures released by the UK Foreign Office reveal that the United Arab Emirates (UAE) is the country where British visitors are most likely to get arrested while visiting. In other words, Dubai or Abu Dhabi may not be the perfect destination for that honeymoon or stag weekend.

Ethnic Hierarchy

There have long been rumblings of criticism about the rigid social, cultural and economic divides between the Emiratis (who make up around just 10% of the population), expatriate Westerners on short-term work visas, and workers from the developing world, particularly India. At last there are signs that these boundaries are blurring, at least at some level, with Westerners encouraged to own property and increasing numbers of educated Indians taking up prominent posts. India is Dubai's largest trading partner: in 2010 non-oil trade between the two countries reached a record Dh183 billion, and this is a trend set to continue.

Human Rights

The government has attempted to address criticism received about human-rights issues. In its 2011 World Report, the international human-rights organisation Human Rights Watch applauded new UAE labour regulations to curb exploitative recruiting agents who entrap foreign workers with recruiting fees and false contracts. The report lauded this positive commitment, which addresses one of the country's most glaring human-rights problems – the abuse of migrant construction workers. The living conditions of such labourers remain a contentious issue. Keep your eyes peeled when you are flying into the airport at Dubai and you may well spot the segregated labour camps on the outskirts of the city. Many consider the abolition of the sponsorship *(kafala)* system (which basically strips workers of any rights) to be key among needed changes. Kuwait announced plans to scrap its *kafala* system in October 2011. It remains to be seen whether the UAE will follow suit.

Arab Spring Fallout

The revolutionary wave of demonstrations (or Arab Spring) that began on 18 December 2010 has led to authorities in the UAE becoming a tad jittery about any online dissent. In November 2011, authorities blocked access to www.localnewsuae.com, a news portal that features wide-ranging articles and blog posts on local and international issues. Downloading social-networking sites, such as Facebook and Twitter, is also still banned. However, if you have these programs already loaded on your device, there should be no problem. More recently, the online UAE discussion forum **UAE Hewar** (www.uaehewar.net), with its emphasis on freedom of expression and politics, was also blocked. 'The UAE should take a long, hard look at what happens to governments that suppress the rights of its citizens to speak out...' commented Sarah Leah Whitson, Middle East director at Human Rights Watch in a January 2011 press release.

The Future

According to statistics released by government economists, there was a 1.8% increase in economic growth during the first quarter of 2011 and unemployment was at its lowest level, both solid indicators of a steady economic recovery. Meanwhile, Nakheel, the Dubai property developer behind the Palm Jumeirah (which was forced to shelve plans for additional islands due to massive debt), is keeping environmentalists happy with its latest project, building a string of artificial reefs off the city state's coast in a bid to attract more aquatic life. Tourism has increased, with 30 new hotels opening in 2011 and a 9% rise in occupancy, and the emirate is apparently on track to achieve the targets set in the Dubai Strategic Plan for 2015. This involves well-publicised initiatives such as boosting cruise tourism with the opening of a new cruise terminal, launching Dubai Green Tourism Awards for environmentally friendly hotels, and establishing a new hotel classification system with five-star properties being classified into a further three categories: platinum, gold and silver.

if UAE were 100 people

19 would be Emirati
23 would be other Arabs and Iranians
50 would be South Asian
8 would be Western European

belief systems

(% of population)

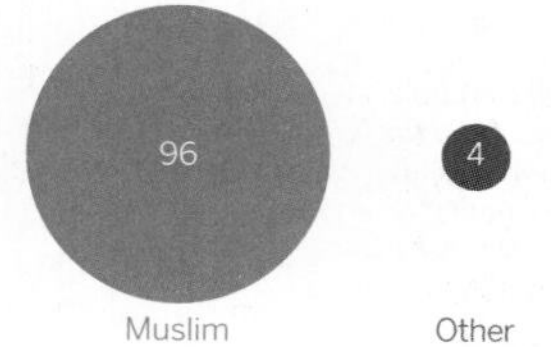

population per sq km

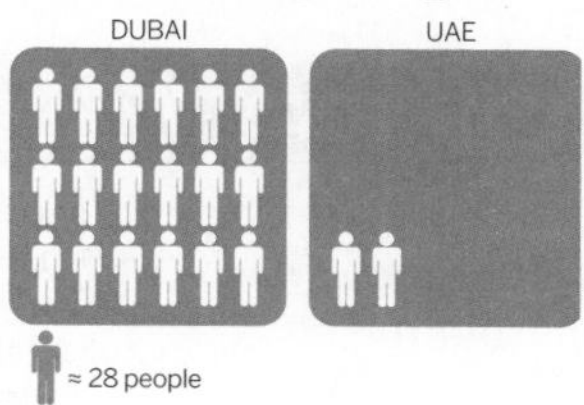

History

Dubai's fast-track transformation from a dusty Arabian outpost to a global leader of tourism and business is an intriguing success story based largely on geography. Located between Dubai Creek and the Gulf, Dubai lies at the heart of lucrative trade routes, whereas Abu Dhabi's wealth is derived largely from oil.

ANCIENT TRADING

It's hard (if not impossible) to imagine that there was ever an Ice Age here, but this period, also known as the Pleistocene epoch, took place roughly 10,000 years ago. Archaeological excavations of sites from around 8000 BC have revealed evidence of human settlement in the United Arab Emirates (UAE). The first signs of trade date back to 5000 BC and documented evidence also suggests that this area, with present-day Oman, was closely associated with the Magan civilisation, which dominated the world's copper trade during the Bronze Age. Mysteriously, all records of the Magan civilisation cease after the 2nd millennium BC, with some historians speculating that the desertification of the area hastened its demise.

One of the most significant events in Dubai's history occurred in the 7th century when the Umayyads, an Islamic tribe from Damascus, introduced the Arabic language and made it part of the Islamic world – a connection still in place today. After their successors, the Baghdad-based Abbasid dynasty, went into decline around AD 1000, the tribes of the Arabian Peninsula asserted themselves in the hinterlands. Meanwhile, the coastal regions were dominated by ports as, once again, trade became the backbone of the local economy, with ships travelling as far as China, returning laden with silk and porcelain.

Historical Reads

Arabia and the Arabs: from the Bronze Age to the Coming of Islam by Robert G Hoyland

The Arabs by Peter Mansfield

Arabian Sands by Wilfred Thesiger

TIMELINE

3000 BC

The area known today as Dubai is populated by nomadic herders of sheep, cattle and goats. The Magan civilisation dominates the world's copper trade.

AD 700

The Umayyads introduce Arabic and Islam to the region. The Umayyad Caliphate was the first dynasty of Islam, lasting from AD 650 to 750.

1580

Gasparo Balbi, a Venetian jeweller, tours the region to investigate its potential for the pearling trade. He notes in his records that he visits a town in the Gulf called 'Dibei'.

EUROPEANS ARRIVE

In the 16th century, Portugal became the first European power to realise that this part of the Gulf might be lucrative. However, their policy of not tolerating rivals was a disaster for Muslim traders, with local trade drying up and tribes fleeing far from the coast. In the 17th and 18th centuries the French and Dutch arrived, and they were similarly eager to control the trading routes to the east. They were followed swiftly by the British in 1766 who were equally intent on ruling the seas.

Throughout this tumultuous time, Dubai remained a small fishing and pearling hamlet, perched on a disputed border between two local powers – the seafaring Qawassim of present-day Ras al-Khaimah and Sharjah, to the north, and the Bani Yas tribal confederation of what is now Abu Dhabi to the south. The region was also affected by rivalries between bigger regional powers – the Wahhabi tribes (of what is now Saudi Arabia), the Ottoman Empire, the Persians and the British.

THE TRUCIAL COAST

In 1833, under the leadership of Maktoum bin Butti (r 1833–52), a tribe from Abu Dhabi overthrew the town. This established the Al-Maktoum dynasty of Dubai, which still rules the emirate today. For Maktoum bin Butti, good relations with the British authorities in the Gulf were essential to safeguard his small upstart sheikhdom against attack from the larger and more powerful surrounding sheikhdoms.

In 1841 the Bur Dubai settlement extended to Deira on the northern side of the Creek, though throughout the 19th century it largely remained a tiny enclave of fishermen, pearl divers, Bedouin, and Indian and Persian merchants. Interestingly, the Indians and Persians (now Iranians) are still largely the custodians of the area, providing the Creek with much of its character today.

Things began to change significantly around the end of the 19th century. In 1892 the British, keen to impose their authority on the region and protect their Indian empire, extended their power through a series of so-called exclusive agreements, under which the sheikhs accepted formal British protection and, in exchange, relinquished all foreign affairs. As a result of these treaties, or truces, Europeans called the area 'the Trucial Coast', a name it retained until the 1971 federation that created the UAE.

In 1894 Dubai's visionary ruler, Sheikh Maktoum bin Hasher al-Maktoum (r 1894–1906), made the masterstroke decision to give foreign traders tax-exempt status, and the free port of Dubai was born, a move that neatly catapulted the emirate way ahead of its rivals.

PEARLING

The heyday of pearling is laced with romanticism. Unfortunately for those who dove in the depths to collect pearls, however, it was a life of hardship and the rewards were no match for the dangers involved. Most divers were slaves from East Africa and the profits of the industry went straight to their master, the boat owner.

1892

The sheikhdoms sign a treaty with Britain: they'd have no dealings with other foreign powers in return for protection from British armed forces.

1930

The Great Depression of 1929–34, paired with the development of a new method of creating pearls artificially, prompts Sheikh Rashid to conclude that the pearling industry is finished.

1940

There is a brief conflict between Dubai and Sharjah following a dispute in the Maktoum family. Hostilities cease after the British cut off the supply lines and both sides run out of gunpowder.

1946

Sheikh Zayed bin Sultan al-Nahyan makes his political debut at the age of 38 when he is appointed ruler's representative in his hometown of Al-Ain.

Further afield, Lingah, across the Strait of Hormuz in Iran, lost its status as a duty-free port, resulting in many disillusioned traders shifting to Dubai. At first the Persians who came to Dubai believed it would be a temporary move. However, by the 1920s it became clear the trade restrictions in southern Iran were there to stay, so they took up permanent residence in the area known today as the Bastakia Quarter.

Dubai's importance to Britain as a port of call continued for half a century, marking the beginning of Dubai's growth as a trading power and fuelling the prosperity that would follow.

THE EXPANDING CITY

By the beginning of the 20th century Dubai was well established and had a population approaching 10,000. Deira was the most populous area at this time, with around 350 shops by 1908 and another 50 in Bur Dubai, where the Indian community was concentrated. To this day, the Bur Dubai Souq shows a strong Indian influence, and Bur Dubai is home to the only Hindu temple in the city.

The development of Dubai as a major trading centre was ironically spurred on by the collapse of the pearling trade, which had been the mainstay of its economy for centuries. The trade had fallen victim to the Great Depression of 1929–34 and to the Japanese discovery (in 1930) of a method of artificial pearl cultivation. Ever resourceful, Sheikh Saeed al-Maktoum (r 1912–58) rapidly realised that alternative sources of revenue were necessary and a new era in Dubai's trade was born: re-exporting. Dubai's enterprising merchants began importing goods to sell on to other ports. In practice, this involved the smuggling of goods, particularly of gold, to India. The goods entered and exited Dubai legally; it was the countries at the other end of the trade that saw it as smuggling.

In 1951 the Trucial States Council was founded, for the first time bringing together the rulers of the sheikhdoms of what would become the UAE, and marking the time modern Dubai would begin to take shape. Savvy Sheikh Rashid spent untold sums on dredging the Creek (it had become badly silted up, reducing the volume of Creek traffic) and building a new breakwater near its mouth. Thus, when oil was discovered in Dubai a few years later in 1966, the cargo channels and infrastructure were already in place. The discovery of oil greatly accelerated the modernisation of the region and was a major factor in the formation of the UAE.

Visitors to Dubai will no doubt notice enormous posters of a smiling sheikh in a pair of Ray Ban–style sunglasses. This is Sheikh Zayed bin Sultan al-Nahyan, the first and, up until his death in 2004, the only president of the UAE. Revered by his people, and often called 'father' by Emiratis, his compassion, modesty and wisdom commanded huge respect across the Middle East.

1951

The British government establishes the Trucial States Council, which brings together the leaders of the sheikhdoms that would later form the UAE.

1958

After almost 20 years of de facto leadership, Sheikh Rashid officially becomes ruler of Dubai. He had been regent since 1939 but could only assume the position of leader after his father's death.

1960

The first commercial oil field is discovered at Babi in Abu Dhabi. Six years later, oil is discovered in Dubai, spurring a period of rapid economic growth.

1968

The British announce that they would end their relationship with the Trucial States by 1971 and local leaders discuss the possibility of a future nation.

THE RECENT PAST

When Britain announced its departure from the region in 1968, an attempt was made to create a nation that included the seven emirates that made up the Trucial States (today's United Arab Emirates) as well as Bahrain and Qatar. While the talks with Bahrain and Qatar collapsed (they both moved on to their own independence), the leader of Abu Dhabi, Sheikh Zayed bin Sultan al-Nahyan, and his counterpart in Dubai, Sheikh Rashid bin Saeed al-Maktoum, strengthened their commitment to creating a single state.

On 2 December 1971, after persistence from Sheikh Zayed, the federation of the UAE was born, consisting of the emirates of Dubai, Abu Dhabi, Ajman, Fujairah, Sharjah and Umm al-Quwain, with Ras al-Khaimah joining in 1972. Impressively, given the volatility in the region, the UAE remains to this day the only federation of Arab states in the Middle East.

Under the agreement, the emirs approved a formula whereby Abu Dhabi and Dubai (in that order) would carry the most weight in the federation, but would leave each emir largely autonomous. Sheikh Zayed became the supreme ruler (president) of the UAE, and Sheikh Rashid of Dubai assumed the role of vice-president.

Since federation, Dubai has been one of the most politically stable city states in the Arab world. However, the fledgling nation has still had its teething problems. Border disputes between the emirates continued throughout the 1970s and '80s, and the level of independence that each emirate enjoys has been the subject of long discussions.

While Dubai and Abu Dhabi had an agreement to cooperate long before the UAE was born, the relationship has not been without its difficulties. Achieving an equitable balance of power between the two emirates, as well as refining a unified vision for the country, was much debated until 1979 when Sheikh Zayed and Sheikh Rashid sealed an agreement in which each gave a little ground on his vision for the country. The result was a much stronger federation in which Dubai remained a bastion of free trade while Abu Dhabi imposed a tighter federal structure on the other emirates. Rashid also agreed to take the title of prime minister as a symbol of his commitment to the federation.

Sheikh Rashid, the driving force behind Dubai's phenomenal growth and 'father of (modern) Dubai', died in 1990 after a long illness and was succeeded as emir by the eldest of his four sons, Sheikh Maktoum bin Rashid al-Maktoum. Maktoum had already been regent for his sick father for several years and continued the expansion of Dubai.

1979

Sheikh Rashid is declared prime minister of the UAE. The post had been held by his son, Sheikh Maktoum, who stepped aside to give his father more power.

1990

Sheikh Rashid dies during the first Gulf War and his son, Sheikh Maktoum, takes over as ruler of Dubai. Five years later, Maktoum's brother Mohammed assumes de facto rule.

FAYEZ NURELDINE/AFP/GETTYIMAGES ©

Sheikh Mohammed bin Rashid al-Maktoum (p154)

Overseeing Dubai's transformation into a 21st-century metropolis is the third son of the dynasty, Sheikh Mohammed bin Rashid al-Maktoum, who was the face of modern Dubai even before he succeeded his older brother as ruler in 2006. Having ruled Dubai as a de facto leader since the mid-1990s, Sheikh Mohammed has brought consistency and continuity to Dubai in a period of tremendous social, cultural and economic change. In February 2008 he named his son Hamdan bin Mohammed bin Rashid al-Maktoum, also known as 'Fazza 3', as the emirate's crown prince and his likely successor. The young prince, a Sandhurst graduate who publishes romantic poetry, is already tremendously popular – check out his fan videos on YouTube or friend him on Facebook.

1996

Two major annual events, the Dubai Shopping Festival and the Dubai World Cup, are launched. The Burj al-Arab opens, enhancing Dubai's reputation as a tourist destination.

2006

Sheikh Mohammed becomes ruler of Dubai after Sheikh Maktoum's passing, and is also confirmed as prime minister and vice-president of the UAE.

2008

The world financial crisis severely affects Dubai's economy, putting the brakes on its surging development and causing a plunge in real estate prices of up to 50%.

2010

The extraordinary Burj Khalifa opens. At 828m it's the world's tallest building. It has more than 160 floors and the highest outdoor observation deck in the world.

Politics & Economy

Despite being the emirate with the highest profile, Dubai is neither the wealthiest nor the most powerful. Those honours belong to Abu Dhabi, the capital of the United Arab Emirates (UAE) and home to most of the country's oil wealth. Dubai is second in line, however, and is the emirate that has truly maximised its tourist potential. In each emirate, power rests with a ruling tribe, which in Dubai's case is the Maktoum family. There are no political parties or general elections in Dubai but even if there were, it would be hard to imagine the Maktoums being deposed, having been in power since 1833.

SOME POLITICAL BACKGROUND

Despite Dubai becoming so strong over the last few years, it has had to fight long and hard to preserve as much of its independence as possible and to minimise the power of the country's federal institutions. As in Ras al-Khaimah, it maintains a legal system that is separate from the federal judiciary.

Politically, the relative interests of the seven emirates are fairly clear. Abu Dhabi is the largest and wealthiest emirate and has the biggest population. It is, therefore, the dominant member of the federation and is likely to remain so for some time. Dubai is the second-largest emirate by population, with both an interest in upholding its free-trade policies and a pronounced independent streak. However, its dependence on Abu Dhabi became clear during the financial turmoil of 2008–9 when the capital had to bail out Dubai on several occasions. The other emirates are dependent on subsidies from Abu Dhabi, though the extent of this dependence varies widely.

Dubai's per capita income is around Dh80,000 per annum, while the annual salary of an unskilled expat labourer is anywhere between Dh6000 and Dh12,000.

The Decision-Makers

The seven rulers (emirs) of the emirates form the Supreme Council, the highest body in the land, which ratifies federal laws and sets general policy. New laws can be passed with the consent of five of the seven rulers. The Supreme Council also elects one of the emirs to a five-year term as the country's president. After the death in late 2004 of the founder of the country and its first president, Sheikh Zayed, power passed peacefully to his son Sheikh Khalifa bin Zayed al-Nahyan.

There is also a Council of Ministers, or cabinet, headed by the prime minister, who appoints ministers from across the emirates. Naturally, the more populous and wealthier emirates such as Abu Dhabi and Dubai have greater representation. The cabinet and Supreme Council are advised, but can't be overruled, by a parliamentary body called the National Council (FNC). See the boxed text (p157) for more information.

Censorship

According to a report issued by the Open Net Initiative (ONI), 'The government of the United Arab Emirates (UAE) censors political and religious content and pervasively filters websites that contain pornography or content relating to alcohol or drug use, gay and lesbian issues, or online dating or gambling.' All journalists working in Dubai know that some topics, such as criticism of the UAE's rulers or anything that could be perceived as negative treatment of Islam, are completely off limits.

OILING THE WHEELS OF SUCCESS

The UAE has the world's seventh-largest oil reserves (after Saudi Arabia, Iran, Iraq, Canada, Kuwait and Venezuela), but the vast majority of it is concentrated in the emirate of Abu Dhabi. It is thought that at current levels of production, reserves will last for only another century and, sensibly, the country is looking at other industries to take over from oil in the future. Dubai handled this with particular foresight, largely thanks to the vision and ambition of Sheikh Mohammed bin Rashid al-Maktoum. Its reserves of oil and gas were never huge, but it used its resources wisely towards financing a modern and efficient infrastructure for trade, manufacturing and tourism. Today, about 82% of the UAE's non-oil GDP is generated in Dubai, and about 95% of Dubai's GDP (US$81 billion in 2008) is not oil-based. Inflation slowed down significantly in 2011 and now hovers around 2.5%.

SHEIKH MOHAMMED – MR DUBAI

When Dubai's current ruler, Sheikh Mohammed bin Rashid al-Maktoum, was named one of the world's 100 most influential people by *Time* magazine in 2008, it surprised no one. Having spent several years as a de facto ruler while he was crown prince, Sheikh Mohammed was the only candidate for the top job when his brother, Sheikh Maktoum, died in early 2006. Although he is surrounded by some of the greatest minds in the Gulf, as well as political and economic experts imported from all over the world, there's no uncertainty about where executive power lies. 'Sheikh Mo', as he is affectionately called, has a flair for generating publicity for the city and was deeply involved in the planning and construction of landmark projects such as the Burj al-Arab, Palm Jumeirah and Burj Khalifa. For the Burj al-Arab project, it's said that the sheikh wanted a design that would be as resonant as the Eiffel Tower and the Sydney Opera House.

In addition to handling the day-to-day running of the emirate, Sheikh Mohammed strengthens the bond between Dubai and the other six emirates in his capacity as prime minister and vice-president of the United Arab Emirates (UAE). At the same time, his ownership of Dubai Holding gives him control of numerous businesses such as the Jumeirah Group (properties including the Burj al-Arab) and TECOM (Internet City). He's also a keen fan of falconry and equestrianism and runs the Godolphin Stables. He is believed to be worth at least US$10 billion.

Visitors from Western countries may feel uncomfortable with the large-scale portraits of the ruler on billboards and buildings around town. Yet these are not simply the propaganda tools of an autocratic regime; many people in Dubai revere their ruler. Few world leaders are able to drive themselves around town, as Sheikh Mohammed does, without a bodyguard and without any fear of being attacked. Although dissenting voices aren't tolerated and the local media is uncritical, most people admire the emirates' leaders for creating a haven of peace and prosperity in a troubled part of the world.

THE ROAD TO DEMOCRACY

Slowly but surely, the UAE is taking tentative steps towards democracy. Since 2006, half the country's Federal National Council (FNC), a 40-person body established to review and debate legislation, has been elected; the other 20 are appointed by each emirate. But the FNC has no real power (it can only advise the government) and only 6689 people – less than 1% of Emiratis and a tiny fraction of the UAE's total population – have been hand-picked to vote for candidates from a list approved by the government. Eight FNC members are women, although only one was elected. While full democracy in the UAE may be decades away, there are plans to grant the FNC some legislative powers and eventually to give the vote to all UAE citizens.

ONE BURST BUBBLE

Until September 2008 it looked as though Dubai had the Midas touch. But then the world financial crisis struck and the emirate's economy collapsed like the proverbial house of cards. Real estate was particularly hard hit, with prices plummeting as much as 50%; Dubai was left with a staggering debt of at least US$80 billion. When the government announced, in November 2009, that it would seek a six-month delay in repaying its debt, including a US$4 billion Islamic bond due in December, it sent worldwide stock markets into a tailspin. Markets stabilised quickly after the Abu Dhabi government rode to the rescue with a US$10 billion loan, which seems generous until you realise that oil-rich Abu Dhabi has a balance sheet of US$600 billion. As a sign of gratitude, in January 2010 Sheikh Mohammed named the world's tallest building – which had thus far been referred to as Burj Dubai – Burj Khalifa in honour of the UAE president and ruler of Abu Dhabi, Sheikh Khalifa bin Zayed al-Nahyan. It remains to be seen whether the loan was merely a stopgap measure or whether it will buy enough time for Dubai to restructure its finances and put itself on a slower but more sustainable growth path. On a positive note, in 2012 the emirate benefited by around $30 billion of maturities, which will doubtless be used to regain access to international markets and ease liquidity pressures.

Dubai's tourism industry has exploded. The city's profusion of quality hotels, long stretches of beach, warm winter weather, shopping incentives, desert activities and relative tolerance of Western habits have helped it become the leading tourist destination in the Gulf.

ONCE A TRADER, ALWAYS A TRADER

Throughout history, trade has been a fundamental part of Dubai's economy. The emirate imports an enormous amount of goods, primarily minerals and chemicals, base metals (including gold), vehicles and machinery, electronics, textiles and foodstuffs; the main importers into Dubai are the US, China, Japan, the UK, South Korea and India. Exports are mainly oil, natural gas, dates, dried fish, cement and electric cables; top export destinations are the other Gulf States, India, Japan, Taiwan, Pakistan and the US. Dubai's re-export trade (where items such as whitegoods come into Dubai from manufacturers and are then sent onwards) makes up about 80% of the UAE's total re-export business. Dubai's re-exports go mainly to Iran, India, Saudi Arabia, Kuwait, China and Afghanistan. Dubai is home to the world's largest man-made harbour and biggest port in the Middle East. Called Jebel Ali, it's at the far western edge of Dubai, en route to Abu Dhabi.

World's Largest Airport

Dubai never shies away from superlatives, which is why it should be no surprise that it is to have the world's biggest airport. Upon completion, Al-Maktoum International Airport in Jebel Ali will boost the emirate's annual passenger potential to an estimated 160 million by 2035 and be capable of handling over 12 million tonnes of cargo annually. It is expected to cost around $34 billion and be 10 times the size of Dubai International Airport and Dubai Cargo Village combined. Freight operations started in June 2010 and passenger flights are expected to begin in 2013. Passenger numbers jumped by 11% in 2011 and the contribution to Dubai's GDP has been significant.

Elsewhere in the Gulf, Qatar and Abu Dhabi are also building megahubs to support their fast-growing national airlines, Qatar Airways and Etihad, respectively. Abu Dhabi's Terminal 3 opened in 2009 to accommodate the approximate 12 million annual passengers, with an additional terminal scheduled to open in 2016.

Economy on the Web

www.kippreport.com

www.uaeinteract.com

www.abudhabi.ae

www.emirateseconomist.blogspot.com

FREE ZONES

The Jebel Ali Free Zone, established in 1985, is home to 5500 companies from 120 countries and has contributed hugely to Dubai's economic diversification. Companies are enticed here by the promise of full foreign ownership, full repatriation of capital and profits, no corporate tax for 15 years, no currency restrictions, and no personal income tax. Other industry-specific free zones, such as Dubai Internet City and Dubai Media City, have added a high-tech information and communication stratum to the city's economy. IT firms based here include Google, HP, Dell and Oracle. Reuters, CNN, CNBC, MBC, Sony, Showtime and Bertelsmann are among the media companies that have set up shop in town.

Identity & Lifestyle

The population in Dubai is one of the most diverse, multicultural and male (three quarters of the population) in the world. In stark contrast to neighbouring Saudi Arabia and nearby Iran, both Dubai and Abu Dhabi are, overall, tolerant and easy-going societies. Most religions are tolerated and places of worship have been built for Christians, Hindus and Sikhs. Notwithstanding, both Dubai and Abu Dhabi's traditional culture and social life is firmly rooted in Islam, and day-to-day activities, relationships, diet and dress are very much dictated by religion.

ROLE OF WOMEN

Living with such a large proportion of expats, and an increasing number of Western cultural influences, has led to both growing conservatism and liberalisation. This is especially noticeable among young women: while some dress in Western fashion (usually those with foreign mothers), others are individualising traditional dress, while yet others are 'covering up'.

Gender roles are changing, with more and more women wanting to establish careers before marriage. Women's contribution to the workforce has grown considerably in the past decade. Successful Emirati women are increasingly serving as role models, such as the United Arab Emirates (UAE) Minister of Trade, Sheikha Lubna al-Qasimi (one of the 100 most powerful women in the world, according to *Forbes* magazine), and Dr Amina Rostamani (CEO of TECOM, a corporation that oversees several free-trade zones).

The UAE Marriage Fund, set up by the federal government in 1994 to facilitate marriages between UAE nationals, provides grants to pay for the exorbitant costs of the wedding and dowry, and promotes mass weddings to enable nationals to save for a down payment on a house.

Marriage

An indirect byproduct of the shifting role of women is the ongoing trend for Emirati men to marry foreign women. One reason is that Emirati women are becoming better educated and as a result are less willing to settle down in the traditional role of an Emirati wife. Other contributing factors are the prohibitive cost of a traditional wedding, plus the dowry the groom must provide – essentially, it can save a lot of dirhams and a lot of hassle to marry a foreign girl.

PRESERVING THE UAE HERITAGE

Some say that Dubai is fake and principally a 'shopping culture'. Take these comments with a pinch of salt – shopping is merely a pastime, albeit an extremely popular one. In both Dubai and Abu Dhabi, Emirati cultural identity is expressed through poetry, traditional song and dance, a love of the desert and nature, and of camels, horses and falconry, all of which remain popular activities. If you're lucky enough to be invited to a wedding (and you should take up the offer), it's a great way to see some of these cultural traditions in action.

The Dubai government has been quite active in preserving and publicly displaying many local sights and traditions that provide insights into traditional and cultural life. The aim of such preservation efforts is not just to attract and entertain tourists, but to educate young Emiratis about the value of their culture and heritage. Families also make an effort to maintain their heritage by taking their children out to the desert frequently and teaching them how to continue traditional practices such as falconry. The love of the desert is also something that is passed from father to son – Emiratis are as comfortable in the sands as they are in Switzerland, where many of them take a summer break away from the heat.

THE EMIRATI LIFESTYLE

Don't be surprised if you hear expats make crude generalisations about Emiratis. You may be told they're all millionaires and live in mansions, or that they refuse to work in ordinary jobs, or that all the men have four wives. Such stereotypes simply reinforce prejudices and demonstrate the lack of understanding between cultures in Dubai and Abu Dhabi.

Not all Emiratis are wealthy. While the traditional tribal leaders, or sheikhs, are often the wealthiest UAE nationals, many have made their fortune through good investments, often dating back to the 1970s. As befits a small oil-producing nation, all Emiratis have access to free

THE FIVE PILLARS OF ISLAM

Islam is the official religion of Dubai and Abu Dhabi, and the majority of Emiratis are Sunni Muslims. Many expatriates also practise Islam, and in some parts of town, mosques have largely Pakistani congregations. The diversity of the large expatriate population means most other religions are also represented.

➡ **Shahadah** The profession of faith: 'There is no god but God, and Mohammed is the messenger of God.'

➡ **Salat** Muslims are required to pray five times every day: at dawn *(fajr)*, noon *(dhuhr)*, mid-afternoon *(asr)*, sunset *(maghrib)* and twilight *(isha'a)*. Loudspeakers on the minarets of mosques transmit the call to prayer *(adhan)* at these times, and you can expect to be woken up at dawn if your hotel is situated in the cluttered streets of Deira or Bur Dubai. During prayers a Muslim must perform a series of prostrations while facing the Kaaba, the ancient shrine at the centre of the Grand Mosque in Mecca. Before a Muslim can pray, however, he or she must perform a series of ritual ablutions; if water isn't available for this, sand or soil can be substituted.

➡ **Zakat** Muslims must give a portion of their income to help the poor. How this has operated in practice has varied over the centuries: either it was seen as an individual duty (as is the case in Dubai and Abu Dhabi) or the state collected it as a form of income tax to be redistributed through mosques or religious charities.

➡ **Sawm** It was during the month of Ramadan in AD 610 that Mohammed received his first revelation. Muslims mark this event by fasting from sunrise until sunset throughout Ramadan. During the fast a Muslim may not take anything into his or her body. Food, drink, smoking and sex are forbidden. Young children, travellers and those whose health will not allow it are exempt from the fast, though those who are able to do so are supposed to make up the days they missed at a later time.

➡ **Hajj** All able Muslims are required to make the pilgrimage to Mecca at least once, if possible during a specific few days in the first and second weeks of the Muslim month of Dhul Hijja, although visiting Mecca and performing the prescribed rituals at any other time of the year is also considered spiritually desirable. Such visits are referred to as *umrah*, or 'little pilgrimages'.

health care and education as well as a marriage fund (although the budgets don't often meet the expenses of elaborate Emirati weddings). These types of social benefits, and charities operated by generous sheikhs such as Sheikh Mohammed, are essential to the survival of poorer Emiratis in modern Dubai.

The upper and middle classes of Emirati society generally have expansive villas in which men and women still live apart, and male family members entertain guests in the *majlis* (meeting room). In all classes of Emirati society, extended families living together is the norm, with the woman moving in with the husband's family after marriage, although some young couples are now choosing to buy their own apartments for a little more privacy than the traditional arrangement allows.

The Impact of Islam

Although Dubai and Abu Dhabi are open and tolerant, they are still Muslim emirates, and followers of Islam follow the laws of Islam. They do not drink alcohol or eat pork – although both are available to non-Muslims in both emirates. Perhaps most noticeable to visitors is the fact that Friday is the holy day here, so the weekend falls on Friday and Saturday. Emirati men are also permitted to have up to four wives, although this is becoming less commonplace. Also worth noting is the fact that the basis of the legal system in Dubai and Abu Dhabi is Sharia'a and Islamic courts work alongside the civil and criminal courts in the UAE.

The Workplace

Most Emiratis work in the public sector, as the short hours, good pay, benefits and early pensions are hard for people to refuse. The UAE government is actively pursuing a policy of 'Emiratisation', which involves encouraging Emiratis to work in the private sector, and encouraging employers to reject negative stereotypes and hire them. In the long term the government hopes to be much less dependent on an imported labour force.

WASTA

When visiting Dubai, you might hear expats talking about '*wasta*'. The term translates loosely as 'influence high up' and having *wasta* can grease the wheels in just about every transaction in Dubai. Most Westerners get a little outraged at the thought of a select few receiving favours because of powerful contacts – until, of course, they want some help themselves.

EXPAT WORKERS

Across the UAE, expats constitute a staggering 79.7% of the population. Although there has been a slump in the number of Western professional expats working in Dubai and Abu Dhabi (largely due to a slowing down of new projects), there is still a healthy quota here, as well as blue-collar workers; most of the latter hail from India, Pakistan and the Philippines and, increasingly, from other parts of Asia, as well as Africa.

Disposable income plays a big part in how people live. At the top end of the pay scale is the professional and wealthy management class, members of which can expect a good salary package, a nice car, a large villa with maid and nanny and a lifestyle that allows them to travel overseas for two months a year. Housewives left with little to do at home spend much of their time with other women in similar circumstances. These 'Jumeirah Janes', as other expats call them with a hint of derision, keep the cosmetics and spa industries alive and the cafes ticking over during the day.

At the other end of the scale is a vast army of service-sector workers, most from India, Pakistan and the Philippines. Working as line cooks and servers and in supermarkets, these expats stand to make more money in the UAE than at home, usually working six days a week and sharing rooms in cheap accommodation.

The Environment

The transformation of Dubai and Abu Dhabi from small towns to major metropolises in the space of a few decades has inevitably had a negative impact on the environment. According to a World Wildlife Fund report in 2010, the United Arab Emirates (UAE) tops the list of the five countries with the biggest ecological footprint. It is not all doom and gloom, however, with various groups and projects trying to raise environmental awareness across the UAE. The most prominent is the extraordinary Masdar City project based in Abu Dhabi.

THE LANDSCAPE

Dubai is capital of the emirate of the same name and extends over 4114 sq km, making it the second-largest of the seven emirates that compose the UAE. Prior to settlement, this area was flat *sabkha* (salt-crusted coastal plain). The sand mostly consists of crushed shell and coral and is fine, clean and white. The *sabkha* was broken only by clumps of desert grasses and a small area of hardy mangroves at the inland end of the Dubai Creek. Photographs of the area from the early 20th century show how strikingly barren the landscape was.

At 67,340 sq km, Abu Dhabi is the largest sheikhdom in the UAE, occupying more than 80% of the UAE's total area. Its coastline is a combination of high-rises, luxury hotels, pristine beaches and landscaped parks.

Beyond the City

East of the city, the *sabkha* gives way to north–south lines of dunes. The farming areas of Al-Khawaneej and Al-Awir, now on the edge of Dubai's suburbia, are fed by wells. Further east, the dunes grow larger and are tinged red with iron oxide. The dunes stop abruptly at the gravel fans at the base of the rugged Hajar Mountains, where there are gorges and waterholes. A vast sea of sand dunes covers the area south of the city, becoming more and more imposing as it stretches into the desert known as the Empty Quarter (Rub' al-Khali), which makes up the southern region of the UAE and the western region of Saudi Arabia. North of Dubai, along the coast, the land is tough desert scrub broken by inlets similar to Dubai Creek, until you reach the mountainous northern emirates.

Away from the coast in Abu Dhabi, the desert interior remains a fertile oasis of soaring dunes, scenic wadis, thickets of date palms and even some historic forts standing where caravans once paused along their ancient trading routes.

PARKS & PLANTS

In the parks of Dubai and Abu Dhabi you will see indigenous tree species such as the date palm and the *neem* (a botanical cousin of mahogany), and a large number of imported species, including eucalyptus. The sandy desert surrounding the city supports wild grasses and the occasional date-palm oasis. In the salty scrublands further down the coast you might spot the dazzle of a desert hyacinth emerging in all its glory after the rains. It has bright-yellow and deep-red dappled flowers.

Decorating the flat plains that stretch away from the foothills of the Hajar Mountains, near Hatta, are different species of flat-topped acacia trees. The *ghaf* also grows in this area; this big tree looks a little like a weeping willow and is incredibly hardy, as its roots stretch down for about 30m, allowing it to tap into deep water reserves. The tree is highly respected in the Arab world, as it provides great shade and food for goats and camels; it's also a good indicator that there's water in the vicinity.

WILDLIFE

The *Handbook of Arabian Medicinal Plants* and *Vegetation of the Arabian Peninsula*, both by SA Ghazanfar, are good illustrated guides to their subject.

Mammals & Reptiles

As in any major city, you don't see much wildlife. On the fringes of Dubai and Abu Dhabi, where the urban sprawl gives way to the desert, you may see a desert fox, sand cat or falcon if you are very lucky. Otherwise, the only animals you are likely to encounter are camels and goats. The desert is also home to various reptile species, including the desert monitor lizard (up to 1m long), the sand skink, the spiny-tailed agama and several species of gecko. The only poisonous snakes are vipers, such as the sawscaled viper, which can be recognised by its distinctive triangular head. There are even two remarkably adapted species of toad, which hibernate for years between floods, burrowed deep in wadis.

Urbanisation, combined with zealous hunting, has brought about the virtual extinction of some species. These include the houbara bustard, the striped hyena and the caracal (a cat that resembles a lynx). The Arabian oryx (also called the white oryx), however, is one success story. As part of a program of the Dubai Desert Conservation Reserve (p127), it has been successfully reintroduced. The Al-Ain Wildlife Park (p129), which is being expanded into a wildlife park with a heavy focus on sustainability, also has a successful breeding program.

Bird Life

The city is a hotspot for birdwatchers; because of the spread of irrigation and greenery, the number and variety of birds are growing. Dubai is on the migration path between Europe, Asia and Africa, and more than 320 migratory species pass through in spring and autumn, or

LOCAL ENVIRONMENTAL ORGANISATIONS

Dubai Turtle Rehabilitation Project (www.facebook.com/turtle.rehabilitation) Located, somewhat strangely, in the basement of the Burj al-Arab, this sanctuary looks after hundreds of sick turtles every year.

Emirates Diving Association (☎393 9390; www.emiratesdiving.com) This association is an active participant in local environmental campaigns, with an emphasis on the marine environment.

Emirates Environmental Group (☎344 8622; www.eeg-uae.org) This non-profit group organises educational programs in schools and businesses as well as community programs, such as clean-up drives.

Emirates Wildlife Society (http://uae.panda.org) Works in association with the World Wildlife Fund on implementing conservation initiatives to protect local biodiversity and promote sustainable lifestyles.

spend winter here. Species native to Arabia include the crab plover, the Socotra cormorant, the black-crowned finch lark and the purple sunbird.

Sea Life

The waters off Dubai teem with around 300 different species of fish. Diners will be most familiar with the hammour, a species of grouper, but the Gulf is also home to an extraordinary range of tropical fish and several species of small sharks. Green turtles and hawksbill turtles used to nest in numbers on Dubai's beaches and today there is a vigorous program to reintroduce them. Check www.dubaiturtles.com for more information.

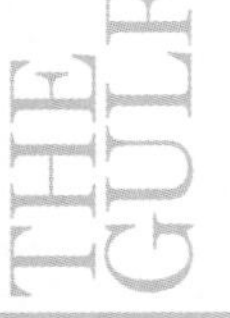

To avoid causing offence, you must not refer to the body of water off the coast of Dubai as the 'Persian Gulf'. This is an exceptionally sensitive issue in Arab Gulf countries, where the water is definitely, emphatically and categorically called the 'Arabian Gulf', even if the rest of the world, including the UN, disagrees.

PROGRESS & SUSTAINABILITY

There's no shortage of sand in Dubai, so converting it into islands that cost several million dollars each looked like a very profitable venture. Today we know that this venture was largely a pipe dream. Worse still, as environmentalists have long argued, Dubai's offshore projects such as Palm Island and the (now defunct) The World have already caused considerable long-term damage. The initial dredging for The World resulted in around 33 million cubic metres of sand and shell from the seabed of the Gulf being redistributed. Critics claim that this work has damaged the marine environment, with dredging destroying the seabed and plumes of sediment from the construction wrecking fragile coral reefs.

Across the UAE, resources are consumed at a much faster rate than they can be replaced, which is why their ecological footprint is so high. It won't be easy to reverse the trend and achieve environmental sustainability because the UAE relies so heavily on imported goods. Nearly everything on the supermarket shelves is brought into the country, and most of what you'll eat in restaurants has been transported from overseas too. There are a few farms in the UAE (including a couple of organic pioneers), but in a country where the economy – and the

ATTACK OF THE KILLER TIDE

The waters off the UAE East Coast used to be a snorkeller's and diver's paradise, teeming with turtles, barracuda, small sharks and tropical fish. Then disaster struck in 2008: the red tide came and stayed for nearly eight months.

Red tide – or, as scientists prefer to call it, 'harmful algal bloom' – is a naturally occurring, cyclical phenomenon caused by a build-up of microscopic algae called *Karenia brevis*. Colouring the water blood-red to cola-brown, it deprives it of oxygen and blocks sunlight, killing fish and coral. The tide usually disappears after a few weeks, but under the right (or rather, wrong) conditions, the organisms continue to multiply. Though it's not toxic to humans, allergic types may come away with stinging and blotched skin if exposed to the water.

During the eight months that the red tide lingered along the UAE coast, it damaged or destroyed 95% of the colourful coral and left hundreds of tons of fish floating belly up, according to Dubai-based **Emirates Diving Association** (EDA; ☎04-393 9390; www.emiratesdiving.com), the UAE's official diving agency.

Scientists are still baffled as to the exact causes of the prolonged tide, but likely culprits include discharge of raw or partially treated sewage, aquaculture farming, spillage from passing freighters and dredging from the construction of nearby artificial islands. Recovery is slow, but corals are reportedly replenishing themselves and marine life is returning as well.

local mentality – is so urbanised, it will take some effort to entice UAE nationals or expatriates to work in the agricultural sector to lessen the nation's dependency on imported goods.

ENVIRONMENTAL AWARENESS

In terms of going green at the micro level, much work needs to be done. Water and energy wastage are major issues. At 550L per day, the UAE has the highest per capita rate of water consumption in the world, and rainfall is infrequent. According to Dr Rashid bin Fahad, the UAE Minister of the Environment, the country relies on desalination for 98% of its drinking-water needs, an expensive and energy-intensive process, but necessary to convert seawater into water clean enough to drink.

It's estimated that a third of the cars on Dubai's roads are gas-guzzling sports utility vehicles (SUVs). But petrol is very cheap and many expatriates like to have a big car for reassurance on Dubai's volatile roads. Many drivers, of course, require 4WD vehicles for their off-road leisure pursuits.

Masdar City

Meanwhile, in Abu Dhabi, the most ambitious environmental project in the region is taking shape, and is scheduled for completion in 2016. When completed, Masdar City will be the world's first carbon-neutral, zero-waste community, powered entirely by renewable energy. The firm of British star architect Norman Foster has provided the blueprint for what will essentially be a living laboratory for around 50,000 people. For more information on this fascinating project, check www.masdar.ae.

Architecture & the Arts

The combination of traditional Arabian architecture and extraordinary futuristic structures is the most obvious reflection of what makes this city tick. Although much of the recent architecture, such as Madinat Jumeirah, sees a return to traditional Arabian forms, projects such as the Burj Khalifa show that the cloud-busting skyscraper isn't going anywhere in Dubai but up. The city's arts scene is not nearly as prevalent and it will be many years before Dubai can compete with the major European cities when it comes to music, theatre, literature and film. The painting and sculpture world is proving to be far more dynamic, however, with the emergence of a number of galleries. Similarly, Abu Dhabi's exciting Saadiyat Island project promises to put this emirate firmly on the art and culture map.

ARCHITECTURE

Traditional Architecture & Wind Towers

On your wanderings around the city, you'll notice that Dubai's traditional architecture consists of essentially four types of buildings: domestic (residential homes), religious (mosques), defensive (forts and watchtowers) and commercial (souqs). Readily available materials, such as gypsum and coral from offshore reefs and from the banks of the Creek, were used in the construction. The Sheikh Saeed al-Maktoum House (p66) in Shindagha is a fine example of this type of residential dwelling. There were two types of traditional house: the *mashait*, a winter house with a courtyard; and the *masayf*, a summer house incorporating a wind tower, a unique form of non-mechanical air-conditioning. You'll see both of these in Bur Dubai's historic Bastakia Quarter (p65).

For a thorough introduction to traditional Arab architecture, visit the excellent Traditional Architecture Museum (p66).

Courtyard Houses

Houses in Dubai and Abu Dhabi were traditionally built around a central courtyard, known as *al-housh* in Arabic. All rooms surrounded the courtyard and all doors and windows opened onto it, except those of the guestrooms, which opened to the outside of the house. A verandah provided shade, kept sun out of rooms at certain times of day, and was usually the place where the women did weaving and sewing. For a great example of a courtyard house, visit the Heritage House (p52) in Deira.

Palm-Leaf Houses

There is something very Robinson Crusoe about the idea of a house made out of palms. Historically, this method of building, known as *barasti*, was also traditional in Dubai and throughout the Gulf, although sadly few ex-

DUBAI'S ICONIC BUILDINGS

➡ **Burj Khalifa** (p79) *The* world's tallest building clocks in at a cloud-tickling 828m. For the design, American architect Adrian Smith found inspiration in the desert flower *Hymenocallis*, whose patterning systems are embodied in Islamic architecture. The tower is designed as three petals arranged around a central core. As it rises from the flat base, the petals are set back in an upward-spiralling pattern.

➡ **Burj al-Arab** (p94) The Burj was completed in 1999, and is set on an artificial island 300m from the shore. The 60-floor, sail-shaped structure is 321m high. A translucent fibreglass wall serves as a shield from the desert sun during the day and as a screen for an impressive light show each night. Until the Burj Khalifa arrived on the scene to steal its thunder, it was *the* iconic symbol of Dubai.

➡ **Dubai Creek Golf & Yacht Club** (Map p208) When you cross the bridges over the Creek from Bur Dubai South, you'll notice the pointed white roof of the clubhouse set amid artificial, undulating hillocks. The idea behind this 1993 design was to incorporate a traditional element – the white sails of a dhow (wooden boat) – into the form and style of the building. While this motif is becoming overused now, the building is ageing well.

➡ **Dubai International Financial Centre** (Map p216) Dubai's stock exchange and leading international financial institutions are housed in a complex of six buildings surrounding a central 80m-high triumphal arch called the Gate. Designed by American firm Gensler Associates, it sits on an axis with the Jumeirah Emirates Towers and the World Trade Centre, effectively framing these two landmarks.

➡ **Dusit Thani Dubai** (p142; next to Interchange No 1) Sheikh Zayed Rd features many modern skyscrapers, but few are as eye-catching as this one. The 153m-high building has an inverted 'Y' shape – two pillars that join to form a tapering tower. It's meant to evoke the Thai joined-hands gesture of greeting, which is appropriate for this Thai hotel chain, but some feel it looks more like a giant tuning fork.

➡ **Jumeirah Emirates Towers** (p140) Designed in an ultramodern style, the twin, triangular, gunmetal-grey towers soar from an oval base on Sheikh Zayed Rd and are among the world's tallest. The taller of the two (355m) houses offices, while the other (305m) is a hotel. Balanced by the curvilinear base structure, the curved motif is also repeated in the upper storeys of the buildings. This is perhaps the best-loved building in the city.

➡ **Jumeirah Beach Hotel** (p142) This long S-shaped construction represents a wave, with the Gulf as its backdrop. The glimmering facades of the hotel and its close neighbour, the Burj al-Arab, are achieved by the use of reflective glass and aluminium. The two structures combined – a huge sail hovering over a breaking wave – symbolise Dubai's maritime heritage.

➡ **National Bank of Dubai** (Map p206) This shimmering building located by Sheraton Dubai Creek Hotel & Towers (off Baniyas Rd) in Deira, overlooking the Creek, has become another quintessential symbol of Dubai. Designed by Carlos Ott and completed in 1997, it combines simple shapes to represent a dhow with a billowing sail. The bronze windows reflect the activity on the Creek and, at sunset, when the light is just right, it's a beautiful sight.

amples of this type of house survive today. It's essentially a skeleton of wooden poles (date-palm trunks) onto which *areesh* (palm leaves) were woven to form a strong structure through which air could circulate, making them much cooler than mudbrick houses in summer. Look for examples of *barasti* houses in the courtyard of the Dubai Museum (p65) and in the Heritage Village (p66).

Modern Architecture

In contrast to the traditional architecture that was all about function over form, and was built with regard for the environment, modern architecture in Dubai and (less so) Abu Dhabi has (until recently) embraced an 'anything goes' ethos with complete disregard for the climate. About 90% of Dubai's architecture can be described as international and is built using concrete, steel and glass. However, many architects have recently started to question the thinking behind building glass towers in a country with extreme heat. The huge cooling costs alone are reason to go for designs that better respond to and integrate with the weather and surroundings. Because these cosmopolitan materials absorb heat and transfer it to other parts of the construction, they also cause damage over time. As a result, high-tech, state-of-the-art materials with greater heat resistance are now starting to be used. Designs that are ageing well – and plenty aren't – are usually the ones produced by established architects, such as Carlos Ott (National Bank of Dubai building), whose fame stems from designing the Opéra de la Bastille in Paris, France.

> Since the financial crisis, many high-profile, commercial and urban-scale projects have been cancelled. Although considerable losses were incurred, Dubai shifted from being a city defined as a fast-paced spectacle to one that possesses a distinctive character and complexity. It suddenly became a very real city. In 2011 the city saw a steady, but slow, rise in construction which meant that there was a lot more time for quality control and planning.
>
> *Sharmeen Syed, architect, urban designer and researcher based in Dubai*

VISUAL ARTS

At the turn of the millennium there were only a handful of galleries in Dubai, most of which offered little more than clichéd watercolours of Arabian horses, camels and the like. Within the space of a few years, the city has become a focal point for contemporary Arabic and Persian art. With customary foresight, Dubai's decision-makers have recognised the potential of the art market in the region and gone all out to make sure it doesn't miss a trick.

The inaugural Gulf Art Fair in 2007 (retitled Art Dubai the following year) brought gallery owners, artists and dealers from around the world to the plush setting of Madinat Jumeirah to talk business. In 2011, Art Dubai's annual event welcomed more than 20,000 visitors and hosted more than 70 of the world's most dynamic galleries.

Top Contemporary Art Galleries

Third Line (p81)

Gallery Isabelle Van Den Eynde (p80)

Courtyard (p82)

JamJar (p81)

Why Dubai?

Dubai's location at the crossroads of the Middle East, the Indian subcontinent and Africa has helped it become an art industry hub. But it's also Dubai's relative openness that makes it such an attractive location for artists hoping to show their work. All the usual taboos, including anything that could be construed as criticism of Dubai, remain off limits. Nudity is a no-no, but Dubai is still more open than cities such as Tehran and Damascus, where some of the artists come from. Major exhibitions at venues such as the British Museum have fuelled a keen interest in Middle Eastern contemporary art, and Dubai is a lot more accessible to Western dealers than other cities

ROCK & ALTERNATIVE MUSIC

- **Abri** Arguably Dubai's top contemporary band playing a mix of soul and jazz.
- **Nervecell** Death-metal band that tours internationally and whose latest album *Psychogenocide* (2011) has enjoyed rave reviews.
- **Nikotin** Another hard-rock band that enjoys a firm UAE following.
- **Crow Murder** Five-piece metal band that plays regular Dubai gigs.
- **Dahab** Acoustic ethnic rock band with '70s influence.
- **Sandwash** Influenced by East African rhythms, rap and R&B.

in the region. On the downside, only a tiny percentage of the artists who exhibit in Dubai were raised in the UAE and there are no government-funded galleries in the country.

Al-Quoz Art District

Perhaps the most surprising thing about Dubai's sudden enthusiasm for art is the development of an art neighbourhood, tucked away in the otherwise uninviting Al-Quoz area. This featureless congregation of industrial estates along the edge of Sheikh Zayed Rd is home to several cutting-edge galleries (p80). Art isn't part of the school curriculum in the UAE, but it is hoped that these galleries will inspire a new generation of homegrown artists.

UAE Art

Dubai isn't the only city in the Gulf experiencing an upsurge in art interest. In Doha, Qatar, the government-funded Museum of Islamic Art opened in December 2008 in a spectacular building by IM Pei, the US-based architect nicknamed the 'mandarin of modernism'.

In Abu Dhabi, an international cast of five Pritzker Prize winners (the 'Oscar awards' of architecture) has been commissioned to build four museums and a performing arts centre on Saadiyat Island (p119). Including Middle Eastern branches of the Louvre (designed by Jean Nouvel) and the Guggenheim (by Frank Gehry), the cultural district is poised to become a major showcase of 21st-century architecture, arts and culture. Of course, such ambitious plans leave Abu Dhabi open to a charge you could also direct at Dubai: that it's spending millions of dollars on importing culture while homegrown artists receive practically no support.

Popular Emirati Musicians

- *Mohammed al-Mazem*
- *Fayez al-Saeed*
- *Ruwaida al-Mahrooqi*
- *Aida al-Manhali*
- *Mehad Hamad*
- *Eda bin Tanaf al-Manhaly*

DANCE

Dubai's contact with East and North African cultures through trade, both seafaring and by camel caravan, has brought many musical and dance influences to the UAE shores. Thus, traditional songs and dances are inspired by the environment – the sea, desert and mountains.

One of the most popular dances is the *ayyalah*, a typical Bedouin dance performed throughout the Gulf. The UAE has its own variation, performed to a simple drumbeat, with anywhere between 25 and 200 men standing with their arms linked in two rows facing each other. They wave walking sticks or swords in front of themselves and sway back and forth, the two rows taking it in turn to sing. It's a war dance and the words expound the virtues of courage and bravery in battle. You can see the dance on video at Dubai Museum (p65).

CONTEMPORARY MUSIC

Emiratis have always acknowledged the importance of music in daily life. Songs have been traditionally composed to accompany different tasks, from hauling water to diving for pearls. The Arabic music you're most likely to hear on the radio, however, is *khaleeji,* the traditional Gulf style, recognisable to those familiar with Arabic pop music. Alongside this, an underground rock and metal music scene is increasingly taking shape, with a few Dubai bands worth noting.

Survival Guide

Transport

GETTING TO DUBAI & ABU DHABI

Most visitors to Dubai arrive by air with convenient flights from most major international cities. The approximate duration time from London is seven hours, from Sydney 14 hours, from New York 12 hours and from Ottawa 14 hours. Dubai also increasingly serves as a major stopover hub between Europe and Asia.

There is road access to Dubai from Oman, which borders the United Arab Emirates (UAE) to the east; and from Saudi Arabia, which is to the south and west of the UAE. You will be required to show your passport and visit visa (if applicable). As this information is highly sensitive and subject to change, always check the www.dubai.ae government website for an update before you travel.

Buses to Abu Dhabi leave from Dubai's Al Ghubaiba station every 40 minutes (single Dh20, return Dh40). The trip takes two hours. Alternatively, it is an easy, direct drive, which will take you roughly the same amount of time.

Flights, tours and rail tickets can be booked online at www.lonelyplanet.com/travel_ services.

THINGS CHANGE...

The information in this chapter is particularly vulnerable to change. Check directly with the airline or a travel agent to make sure you understand how a fare (and ticket you may buy) works and be aware of the security requirements for international travel. Shop carefully. The details given in this chapter should be regarded as pointers and are not a substitute for your own careful, up-to-date research.

Air

All UAE airports have short- and long-term parking facilities. Tariffs range from Dh10 per hour to Dh125 per day in the short-term car park; travellers can leave their cars for up to 10 days in the long-stay. Always ask about airport transfers to your hotel when making your reservation.

Dubai

Located in the north of the city, on the border with the Sharjah emirate, **Dubai International Airport** (DXB; off Map p208; ☎04-224 5555, flight enquiries 04-224 5777; www.dubaiairport.com) is the busiest airport in the Middle East. There are three terminals:

- **Terminal 1** Main terminal used for major international airlines.
- **Terminal 2** For small airlines and charters mainly en route to Iran, Eastern Africa and some Eastern European countries.
- **Terminal 3** Used exclusively by Emirates Airlines.

In 2011, the airport hit the headlines as being the first Middle Eastern airport to offer modular sleep pods for weary visitors. They are located in Terminal 1.

For details on getting to and from Dubai International Airport, see p15.

Abu Dhabi

About 30km northeast of the city centre, **Abu Dhabi International Airport** (AUH; ☎02-505 5555, flight information 02-575 7500; www.abudhabiairport.ae) has three terminals, including Etihad Airways' exclusive base, Terminal 3.

Passengers travelling to Abu Dhabi International Airport on Etihad Airways can use free shuttle buses to/from Dubai. Otherwise, there is no direct public transport from the airport.

Sharjah

About 15km east of the Dubai–Sharjah border, **Sharjah International Airport** (SAI; ☎06-558 1111; www.shj-airport.gov.ae) has significantly increased its capacity since becoming the hub of Air Arabia, the region's first budget airline.

To get to/from the airport you have to take a taxi (approximately Dh55 from Dubai), as there's no public transport.

CLIMATE CHANGE & TRAVEL

Every form of transport that relies on carbon-based fuel generates CO_2, the main cause of human-induced climate change. Modern travel is dependent on aeroplanes, which might use less fuel per kilometre per person than most cars but travel much greater distances. The altitude at which aircraft emit gases (including CO_2) and particles also contributes to their climate change impact. Many websites offer 'carbon calculators' that allow people to estimate the carbon emissions generated by their journey and, for those who wish to do so, to offset the impact of the greenhouse gases emitted with contributions to portfolios of climate-friendly initiatives throughout the world. Lonely Planet offsets the carbon footprint of all staff and author travel.

Bus

Well-maintained minibuses or buses operated by the Dubai-based **Roads & Transport Authority** (RTA; www.rta.ae) travel to all the emirates, but only services to Sharjah and Ajman return passengers to Dubai. From the other towns, you have to come back by local taxi or local bus. Routes are generally served between 6am and 11pm. Buses are air-conditioned but can be overcrowded. Maps and timetables are available online and at the two main bus stations, which are Al-Ittihad in Deira and Al-Ghubaiba in Bur Dubai.

Al-Ittihad Bus Station

Several services depart from **Al-Ittihad bus station** (Map p206; cnr of Omar ibn al-Khattab & Al-Rigga Rds, Deira), next to the Union metro station. These include buses to Fujairah (Dh25, two to 2½ hours, every 45 minutes), Ajman (Dh7, one to 1½ hours, every 20 minutes), Ras al-Khaimah (Dh20, two hours, every 45 minutes), Sharjah (Dh5, 40 to 60 minutes, every 10 minutes) and Umm al-Quwain (Dh10, 1½ hours, every 45 minutes).

Al-Ghubaiba Bus Station

Bus services from **Al-Ghubaiba bus station** (Map p210; Al-Ghubaiba Rd, Bur Dubai), next to Carrefour supermarket, include Abu Dhabi (Dh20, two hours, every 40 minutes), Al-Ain (Dh20, 1½ hours, hourly) and Sharjah (Dh5, 40 to 50 minutes, every 10 minutes).

GETTING AROUND DUBAI

If you packed your trainers hoping to do a lot of walking, you will be disappointed. Negotiating the city by foot, even combined with public transport, is highly challenging, not only because of the heat, but also due to the lack of pavements, traffic lights and pedestrian crossings. It is not unheard of here to be forced to take a taxi, merely to reach the other side of the road.

Most visitors get around town via taxis. The Dubai metro is also an excellent mode of transport with two lines and sparkling-clean trains. Although bus lines offer good coverage, they are slow and have baffling timetables.

There is a good service of feeder buses that link the Burj Khalifa metro station with Dubai Mall, and the Mall of the Emirates metro station with the mall (although this is walkable). There are also shuttle buses that connect both malls with a number of local hotels.

Taxi

Taxis are operated by **Dubai Taxi Corporation** (DTC; ☎04-208 0808; www.dubaitaxi.ae) and are metered, relatively inexpensive and the fastest and most comfortable way to get around, except during rush-hour traffic.

Fares

- Daytime flagfall for street taxis is Dh3.
- Taxis ordered in advance or from your hotel have a flagfall of Dh6.
- The cost is Dh1.60 per kilometre, and Dh1.70 for larger people-carriers.
- From 10pm to 6am the starting fare is Dh3.50 (Dh7 when reserved).
- Trips originating at the airport have a flagfall of Dh25.

Reaching your Destination

Most taxi drivers speak at least some English but destinations are generally not given via a street address. Instead, mention the nearest landmark (eg a hotel, mall, roundabout, major building). If you're going to a private residence, phone your host and ask them to give the cabbie directions.

Taxi Trouble Spots

It's usually fairly easy to catch a taxi, but there are a few places where long waits are common. Expect lengthy queues at the major shopping malls on weekday evenings (especially Thursday) and Friday afternoons. There's also a chronic taxi shortage near the *abra* (water taxi) stations in Deira, by the shopping district of Karama, in Bur Dubai by the bus station, and along The Walk at JBR in Dubai Marina. Finding an available taxi is especially tough between 4pm and 5.30pm when most drivers end their shifts and have to deliver their cars to their partners.

Taxi Companies

Cars Taxis (☎04-269 3344; blue roof)

Dubai Transport Company (☎04-208 0808; red roof)

Metro Taxis (☎04-267 3222; orange roof)

National Taxis (☎04-339 0002; yellow roof)

Ladies Taxi (☎04-208 0808; pink roof)

It's perfectly fine for women to ride alone in a taxi, even at night. However, if you prefer, you can also call the last number of the above list (flagfall Dh7) and request a Ladies Taxi, complete with pink roof and lady drivers.

Car

If you are planning on taking an excursion from Dubai, consider hiring your own wheels so you can get off the major highways and stop and explore as you please. Well-maintained multilane highways link the cities. Petrol stations are plentiful and petrol is sold by the imperial gallon (an imperial gallon is just over 4.5L) and costs around Dh8 per gallon.

If you decide to drive around the city, bear in mind that traffic congestion in Dubai can be a nightmare at peak hours, ie between 7am and 9am, 1pm and 2pm and most of the evening from 5pm onwards. The worst congestion is around the approaches to Al-Maktoum and Al-Garhoud Bridges and along Al-Ittihad Rd towards Sharjah. Accidents are frequent; tune into the radio to get traffic updates.

Car Hire

To hire a car, you must be over the age of 21 and have a valid credit card and international driving licence, in addition to your home licence.

Daily rates start at about Dh200 for a small manual car, including comprehensive insurance and unlimited kilometres. Expect surcharges for airport rentals, additional drivers, one-way hire and drivers under 25 years of age. Most companies have child and infant safety seats for a fee, but these must be reserved well in advance. Check for deals with the online travel agencies, travel agents or car-rental brokers such as **Auto Europe** (www.autoeurope.com) and **Holiday Autos** (www.holidayautos.co.uk).

Dubai has scores of car-rental agencies, from major global players to no-name local companies. The former may charge more but you get peace of mind knowing that you can get full insurance and round-the-clock assistance.

The following international agencies have offices in the airport arrivals hall, around town and in major hotels.

Avis (☎airport 04-220 3800, head office 04-295 7121; www.avis.com)

Budget (☎airport 04-282 2727, head office 04-282 2727; www.budget-uae.com)

Europcar (☎airport 04-224 5240, head office 04-339 4433; www.europcar-dubai.com)

Hertz (☎airport 04-224 5222, head office 04-206 0206; www.hertz-uae.com)

Thrifty (☎airport 04-224 5404, head office 04-331 8772; www.thrifty.com)

Insurance

You will be offered a choice of insurance plans. If possible, opt for the most comprehensive as minor prangs are common here. If you have a breakdown, contact the **Arabian Automobile Association** (AAA; ☎800 4900; www.aaauae.com) or the **International Automobile Touring Club** (IATC; ☎800 5200; www.iatcuae.com).

Parking

Increasingly, the busier city streets of Dubai have a strictly enforced four-hour limit on parking. Tickets are purchased from an orange machine and displayed on your dashboard. Rates start at Dh1 for the first hour, Dh5 for two hours, Dh8 for three and Dh11 for four hours. Parking rates apply from 8am to 1pm and from 4pm to 9pm Saturday to Thursday. Pay with cash or by credit card. Parking in the centre of Dubai is free on Friday and holidays. Fines for not buying a ticket start at Dh100.

Road Rules

- ➡ Driving is on the right.
- ➡ The speed limit is 60km/h on city streets, 80km/h on major city roads and 200km/h on dual-lane highways.

ACCIDENT ALERT

If you are unfortunate enough to have an accident, no matter how small, you are required to wait at the scene and report it to the **police** (☎999). Unless your car is causing a major traffic jam, do NOT move it until the police arrive. If there has been an injury, or it's not blindingly obvious who was at fault, don't move the vehicles at all. For insurance-claim purposes you must have a police report, and if you move your car, the police may not be able to issue a complete report. Outside Dubai you should leave your car exactly where it is, no matter how bad an obstruction it is causing, and call the police immediately.

- Seatbelts are compulsory and it is illegal to use a hand-held mobile phone while driving.
- There's a zero-tolerance policy on drinking and driving. See the boxed text (p176).
- Never make an offensive hand gesture to another driver; it could end in deportation or a prison sentence.
- Tailgating, although common, is illegal and can result in a fine.
- Don't cross yellow lines.

Local Transport

Dubai's local public transport is also operated by the RTA and consists of the Dubai metro, buses, water buses and *abras* (water taxis). For trip planning and general information, call the 24-hour hotline on ☎800 9090 or go online at www.rta.ae.

Abras

*Abra*s are motorised traditional wooden boats linking Bur Dubai and Deira across the Creek on two routes:

Route 1 – Bur Dubai Abra Station (Map p210) to Deira Old Souq Abra Station (Map p206); daily between 5am and midnight.

Route 2 – Dubai Old Souq Abra Station (Map p210) to Al-Sabkha Abra Station (Map p206) around the clock.

*Abra*s leave when full (around 20 passengers), which rarely takes more than a few minutes. The fare is Dh1 and you pay the driver halfway across the Creek. Chartering your own *abra* costs Dh100 per hour.

Dubai Metro

Dubai's metro opened in 2010 with the Red Line, which runs for 52.1km from near Dubai International Airport to Jebel Ali past Dubai Marina, mostly paralleling Sheikh Zayed Rd.

A second line, the 22.5km Green Line, linking the Dubai Airport Free Zone with Dubai Healthcare City, opened in mid-2011. It intersects with the Red Line at Union and Khalid bin al-Waleed (next to BurJuman shopping mall) stations. At each station, cabs and feeder buses stand by to take you to your final destination. Don't forget to swipe your Nol (fare) card (p176) on the latter as inspectors regularly check and will issue an on-the-spot Dh200 fine for ticket evasion.

Trains run roughly every 10 minutes from 6am to 11pm Saturday to Thursday, and 1pm to midnight on Fridays. Each train consists of four standard cars and one car that's divided into a women-only section and a 'Gold Class' section where a double fare buys carpets and leather seats. Women may of course travel in any of the other cars as well.

Fares vary from Dh1.80 for stops within a single zone to Dh5.80 for stops exceeding two zones. All metro stations stock leaflets, in English, clearly mapping the zones. Note that if you exit a station with insufficient credit you will have to pay the equivalent of a day pass (Dh14).

MOTORING MAYHEM

Driving in the United Arab Emirates (UAE) is not for the faint of heart. Although it's not as chaotic as in other parts of the Middle East, drivers tend to cut in front of you, turn without indicating and view roundabouts as a lane-less free-for-all. Out on the freeway, driving in the lane closest to the centre of the road at speeds of less than 160km/h will invoke some serious headlight flashing from the latest-model Mercedes trying to break the Dubai–Abu Dhabi land-speed record.

So it's no surprise that the UAE has one of the world's highest rates of road deaths per capita. Inappropriate speed and reckless driving are the major causes, as well as pedestrians crossing against the lights or not at crossings.

On a more positive note, the situation seems to be gradually improving with a decline in deaths due to traffic accidents of around 7.5% in 2010 when compared to the previous year.

Local Buses

RTA (www.rta.ae) operates local buses on 79 routes primarily serving the needs of low-income commuters. Buses are clean, comfortable, air-conditioned and cheap (Dh2 per ride), but they're slow. The first few rows of seats are generally reserved for women and children.

For information and trip planning check the website. Free route maps and timetables can also be picked up from major bus stations.

Monorail

The elevated, driverless Palm Jumeirah Monorail connects the Palm Jumeirah with Dubai Marina. There are only two stations: Gateway Towers near the bottom of the trunk and the Aquaventure Park at the Atlantis hotel. The 5.45km trip takes about five minutes and costs Dh15 (Dh25 round trip).

Water Buses

Air-conditioned water buses travel along four Creek-crossing routes from 6am to 11pm daily. Routes B1 and B4 operate every 30 minutes, B2 and B3 at 15-minute intervals. Tickets are Dh4.

Route B1 – Bur Dubai Station (Map p210) to Al-Sabkha Station (Map p206)

Route B2 – Dubai Old Souq Station (Map p210) to Baniyas Station (Map p206)

Route B3 – Al-Seef Station (Map p206) to Al-Sabkha via Baniyas

Route B4 – Bur Dubai Station to Creek Park Water Bus Station (Map p214) via Al-Seef Station

A fifth route, the tourist-geared B5, travels between **Shindagha Station** (Map p210) near Heritage Village and Creek Park Water Bus Station every 30 minutes, stopping at Bur Dubai Station, Deira Old Souq Station and Al-Seef Station. All-day tickets cost Dh50 (Dh25 for children over six years). The entire journey lasts 45 minutes but you're free to get on and off throughout the ticket's validity (9am to midnight). You can also pay your fare using a prepaid Nol Card.

JUST SAY NO! REALLY.

Drinking and driving are never a good idea but in Dubai you'd be outright crazy to do so. Let's make it absolutely clear: if you've had as much as one sip, you've had too much. Dubai has a zero-tolerance policy on drink-driving, and if your vehicle is stopped and you're found to have been driving under the influence of alcohol, you'll be a guest of Dubai police for up to 30 days.

If you are involved in a traffic accident, it's a case of being guilty until proven innocent, which means you may be held by the police until an investigation determines whose fault the accident was.

NOL CARDS

Before you can hop aboard a local bus or the metro, you must purchase a rechargeable Nol Card (*nol* is Arabic for fare) from ticket offices in any metro and some bus stations. There are also ticket vending machines (with English instructions) in all metro and bus stations, at some bus stops and other places such as malls and the airport.

There are four categories of Nol Card: red, silver, gold and blue (aimed at residents). If you're only going to use public transport a few times, get a Red Card, which costs Dh2 and may be recharged for up to 10 journeys. Fares depend on distance and are divided into five zones. For Red Cards the cost ranges from Dh2.50 to Dh6.50.

Those travelling more frequently should get a Silver Card for Dh20 (including Dh14 of credit). These are equipped with an 'e-purse', meaning that the correct fare is deducted automatically every time you swipe the card at the station turnstiles, up to a daily maximum of Dh14. Fares start at just Dh1.80 for one zone.

The Gold Card has the same features as the Silver Card but gives you access to the Gold Class carriage and is roughly double the price.

Day passes for unlimited travel in all zones are Dh14 (not available for Gold Class). Children under five years of age travel free.

For full details, see www.nol.ae.

TOURS

The following reputable companies are all well established and licensed by the Department of Tourism & Commerce Marketing (DTCM). They offer a wide choice of tours, ranging from city excursions of Dubai, Al-Ain and Sharjah to more active trips, such as trekking in the Hajar Mountains or overnight safaris. Check the websites for more details and prices. Note that some tours only depart with a minimum number of passengers. If you have a choice, Arabian Adventures has a particularly good reputation and repeatedly receives positive feedback from tourists.

Alpha Tours (04-294-9888; www.alphatoursdubai.com)

Arabian Adventures (04-303 4888; www.arabian-adventures.com)

Desert Rangers (04-357 2233; www.desertrangers.com)

Hormuz Tourism (04-228 0668; www.hormuztourism.com)

Knight Tours (04-343 7725; www.knighttours.co.ae)

Lama Tours (04-334 4330; www.lama.ae)

Orient Tours (04 282 8238; www.orienttours.ae)

Bus Tours

Big Bus Company (04-340 7709; www.bigbustours.com; 24hr tickets adult/child Dh220/100, 48hr tickets Dh295/130) These 'hop on, hop off' city tours aboard open-topped double-decker buses are a good way for Dubai first-timers to get their bearing. Tickets are sold online, on the bus or at hotels. Pick up a flyer or check the web for pick-up points.

Directory A–Z

Business Hours

Reviews in this guidebook won't list business hours unless they differ from the following standards. The United Arab Emirates (UAE) weekend is on Friday and Saturday. Note that hours are more limited during Ramadan.

Banks 8am to 1pm (some until 3pm) Sunday to Thursday, 8am to noon Saturday.

Government offices 7.30am to 2pm (or 3pm) Sunday to Thursday.

Private offices 8am to 5pm or 9am to 6pm, or split shifts 8am to 1pm and 3pm (or 4pm) to 7pm Sunday to Thursday.

Restaurants noon to 3pm and 7.30pm to midnight.

Shopping malls 10am to 10pm Sunday to Wednesday, 10am to midnight Thursday to Saturday.

Souqs 9am to 1pm and 4pm to 9pm Saturday to Thursday, 4pm to 9pm Friday.

Supermarkets 9am to midnight daily; some open 24 hours.

Courses

The following centres offer Arabic language courses:

Arabic Language Centre (☎04-331 5600; www.arabiclanguagecentre.com; Dubai World Trade Centre, Sheikh Zayed Rd) Runs six courses a year in Arabic from beginner to advanced levels.

Berlitz Language School (☎04-344 0034; www.berlitz.ae; Jumeirah Rd) Offers courses in a number of languages, including Arabic and Urdu. The latter is useful to know to some extent, as this is the language of many of the Pakistani expats in the UAE.

Polyglot Language Institute (☎04-222 3429; www.polyglot.ae; Al-Masaeed Bldg, Al-Maktoum Rd, Deira) Beginner courses and conversation classes in Arabic, French, German and English.

Customs Regulations

Anyone aged over 18 years is allowed to bring in the following duty-free:

- 400 cigarettes plus 50 cigars plus 500g of loose tobacco.
- 4L of alcohol or two cartons (24 cans) of beer (non-Muslims only).
- Total price of gifts not exceeding Dh3000 in value.

You are *not* allowed to bring in:

- Alcohol if you cross into the UAE by land.
- Materials (ie books) that insult Islam.
- Firearms, pork, pornography or Israeli products.

You must declare to Customs:

- Cash (or equivalent) over Dh40,000.
- Total price of gifts with a value of more than Dh3000.
- Medicines (you must be able to produce a prescription).

Electricity

The electric voltage is 220V AC. British-style three-pin wall sockets are standard, although most appliances are sold with two-pin plugs. Adaptors are inexpensive and available in supermarkets.

Embassies & Consulates

Generally speaking, an embassy will not be much help in emergencies if the trouble you're in is your own fault. Remember that you are bound by the laws of the UAE. Your embassy will not be very sympathetic if you end up in jail after committing a crime locally, even if your actions are legal in your own country.

In genuine emergencies you might get some assistance, but only if other channels have been exhausted. For example, if you need to get home urgently a free flight is exceedingly unlikely – the embassy would expect you to have insurance. If you have all your money and documents stolen, it might assist with getting a new passport, but a loan for onward travel is out of the question.

Most countries have diplomatic representation in the UAE, including the following:

Australia (☎04-508 7100; www.uae.embassy.gov.au; 25th fl, BurJuman Business Tower, Trade Centre Rd, Bur Dubai; ⌚8am-1pm & 1.30-4.30pm Sun-Thu)

Canada (☎04-314 5555; dubai@international.gc.ca; 7th fl, Bank St Bldg, Khalid bin al-Waleed Rd, next to Citibank, Bur Dubai; ⌚8am-4pm Sun-Thu)

France (☎04-332 9040; http://consulfrance-dubai.org; 18th fl, API World Tower, Sheikh Zayed Rd, Trade Centre District; ⌚8am-1pm Sat-Thu)

Germany (☎04-397 2333; www.dubai.diplo.de; 1st fl, Sharaf Bldg, Khalid bin al-Waleed Rd, opposite BurJuman Centre, Bur Dubai; ⌚8-11am Sun-Thu)

Netherlands (☎04-352 8700; www.netherlands.ae; 5th fl, Royal Bank of Scotland Bldg, Khalid bin al-Waleed Rd, Mankhool, Bur Dubai; ⌚9am-noon Sat-Thu)

Oman (☎04-397 1000; www.ocodubai.com; Consulate Zone, near Khalid bin al-Waleed Rd, Umm Hurair; ⌚7.30am-2.30pm Sun-Thu)

UK (☎04-309 4444; http://ukinuae.fco.gov.uk/en; Consulate Zone, Al-Seef Rd, Umm Hurair; ⌚7.30am-2.30pm Sun-Thu)

USA (☎04-309 4000; http://dubai.usconsulate.gov; Consulate General Compound, cnr Al-Seef Rd & Sheikh Khalifa bin Zayed Rd, Bur Dubai; ⌚12.30-3pm Sun-Thu)

Emergency

Police (emergency ☎999, headquarters ☎04-229 2222)

Fire department (☎997)

Ambulance (☎998/999)

Gay & Lesbian Travellers

While Dubai and Abu Dhabi are certainly not 'gay' destinations along the lines of Berlin, Sitjes or Amsterdam, same-sex couples are unlikely to encounter problems as long as they respect local customs. Open displays of affection are likely to land you in trouble (the same goes for heterosexuals, of course) but sharing a room will barely raise an eyebrow.

Homosexual acts are illegal under UAE law and can incur a jail term. You will see men walking hand in hand, but that's a sign of friendship and no indication of sexual orientation. Although no bars, clubs or cafes would dare identify themselves as gay-friendly for fear of being raided and shut down, there are venues in the city that attract a sizeable gay and lesbian crowd. It is sometimes possible to get info on these venues from websites, but you can't access gay- and lesbian-interest websites from inside the UAE.

For more on the subject, an interesting read is *Gay Travels in the Muslim World* by Michael Luongo. You can also check the www.al-bab.com Middle East gay news website for any changes in the law.

Internet Access

Dubai and Abu Dhabi are extremely well wired and you should have no trouble getting online.

Banned Websites

The internet is accessed through a proxy server that blocks pornography, gay-interest sites, websites considered critical of Islam or the UAE's leaders, dating and gambling sites, drug-related material and the entire Israeli domain. To the irritation of the country's huge foreign workforce, peer-to-peer and Voice over Internet Protocol (VoIP) software such as Skype is banned in the UAE, although if the programs are already installed on your computer before you arrive you should be able to use them with no problem.

Internet Access

Nearly every hotel and hotel apartment offers in-room internet access, either broadband or wireless, although rates are usually extortionate (Dh40 to Dh60 per hour is not uncommon). Sometimes it's more economical to prepay for 24 hours.

A cheaper way to connect is through Etisalat Hotspots, which are available at all branches of Starbucks, Barista and Coffee Bean & Tea Leaf, as well as at major shopping malls and various restaurants and cafes (see www.etisalat.ae for the full list). You gain access by buying a prepaid card from the venue itself, or by using your credit card. Enter your card number and mobile

PRACTICALITIES

Currency

UAE dirham (Dh) is divided into 100 fils. Notes come in denominations of five, 10, 20, 50, 100, 200, 500 and 1000. There are Dh1, 50 fils, 25 fils, 10 fils and 5 fils coins. The most convenient way to bring your money is in the form of a debit or credit card, with some extra cash for use in case of an emergency.

Newspapers & Magazines

English-language newspapers in Dubai include the free *7 Days* (www.7days.ae), the government-owned and infuriatingly obsequious *Emirates Business 24/7* (www.business24-7.ae), the high-design weekly tabloid *Xpress* (www.xpress4me.com), and the long-established dailies (*Gulf News*, *Khaleej Times* and *Gulf Today*). In 2008 the Abu Dhabi government launched *The National* (www.thenational.ae), the region's most ambitious English-language daily newspaper to date.

Time Out Dubai is produced weekly and has detailed listings and stories on upcoming events. It costs Dh7, although you'll find it free in Dubai's better hotel rooms. *What's On* is the other listings monthly and costs Dh10, although it's a lot tamer than the competition.

Radio

The quality of radio programming in Dubai is improving (especially talk radio), but it's generally a cringe-worthy and ad-saturated affair wherever you point the dial.

BBC Worldwide (87.9) Broadcasts from 9am to 6pm.

Channel 4 FM (104.8) Contemporary Top 40.

Dubai Eye (103.8) News, talk and sports.

Dubai FM (92) Classic hits from the '80s,'90s etc, as well as dance and lounge on weekends.

Emirates Radio 1 (104.1) Popular music.

Emirates Radio 2 (99.3) Eclectic programming.

It's worth searching through the dial, as there are stations playing Hindi, Arabic and Indian regional music, and stations where you can hear recitations of the Quran – very soothing when you're stuck in Dubai's horrific traffic.

Smoking

Dubai and Abu Dhabi have a comprehensive smoking ban that essentially extends to all public places, with the exception of nightclubs and enclosed bars. Shopping malls, hotels, restaurants and cafes may have designated smoking rooms but these must be clearly marked, properly ventilated, and cannot be entered by people aged under 20 years. Hotels have rooms where smoking is permitted. The fine for lighting up in a nonsmoking area can range from Dh1000 to Dh8000. There are also fines for throwing cigarette butts into the street. In 2009 the ban was extended to include *sheesha* smoking in parks, beaches and public recreation areas.

phone number in the fields provided, and you'll be sent an access code by text message. Internet access costs Dh15 for one continuous hour, Dh30 for three continuous hours, Dh80 for six hours over a 30-day period and Dh120 for 12 hours over a 60-day period. Some restaurants and cafes also offer wi-fi access, sometimes free with purchase. Most shopping malls offer free wi-fi access, although you may need a UAE mobile phone number to access.

If you don't own a computer, nearly all hotels have business centres, and internet cafes charge as little as Dh2 per hour for access.

Legal Matters

Drugs in Dubai and Abu Dhabi are simply a bad, bad idea. The UAE has a small but growing drug problem, and

DRUGS: ZERO TOLERANCE

We can't shout the following words loudly enough: do not attempt to carry illegal drugs into Dubai! In fact, even if you're not attempting to import drugs, you should double-check that there isn't the faintest speck of anything illegal anywhere in your baggage or on your person. You must also ensure that medicines and drugs legal in your country are legal in Dubai before travelling with them. If you have illegal substances in your bloodstream, this counts as possession, and a urine test could see you found guilty. Several drugs available over the supermarket counter in other countries are banned substances in the United Arab Emirates (UAE).

The following cases illustrate how strict Dubai's drug laws are:

- A British tourist was arrested at Dubai airport after 0.03g of cannabis, an amount smaller than a grain of sugar and invisible to the human eye, was detected on the stub of a cigarette stuck to the sole of his shoe. He was sentenced to four years in prison.
- A British TV producer was arrested and held for possessing the health supplement melatonin, which is taken to alleviate jet lag and is legal in the UK. After being cleared of importing an illegal substance, he was held for more than a month without charges in a Dubai prison while the rest of his possessions were tested.
- A Saudi man was sentenced to four years in prison after a tiny, dried-up leaf of qat (a mild stimulant, which is legal in Yemen) was found on his clothing.
- A Swiss man was reportedly imprisoned after customs officials found three poppy seeds on his clothes. These had fallen off a bread roll he ate at Heathrow.
- A British woman was held in custody for two months before UAE customs officers accepted that the codeine she was using for her back problem had been prescribed by a doctor.
- BBC1 radio host and drum 'n' bass DJ Grooverider was sentenced to four years in prison after 2.16g of cannabis was found in his luggage upon arrival at the airport. He was released after 10 months.

the authorities are cracking down hard on it. The minimum penalty for possession of even trace amounts is four years in prison, and the death penalty is still on the books for importing or dealing in drugs (although in fact it usually ends up being a very long jail term). For more information, see the boxed text (above). Jail sentences for being involved in drugs by association are also fairly common. That means that even if you are in a room where there are drugs, but are not partaking, you could be in as much trouble as those who are. The secret police are pervasive, and they include officers of many nationalities.

There are also import restrictions for prescription medications that are legal in most countries, such as diazepam (Valium), dextromethorphan (Robitussin), fluoxetine (Prozac) and anything containing codeine. Check with the UAE embassy in your home country for the full list. If you need to take such medications, carry the original prescription and a letter from your doctor.

Other common infractions that may incur a fine, jail time or even deportation include drinking alcohol in an unlicensed public place; buying alcohol without a local licence; writing bad cheques; unmarried cohabitation; and public eating, drinking and smoking during daylight hours in Ramadan. Another big no-no is sexual or indecent public behaviour. Although Dubai has the most tolerant social codes in the Middle East, police can still crack down on people appearing to push the limits.

If arrested, you have the right to a phone call, which you should make as soon as possible (ie before you are detained in a police cell or prison pending investigation, where making contact with anyone could be difficult). Call your embassy or consulate first so they can get in touch with your family and possibly recommend a lawyer.

Dubai Police has established a **Department of Tourist Security** (☎800 4438; ⏲24hr) to help visitors with any legal complications they may face on their trip.

You can also check the Dubai Code of Ethics published in March 2009 on www.dubai.ae.

Medical Services

Pharmacies are plentiful in Dubai and Abu Dhabi. See the daily newspapers for a list of pharmacies that are open 24 hours, or call ☎04-223 2323.

As a visitor you will receive medical care, but you will be charged for it, so don't leave home without travel health insurance. The standard of medical services is quite good.

For house calls, contact **Health Call** (☎04-363 5343; http://health-call.com; per visit Dh600-800), which will send out Western-trained doctors around the clock.

The following government hospitals have 24/7 emergency rooms:

Al-Wasl Hospital (☎04-219 3000; Oud Metha Rd, south of Al-Qataiyat Rd, Za'abeel)

Dubai Hospital (☎04-219 5000; Abu Baker al-Siddiq Rd, near cnr Al-Khaleej Rd)

Rashid Hospital (☎04-337 4000; off Oud Metha Rd, near Al-Maktoum Bridge, Bur Dubai)

For more information on all Dubai hospitals, check the www.dha.gov.ae government health authority website. For non-urgent care, contact the following or ask your consulate for a referral:

Al-Zahra Medical Centre (☎04-331 5000; www.al-zahra.com; Al Safa Tower, Sheikh Zayed Rd, near Emirates Tower metro station)

American Hospital (☎04-336 7777, emergency ☎04-309 6877; www.ahdubai.com; opposite Mövenpick Hotel, Oud Metha) Has a walk-in clinic (no appointment needed) open 10am to 5pm daily, as well as a 24-hour emergency room.

Dubai London Clinic (☎04-344 6663; www.dubailondonclinic.com; Jumeirah Rd, Umm Suqeim; ⌚8am-7pm Sat-Wed, 8am-5pm Thu)

Money

ATMs

Many credit and debit cards can be used for withdrawing money from ATMs that display the relevant symbols, such as Visa and MasterCard. Remember that there is usually a charge (around 1.5% to 2%) on ATM cash withdrawals abroad.

Changing Money

If you need to change money, exchange offices tend to offer better rates than banks. Reliable exchanges include **Al-Rostamani** (☎04-295 6777; www.alrostamaniexchange.com) and **UAE Exchange** (☎04-229 7373; www.uaeexchange.com), with multiple branches around town at locations including Mall of the Emirates, Dubai International Airport and Ibn Battuta Mall.

Currencies of neighbouring countries are all recognised and easily changed, with the exception of the Yemeni rial.

Credit Cards

Visa, MasterCard and American Express are widely accepted at shops, hotels and restaurants throughout Dubai and Abu Dhabi, and debit cards are accepted at bigger retail outlets.

Tipping

By law, only food and beverage outlets in hotels are entitled to tack a service charge (usually 10%) on to bills. Independent restaurants are not officially permitted to do so, although many seem to thumb their nose at the regulation. Unfortunately, the service charge rarely ends up in the pockets of the person who served you, which is why it's nice to give them a few extra dirham in cash if they did a good job.

Post

Your hotel should be able to send mail for you, but otherwise stamps are available at local post offices operated by **Emirates Post** (www.emiratespost.com). A letter to Europe costs Dh5, while a postcard costs Dh3.25 and a 1kg parcel costs Dh96.50. Rates to the US or Canada are almost identical: Dh5.75 for letters, Dh3.75 for postcards and Dh99 for the 1kg parcel. Mail generally takes about a week to 10 days to Europe or the USA, and eight to 15 days to Australia.

Major post offices:

Al-Musallah Post Office (Al-Fahidi Roundabout, Bur Dubai)

Al-Rigga Post Office (Near Clock Tower Roundabout, Deira)

Central Post Office (Za'abeel Rd, Bur Dubai)

Dubai International Airport (⌚24hr) Near Gate 18 of Terminal 1.

Jumeirah Post Office (Al-Wasl Rd, Jumeirah)

Satwa Post Office (Al-Satwa Rd, Jumeirah)

Courier Service

If you need to send something in a hurry, contact the following courier agencies for office locations and hours:

Aramex (☎04-600 544 000; www.aramex.com)

DHL (☎800 4004; www.dhl.co.ae)

FedEx (☎800 4050; www.fedex.com)

UPS (☎800 4774; www.ups.com)

Public Holidays

Hejira is the Islamic New Year. Eid al-Fitr marks the end of Ramadan fasting and is a three-day celebration spent feasting and visiting friends and family. Eid al-Adha is a four-day celebration following the main pilgrimage to Mecca, the hajj. Secular holidays are New Year's Day (1 January) and National Day (2 December). If a public holiday falls on a

ISLAMIC HOLIDAYS

ISLAMIC YEAR	HEJIRA	PROPHET'S BIRTHDAY	RAMADAN	EID AL-FITR	EID AL-ADHA
1434	15 Nov 2012	24 Jan 2013	09 Jul 2013	08 Aug 2013	15 Oct 2013
1435	4 Nov 2013	13 Jan 2014	28 Jun 2014	28 Jul 2014	4 Oct 2014

weekend (ie Friday or Saturday), the holiday is usually taken at the beginning of the next working week.

Ramadan

This is the month during which Muslims fast during daylight hours. They must also refrain from sex, swearing, smoking or any other indulgence. This is to clean the mind and body to better focus on the person's relationship with Allah.

During Ramadan, government offices ease back to about six hours' work a day. Bars and pubs are closed until 7pm each night, live music is prohibited and dance clubs are closed throughout the month. Camel racing ceases, too. Some restaurants do not serve alcohol during this month. Everyone, regardless of their religion, is required to observe the fast in public.

Relocating

If you like Dubai so much you don't want to leave, you may not have to. In most cases, relocating to Dubai is easy. To secure a three-year residency permit, you need either an employer to sponsor you; a spouse with a job who can sponsor you; or ownership of freehold property, which comes with a renewable residency permit. The situation is similar in Abu Dhabi.

It seems almost inconceivable that 25 years ago foreign workers in Dubai were eligible for a 'hardship allowance' – financial compensation for having to live in a boring, conservative and unbearably hot place. Back then, working hours were short and salaries were high. Today some people will accept a drop in salary to experience the much-feted 'Dubai dream', despite the fact that inflation is on the rise, rents are still sky-high (though they've dropped as much as 40% since the economic downturn) and wages haven't increased in years (and are now on a par with salaries in the West). For many, these conditions are offset by the fact that the salary is tax-free, and that myriad perks are still considered standard in many expat packages, such as a relocation allowance, annual plane tickets home, housing, health insurance, children's education allowance and long paid holidays.

These days many people are moving to Dubai (and Abu Dhabi) for reasons that have less to do with financial reward and more to do with job satisfaction and being part of the developments taking place in the region. The opportunities for career progression are fantastic. Competition exists, but it's nowhere near as tough as it is elsewhere. Whereas the expat of the oil-boom days was in his or her 40s or 50s, white, middle class, and more than likely worked in oil, gas, petroleum, construction, nursing, teaching or foreign relations, times have changed. The new expats come in all ages, races, nationalities and classes, and the work itself is more glamorous, with the most coveted opportunities being in tourism, hospitality, marketing, PR and advertising, real estate development, project management, architecture, interior design, fashion and entertainment. While the opportunities are fantastic, the work culture can be intense. Late nights and weekends in the office are commonplace and it can be tricky achieving the right work-life balance.

While Dubai may not be as culturally active as many other cities (there's very little theatre, live music or quality cinema), it's easier to get noticed if you are a budding playwright, actor, musician or film director. The opportunities to travel from Dubai are fantastic, with the Indian subcontinent, Eastern Europe, East Africa and all of the Middle East accessible within a few hours' flying time. And then there's the fine dining, the beaches, the desert trips at weekends, the inspiring multiculturalism and the chance to learn about the Arab world and Islam.

For a detailed guide to relocating to the Gulf, see Lonely Planet's *Oman, UAE & Arabian Peninsula* guide.

Safe Travel

On the whole, Dubai is a very safe city, but you should exercise the same sort of caution with your personal safety as you would anywhere. Due to Dubai's location at the heart of the Gulf, the US Department of State and British Foreign Office both warn travellers of a general threat from terrorism.

One very real danger in Dubai is bad driving. We also don't recommend that you swim, waterski or jet-ski in the Creek. The tides in the Gulf are not strong enough to regularly flush out the Creek, so it is not a clean waterway, despite what the tourist authorities might tell you. Also, be careful when swimming in the open sea. Despite the small surf, currents can be very strong and drownings are not uncommon.

Telephone

The UAE has an efficient communications system that connects callers with anywhere in the world, even from the most remote areas. There are two mobile networks: Etisalat and Du. Both are government-owned and there is little difference between the two.

Local calls (within the same area code) are free. Coin phones have been almost completely superseded by cardphones. Phonecards are available in various denominations from grocery stores, supermarkets and petrol stations. Do not buy them from street vendors.

To phone another country from the UAE, dial ☎00 followed by the country code. If you want to call the UAE, the country code is ☎971. The area code for Dubai is ☎04, though if you are calling from outside the UAE you drop the zero.

Directory enquiries (☎181)

International directory assistance (☎151)

Mobile Phones

The UAE's mobile phone network uses the GSM 900 MHz and 1800 MHz standard, the same as Europe, Asia and Australia. Mobile numbers begin with either 050 (Etisalat) or 055 (Du). If you don't have a worldwide roaming service, consider buying a pay-as-you-go mobile with credit for around Dh125. Alternatively, prepaid SIM card are widely available, for example at Dubai Duty Free at the airport, at any Etisalat office or at licensed mobile phone shops. You need to bring an unlocked handset for this, so make sure your phone is unlocked and you are able to switch SIM cards. The excellent-value Ahlan Visitor's Mobile Package lasts 90 days, costs Dh60 and includes Dh25 of credit. Domestic calls cost Dh0.50 a minute and international calls are priced at Dh2.50 a minute. Domestic text messages cost Dh0.30, international messages cost Dh0.90. Recharge cards in denominations of Dh25, Dh50, Dh100, Dh200 and Dh500 are sold at grocery stores, supermarkets and petrol stations. Once again, do not buy them from street vendors.

Time

Dubai and Abu Dhabi are four hours ahead of GMT. The time does not change during the summer. Not taking daylight saving into account, when it's noon in Dubai, the time elsewhere is as follows:

CITY	TIME
Auckland	8pm
London	8am
Los Angeles	midnight
New York	3am
Paris & Rome	9am
Perth & Hong Kong	4pm
Sydney	6pm

Toilets

The best advice is to go when you can. Public toilets in shopping centres, museums, restaurants and hotels are Western-style and are generally extremely clean and well maintained. Those in souqs and bus stations are usually only for men. Outside the cities you might have to contend with hole-in-the-ground loos at the back of restaurants or petrol stations, although these are increasingly rare. You'll always find a hose and nozzle next to the toilet, which is used to rinse yourself before using the toilet paper.

Tourist Information

The **Department of Tourism & Commerce Marketing** (DTCM; ☎04-223 0000; www.dubaitourism.ae) operates 24-hour information kiosks in the Terminal 1 and 3 arrivals areas of Dubai International Airport, as well as booths at the following malls: Deira City Centre, BurJuman, Wafi Mall, Ibn Battuta and Mercato Mall. Officially, these are open from 10am to 10pm, but we frequently found them unstaffed, leaving you to pick through a meagre assortment of flyers and brochures by yourself.

Travellers with Disabilities

Dubai and Abu Dhabi have made a big effort in recent years to improve services for people with disabilities. The **Department of Tourism & Commerce Marketing** (DTCM; ☎04-223 0000; www.dubaitourism.ae) website includes a Special Needs Tourism section, which contains information on wheelchair-accessible parks, heritage sites, cinemas, malls and tour operators.

The airport is well equipped with low check-in counters, luggage trolleys, automatic doors, lifts and quick check-in. **Dubai Taxi** (☎04-208 0808, 04-224 5331; www.dubaitaxi.ae) has special vans with wheelchair lifts for Dh50 per hour, but they must be ordered 24 hours in

VIS-À-VIS OMAN

If you are from one of the 34 countries eligible to get an on-the-spot visa at Dubai airport, you won't need to obtain a separate visa for Oman. Everyone else has to apply in advance at the Omani embassy in Abu Dhabi. If you are visiting Oman on a tourist visa, these same 34 nationalities can enter the UAE by land, air or sea without visa charges.

advance. Some local buses and all water taxis are wheelchair-accessible. Dubai's metro has lifts and grooved guidance paths in stations and wheelchair spaces in each train compartment. Most parking areas in town contain spaces for drivers with disabilities.

Top-end hotels are the ones most likely to have rooms with extra-wide doors and spacious bathrooms. However, it's best to discuss your particular needs when making a reservation. For other venues, call ahead to find what access to expect. Wheelchair ramps, for instance, are still a rarity, even in public buildings and at tourist attractions. Exceptions include the Dubai Museum and Heritage Village.

Visas

Entry requirements to the UAE are in constant flux, which is why you should double-check all information in this section by checking the official tourism website (www.dubaitourism.ae) before you make final plans.

At the time of writing, citizens of 34 developed countries, including nearly all of Western Europe plus Australia, Brunei, Canada, Hong Kong, Japan, Malaysia, New Zealand, Singapore, South Korea and the USA, get free on-the-spot visas on arrival in the UAE at air, land and sea ports. Visas are valid for 30 days with an additional grace period of 10 days. Don't risk outstaying your visa as the fine is, at present, Dh100 a day, which can soon add up.

If you're a citizen of a country not included in the list above, a visit visa must be arranged through a sponsor – such as your Dubai hotel or tour operator – prior to your arrival in the UAE. The non-renewable visas cost Dh100 and are valid for 30 days. Citizens of Gulf Cooperative Council (GCC) countries only need a valid passport to enter the UAE and can stay as long as they want. It is generally not possible to enter with an Israeli passport, but there's no problem entering the UAE with an Israeli stamp in a non-Israeli passport.

Note that passports must be valid for at least six months from the date of arrival.

Visa Extensions

Visit visas can be extended once for 30 days by the **Department of Immigration & Naturalisation** (☎04-398 0000; Sheikh Khalifa bin Zayed Rd, near Bur Dubai Police Station) for Dh500 and a fair amount of paperwork. You may be asked to provide proof of funds. It's much easier, and usually cheaper, to leave the country for a few hours and head back for a new stamp.

Visas can only be extended in the city or emirate you arrived in, so if you landed in Sharjah, you can't get your visa extended in Dubai.

Women Travellers

Many women imagine that travel to Dubai and within the UAE is much more difficult than it actually is. No, you don't have to wear a burka, headscarf or veil. Yes, you can drive a car. No, you won't be constantly harassed. In fact, Dubai is one of the safest Middle East destinations for women travellers. It's totally fine to take cabs, stay alone in hotels (although you may want to avoid the fleabag hotels in Deira and Bur Dubai) and walk around on your own in most areas. Having said that, this does not mean that some of the problems that accompany travel just about anywhere in the world will not arise in Dubai as well, such as unwanted male attention and long, lewd stares, especially on public beaches. Try not to be intimidated, and appear self-confident. For a few simple techniques on how to avoid harassment, see the boxed text (p185).

Although prostitution does not officially exist, authorities do little to suppress the small army of 'working women' catering to both expats and Emiratis in clubs, bars and on the backstreets of Deira and Bur Dubai. In terms of dress, they're often indistinguishable from other women, which is confusing to the men and opens up the possibility of respectable women being solicited erroneously. While this can be offensive, just imagine how embarrassed the guy must feel about his mistake.

Attitudes Towards Women

Some of the biggest misunderstandings between Middle Easterners and Westerners occur over the issue of women. Half-truths and stereotypes exist on both sides: many Westerners assume that all Middle Eastern women are veiled, repressed victims, while a large number of locals see Western women as sex-obsessed and immoral.

Traditionally, the role of a woman in the region is to be a mother and matron of the household, while the man is the financial provider. However, as with any society, the reality is far more nuanced. There are thousands of middle- and upper-middle-class professional women in the UAE who, like their counterparts in the West, juggle work and family responsibilities.

The issue of sex is where the differences between the cultures are particularly apparent. Premarital sex (or indeed any sex outside marriage) is taboo, although, as with anything forbidden, it still happens. Emirati women are expected to be virgins when they marry, and a family's reputation can rest upon this point. The presence of foreign women provides, in the eyes of some Arab men, a chance to get around these norms with ease and without consequences. Hence the occasional hassle.

What to Wear

Even though you'll see plenty of Western women wearing skimpy shorts and tank-tops in shopping malls and other public places, you should not assume that it's acceptable to do so. While they're too polite a host to actually say anything, most Emiratis find this disrespectful. Despite Dubai's relative liberalism, you are in a country that holds its traditions dear. When it comes to beach parties and nightclubs almost anything goes, but take a taxi there and back.

Generally speaking, dressing 'modestly' has the following advantages: it attracts less attention to you; you will get a warmer welcome from locals (who greatly appreciate your willingness to respect their customs); and it'll prove more comfortable in the heat. Dressing modestly means covering your shoulders, knees and neckline. Baggy T-shirts and loose cotton trousers or over-the-knee skirts will not only keep you cool but will also protect your skin from the sun. If you travel outside Dubai (and Abu Dhabi), keep in mind that everywhere else in the UAE is far more conservative.

Work

You can pre-arrange work in the UAE, but if you enter the country on a visit visa and then find work, you will have to leave the country for one day and re-enter under your employer's sponsorship.

If you have arranged to work in Dubai, you will enter the country on a visit visa sponsored by your employer while your residence visa is processed. This process involves a blood test for HIV/AIDS and lots of paperwork. Those on a residence visa who are sponsored by a spouse who is in turn sponsored by an employer are not officially permitted to work. This rule is often broken, and it is possible to find work in the public or private sector. If you are in this situation, remember that your spouse, and not the company you work for, is your sponsor. One effect of this is that you may only be able to apply for a tourist visa to another Gulf Arab country with a consent letter from your spouse. In some cases you will need to be accompanied by your spouse, who has company sponsorship. Similarly, if you want to apply for a driving licence, you will also need a consent letter from your spouse.

If you obtain your residence visa through an employer and then quit because you've found something better, you may find yourself under a six-month ban from working in the UAE.

TOP 10 TIPS FOR WOMEN TRAVELLERS

- Wear a wedding ring – it will make you appear less 'available'.
- If you're unmarried but travelling in male company, say that you're married rather than girlfriend/boyfriend.
- Avoid direct eye contact with men (dark sunglasses help).
- Don't sit in the front seat of taxis unless the driver is a woman.
- On public transport, sit in the women's section towards the front.
- If you need help for any reason (directions, etc), ask a woman first.
- If dining alone, eat at Western-style places or ask to be seated in the 'family' section of local eateries.
- It's perfectly acceptable for women to go straight to the front of a queue (eg at banks or post offices) or ask to be served first before any men who might be waiting.
- If someone follows you in his car, take a picture of his licence plate or just get your mobile phone out (if it doesn't have a camera, simply pretend it does).
- If you're being followed, go to the nearest public place, preferably a hotel lobby. If this doesn't discourage them, ask the receptionist to call the police, which usually makes them slink away.

This rule is designed to stop people from job-hopping.

If you are employed in Dubai and have any work-related problems, you can call the **Ministry of Labour Helpline** (☎800 665; www.mol.gov.ae) for advice.

Finding Work

While plenty of people turn up in Dubai on a visit visa, decide they like the look of the place and then scout around for a job, this isn't really the most effective way to go about it. First, most employees are on a contract that's generally for three years. Secondly, there are a lot of sums to be done before you can really figure out whether the amount you're offered is going to make financial sense. Things such as a housing allowance, medical coverage, holidays and schooling (for those with kids) have to be taken into account before you can decide.

Target who you want to work for and try to set up meetings before you arrive. Email and follow up with a phone call or two. Employers in Dubai are very fond of people with qualifications. However, it's of little consequence which higher learning establishment you attended. Teachers, nurses and those in engineering are highly valued in Dubai and Abu Dhabi and are well paid.

The *Khaleej Times* and the *Gulf News* publish employment supplements several times a week. When you find a job, you will be offered an employment contract in Arabic and English. Get the one in Arabic translated before you sign it.

Business Aid Centre (☎04-337 5747; www.bacdubai.com)

SOS Recruitment Consultants (☎04-396 5600; www.sosrecruitment.net)

Language

Arabic is the official language of the UAE, but English is widely understood. Note that there are significant differences between the MSA (Modern Standard Arabic) – the official lingua franca of the Arab world, used in schools, administration and the media – and the colloquial language, ie the everyday spoken version. The Arabic variety spoken in the UAE (and provided in this chapter) is known as Gulf Arabic.

Read our coloured pronunciation guides as if they were English and you'll be understood. Note that a is pronounced as in 'act', aa as the 'a' in 'father', ai as in 'aisle', aw as in 'law', ay as in 'say', ee as in 'see', i as in 'hit', oo as in 'zoo', u as in 'put', gh is a guttural sound (like the Parisian French 'r'), r is rolled, dh is pronounced as the 'th' in 'that', th as in 'thin', ch as in 'cheat' and kh as the 'ch' in the Scottish *loch*. The apostrophe (') indicates the glottal stop (like the pause in the middle of 'uh-oh'). The stressed syllables are indicated with italics.

BASICS

Hello.	اهلا و سهلا.	*ah*·lan was *ah*·lan
Goodbye.	مع السلامة.	ma' sa·*laa*·ma
Yes./No.	نعم./لا.	*na*·'am/la
Please.	من فضلك. من فضلِك.	min *fad*·lak (m) min *fad*·lik (f)
Thank you.	شكران.	*shuk*·ran
Excuse me.	اسمح. اسمحي لي.	is·*mah* (m) is·mah·*ee* lee (f)
Sorry.	مع الاسف.	ma' al·*as*·af

WANT MORE?

For in-depth language information and handy phrases, check out Lonely Planet's *Middle East Phrasebook*. You'll find it at **shop.lonelyplanet.com**, or you can buy Lonely Planet's iPhone phrasebooks at the Apple App Store.

How are you?
كيف حالك/حالِك؟ — kayf *haa*·lak/*haa*·lik (m/f)

Fine, thanks. And you?
بخير الحمد الله. — bi·*khayr* il·*ham*·du·li·laa
و انتَ/و انتِ؟ — *win*·ta/*win*·ti (m/f)

What's your name?
اش اسمَك/اسمِك؟ — aash *is*·mak/*is*·mik (m/f)

My name is ...
اسمي ... — *is*·mee ...

Do you speak English?
تتكلم انجليزية؟ — tit·*kal*·am in·glee·*zee*·ya (m)
تتكلمي انجليزية؟ — tit·*ka*·la·mee in·glee·*zee*·ya (f)

I don't understand.
مو فاهم. — moo *faa*·him

Can I take a photo?
ممكن اتصور؟ — *mum*·kin at·*saw*·ar

ACCOMMODATION

Where's a ...?	وين ...؟	wayn ...
campsite	مخيم	moo·*khay*·am
hotel	فندق	*fun*·dug

Do you have a ... room?	عندك/عندك غرفة ...؟	*'and*·ak/*'and*·ik *ghur*·fa ... (m/f)
single	لشخص واحد	li·*shakhs waa*·hid
double	لشخسين	li·shakh·*sayn*
twin	مع سريرين	ma' sa·ree·*rayn*

How much is it per ...?	بكم كل ...؟	bi·*kam* kul ...
night	ليلة	*lay*·la
person	شخص	shakhs

Can I get another (blanket)?
احتاج الى (برنوس) — ah·*taaj* i·*la* (bar·*noos*)
الثاني من فضلك؟ — i·*thaa*·nee min *fad*·lak

The (air conditioning) doesn't work.
(الكنديشان) — (il·kan·*day*·shan)
ما يشتغل. — ma yish·*ta*·ghil

Signs

Entrance	مدخل
Exit	خروج
Open	مفتوح
Closed	مقفول
Information	معلومات
Prohibited	ممنوع
Toilets	المرحاض
Men	رجال
Women	نساء

DIRECTIONS

Where's the ...? من وين ...؟ min wayn ...

bank	البنك	il·*bank*
market	السوق	i·*soog*
post office	مكتب البريد	*mak*·tab il·ba·*reed*

Can you show me (on the map)?
لو سمحت وريني (علخريطة)؟ law sa·*maht* wa·*ree*·nee ('al·kha·*ree*·ta)

What's the address?
ما العنوان؟ ma il·'un·*waan*

Could you please write it down?
لو سمحت اكتبه لي؟ law sa·*maht* ik·ti·*boo* lee (m)
لو سمحت اكتبيه لي؟ law sa·*maht* ik·ti·*bee* lee (f)

How far is it?
كم بعيد؟ kam ba·*'eed*

How do I get there?
كيف ممكن اوصل هناكا؟ kayf *mum*·kin *aw*·sil *hoo*·naak

Turn left/right.
لف يسار/يمين. lif yee·*saar*/yee·*meen* (m)
لفي يسار/يمين. *li*·fee yee·*saar*/yee·*meen* (f)

It's ... هو ... *hoo*·wa ... (m)
هي ... *hee*·ya ... (f)

behind ...	ورا ...	wa·*raa* ...
in front of ...	قدام ...	gu·*daam* ...
near to ...	قريب من ...	ga·*reeb* min ...
next to ...	جنب ...	janb ...
on the corner	علزاوية	'a·*zaa*·wee·ya
opposite ...	مقابل ...	moo·*gaa*·bil ...
straight ahead	سيدا	*see*·da

EATING & DRINKING

Can you recommend a ...? ممكن تنصح/تنصحي ...؟ *mum*·kin *tan*·sah/*tan*·sa·hee ... (m/f)

bar	بار	baar
cafe	قهوة	*gah*·wa
restaurant	مطعم	*ma*·ta'm

I'd like a/the ..., please. اريد ... من فضلك. a·*reed* ... min *fad*·lak

nonsmoking section	المكان ممنوع تدخين	il·ma·*kaan* mam·*noo*·a' tad·*kheen*
table for (four)	طاولة (اربعة) اشخاص	*taa*·wi·lat (*ar*·ba') ash·*khaas*

What would you recommend?
اش تنصح؟ aash *tan*·sah (m)
اش تنصحي؟ aash *tan*·sa·hee (f)

What's the local speciality?
اش الطبق المحلي؟ aash i·*ta*·bak il·*ma*·ha·lee

Do you have vegetarian food?
عندك طعم نباتي؟ *'an*·dak *ta*·'am na·*baa*·tee

I'd like (the) ..., please. عطني/عطيني الـ ... من فضلك. *'a*·ti·nee/*'a*·*tee*·nee il ... min *fad*·lak (m/f)

bill	قائمة	*kaa*·'i·ma
drink list	قائمة المشروبات	*kaa*·'i·mat il·mash·roo·*baat*
menu	قائمة الطعام	*kaa*·'i·mat i·ta·*'aam*
that dish	الطبق هاذاك	i·*tab*·ak *haa*·dhaa·ka

Could you prepare a meal without ...? ممكن تطبخها/تطبخيها بدون ...؟ *mum*·kin *tat*·bakh·ha/*tat*·bakh·ee·ha bi·*doon* ... (m/f)

butter	زبدة	*zib*·da
eggs	بيض	bayd
meat stock	مرق لهم	ma·*rak la*·ham

I'm allergic to ... عندي حساسية لـ ... *'an*·dee ha·*saa*·see·ya li ...

dairy produce	الألبان	il·al·*baan*
gluten	قمح	*ka*·mah
nuts	كرزات	ka·ra·*zaat*
seafood	السمك و المحارات	i·*sa*·mak wa al·ma·haa·*raat*

coffee ...	نقهوة ...	*kah*·wa ...
tea ...	شاي ...	shay ...
with milk	بالحليب	bil·ha·*leeb*
without sugar	بدون شكر	bi·*doon shi*·ker

bottle/glass of beer	بوتل/قلاس بيرة	*boo*·til/glaas *bee*·ra
(orange) juice	عصير (برتقال)	'a·*seer* (bor·too·*gaal*)
(mineral) water	ماي (معدني)	may (*ma'a*·da·nee)

... wine	... خمر ...	... *kha*·mar
red	احمر	*ah*·mer
sparkling	فوار	fa·*waar*
white	ابيض	*ab*·yad

EMERGENCIES

Help!
مساعد! moo·*saa*·'id (m)
مساعدة! moo·*saa*·'id·a (f)

Go away!
ابعد!/ابعدي! *ib*·'ad/*ib*·'ad·ee (m/f)

Call ...!
تصل على ...! ti·*sil* 'a·la ... (m)
تصلي على ...! *ti*·*si*·lee 'a·la ... (f)

a doctor	طبيب	ta·*beeb*
the police	الشرطة	i·*shur*·ta

I'm lost.
انا ضعت. *a*·na duht

Where are the toilets?
وين المرحاض؟ wayn il·mir·*haad*

I'm sick.
انا مريض. *a*·na ma·*reed* (m)
انا مريضة. *a*·na ma·*ree*·da (f)

I'm allergic to (antibiotics).
عندي حساسية لـ (مضاد حيوي). *'and*·ee ha·saa·*see*·ya li (moo·*daad hay*·a·we)

SHOPPING & SERVICES

Where's a ...?
من وين ...؟ min wayn ...

department store	محل ضخم	ma·*hal dukh*·um
grocery store	محل ابقالية	ma·*hal* ib·gaa·*lee*·ya
newsagency	محل يبيع جرائد	ma·*hal* yi·*bee*·a' ja·*raa*·id
souvenir shop	محل سياحي	ma·*hal* say·*aa*·hee
supermarket	سوبرمركت	*soo*·ber·mar·ket

I'm looking for ...
مدور على ... moo·*daw*·ir *'a*·la ... (m)
مدورة على ... moo·*daw*·i·ra 'a·la ... (f)

Can I look at it?
ممكن اشوف؟ *mum*·kin a·*shoof*

Do you have any others?
عندَك اخرين؟ *'and*·ak ukh·*reen* (m)
عندِك اخرين؟ *'and*·ik ukh·*reen* (f)

It's faulty.
فيه خلل. fee *kha*·lal

How much is it?
بكم؟ bi·*kam*

Can you write down the price?
ممكن تكتبلي/تكتبيلي السعر؟ *mum*·kin tik·*tib*·lee/tik·*tib*·ee·lee i·*si'r* (m/f)

That's too expensive.
غالي جدا. *ghaa*·lee *jid*·an

What's your lowest price?
اش السعر الاخر؟ aash i·*si'r* il·*aa*·khir

There's a mistake in the bill.
فيه غلط في الفطورة. fee *gha*·lat fil fa·*too*·ra

Where's ...?
من وين ...؟ min wayn ...

a foreign exchange office	صراف	si·*raaf*
an ATM	مكينة صرف	ma·*kee*·nat sarf

What's the exchange rate?
ما هو السعر؟ maa *hoo*·wa i·*sa'r*

Where's the local internet cafe?
من وين انترنيت كفي؟ min wayn *in*·ter·net ka·*fay*

How much is it per hour?
بكم كل ساعة؟ bi·*kam* kul *saa*·a'

Where's the nearest public phone?
وين اقرب تلفون عمومي؟ wayn *ak*·rab til·*foon* 'u·*moo*·mee

I'd like to buy a phonecard.
اريد اشري كرت لتلفون. a·*reed ish*·ree kart li·til·*foon*

TIME & DATES

What time is it?
الساعة كم؟ i·*saa*·a' kam

It's one o'clock.
الساعة واحدة. i·*saa*·a' *waa*·hi·da

It's (two) o'clock.
الساعة (ثنتين). i·*saa*·a' (thin·*tayn*)

Half past (two).
الساعة (ثنتين) و نس. i·*saa*·a' (thin·*tayn*) wa nus

At what time ...?
الساعة كم ...؟ i·*saa*·a' kam ...

At ...
الساعة ... i·*saa*·a'...

yesterday ...	البارح ...	il·*baa*·rih ...
tomorrow ...	باكر ...	*baa*·chir ...
morning	صباح	sa·*baah*
afternoon	بعد الظهر	ba'd a·*thuhr*
evening	مساء	*mi*·saa

Question Words

When?	متى؟	*ma*·ta
Where?	وين؟	wayn
Who?	من؟	man
Why?	لاش؟	laysh

Monday	يوم الاثنين	yawm al·ith·*nayn*
Tuesday	يوم الثلاثة	yawm a·tha·*laa*·tha
Wednesday	يوم الاربعة	yawm al·*ar*·ba'
Thursday	يوم الخميس	yawm al·kha·*mees*
Friday	يوم الجمعة	yawm al·*jum*·a'
Saturday	يوم السبت	yawm a·*sibt*
Sunday	يوم الاحد	yawm al·*aa*·had

TRANSPORT

Is this the ... (to Riyadh)?	هاذا ال ... يروح (لرياض)؟	*haa*·dha al ... yi·*roh* (li·ree·*yaad*)
boat	سفينة	sa·*fee*·na
bus	باص	baas
plane	طيارة	tay·*aa*·ra
train	قطار	gi·*taar*

What time's the ... bus?	الساعة كم الباص ...؟	a·*saa*·a' kam il·*baas* ...
first	الاول	il·*aw*·al
last	الاخر	il·*aa*·khir
next	القادم	il·*gaa*·dim

Numbers

1	١	واحد	*waa*·hid
2	٢	اثنين	ith·*nayn*
3	٣	ثلاثة	tha·*laa*·tha
4	٤	اربع	ar·*ba'*
5	٥	خمسة	*kham*·sa
6	٦	ستة	*si*·ta
7	٧	سبعة	*sa*·ba'
8	٨	ثمانية	tha·*maan*·ya
9	٩	تسعة	*tis*·a'
10	١٠	عشرة	*'ash*·ar·a
20	٢٠	عشرين	'ash·*reen*
30	٣٠	ثلاثين	tha·la·*theen*
40	٤٠	اربعين	ar·ba'·*een*
50	٥٠	خمسين	kham·*seen*
60	٦٠	ستين	sit·*een*
70	٧٠	سبعين	sa·ba'·*een*
80	٨٠	ثمانين	tha·ma·*neen*
90	٩٠	تسعين	ti·sa'·*een*
100	١٠٠	مية	*mee*·ya
1000	١٠٠٠	الف	alf

Note that Arabic numerals, unlike letters, are read from left to right.

One ... ticket (to Doha), please.	تذكرة ... (الدوحة) من فضلك.	*tadh*·ka·ra ... (a·*do*·ha) min *fad*·lak
one-way	ذهاب بص	dhee·*haab* bas
return	ذهاب و اياب	dhee·*haab* wa ai·*yaab*

How long does the trip take?
كم الرحلة تستغرق؟ kam i·*rah*·la tis·*tagh*·rik

Is it a direct route?
الرحلة متواصلة؟ i·*rah*·la moo·ta·*waa*·si·la

What station/stop is this?
ما هي المحطة هاذي؟ maa *hee*·ya il·ma·*ha*·ta *haa*·dhee

Please tell me when we get to (Al-Ain).
لو سمحت خبرني/خبريني وقت ما نوصل الي (العين). law sa·*maht* kha·*bir*·nee/kha·*bir*·ee·nee wokt ma *noo*·sil i·*la* (al·*'ain*) (m/f)

How much is it to (Sharjah)?
بكم الى (شارقة)؟ bi·*kam* i·*la* (*shaa*·ri·ka)

Please take me to (this address).
من فضلك خذني (علعنوان هاذا). min *fad*·lak *khudh*·nee ('al·'un·*waan haa*·dha)

Please stop here.
لو سمحت وقف هنا. law sa·*maht wa*·gif *hi*·na

Please wait here.
لو سمحت استنا هنا. law sa·*maht* is·*ta*·na *hi*·na

I'd like to hire a ...	اريد استأجر ...	a·*reed* ist·*'aj*·ir ...
4WD	سيارة فيها دبل	say·*aa*·ra *fee*·ha *da*·bal
car	سيارة	say·*aa*·ra

with ...	مع ...	ma' ...
a driver	دريول	*dray*·wil
air conditioning	كنديشان	kan·*day*·shan

How much for ... hire?	كم الإيجار ...؟	kam il·ee·*jaar* ...
daily	كل يوم	kul yawm
weekly	كل اسبوع	kul us·*boo*·a'

Is this the road to (Abu Dhabi)?
هاذا الطريق الى (ابو ظبي)؟ *haa*·dha i·ta·*reeg* i·*la* (a·*boo da*·bee)

I need a mechanic.
احتاج ميكانيك. ah·*taaj* mee·kaa·*neek*

I've run out of petrol.
ينضب البنزين. *yan*·dab al·ban·*zeen*

I have a flat tyre.
عندي بنشار. *'and*·ee *ban*·shar

ARABIC ALPHABET

Arabic is written from right to left. The form of each letter changes depending on whether it's at the start, in the middle or at the end of a word or whether it stands alone.

Word-Final	Word-Medial	Word-Initial	Alone	Letter
ـا	ـاـ	اـ	ا	alef'
ـب	ـبـ	بـ	ب	'ba
ـت	ـتـ	تـ	ت	'ta
ـث	ـثـ	ثـ	ث	'tha
ـج	ـجـ	جـ	ج	jeem
ـح	ـحـ	حـ	ح	'ha
ـخ	ـخـ	خـ	خ	'kha
ـد	ـد ـ	د ـ	د	daal
ـذ	ـذ ـ	ذـ	ذ	dhaal
ـر	ـرـ	رـ	ر	'ra
ـز	ـزـ	زـ	ز	'za
ـس	ـسـ	سـ	س	seen
ـش	ـشـ	شـ	ش	sheen
ـص	ـصـ	صـ	ص	saad
ـض	ـضـ	ضـ	ض	daad
ـط	ـطـ	طـ	ط	'ta
ـظ	ـظـ	ظـ	ظ	'dha
ـع	ـعـ	عـ	ع	ain'
ـغ	ـغـ	غـ	غ	ghain
ـف	ـفـ	فـ	ف	'fa
ـق	ـقـ	قـ	ق	kuf
ـك	ـكـ	كـ	ك	kaf
ـل	ـلـ	لـ	ل	lam
ـم	ـمـ	مـ	م	mim
ـن	ـنـ	نـ	ن	nun
ـه	ـهـ	هـ	ه	'ha
ـو	ـو ـ	و ـ	و	waw
ـي	ـيـ	يـ	ي	'ya
	ء			hamza
ـأَ	ـئَ ـؤَ	أَ	أَ	a
ـأُ	ـئُ ـؤُ	أُ	أُ	u
ـإِ	ـئِ ـؤِ	إِ	إِ	i
ـأْ	ـئْ ـؤْ	أْ	أْ	' (glottal stop)
ـَا	ـَا ـ	آ	آ	aa
ـُو	ـُوْ ـ	أُو	أُو	oo
ـِيْ	ـِيْـ	إِيْ	إِيْ	ee
ـَوْ	ـَوْـ	أَوْ	أَوْ	aw
ـَي	ـَيْـ	أَيْ	أَيْ	ay

GLOSSARY

abaya – woman's full-length black robe

abra – small, flat-decked boat; water taxi

adhan – call to prayer

agal – head ropes used to hold a *gutra* in place

al-housh – courtyard

areesh – palm fronds used to construct houses

asr – mid-afternoon

attar – perfume

ayyalah – Bedouin dance

azan – call to prayer

barasti – traditional Gulf method of building palm-leaf houses; house built with palm leaves

barjeel – wind tower; architectural feature of *masayf* houses designed to keep the house cool

bateel – young shoot of date-palm plant

Bedouin (plural Bedu) – a nomadic desert dweller

burj – tower

burka – a long, enveloping garment worn in public by Muslim women

corniche – seaside road

dosa – paper-thin lentil-flour pancakes

dhow – traditional sailing vessel of the Gulf

dhuhr – noon

dishdasha – man's long shirt-dress

eid – Islamic feast

fajr – dawn

falaj – traditional irrigation channel

ghaf – big hardy tree that looks a little like a weeping willow

Gulf Cooperative Council (GCC) – members are Saudi Arabia, Kuwait, Bahrain, Qatar, Oman and the UAE

gutra – white headcloth worn by men

hajj – Muslim pilgrimage to Mecca

halal – meat from animals killed according to Islamic law

hammam – bathhouse

hammour – common species of fish in Gulf waters

haram – forbidden by Islamic law

Hejira – meaning 'flight'; the Islamic calendar is called the Hejira calendar

imam – prayer leader, Muslim cleric

insha'alla – 'if Allah wills it'; 'God willing'

isha'a – twilight

jebel – hill, mountain

kandoura – casual shirt-dress worn by men and women

khaleeji – traditional Gulf-style music

khanjar – traditional curved dagger

khor – inlet or creek

maghrib – sunset

majlis – formal meeting room or reception area

Majlis, the – parliament

mandir – temple

masayf – traditional summer house incorporating a *barjeel*

masgouf – fish dish

mashait – traditional winter house incorporating a courtyard

masjid – mosque

mathaf – museum

mihrab – niche in a mosque indicating the direction of Mecca

mina – port

mullah – Muslim scholar, teacher or religious leader

neem – a botanical cousin of mahogany

oud – wooden Arabian lute; also the wood used to burn with frankincense

Ramadan – Muslim month of fasting

sabkha – salt-crusted coastal plain

shayla – headscarf

sheesha – tall, glass-bottomed smoking implement; also called a water pipe or hubbly-bubbly

sheikh – venerated religious scholar, tribal chief, ruler or elderly man worthy of respect

sheikha – daughter of a *sheikh*

souq – market

Trucial States – former name of the United Arab Emirates; also called Trucial Coast and Trucial sheikhdoms

umrah – little pilgrimage

wasta – influence gained by connections in high places

wind tower – *barjeel*; architectural feature of *masayf* houses designed to keep the house cool

Behind the Scenes

SEND US YOUR FEEDBACK

We love to hear from travellers – your comments keep us on our toes and help make our books better. Our well-travelled team reads every word on what you loved or loathed about this book. Although we cannot reply individually to postal submissions, we always guarantee that your feedback goes straight to the appropriate authors, in time for the next edition. Each person who sends us information is thanked in the next edition – and the most useful submissions are rewarded with a selection of digital PDF chapters.

Visit **lonelyplanet.com/contact** to submit your updates and suggestions or to ask for help. Our award-winning website also features inspirational travel stories, news and discussions.

Note: We may edit, reproduce and incorporate your comments in Lonely Planet products such as guidebooks, websites and digital products, so let us know if you don't want your comments reproduced or your name acknowledged. For a copy of our privacy policy visit lonelyplanet.com/privacy.

OUR READERS

Many thanks to the travellers who used the last edition and wrote to us with helpful hints, useful advice and interesting anecdotes:

Sergio Boccia, Mary-Clare Buckle, Debra Dorn, Liliane Foederer, Klaus Hindso, John Mitchell and Flavia Romano Rodrigues.

AUTHOR THANKS

Josephine Quintero

Where to start! So many people provided me with invaluable help during my research trip. Top of the list has to be Richard and Angela Carey-Brown in Abu Dhabi, followed closely by Peter and Jan Casey, who I shared many a meal and bottle of wine with in Dubai. I would also like to thank Brian Hollis, David Quinn, Farah Atoui from Art Dubai, Ilka Becker from Arabian Adventures, Sharmeen Sayed, Yasmine Behnam and Robin Chapman for his cat sitting and support. A mighty *shukran* to you all.

ACKNOWLEDGMENTS

Cover photograph: Burj al-Arab, Dubai; Merten Snijders/Lonely Planet Images.

Many of the images in this guide are available for licensing from Lonely Planet Images: www.lonelyplanetimages.com.

THIS BOOK

This 7th edition of *Dubai & Abu Dhabi* was written and researched by Josephine Quintero. The 6th edition was written by Andrea Schulte-Peevers and the 5th edition was written by Matthew Lee and John A Vlahides. This guidebook was commissioned in Lonely Planet's Melbourne office and produced by the following:

Commissioning Editors Sam Trafford, William Gourlay
Coordinating Editors Susie Ashworth, Carolyn Bain
Coordinating Cartographers Valentina Kremenchutskaya, Jolyon Philcox
Coordinating Layout Designer Wendy Wright
Managing Editors Brigitte Ellemor, Martine Power, Angela Tinson
Senior Editors Andi Jones, Susan Paterson
Managing Cartographers Adrian Persoglia, Amanda Sierp
Managing Layout Designer Jane Hart
Assisting Editors Kate Mathews, Joanne Newell
Assisting Cartographers Corey Hutchison, Eve Kelly, Peter Shields
Assisting Layout Designer Yvonne Bischofberger
Cover Research Naomi Parker
Internal Image Research Jane Hart
Language Content Branislava Vladisavljevic
Thanks to Shahara Ahmed, Anita Banh, Janine Eberle, Ryan Evans, Larissa Frost, Laura Jane, Trent Paton, Suzannah Shwer, Laura Stansfeld, John Taufa, Gerard Walker

See also separate subindexes for:
- EATING P199
- DRINKING & NIGHTLIFE P200
- ENTERTAINMENT P201
- SHOPPING P201
- SPORTS & ACTIVITIES P202
- SLEEPING P202

Index

Sights 000
Map Pages **000**
Photo Pages **000**

Sights 000
Map Pages **000**
Photo Pages **000**

EATING

Sights 000
Map Pages **000**
Photo Pages **000**

DRINKING & NIGHTLIFE

ENTERTAINMENT

SHOPPING

SPORTS & ACTIVITIES

SLEEPING

Dubai Maps

Map Legend

Sights
- Beach
- Buddhist
- Castle
- Christian
- Hindu
- Islamic
- Jewish
- Monument
- Museum/Gallery
- Ruin
- Winery/Vineyard
- Zoo
- Other Sight

Eating
- Eating

Drinking & Nightlife
- Drinking & Nightlife
- Cafe

Entertainment
- Entertainment

Shopping
- Shopping

Sleeping
- Sleeping
- Camping

Sports & Activities
- Diving/Snorkelling
- Canoeing/Kayaking
- Skiing
- Surfing
- Swimming/Pool
- Walking
- Windsurfing
- Other Sports & Activities

Information
- Post Office
- Tourist Information

Transport
- Airport
- Border Crossing
- Bus
- Cable Car/ Funicular
- Cycling
- Ferry
- Metro
- Monorail
- Parking
- S-Bahn
- Taxi
- Train/Railway
- Tram
- Tube Station
- U-Bahn
- Other Transport

Routes
- Tollway
- Freeway
- Primary
- Secondary
- Tertiary
- Lane
- Unsealed Road
- Plaza/Mall
- Steps
- Tunnel
- Pedestrian Overpass
- Walking Tour
- Walking Tour Detour
- Path

Boundaries
- International
- State/Province
- Disputed
- Regional/Suburb
- Marine Park
- Cliff
- Wall

Geographic
- Hut/Shelter
- Lighthouse
- Lookout
- Mountain/Volcano
- Oasis
- Park
- Pass
- Picnic Area
- Waterfall

Hydrography
- River/Creek
- Intermittent River
- Swamp/Mangrove
- Reef
- Canal
- Water
- Dry/Salt/ Intermittent Lake
- Glacier

Areas
- Beach/Desert
- Cemetery (Christian)
- Cemetery (Other)
- Park/Forest
- Sportsground
- Sight (Building)
- Top Sight (Building)

MAP INDEX

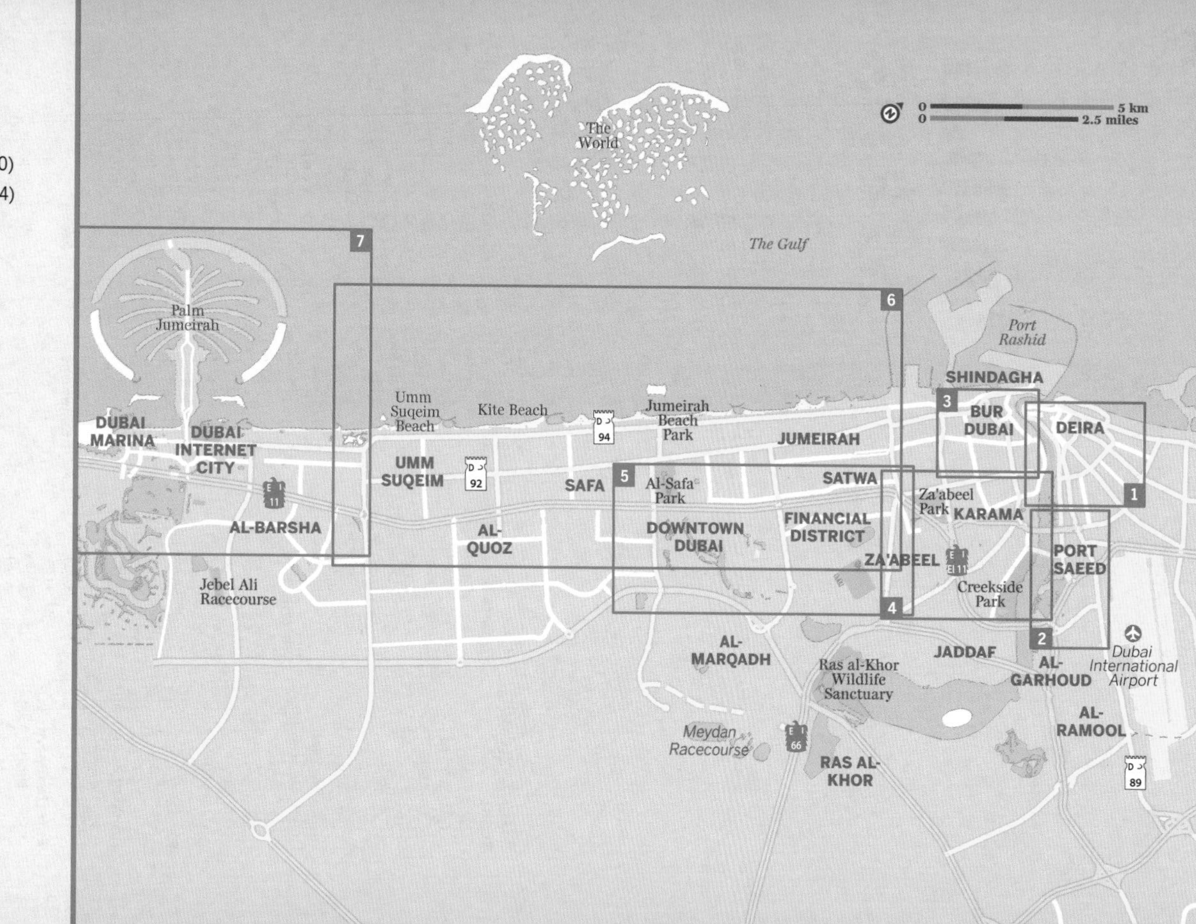

0 5 km
0 2.5 miles
The World
The Gulf
Port Rashid
SHINDAGHA
BUR DUBAI
DEIRA
Palm Jumeirah
Umm Suqeim Beach
Kite Beach
Jumeirah Beach Park
JUMEIRAH
DUBAI MARINA
DUBAI INTERNET CITY
UMM SUQEIM
SAFA
Al-Safa Park
SATWA
Za'abeel Park
KARAMA
AL-BARSHA
AL-QUOZ
DOWNTOWN DUBAI
FINANCIAL DISTRICT
ZA'ABEEL
PORT SAEED
Creekside Park
Jebel Ali Racecourse
AL-MARQADH
Ras al-Khor Wildlife Sanctuary
JADDAF
AL-GARHOUD
Dubai International Airport
AL-RAMOOL
Meydan Racecourse
RAS AL-KHOR
94
92
89
11
66
1
2
3
4
5
6
7

DEIRA NORTH *Map on p206*

Sights (p52)

1 Al-Ahmadiya School........A1
2 Deira Covered Souq........C2
3 Deira Gold Souq........B1
4 Deira Spice Souq........A1
5 Fish Market........C1
6 Heritage House........A1
7 National Bank of Dubai........C6
8 New Naif Market........C2
9 Perfume Souq........B2

Eating (p54)

10 Abesinian Restaurant........E2
11 Afghan Khorasan Kebab House........C2
12 Al-Baghdadi Home........F5
13 Al-Mansour Dhow........C5
14 Aroos Damascus........E6
Ashiana........(see 27)
15 Ashwaq Cafeteria........C2
China Club........(see 24)
16 Fruit & Vegetable Market........C1
Glasshouse Mediterranean Brasserie........(see 22)
17 Pinoy Grill........D6
Shabestan........(see 24)
18 Spice Island........G7
Sumibiya........(see 24)
Table 9........(see 22)
19 Xiao Wei Yang........C4
Yum!........(see 24)

Drinking & Nightlife (p57)

Issimo........(see 22)
Ku-Bu........(see 24)

Shopping (p58)

20 Al-Ghurair City........D6
Deira Covered Souq........(see 2)
Deira Gold Souq........(see 3)
Deira Spice Souq........(see 4)
Fish Market........(see 5)
21 Gift Village........C3
Perfume Souq........(see 9)

Sleeping (p137)

22 Hilton Dubai Creek........C7
23 Landmark Hotel........C3
24 Radisson Blu Hotel........C5
25 Riviera Hotel........C4
26 Sheraton Deira........H6
27 Sheraton Dubai Creek Hotel & Towers........C6

Key on p205

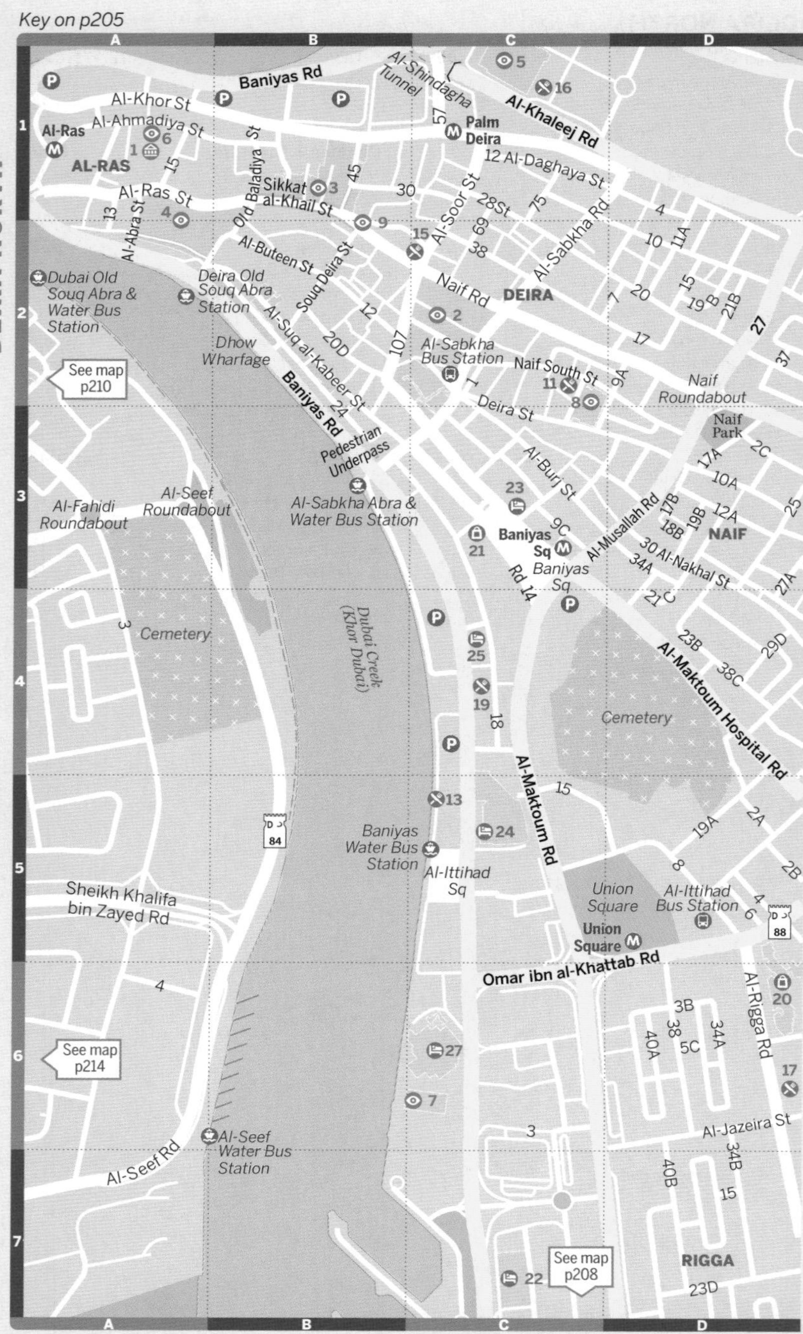
A
B
C
D
Baniyas Rd
Al-Khor St
Al-Ahmadiya St
Al-Ras
AL-RAS
Al-Ras St
Al-Abra St
Old Baladiya St
Sikkat al-Khail St
Al-Shindagha Tunnel
Al-Khaleej Rd
Palm Deira
12 Al-Daghaya St
Al-Soor St
28St
Al-Sabkha Rd
Al-Buteen St
Souq Deira St
Naif Rd
DEIRA
Dubai Old Souq Abra & Water Bus Station
Deira Old Souq Abra Station
Al-Suq al-Kabeer St
Dhow Wharfage
Al-Sabkha Bus Station
Naif South St
Deira St
Naif Roundabout
Naif Park
See map p210
Baniyas Rd
Pedestrian Underpass
Al-Burj St
Al-Musallah Rd
Al-Fahidi Roundabout
Al-Seef Roundabout
Al-Sabkha Abra & Water Bus Station
Baniyas Sq
NAIF
30 Al-Nakhal St
Rd 14
Cemetery
Dubai Creek (Khor Dubai)
Al-Maktoum Hospital Rd
Cemetery
Al-Maktoum Rd
Baniyas Water Bus Station
Al-Ittihad Sq
Sheikh Khalifa bin Zayed Rd
Union Square
Al-Ittihad Bus Station
Union Square
Omar ibn al-Khattab Rd
Al-Rigga Rd
See map p214
Al-Jazeira St
Al-Seef Water Bus Station
Al-Seef Rd
RIGGA
See map p208
A
B
C
D

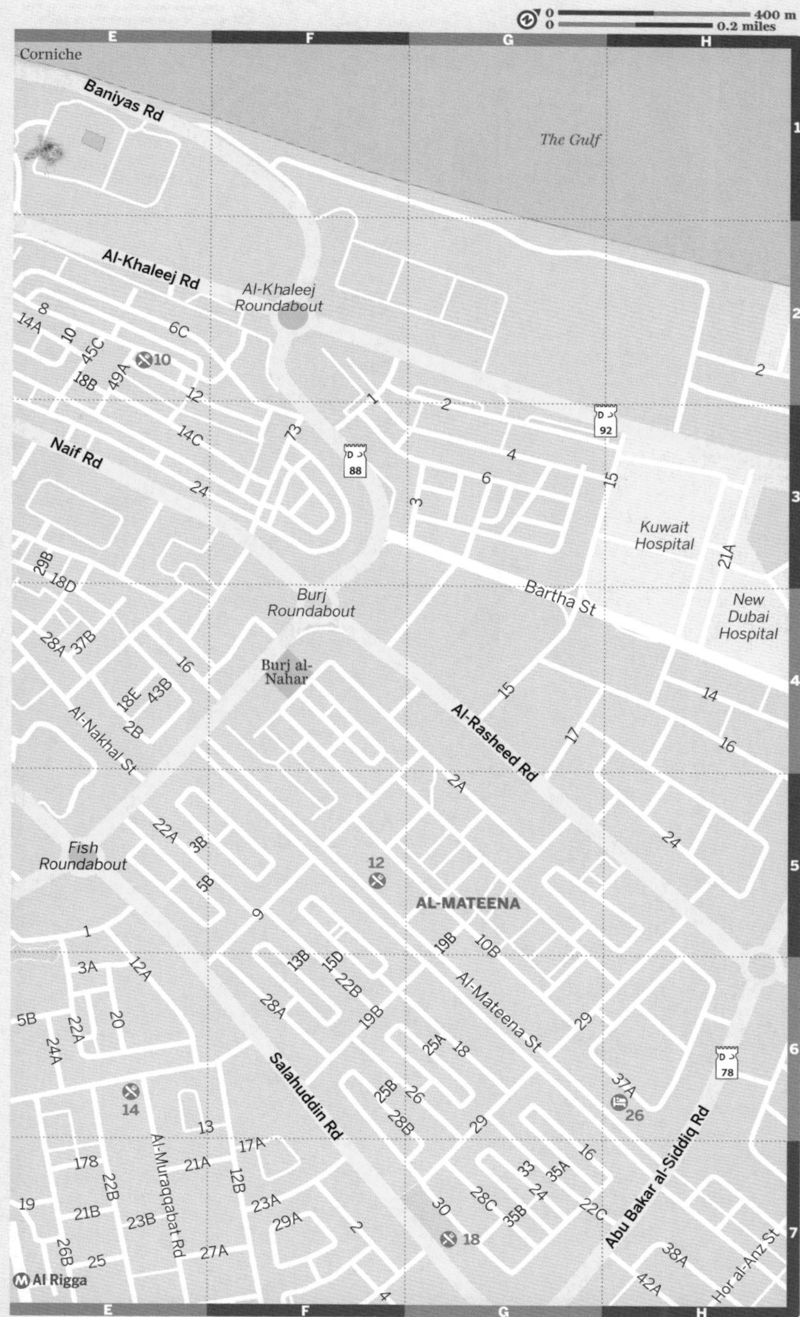

0 400 m
0 0.2 miles
Corniche
Baniyas Rd
The Gulf
Al-Khaleej Rd
Al-Khaleej Roundabout
Naif Rd
Kuwait Hospital
Bartha St
Burj Roundabout
New Dubai Hospital
Burj al-Nahar
Al-Rasheed Rd
Al-Nakhal St
Fish Roundabout
AL-MATEENA
Al-Mateena St
Salahuddin Rd
Abu Bakar al-Siddiq Rd
Al-Muraqqabat Rd
Hor al-Anz St
Al Rigga

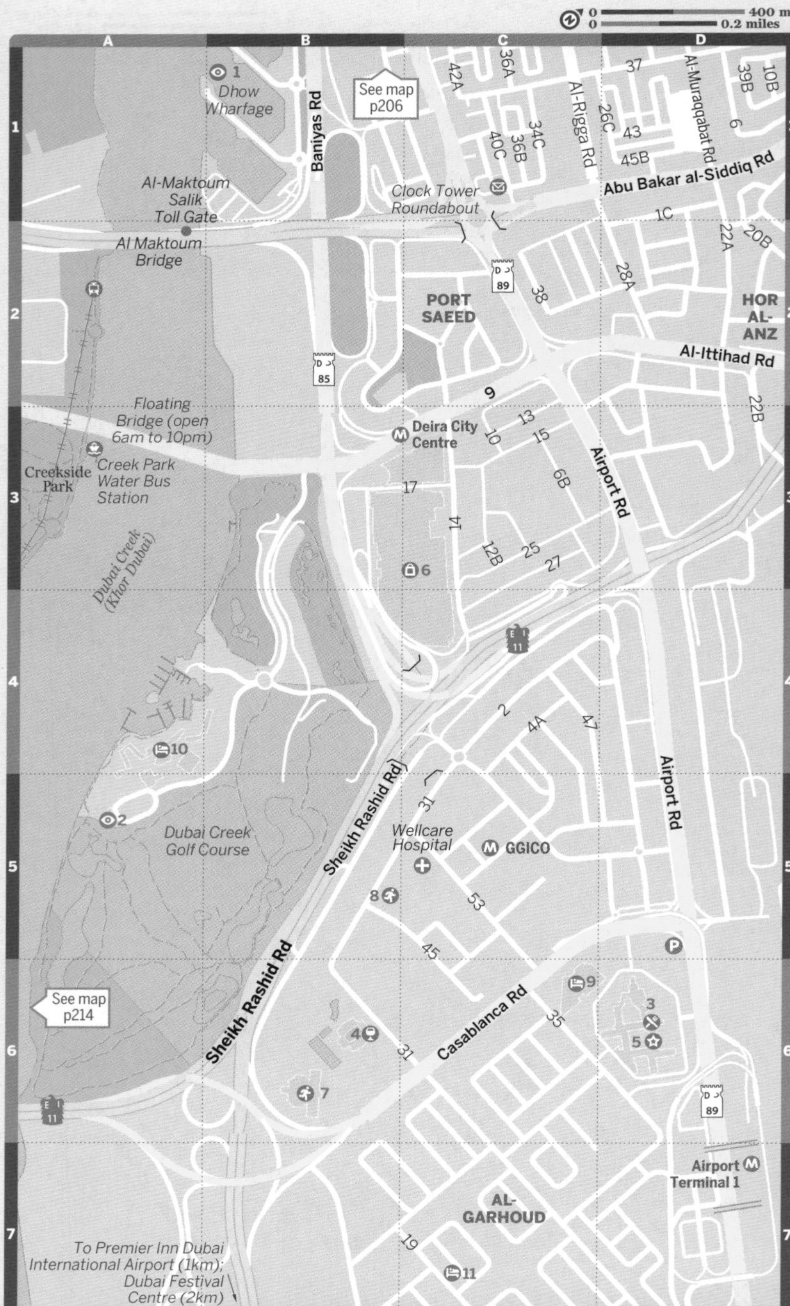

400 m
0.2 miles
Dhow Wharfage
See map p206
Baniyas Rd
Al-Rigga Rd
Al-Muraqqabat Rd
Abu Bakar al-Siddiq Rd
Al-Maktoum Salik Toll Gate
Al Maktoum Bridge
Clock Tower Roundabout
PORT SAEED
HOR AL-ANZ
Al-Ittihad Rd
Floating Bridge (open 6am to 10pm)
Deira City Centre
Creekside Park
Creek Park Water Bus Station
Airport Rd
Dubai Creek (Khor Dubai)
Sheikh Rashid Rd
Wellcare Hospital
GGICO
Dubai Creek Golf Course
See map p214
Casablanca Rd
Airport Terminal 1
AL-GARHOUD
To Premier Inn Dubai International Airport (1km); Dubai Festival Centre (2km)

DEIRA SOUTH

Sights (p52)

1 Dhow Wharfage B1
2 Dubai Creek Golf & Yacht Club A5

Eating (p54)

Cafe Arabesque .... (see 10)
Carrefour .... (see 6)
Paul .... (see 6)
Thai Kitchen .... (see 10)
Traiteur .... (see 10)
3 Yalumba D6

Drinking & Nightlife (p57)

4 Irish Village B6
QD's .... (see 2)
Terrace .... (see 10)

Entertainment (p58)

5 Jules Bar D6

Shopping (p58)

Al Washia .... (see 6)
Bateel .... (see 6)
Damas .... (see 6)
6 Deira City Centre C3
Early Learning Centre .... (see 6)
Lush .... (see 6)
Mango Touch .... (see 6)
Mikyajy .... (see 6)
Virgin Megastore .... (see 6)
Women's Secret .... (see 6)
Zara .... (see 6)

Sports & Activities (p61)

Amara .... (see 10)
7 Aviation Club B6
8 Bliss Relaxology B5

Sleeping (p137)

9 Al-Bustan Rotana C6
10 Park Hyatt Dubai A4
11 Villa 47 .... C7

Key on p212

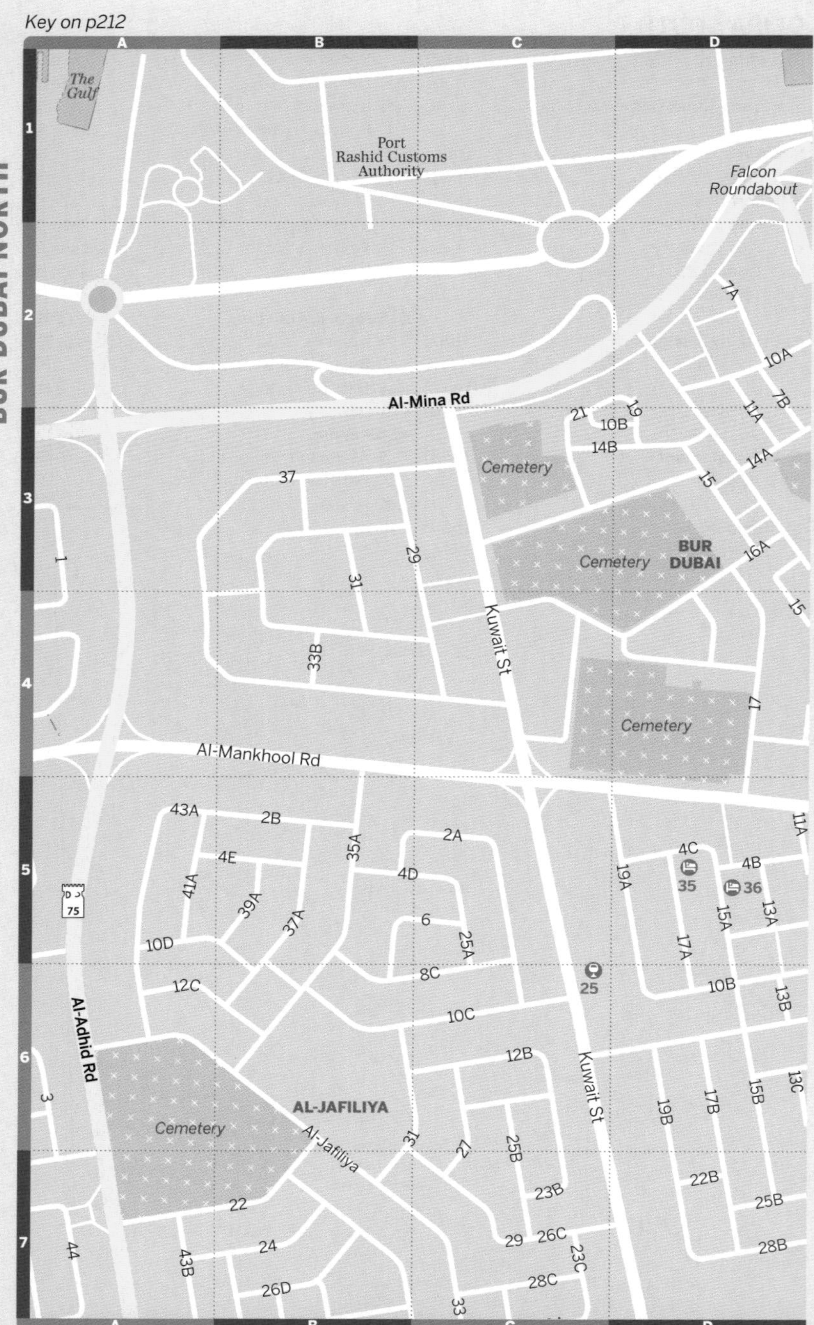
BUR DUBAI NORTH
The Gulf
Port Rashid Customs Authority
Falcon Roundabout
Al-Mina Rd
Cemetery
BUR DUBAI
Kuwait St
Al-Mankhool Rd
Al-Adhid Rd
AL-JAFILIYA
Al-Jafiliya
35
36
25
75

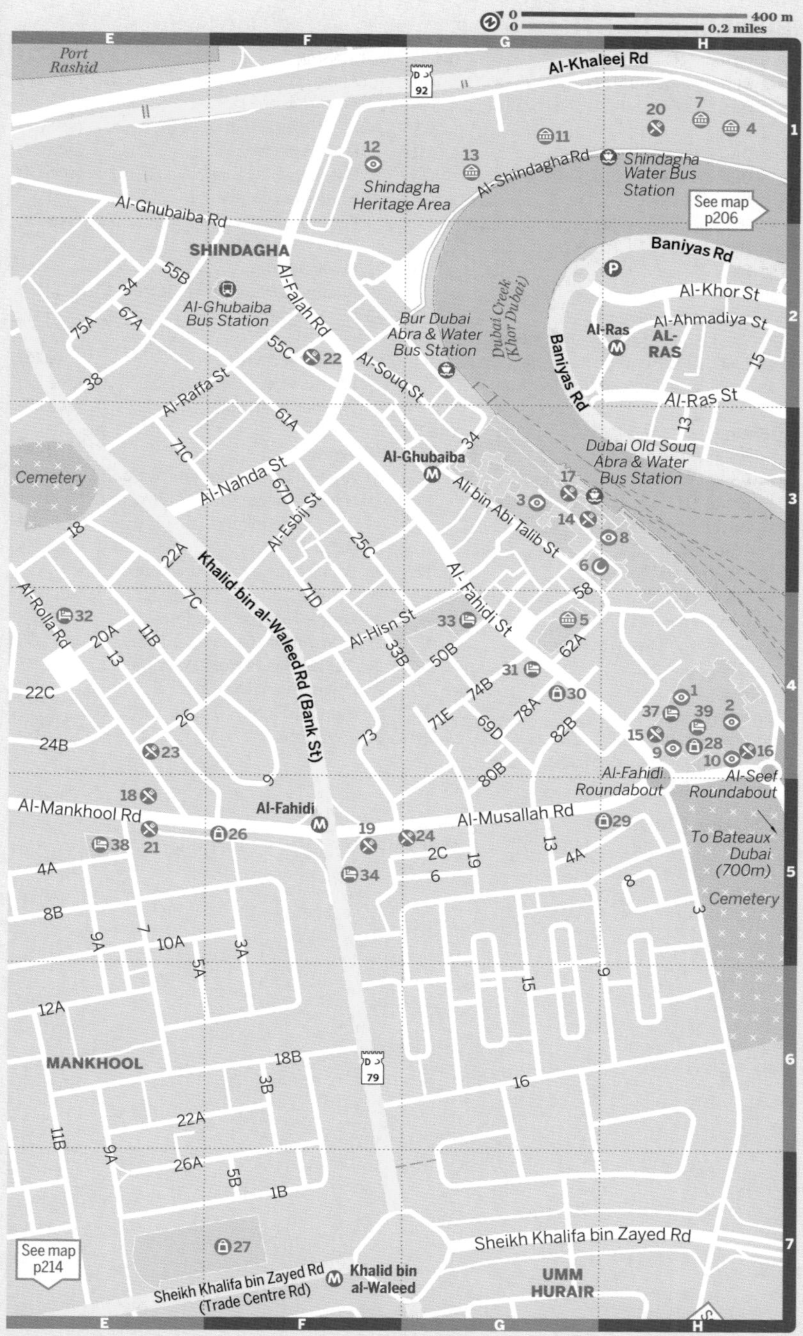

BUR DUBAI NORTH
400 m
0.2 miles
Port Rashid
Al-Khaleej Rd
Shindagha Heritage Area
Al-Shindagha Rd
Shindagha Water Bus Station
See map p206
Al-Ghubaiba Rd
SHINDAGHA
Baniyas Rd
Al-Khor St
Al-Ghubaiba Bus Station
Al-Falah Rd
Bur Dubai Abra & Water Bus Station
Dubai Creek (Khor Dubai)
Al-Ras
AL-RAS
Al-Ahmadiya St
Al-Souq St
Al-Raffa St
Al-Ras St
Al-Ghubaiba
Dubai Old Souq Abra & Water Bus Station
Cemetery
Al-Nahda St
Ali bin Abi Talib St
Al-Esbij St
Khalid bin al-Waleed Rd (Bank St)
Al-Rolla Rd
Al-Fahidi St
Al-Hisn St
Al-Fahidi Roundabout
Al-Seef Roundabout
Al-Mankhool Rd
Al-Fahidi
Al-Musallah Rd
To Bateaux Dubai (700m)
Cemetery
MANKHOOL
Sheikh Khalifa bin Zayed Rd
See map p214
Sheikh Khalifa bin Zayed Rd (Trade Centre Rd)
Khalid bin al-Waleed
UMM HURAIR

BUR DUBAI NORTH *Map on p210*

Sights (p65)

1 Al-Serkal Cultural Foundation ... H4
2 Bastakia Quarter ... H4
3 Bur Dubai Souq ... G3
4 Diving Village ... H1
5 Dubai Museum ... G4
6 Grand Mosque ... G3
7 Heritage Village ... H1
8 Hindi Lane ... H3
9 Majlis Gallery ... H4
10 Sheikh Mohammed Centre for Cultural Understanding ... H4
11 Sheikh Saeed al-Maktoum House ... G1
12 Shindagha Heritage Area ... F1
13 Traditional Architecture Museum ... G1

Eating (p67)

Antique Bazaar ... (see 34)
14 Bait Al Wakeel ... G3
15 Basta Art Cafe ... H4
16 Bastakiah Nights ... H4
17 Blue Barjeel ... G3
18 Choithram ... E5
19 Curry Leaf ... F5
20 Kan Zaman ... H1
21 Lebanese Village Restaurant ... E5
Olive Gourmet ... (see 27)
Paul ... (see 27)
22 Saravanaa Bhavan ... F2
23 Shiv Ganya ... E4
24 Special Ostadi ... G5
XVA Cafe ... (see 39)

Drinking & Nightlife (p72)

Old Vic ... (see 38)
25 Submarine ... C6

Shopping (p72)

Ajmal ... (see 27)
26 Al-Ain Centre ... F5
Al-Orooba Oriental ... (see 27)
Bang & Olufson ... (see 27)
Bateel ... (see 27)
27 BurJuman Centre ... F7
Faces ... (see 27)
Galaxy Piano ... (see 27)
28 Royal Saffron ... H4
29 Shoppers Department Store ... H5
30 Silk Wonders ... G4

Sports & Activities (p75)

Fitness First ... (see 27)
Wonder Bus Tours ... (see 27)

Sleeping (p138)

31 Arabian Courtyard Hotel & Spa ... G4
32 Dar al Sondos Hotel Apartments by Le Meridien ... E4
33 Dubai Nova ... G4
34 Four Points by Sheraton Bur Dubai ... F5
35 Four Points by Sheraton Downtown Dubai ... D5
36 Golden Sands Hotel Apartments ... D5
37 Orient Guest House ... H4
38 Ramada Hotel ... E5
39 XVA Hotel ... H4

BUR DUBAI SOUTH *Map on p214*

Key on p213

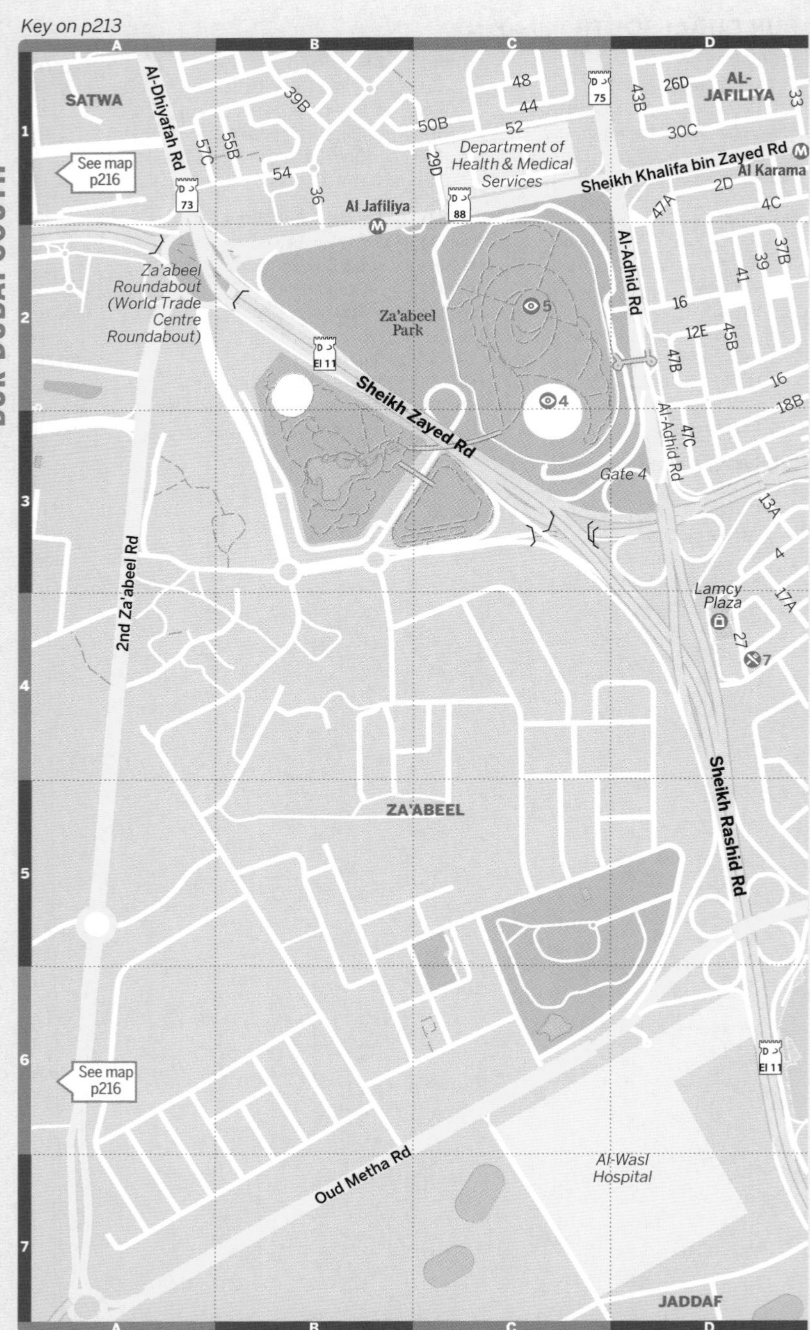

BUR DUBAI SOUTH
A
B
C
D
1
2
3
4
5
6
7
SATWA
Al-Dhiyafah Rd
39B
57C
55B
54
36
48
44
50B
52
29D
Department of Health & Medical Services
26D
43B
AL-JAFILIYA
33
30C
Sheikh Khalifa bin Zayed Rd
Al Karama
2D
4C
47A
Al Jafiliya
73
88
75
See map p216
Za'abeel Roundabout (World Trade Centre Roundabout)
Za'abeel Park
5
4
Al-Adhid Rd
16
37B
39
41
12E
45B
47B
16
18B
47C
Al-Adhid Rd
El 11
Sheikh Zayed Rd
Gate 4
13A
4
17A
Lamcy Plaza
27
7
2nd Za'abeel Rd
ZA'ABEEL
Sheikh Rashid Rd
See map p216
El 11
Oud Metha Rd
Al-Wasl Hospital
JADDAF

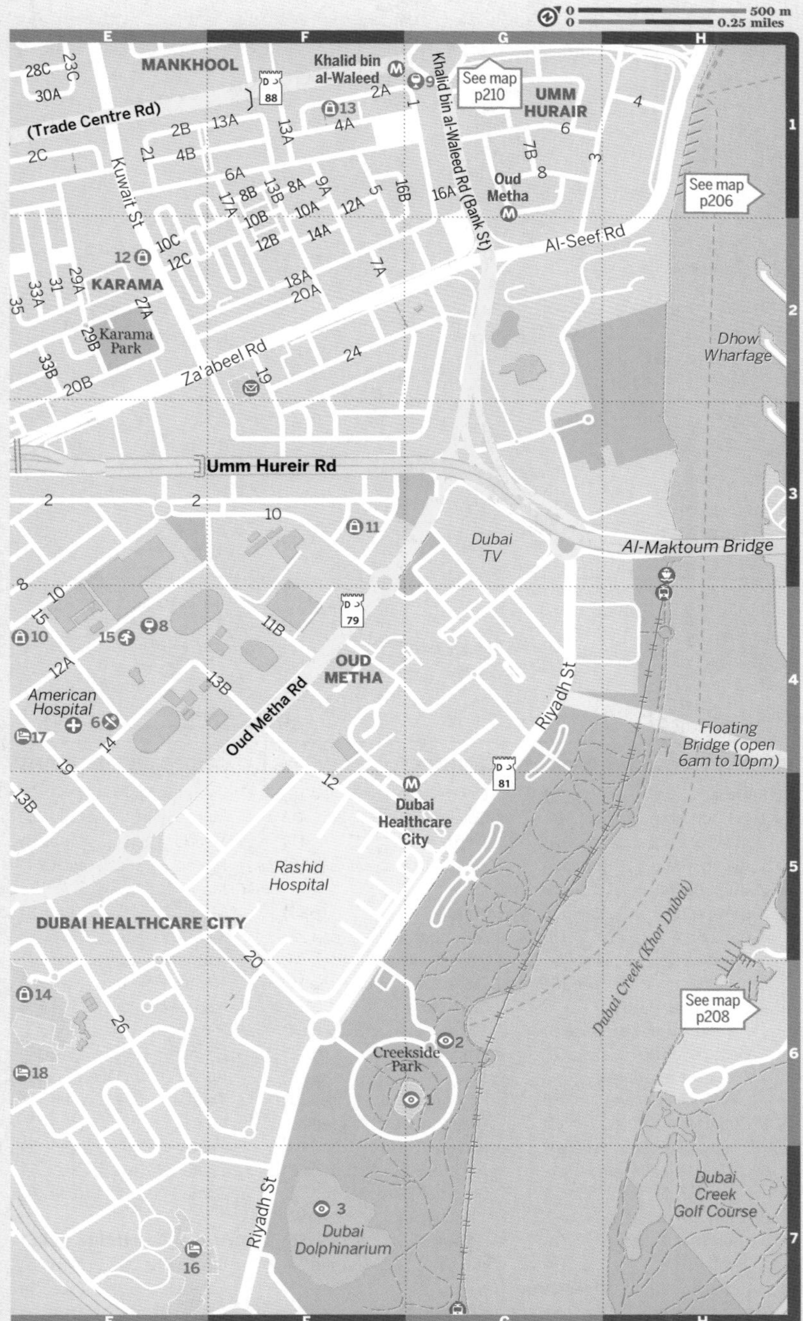

500 m
0.25 miles
MANKHOOL
Khalid bin al-Waleed
(Trade Centre Rd)
UMM HURAIR
See map p210
See map p206
Oud Metha
Kuwait St
Khalid bin al-Waleed Rd (Bank St)
Al-Seef Rd
KARAMA
Karama Park
Za'abeel Rd
Dhow Wharfage
Umm Hureir Rd
Dubai TV
Al-Maktoum Bridge
OUD METHA
Oud Metha Rd
American Hospital
Riyadh St
Floating Bridge (open 6am to 10pm)
Dubai Healthcare City
Rashid Hospital
DUBAI HEALTHCARE CITY
Dubai Creek (Khor Dubai)
See map p208
Creekside Park
Dubai Dolphinarium
Dubai Creek Golf Course

Sights (p79)

1 1x1 Contemporary Art .. C4
Art Sawa .... (see 10)
Ayyam Gallery ...... (see 10)
2 Burj Khalifa D2
3 Carbon 12 .... D4
4 Cartoon Art Gallery D4
5 Courtyard D4
Cuadro .... (see 10)
Dubai Aquarium & Underwater Zoo .. (see 8)
6 Dubai Fountain D3
7 Dubai International Financial Centre F2
8 Dubai Mall E3
Empty Quarter ..... (see 10)
9 Gallery Isabelle van den Eynde C4
10 Gate Village F2
11 Green Art Gallery C4
12 JamJar B4
KidZania .... (see 8)
13 Meem Gallery A4
Opera Gallery .... (see 10)
14 Souq al-Bahar D3
15 Third Line D4
XVA Gallery .... (see 10)

Eating (p83)

Al-Nafoorah .... (see 23)
Asado .... (see 33)
Baker & Spice ...... (see 14)
Cold Stone Creamery .... (see 8)
Emporio Armani Caffé .... (see 8)
Exchange Grill ...... (see 31)
Fazaris .... (see 27)
Frozen Yoghurt Factory .... (see 8)
Gourmet Burger Kitchen .... (see 7)
Hoi An .... (see 35)
Hukama .... (see 27)
Ivy .... (see 23)
Karma Kafe .... (see 14)
La Petite Maison .. (see 10)
Marrakech .... (see 35)
Milano .... (see 8)
More .... (see 24)
16 More E2
More .... (see 8)
Morelli's Gelato ..... (see 8)
na3na3 .... (see 28)
Noodle House ...... (see 23)
Noodle House .... (see 8)
Rib Room .... (see 23)
Rivington Grill .... (see 14)
Spectrum on One. (see 31)
Thiptara .... (see 33)
Vu's .... (see 23)
Zaatar W Zeit .... (see 8)
17 Zaatar W Zeit E1
Zuma .... (see 10)

Drinking & Nightlife (p86)

Agency .... (see 23)
Calabar .... (see 27)
Cavalli Club .... (see 31)

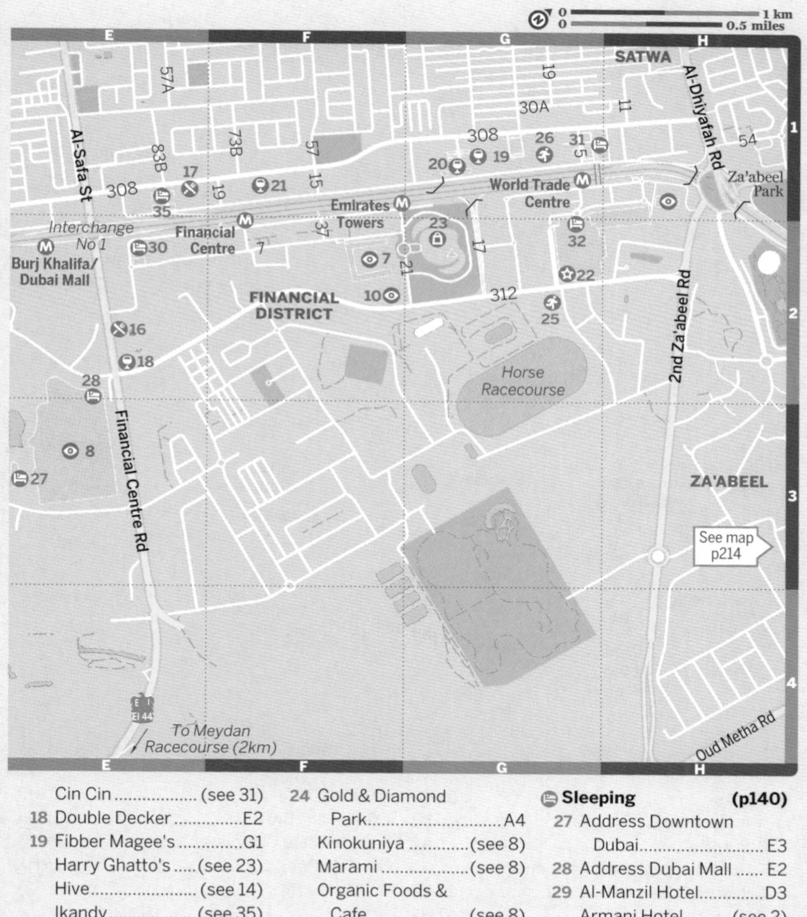

Cin Cin .... (see 31)
18 Double Decker E2
19 Fibber Magee's G1
Harry Ghatto's ..... (see 23)
Hive .... (see 14)
Ikandy .... (see 35)
Neos .... (see 27)
Nezesaussi .... (see 29)
Vu's Bar .... (see 23)
20 Zinc G1
21 Zyara F1

Entertainment (p87)

22 Blue Bar G2
Reel Cinemas .... (see 8)

Shopping (p88)

Armani Junior .... (see 8)
23 Boulevard at Jumeirah Emirates Towers G2
Candylicious .... (see 8)
Dubai Mall .... (see 8)
24 Gold & Diamond Park A4
Kinokuniya .... (see 8)
Marami .... (see 8)
Organic Foods & Cafe .... (see 8)
Souq al-Bahar ...... (see 14)
Taharan Persian Carpets & Antiques .... (see 14)

Sports & Activities (p89)

1847 .... (see 23)
25 Dubai Creek Striders G2
Dubai Ice Rink .... (see 8)
26 Gems of Yoga G1
Sega Republic .... (see 8)
Spa at the Palace – The Old Town .... (see 33)
Talise .... (see 23)

Sleeping (p140)

27 Address Downtown Dubai E3
28 Address Dubai Mall E2
29 Al-Manzil Hotel D3
Armani Hotel .... (see 2)
30 Dusit Thani Dubai E2
31 Fairmont G1
32 Ibis World Trade Centre G2
Jumeirah Emirates Towers .... (see 23)
33 Palace – The Old Town D3
34 Qamardeen Hotel D3
35 Shangri-La E1

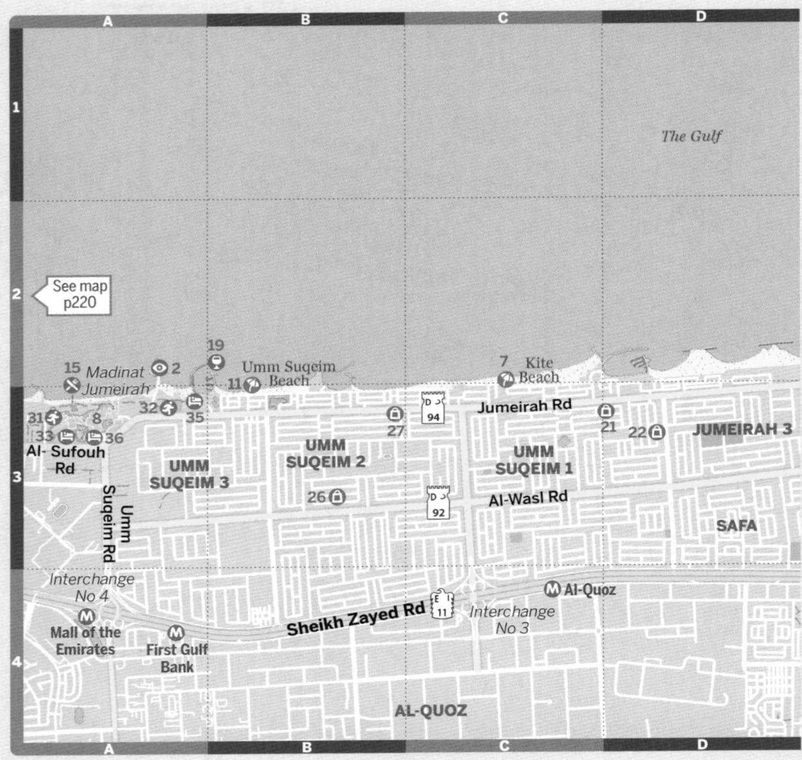

Sights **(p93)**

1 Al-Safa Park E3
2 Burj al-Arab A2
3 Dubai International Art Centre G2
4 Jumeirah Beach Park E2
5 Jumeirah Mosque H2
6 Jumeirah Open Beach H2
7 Kite Beach C2
8 Madinat Jumeirah A3
9 Majlis Ghorfat Um-al-Sheef E3
10 Pro Art Gallery H2
11 Umm Suqeim Beach B2

Eating **(p95)**

Al-Mahara .... (see 2)
Bella Donna .... (see 25)
Japengo Café .... (see 10)
12 Lime Tree Cafe H2
13 Noodle Bowl H3
Pai Thai .... (see 33)
14 Pars Iranian Kitchen H3
Paul .... (see 25)
15 Pierchic A2
16 Ravi H3
17 Smiling BKK G3
The Meat Company .... (see 8)
18 THE One H2
Zheng He's .... (see 36)

Drinking & Nightlife **(p97)**

19 360° B2
Agency .... (see 8)
Bahri Bar .... (see 36)
Bar Zar .... (see 8)
Boudoir .... (see 34)
Koubba .... (see 33)
Left Bank .... (see 8)
Legends .... (see 37)
Malecon .... (see 34)
Sho Cho .... (see 34)
Skyview Bar .... (see 2)
Trilogy .... (see 8)
Uptown Bar .... (see 35)

Entertainment **(p98)**

First Group Theatre at Madinat .... (see 8)

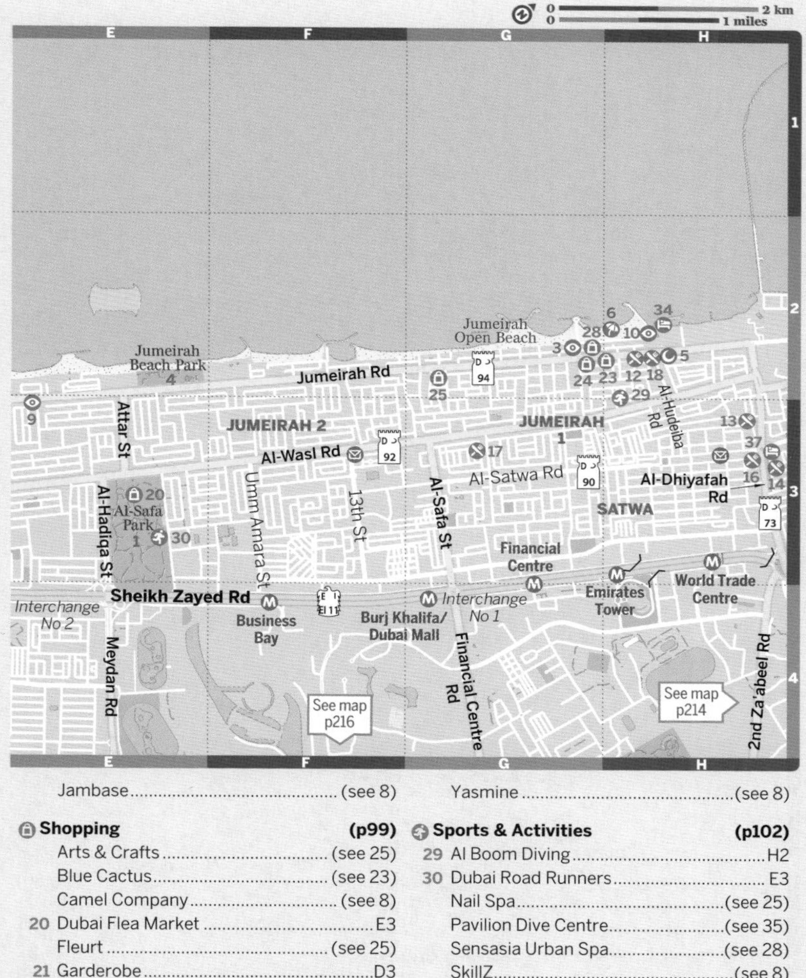

Jambase .... (see 8)
Yasmine .... (see 8)

Shopping (p99)

	Arts & Crafts	(see 25)
	Blue Cactus	(see 23)
	Camel Company	(see 8)
20	Dubai Flea Market	E3
	Fleurt	(see 25)
21	Garderobe	D3
	House of Prose	(see 24)
22	If	D3
23	Jumeirah Centre	H2
24	Jumeirah Plaza	G2
	Lata's	(see 8)
	Luxecouture	(see 8)
25	Mercato Mall	G2
26	O' de Rose	B3
	S*uce	(see 28)
	S*uce Light	(see 23)
27	Showcase Antiques, Art & Frames	B3
	Souq Madinat Jumeirah	(see 8)
	Topshop	(see 25)
28	Village Mall	G2

Sports & Activities (p102)

29	Al Boom Diving	H2
30	Dubai Road Runners	E3
	Nail Spa	(see 25)
	Pavilion Dive Centre	(see 35)
	Sensasia Urban Spa	(see 28)
	SkillZ	(see 8)
31	Talise	A3
32	Wild Wadi Waterpark	A3

Sleeping (p142)

33	Al-Qasr, Madinat Jumeirah	A3
	Burj al-Arab	(see 2)
34	Dubai Marine Beach Resort & Spa	H2
35	Jumeirah Beach Hotel	A3
36	Mina A' Salam, Madinat Jumeirah	A3
37	Rydges Plaza	H3

Key on p222

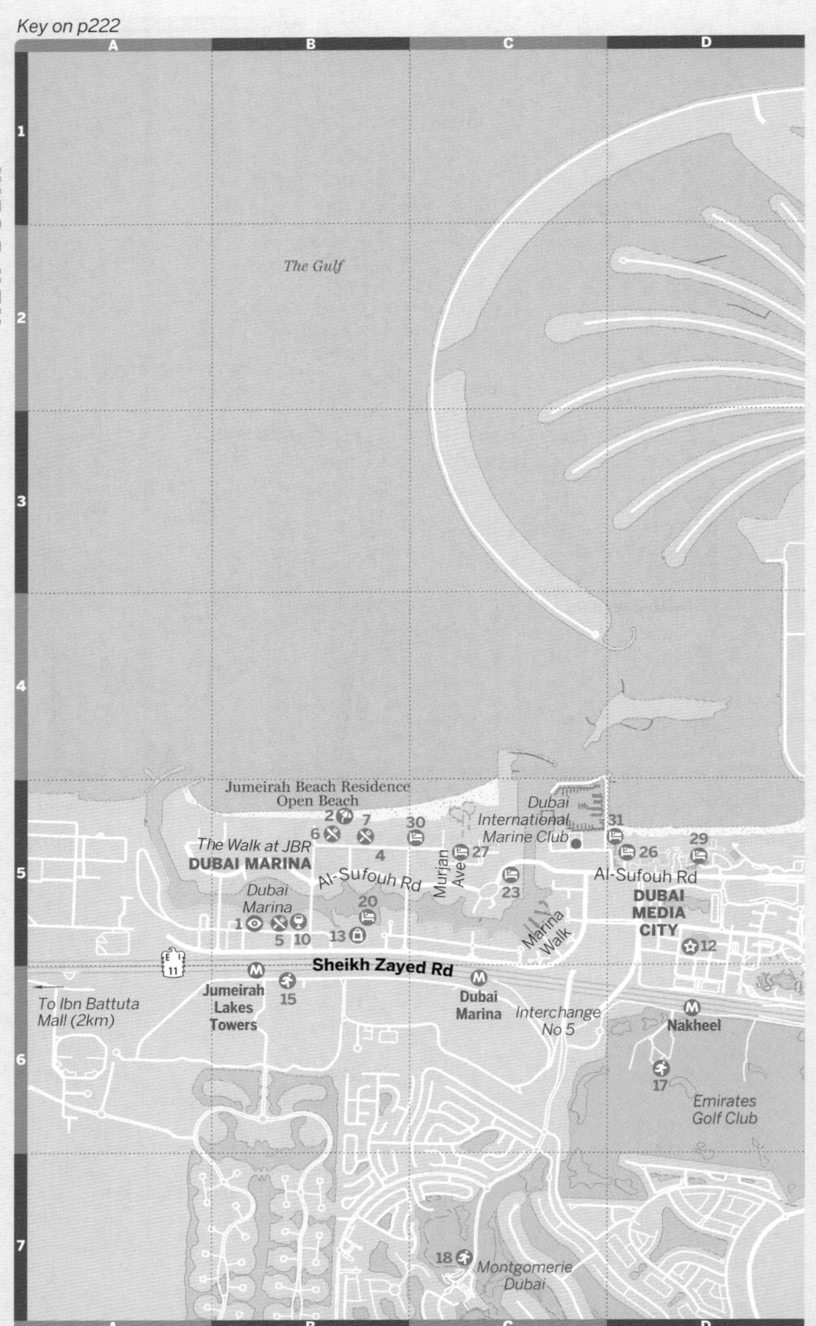

A
B
C
D
1
2
3
4
5
6
7
The Gulf
Jumeirah Beach Residence Open Beach
The Walk at JBR
DUBAI MARINA
Dubai Marina
Al-Sufouh Rd
Murjan Ave
Dubai International Marine Club
Marina Walk
DUBAI MEDIA CITY
Sheikh Zayed Rd
Jumeirah Lakes Towers
Dubai Marina
Interchange No 5
Nakheel
To Ibn Battuta Mall (2km)
Emirates Golf Club
Montgomerie Dubai
E 11
1
2
4
5
6
7
10
12
13
15
17
18
20
23
26
27
29
30
31

0 1 km
0 0.5 mile
E
F
G
H
1
2
3
4
5
6
7
Atlantis - The Palm
Aquaventure
14
9
Palm Jumeirah
Palm Jumeirah Monorail
Gateway Towers
Madinat Jumeirah
Al-Sufouh Rd
DUBAI INTERNET CITY
See map p218
Umm Suqeim Rd
AL-SUFOUH
TECOM/Dubai Internet City
E 11
Sheikh Zayed Rd
8
Al Barsha Salik Toll Gate
Sadaf
TECOM
Mall of the Emirates
22
25
24
11
4A
3
AL-BARSHA
21
19
6A
15
28
16

NEW DUBAI *Map on p220*

Our Story

A beat-up old car, a few dollars in the pocket and a sense of adventure. In 1972 that's all Tony and Maureen Wheeler needed for the trip of a lifetime – across Europe and Asia overland to Australia. It took several months, and at the end – broke but inspired – they sat at their kitchen table writing and stapling together their first travel guide, *Across Asia on the Cheap*. Within a week they'd sold 1500 copies. Lonely Planet was born.

Today, Lonely Planet has offices in Melbourne, London and Oakland, with more than 600 staff and writers. We share Tony's belief that 'a great guidebook should do three things: inform, educate and amuse'.

Our Writer

Josephine Quintero

Josephine has enjoyed a long and varied career in journalism and travel writing and has been a Lonely Planet author for several years. A University of California, Berkeley graduate, she worked on a wine magazine in the Napa Valley (California) before moving, ironically, to relatively 'dry' Kuwait. Josephine was editor of the *Kuwaiti Digest* (an oil company magazine), during which time she travelled extensively throughout the Middle East and the Gulf, including the contrasting destinations of Yemen and Dubai. After being abruptly ousted from her home by Saddam Hussein's troops, she moved to Spain, and was delighted to have an opportunity to return to the Gulf and explore this extraordinary and tantalising destination in depth. Highlights on this trip included discovering the Deira souqs – along with avocado smoothies. Fabulous!

Read more about Josephine at:
lonelyplanet.com/members/josephinequintero

Published by Lonely Planet Publications Pty Ltd
ABN 36 005 607 983
7th edition – September 2012
ISBN 978 1 74220 022 4

10 9 8 7 6 5 4 3 2
Printed in China